ESSAYS

By ARTHUR SCHOPENHAUER

Translated by T. BAILEY SAUNDERS

Essays
By Arthur Schopenhauer
Translated by T. Bailey Saunders

Print ISBN 13: 978-1-4209-7062-3
eBook ISBN 13: 978-1-4209-7063-0

This edition copyright © 2020. Digireads.com Publishing.

Cover Image: a detail of a portrait of Arthur Schopenhauer, by Bohumil Kubista (1884-1918), c. 1908 / Photo © Fine Art Images / Bridgeman Images.

Please visit *www.digireads.com*

CONTENTS

RELIGION: A DIALOGUE, ETC.

THE ART OF LITERATURE.

STUDIES IN PESSIMISM.

THE ART OF CONTROVERSY.

ON HUMAN NATURE.

Religion: A Dialogue, etc.

RELIGION: A DIALOGUE

Demopheles. Between ourselves, my dear fellow, I don't care about the way you sometimes have of exhibiting your talent for philosophy; you make religion a subject for sarcastic remarks, and even for open ridicule. Every one thinks his religion sacred, and therefore you ought to respect it.

Philalethes. That doesn't follow! I don't see why, because other people are simpletons, I should have any regard for a pack of lies. I respect truth everywhere, and so I can't respect what is opposed to it. My maxim is *Vigeat veritas et pereat mundus*, like the lawyers' *Fiat justitia et pereat mundus*. Every profession ought to have an analogous advice.

Demopheles. Then I suppose doctors should say *Fiant pilulae et pereat mundus,*—there wouldn't be much difficulty about that!

Philalethes. Heaven forbid! You must take everything *cum grano salis.*

Demopheles. Exactly; that's why I want you to take religion *cum grano salis.* I want you to see that one must meet the requirements of the people according to the measure of their comprehension. Where you have masses of people of crude susceptibilities and clumsy intelligence, sordid in their pursuits and sunk in drudgery, religion provides the only means of proclaiming and making them feel the hight import of life. For the average man takes an interest, primarily, in nothing but what will satisfy his physical needs and hankerings, and beyond this, give him a little amusement and pastime. Founders of religion and philosophers come into the world to rouse him from his stupor and point to the lofty meaning of existence; philosophers for the few, the emancipated, founders of religion for the many, for humanity at large. For, as your friend Plato has said, the multitude can't be philosophers, and you shouldn't forget that. Religion is the metaphysics of the masses; by all means let them keep it: let it therefore command external respect, for to discredit it is to take it away. Just as they have popular poetry, and the popular wisdom of proverbs, so they must have popular metaphysics too: for mankind absolutely needs *an interpretation of life*; and this, again, must be suited to popular comprehension. Consequently, this interpretation is always an allegorical investiture of the truth: and in practical life and in its effects on the feelings, that is to say, as a rule of action and as a comfort and consolation in suffering and death, it accomplishes perhaps just as much as the truth itself could achieve if we possessed it. Don't take offense at its unkempt, grotesque and apparently absurd form; for with your education and learning, you have no idea of the roundabout ways by which people in their crude state have to receive their knowledge of deep truths. The various religions are only various forms in which the truth, which taken by itself is above their comprehension, is grasped and realized by the masses; and truth becomes inseparable from these forms. Therefore, my dear sir, don't take it amiss if I say that to make a mockery of these forms is both shallow and unjust.

Philalethes. But isn't it every bit as shallow and unjust to demand that there shall be no other system of metaphysics but this one, cut out as it is to suit the requirements and comprehension of the masses? that its doctrine shall be the limit of human speculation, the standard of all thought, so that the metaphysics of the few, the emancipated, as you call them, must be devoted only to confirming, strengthening, and explaining the metaphysics of the masses? that the highest powers of human intelligence shall remain unused and undeveloped, even be nipped in the bud, in order that their activity may not thwart the popular metaphysics? And isn't this just the very claim which religion sets up? Isn't it a little too much to have tolerance and delicate forbearance preached by what is intolerance and cruelty itself? Think of the heretical tribunals, inquisitions, religious wars, crusades, Socrates' cup of poison, Bruno's and Vanini's death in the flames! Is all this to-day quite a thing of the past? How can genuine philosophical effort, sincere search after truth, the noblest calling of the noblest men, be let and hindered more completely than by a conventional system of metaphysics enjoying a State monopoly, the principles of which are impressed into every head in earliest youth, so earnestly, so deeply, and so firmly, that, unless the mind is miraculously elastic, they remain indelible. In this way the groundwork of all healthy reason is once for all deranged; that is to say, the capacity for original thought and unbiased judgment, which is weak enough in itself, is, in regard to those subjects to which it might be applied, for ever paralyzed and ruined.

Demopheles. Which means, I suppose, that people have arrived at a conviction which they won't give up in order to embrace yours instead.

Philalethes. Ah! if it were only a conviction based on insight. Then one could bring arguments to bear, and the battle would be fought with equal weapons. But religions admittedly appeal, not to conviction as the result of argument, but to belief as demanded by revelation. And as the capacity for believing is strongest in childhood, special care is taken to make sure of this tender age. This has much more to do with the doctrines of belief taking root than threats and reports of miracles. If, in early childhood, certain fundamental views and doctrines are paraded with unusual solemnity, and an air of the greatest earnestness never before visible in anything else; if, at the same time, the possibility of a doubt about them be completely passed over, or touched upon only to indicate that doubt is the first step to eternal perdition, the resulting impression will be so deep that, as a rule, that is, in almost every case, doubt about them will be almost as impossible as doubt about one's own existence. Hardly one in ten thousand will have the strength of mind to ask himself seriously and earnestly—is that true? To call such as can do it strong minds, *esprits forts*, is a description more apt than is generally supposed. But for the ordinary mind there is nothing so absurd or revolting but what, if inculcated in that way, the strongest belief in it will strike root. If, for example, the killing of a heretic or infidel were essential to the future salvation of his soul, almost every one would make it the chief event of his life, and in dying would draw consolation and strength from the remembrance that he had succeeded. As a matter of fact, almost every Spaniard in days gone by used to look upon an *auto da fe* as the most pious of all acts and one most agreeable to God. A parallel to this may be found in the way in which the Thugs (a religious sect in India, suppressed a short time ago by the English, who executed numbers of them) express their sense of religion and their veneration for the goddess Kali; they take every opportunity of murdering their friends and traveling companions, with the object of getting possession of their goods, and in the serious conviction that they are thereby doing a praiseworthy action, conducive to their eternal welfare. [Cf. Illustrations of the history and practice of the Thugs, London, 1837; also the *Edinburg Review*, Oct.-Jan., 1836-7.] The power of religious dogma, when inculcated early, is such as to stifle conscience, compassion, and finally every feeling of humanity. But if you want to see with your own eyes and close at hand what timely inoculation will accomplish, look at the English. Here is a nation favored before all others by nature; endowed, more than all others, with discernment, intelligence, power of judgment, strength of character; look at them, abased and made ridiculous, beyond all others, by their stupid ecclesiastical superstition, which appears amongst their other abilities like a fixed idea or monomania. For this they have to thank the circumstance that education is in the hands of the clergy, whose endeavor it is to impress all the articles of belief, at the earliest age, in a way that amounts to a kind of paralysis of the brain; this in its turn expresses itself all their life in an idiotic bigotry, which makes otherwise most sensible and intelligent people amongst them degrade themselves so that one can't make head or tail of them. If you consider how essential to such a masterpiece is inoculation in the tender age of childhood, the missionary system appears no longer only as the acme of human importunity, arrogance and impertinence, but also as an absurdity, if it doesn't confine itself to nations which are still in their infancy, like Caffirs, Hottentots, South Sea Islanders, etc. Amongst these races it is successful; but in India, the Brahmans treat the discourses of the missionaries with contemptuous smiles of approbation, or simply shrug their shoulders. And one may say generally that the proselytizing efforts of the missionaries in India, in spite of the most advantageous facilities, are, as a rule, a failure. An authentic report in the Vol. XXI. of the Asiatic Journal (1826) states that after so many years of missionary activity not more than three hundred living converts were to be found in the whole of India, where the population of the English possessions alone comes to one hundred and fifteen millions; and at the same time it is admitted that the Christian converts are distinguished for their extreme immorality. Three hundred venal and bribed souls out of so many millions! There is no evidence that things have gone better with Christianity in India since then, in spite of the fact that the missionaries are now trying, contrary to stipulation and in schools exclusively designed for secular English instruction, to work upon the children's minds as they please, in order to smuggle in Christianity; against which the Hindoos are most jealously on their guard. As I have said, childhood is the time to sow the seeds of belief, and not manhood; more especially where an earlier faith has taken root. An acquired conviction such as is feigned by adults is, as a rule, only the mask for some kind of personal interest. And it is the feeling that this is almost bound to be the case which makes a man who has changed his religion in mature years an object of contempt to most people everywhere; who thus show that they look upon religion, not as a matter of reasoned conviction, but merely as a belief inoculated in childhood, before any test can be applied. And that they are right in their view of religion is also obvious from the way in which not only the masses, who are blindly credulous, but also the clergy of every religion, who, as such, have faithfully and zealously studied its sources, foundations, dogmas and disputed points, cleave as a body to the religion of their particular country; consequently for a minister of one religion or confession to go over to another is the rarest thing in the world. The Catholic clergy, for example, are fully convinced of the truth of all the tenets of their Church, and so are the Protestant clergy of theirs, and both defend the principles of their creeds with like zeal. And yet the conviction is governed merely by the country native to each; to the South German ecclesiastic the truth of the Catholic dogma is quite obvious, to the North German, the Protestant. If then, these convictions are based on objective reasons, the reasons must be climatic, and thrive, like plants, some only here, some only there. The convictions of those who are thus locally convinced are taken on trust and believed by the masses everywhere.

Demopheles. Well, no harm is done, and it doesn't make any real difference. As a fact, Protestantism is more suited to the North, Catholicism to the South.

Philalethes. So it seems. Still I take a higher standpoint, and keep in view a more important object, the progress, namely, of the knowledge of truth among mankind. And from this point of view, it is a terrible thing that, wherever a man is born, certain propositions are inculcated in him in earliest youth, and he is assured that he may never have any doubts about them, under penalty of thereby forfeiting eternal salvation; propositions, I mean, which affect the foundation of all our other knowledge and accordingly determine for ever, and, if they are false, distort for ever, the point of view from which our knowledge starts; and as, further, the corollaries of these propositions touch the entire system of our intellectual attainments at every point, the whole of human knowledge is thoroughly adulterated by them. Evidence of this is afforded by every literature; the most striking by that of the Middle Age, but in a too considerable degree by that of the fifteenth and sixteenth centuries. Look at even the first minds of all those epochs; how paralyzed they are by false fundamental positions like these; how, more especially, all insight into the true constitution and working of nature is, as it were, blocked up. During the whole of the Christian period Theism lies like a mountain on all intellectual, and chiefly on all philosophical efforts, and arrests or stunts all progress. For the scientific men of these ages God, devil, angels, demons hid the whole of nature; no inquiry was followed to the end, nothing ever thoroughly examined; everything which went beyond the most obvious casual nexus was immediately set down to those personalities. "*It was at once explained by a reference to God, angels or demons,*" as Pomponatius expressed himself when the matter was being discussed, "*and philosophers at any rate have nothing analogous.*" There is, to be sure, a suspicion of irony in this statement of Pomponatius, as his perfidy in other matters is known; still, he is only giving expression to the general way of thinking of his age. And if, on the other hand, any one possessed the rare quality of an elastic mind, which alone could burst the bonds, his writings and he himself with them were burnt; as happened to Bruno and Vanini. How completely an ordinary mind is paralyzed by that early preparation in metaphysics is seen in the most vivid way and on its most ridiculous side, where such a one undertakes to criticise the doctrines of an alien creed. The efforts of the ordinary man are generally found to be directed to a careful exhibition of the incongruity of its dogmas with those of his own belief: he is at great pains to show that not only do they not say, but certainly do not mean, the same thing; and with that he thinks, in his simplicity, that he has demonstrated the falsehood of the alien creed. He really never dreams of putting the question which of the two may be right; his own articles of belief he looks upon as *à priori* true and certain principles.

Demopheles. So that's your higher point of view? I assure you there is a higher still. *First live, then philosophize* is a maxim of more comprehensive import than appears at first sight. The first thing to do is to control the raw and evil dispositions of the masses, so as to keep them from pushing injustice to extremes, and from committing cruel, violent and disgraceful acts. If you were to wait until they had recognized and grasped the truth, you would undoubtedly come too late; and truth, supposing that it had been found, would surpass their powers of comprehension. In any case an allegorical investiture of it, a parable or myth, is all that would be of any service to them. As Kant said, there must be a public standard of Right and Virtue; it must always flutter high overhead. It is a matter of indifference what heraldic figures are inscribed on it, so long as they signify what is meant. Such an allegorical representation of truth is always and everywhere, for humanity at large, a serviceable substitute for a truth to which it can never attain,—for a philosophy which it can never grasp; let alone the fact that it is daily changing its shape, and has in no form as yet met with general acceptance. Practical aims, then, my good Philalethes, are in every respect superior to theoretical.

Philalethes. What you say is very like the ancient advice of Timæus of Locrus, the Pythagorean, *stop the mind with falsehood if you can't speed it with truth.* I almost suspect that your plan is the one which is so much in vogue just now, that you want to impress upon me that

> The hour is nigh
> When we may feast in quiet.

You recommend us, in fact, to take timely precautions, so that the waves of the discontented raging masses mayn't disturb us at table. But the whole point of view is as false as it is now-a-days popular and commended; and so I make haste to enter a protest against it. It is *false,* that state, justice, law cannot be upheld without the assistance of religion and its dogmas; and that justice and public order need religion as a necessary complement, if legislative enactments are to be carried out. It is *false,* were it repeated a hundred times. An effective and striking argument to the contrary is afforded by the ancients, especially the Greeks. They had nothing at all of what we understand by religion. They had no sacred documents, no dogma to be learned and its acceptance furthered by every one, its principles to be inculcated early on the young. Just as little was moral doctrine preached by the ministers of religion, nor did the priests trouble themselves about morality or about what the people did or left undone. Not at all. The duty of the priests was confined to temple-ceremonial, prayers, hymns, sacrifices, processions, lustrations and the like, the object of which was anything but the moral improvement of the individual. What was called religion consisted, more especially in the cities, in giving temples here and there to some of the gods of the greater tribes, in which the worship described was carried on as a state matter, and was consequently, in fact, an affair of police. No one, except the functionaries performing, was in any way compelled to attend, or even to believe in it. In the whole of antiquity there is no trace of any obligation to believe in any particular dogma. Merely in the case of an open denial of the existence of the gods, or any other reviling of them, a penalty was imposed, and that on account of the insult offered to the state, which served those gods; beyond this it was free to everyone to think of them what he pleased. If anyone wanted to gain the favor of those gods privately, by prayer or sacrifice, it was open to him to do so at his own expense and at his own risk; if he didn't do it, no one made any objection, least of all the state. In the case of the Romans, everyone had his own Lares and Penates at home; they were, however, in reality, only the venerated busts of ancestors. Of the immortality of the soul and a life beyond the grave, the ancients had no firm, clear or, least of all, dogmatically fixed idea, but very loose, fluctuating, indefinite and problematical notions, everyone in his own way: and the ideas about the gods were just as varying, individual and vague. There was, therefore, really no *religion*, in our sense of the word, amongst the ancients. But did anarchy and lawlessness prevail amongst them on that account? Is not law and civil order, rather, so much their work, that it still forms the foundation of our own? Was there not complete protection for property, even though it consisted for the most part of slaves? And did not this state of things last for more than a thousand years? So that I can't recognize, I must even protest against the practical aims and the necessity of religion in the sense indicated by you, and so popular now-a-days, that is, as an indispensable foundation of all legislative arrangements. For, if you take that point of view, the pure and sacred endeavor after truth would, to say the least, appear quixotic, and even criminal, if it ventured, in its feeling of justice, to denounce the authoritative creed as a usurper who had taken possession of the throne of truth and maintained his position by keeping up the deception.

Demopheles. But religion is not opposed to truth; it itself teaches truth. And as the range of its activity is not a narrow lecture room, but the world and humanity at large, religion must conform to the requirements and comprehension of an audience so numerous and so mixed. Religion must not let truth appear in its naked form; or, to use a medical simile, it must not exhibit it pure, but must employ a mythical vehicle, a medium, as it were. You can also compare truth in this respect to certain chemical stuffs which in themselves are gaseous, but which for medicinal uses, as also for preservation or transmission, must be bound to a stable, solid base, because they would otherwise volatilize. Chlorine gas, for example, is for all purposes applied only in the form of chlorides. But if truth, pure, abstract and free from all mythical alloy, is always to remain unattainable, even by philosophers, it might be compared to fluorine, which cannot even be isolated, but must always appear in combination with other elements. Or, to take a less scientific simile, truth, which is inexpressible except by means of myth and allegory, is like water, which can be carried about only in vessels; a philosopher who insists on obtaining it pure is like a man who breaks the jug in order to get the water by itself. This is, perhaps, an exact analogy. At any rate, religion is truth allegorically and mythically expressed, and so rendered attainable and digestible by mankind in general. Mankind couldn't possibly take it pure and unmixed, just as we can't breathe pure oxygen; we require an addition of four times its bulk in nitrogen. In plain language, the profound meaning, the high aim of life, can only be unfolded and presented to the masses symbolically, because they are incapable of grasping it in its true signification. Philosophy, on the other hand, should be like the Eleusinian mysteries, for the few, the *élite*.

Philalethes. I understand. It comes, in short, to truth wearing the garment of falsehood. But in doing so it enters on a fatal alliance. What a dangerous weapon is put into the hands of those who are authorized to employ falsehood as the vehicle of truth! If it is as you say, I fear the damage caused by the falsehood will be greater than any advantage the truth could ever produce. Of course, if the allegory were admitted to be such, I should raise no objection; but with the admission it would rob itself of all respect, and consequently, of all utility. The allegory must, therefore, put in a claim to be true in the proper sense of the word, and maintain the claim; while, at the most, it is true only in an allegorical sense. Here lies the irreparable mischief, the permanent evil; and this is why religion has always been and always will be in conflict with the noble endeavor after pure truth.

Demopheles. Oh no! that danger is guarded against. If religion mayn't exactly confess its allegorical nature, it gives sufficient indication of it.

Philalethes. How so?

Demopheles. In its mysteries. "Mystery," is in reality only a technical theological term for religious allegory. All religions have their mysteries. Properly speaking, a mystery is a dogma which is plainly absurd, but which, nevertheless, conceals in itself a lofty truth, and one which by itself would be completely incomprehensible to the ordinary understanding of the raw multitude. The multitude accepts it in this disguise on trust, and believes it, without being led astray by the absurdity of it, which even to its intelligence is obvious; and in this way it participates in the kernel of the matter so far as it is possible for it to do so. To explain what I mean, I may add that even in philosophy an attempt has been made to make use of a mystery. Pascal, for example, who was at once a pietist, a mathematician, and a philosopher, says in this threefold capacity: *God is everywhere center and nowhere periphery.* Malebranche has also the just remark: *Liberty is a mystery.* One could go a step further and maintain that in religions everything is mystery. For to impart truth, in the proper sense of the word, to the multitude in its raw state is absolutely impossible; all that can fall to its lot is to be enlightened by a mythological reflection of it. Naked truth is out of place before the eyes of the profane vulgar; it can only make its appearance thickly veiled. Hence, it is unreasonable to require of a religion that it shall be true in the proper sense of the word; and this, I may observe in passing, is now-a-days the absurd contention of Rationalists and Supernaturalists alike. Both start from the position that religion must be the real truth; and while the former demonstrate that it is not the truth, the latter obstinately maintain that it is; or rather, the former dress up and arrange the allegorical element in such a way, that, in the proper sense of the word, it could be true, but would be, in that case, a platitude; while the latter wish to maintain that it is true in the proper sense of the word, without any further dressing; a belief, which, as we ought to know is only to be enforced by inquisitions and the stake. As a fact, however, myth and allegory really form the proper element of religion; and under this indispensable condition, which is imposed by the intellectual limitation of the multitude, religion provides a sufficient satisfaction for those metaphysical requirements of mankind which are indestructible. It takes the place of that pure philosophical truth which is infinitely difficult and perhaps never attainable.

Philalethes. Ah! just as a wooden leg takes the place of a natural one; it supplies what is lacking, barely does duty for it, claims to be regarded as a natural leg, and is more or less artfully put together. The only difference is that, whilst a natural leg as a rule preceded the wooden one, religion has everywhere got the start of philosophy.

Demopheles. That may be, but still for a man who hasn't a natural leg, a wooden one is of great service. You must bear in mind that the metaphysical needs of mankind absolutely require satisfaction, because the horizon of men's thoughts must have a background and not remain unbounded. Man has, as a rule, no faculty for weighing reasons and discriminating between what is false and what is true; and besides, the labor which nature and the needs of nature impose upon him, leaves him no time for such enquiries, or for the education which they presuppose. In his case, therefore, it is no use talking of a reasoned conviction; he has to fall back on belief and authority. If a really true philosophy were to take the place of religion, nine-tenths at least of mankind would have to receive it on authority; that is to say, it too would be a matter of faith, for Plato's dictum, that the multitude can't be philosophers, will always remain true. Authority, however, is an affair of time and circumstance alone, and so it can't be bestowed on that which has only reason in its favor, it must accordingly be allowed to nothing but what has acquired it in the course of history, even if it is only an allegorical representation of truth. Truth in this form, supported by authority, appeals first of all to those elements in the human constitution which are strictly metaphysical, that is to say, to the need man feels of a theory in regard to the riddle of existence which forces itself upon his notice, a need arising from the consciousness that behind the physical in the world there is a metaphysical, something permanent as the foundation of constant change. Then it appeals to the will, to the fears and hopes of mortal beings living in constant struggle; for whom, accordingly, religion creates gods and demons whom they can cry to, appease and win over. Finally, it appeals to that moral consciousness which is undeniably present in man, lends to it that corroboration and support without which it would not easily maintain itself in the struggle against so many temptations. It is just from this side that religion affords an inexhaustible source of consolation and comfort in the innumerable trials of life, a comfort which does not leave men in death, but rather then only unfolds its full efficacy. So religion may be compared to one who takes a blind man by the hand and leads him, because he is unable to see for himself, whose concern it is to reach his destination, not to look at everything by the way.

Philalethes. That is certainly the strong point of religion. If it is a fraud, it is a pious fraud; that is undeniable. But this makes priests something between deceivers and teachers of morality; they daren't teach the real truth, as you have quite rightly explained, even if they knew it, which is not the case. A true philosophy, then, can always exist, but not a true religion; true, I mean, in the proper understanding of the word, not merely in that flowery or allegorical sense which you have described; a sense in which all religions would be true, only in various degrees. It is quite in keeping with the inextricable mixture of weal and woe, honesty and deceit, good and evil, nobility and baseness, which is the average characteristic of the world everywhere, that the most important, the most lofty, the most sacred truths can make their appearance only in combination with a lie, can even borrow strength from a lie as from something that works more powerfully on mankind; and, as revelation, must be ushered in by a lie. This might, indeed, be regarded as the *cachet* of the moral world. However, we won't give up the hope that mankind will eventually reach a point of maturity and education at which it can on the one side produce, and on the other receive, the true philosophy. *Simplex sigillum veri*: the naked truth must be so simple and intelligible that it can be imparted to all in its true form, without any admixture of myth and fable, without disguising it in the form of *religion*.

Demopheles. You've no notion how stupid most people are.

Philalethes. I am only expressing a hope which I can't give up. If it were fulfilled, truth in its simple and intelligible form would of course drive religion from the place it has so long occupied as its representative, and by that very means kept open for it. The time would have come when religion would have carried out her object and completed her course: the race she had brought to years of discretion she could dismiss, and herself depart in peace: that would be the *euthanasia* of religion. But as long as she lives, she has two faces, one of truth, one of fraud. According as you look at one or the other, you will bear her favor or ill-will. Religion must be regarded as a necessary evil, its necessity resting on the pitiful imbecility of the great majority of mankind, incapable of grasping the truth, and therefore requiring, in its pressing need, something to take its place.

Demopheles. Really, one would think that you philosophers had truth in a cupboard, and that all you had to do was to go and get it!

Philalethes. Well, if we haven't got it, it is chiefly owing to the pressure put upon philosophy by religion at all times and in all places. People have tried to make the expression and communication of truth, even the contemplation and discovery of it, impossible, by putting children, in their earliest years, into the hands of priests to be manipulated; to have the lines, in which their fundamental thoughts are henceforth to run, laid down with such firmness as, in essential matters, to be fixed and determined for this whole life. When I take up the writings even of the best intellects of the sixteenth and seventeenth centuries, (more especially if I have been engaged in Oriental studies), I am sometimes shocked to see how they are paralyzed and hemmed in on all sides by Jewish ideas. How can anyone think out the true philosophy when he is prepared like this?

Demopheles. Even if the true philosophy were to be discovered, religion wouldn't disappear from the world, as you seem to think. There can't be one system of metaphysics for everybody; that's rendered impossible by the natural differences of intellectual power between man and man, and the differences, too, which education makes. It is a necessity for the great majority of mankind to engage in that severe bodily labor which cannot be dispensed with if the ceaseless requirements of the whole race are to be satisfied. Not only does this leave the majority no time for education, for learning, for contemplation; but by virtue of the hard and fast antagonism between muscles and mind, the intelligence is blunted by so much exhausting bodily labor, and becomes heavy, clumsy, awkward, and consequently incapable of grasping any other than quite simple situations. At least nine-tenths of the human race falls under this category. But still the people require a system of metaphysics, that is, an account of the world and our existence, because such an account belongs to the most natural needs of mankind, they require a popular system; and to be popular it must combine many rare qualities. It must be easily understood, and at the same time possess, on the proper points, a certain amount of obscurity, even of impenetrability; then a correct and satisfactory system of morality must be bound up with its dogmas; above all, it must afford inexhaustible consolation in suffering and death; the consequence of all this is, that it can only be true in an allegorical and not in a real sense. Further, it must have the support of an authority which is impressive by its great age, by being universally recognized, by its documents, their tone and utterances; qualities which are so extremely difficult to combine that many a man wouldn't be so ready, if he considered the matter, to help to undermine a religion, but would reflect that what he is attacking is a people's most sacred treasure. If you want to form an opinion on religion, you should always bear in mind the character of the great multitude for which it is destined, and form a picture to yourself of its complete inferiority, moral and intellectual. It is incredible how far this inferiority goes, and how perseveringly a spark of truth will glimmer on even under the crudest covering of monstrous fable or grotesque ceremony, clinging indestructibly, like the odor of musk, to everything that has once come into contact with it. In illustration of this, consider the profound wisdom of the Upanishads, and then look at the mad idolatry in the India of to-day, with its pilgrimages, processions and festivities, or at the insane and ridiculous goings-on of the Saniassi. Still one can't deny that in all this insanity and nonsense there lies some obscure purpose which accords with, or is a reflection of the profound wisdom I mentioned. But for the brute multitude, it had to be dressed up in this form. In such a contrast as this we have the two poles of humanity, the wisdom of the individual and the bestiality of the many, both of which find their point of contact in the moral sphere. That saying from the Kurral must occur to everybody. *Base people look like men, but I have never seen their exact counterpart.* The man of education may, all the same, interpret religion to himself *cum grano salis*; the man of learning, the contemplative spirit may secretly exchange it for a philosophy. But here again one philosophy wouldn't suit everybody; by the laws of affinity every system would draw to itself that public to whose education and capacities it was most suited. So there is always an inferior metaphysical system of the schools for the educated multitude, and a higher one for the *élite*. Kant's lofty doctrine, for instance, had to be degraded to the level of the schools and ruined by such men as Fries, Krug and Salat. In short, here, if anywhere, Goethe's maxim is true, *One does not suit all.* Pure faith in revelation and pure metaphysics are for the two extremes, and for the intermediate steps mutual modifications of both in innumerable combinations and gradations. And this is rendered necessary by the immeasurable differences which nature and education have placed between man and man.

Philalethes. The view you take reminds me seriously of the mysteries of the ancients, which you mentioned just now. Their fundamental purpose seems to have been to remedy the evil arising from the differences of intellectual capacity and education. The plan was, out of the great multitude utterly impervious to unveiled truth, to select certain persons who might have it revealed to them up to a given point; out of these, again, to choose others to whom more would be revealed, as being able to grasp more; and so on up to the Epopts. These grades correspond to the little, greater and greatest mysteries. The arrangement was founded on a correct estimate of the intellectual inequality of mankind.

Demopheles. To some extent the education in our lower, middle and high schools corresponds to the varying grades of initiation into the mysteries.

Philalethes. In a very approximate way; and then only in so far as subjects of higher knowledge are written about exclusively in Latin. But since that has ceased to be the case, all the mysteries are profaned.

Demopheles. However that may be, I wanted to remind you that you should look at religion more from the practical than from the theoretical side. *Personified* metaphysics may be the enemy of religion, but all the same *personified* morality will be its friend. Perhaps the metaphysical element in all religions is false; but the moral element in all is true. This might perhaps be presumed from the fact that they all disagree in their metaphysics, but are in accord as regards morality.

Philalethes. Which is an illustration of the rule of logic that false premises may give a true conclusion.

Demopheles. Let me hold you to your conclusion: let me remind you that religion has two sides. If it can't stand when looked at from its theoretical, that is, its intellectual side; on the other hand, from the moral side, it proves itself the only means of guiding, controlling and mollifying those races of animals endowed with reason, whose kinship with the ape does not exclude a kinship with the tiger. But at the same time religion is, as a rule, a sufficient satisfaction for their dull metaphysical necessities. You don't seem to me to possess a proper idea of the difference, wide as the heavens asunder, the deep gulf between your man of learning and enlightenment, accustomed to the process of thinking, and the heavy, clumsy, dull and sluggish consciousness of humanity's beasts of burden, whose thoughts have once and for all taken the direction of anxiety about their livelihood, and cannot be put in motion in any other; whose muscular strength is so exclusively brought into play that the nervous power, which makes intelligence, sinks to a very low ebb. People like that must have something tangible which they can lay hold of on the slippery and thorny pathway of their life, some sort of beautiful fable, by means of which things can be imparted to them which their crude intelligence can entertain only in picture and parable. Profound explanations and fine distinctions are thrown away upon them. If you conceive religion in this light, and recollect that its aims are above all practical, and only in a subordinate degree theoretical, it will appear to you as something worthy of the highest respect.

Philalethes. A respect which will finally rest upon the principle that the end sanctifies the means. I don't feel in favor of a compromise on a basis like that. Religion may be an excellent means of training the perverse, obtuse and ill-disposed members of the biped race: in the eyes of the friend of truth every fraud, even though it be a pious one, is to be condemned. A system of deception, a pack of lies, would be a strange means of inculcating virtue. The flag to which I have taken the oath is truth; I shall remain faithful to it everywhere, and whether I succeed or not, I shall fight for light and truth! If I see religion on the wrong side—

Demopheles. But you won't. Religion isn't a deception: it is true and the most important of all truths. Because its doctrines are, as I have said, of such a lofty kind that the multitude can't grasp them without an intermediary, because, I say, its light would blind the ordinary eye, it comes forward wrapt in the veil of allegory and teaches, not indeed what is exactly true in itself, but what is true in respect of the lofty meaning contained in it; and, understood in this way, religion is the truth.

Philalethes. It would be all right if religion were only at liberty to be true in a merely allegorical sense. But its contention is that it is downright true in the proper sense of the word. Herein lies the deception, and it is here that the friend of truth must take up a hostile position.

Demopheles. The deception is a *sine qua non*. If religion were to admit that it was only the allegorical meaning in its doctrine which was true, it would rob itself of all efficacy. Such rigorous treatment as this would destroy its invaluable influence on the hearts and morals of mankind. Instead of insisting on that with pedantic obstinacy, look at its great achievements in the practical sphere, its furtherance of good and kindly feelings, its guidance in conduct, the support and consolation it gives to suffering humanity in life and death. How much you ought to guard against letting theoretical cavils discredit in the eyes of the multitude, and finally wrest from it, something which is an inexhaustible source of consolation and tranquillity, something which, in its hard lot, it needs so much, even more than we do. On that score alone, religion should be free from attack.

Philalethes. With that kind of argument you could have driven Luther from the field, when he attacked the sale of indulgences. How many a one got consolation from the letters of indulgence, a consolation which nothing else could give, a complete tranquillity; so that he joyfully departed with the fullest confidence in the packet of them which he held in his hand at the hour of death, convinced that they were so many cards of admission to all the nine heavens. What is the use of grounds of consolation and tranquillity which are constantly overshadowed by the Damocles-sword of illusion? The truth, my dear sir, is the only safe thing; the truth alone remains steadfast and trusty; it is the only solid consolation; it is the indestructible diamond.

Demopheles. Yes, if you had truth in your pocket, ready to favor us with it on demand. All you've got are metaphysical systems, in which nothing is certain but the headaches they cost. Before you take anything away, you must have something better to put in its place.

Philalethes. That's what you keep on saying. To free a man from error is to give, not to take away. Knowledge that a thing is false is a truth. Error always does harm; sooner or later it will bring mischief to the man who harbors it. Then give up deceiving people; confess ignorance of what you don't know, and leave everyone to form his own articles of faith for himself. Perhaps they won't turn out so bad, especially as they'll rub one another's corners down, and mutually rectify mistakes. The existence of many views will at any rate lay a foundation of tolerance. Those who possess knowledge and capacity may betake themselves to the study of philosophy, or even in their own persons carry the history of philosophy a step further.

Demopheles. That'll be a pretty business! A whole nation of raw metaphysicians, wrangling and eventually coming to blows with one another!

Philalethes. Well, well, a few blows here and there are the sauce of life; or at any rate a very inconsiderable evil compared with such things as priestly dominion, plundering of the laity, persecution of heretics, courts of inquisition, crusades, religious wars, massacres of St. Bartholomew. These have been the result of popular metaphysics imposed from without; so I stick to the old saying that you can't get grapes from thistles, nor expect good to come from a pack of lies.

Demopheles. How often must I repeat that religion is anything but a pack of lies? It is truth itself, only in a mythical, allegorical vesture. But when you spoke of your plan of everyone being his own founder of religion, I wanted to say that a particularism like this is totally opposed to human nature, and would consequently destroy all social order. Man is a metaphysical animal,—that is to say, he has paramount metaphysical necessities; accordingly, he conceives life above all in its metaphysical signification, and wishes to bring everything into line with that. Consequently, however strange it may sound in view of the uncertainty of all dogmas, agreement in the fundamentals of metaphysics is the chief thing, because a genuine and lasting bond of union is only possible among those who are of one opinion on these points. As a result of this, the main point of likeness and of contrast between nations is rather religion than government, or even language; and so the fabric of society, the State, will stand firm only when founded on a system of metaphysics which is acknowledged by all. This, of course, can only be a popular system,—that is, a religion: it becomes part and parcel of the constitution of the State, of all the public manifestations of the national life, and also of all solemn acts of individuals. This was the case in ancient India, among the Persians, Egyptians, Jews, Greeks and Romans; it is still the case in the Brahman, Buddhist and Mohammedan nations. In China there are three faiths, it is true, of which the most prevalent—Buddhism—is precisely the one which is not protected by the State; still, there is a saying in China, universally acknowledged, and of daily application, that "the three faiths are only one,"—that is to say, they agree in essentials. The Emperor confesses all three together at the same time. And Europe is the union of Christian States: Christianity is the basis of every one of the members, and the common bond of all. Hence Turkey, though geographically in Europe, is not properly to be reckoned as belonging to it. In the same way, the European princes hold their place "by the grace of God:" and the Pope is the vicegerent of God. Accordingly, as his throne was the highest, he used to wish all thrones to be regarded as held in fee from him. In the same way, too, Archbishops and Bishops, as such, possessed temporal power; and in England they still have seats and votes in the Upper House. Protestant princes, as such, are heads of their churches: in England, a few years ago, this was a girl eighteen years old. By the revolt from the Pope, the Reformation shattered the European fabric, and in a special degree dissolved the true unity of Germany by destroying its common religious faith. This union, which had practically come to an end, had, accordingly, to be restored later on by artificial and purely political means. You see, then, how closely connected a common faith is with the social order and the constitution of every State. Faith is everywhere the support of the laws and the constitution, the foundation, therefore, of the social fabric, which could hardly hold together at all if religion did not lend weight to the authority of government and the dignity of the ruler.

Philalethes. Oh, yes, princes use God as a kind of bogey to frighten grown-up children to bed with, if nothing else avails: that's why they attach so much importance to the Deity. Very well. Let me, in passing, recommend our rulers to give their serious attention, regularly twice every year, to the fifteenth chapter of the First Book of Samuel, that they may be constantly reminded of what it means to prop the throne on the altar. Besides, since the stake, that *ultima ration theologorum*, has gone out of fashion, this method of government has lost its efficacy. For, as you know, religions are like glow-worms; they shine only when it is dark. A certain amount of general ignorance is the condition of all religions, the element in which alone they can exist. And as soon as astronomy, natural science, geology, history, the knowledge of countries and peoples have spread their light broadcast, and philosophy finally is permitted to say a word, every faith founded on miracles and revelation must disappear; and philosophy takes its place. In Europe the day of knowledge and science dawned towards the end of the fifteenth century with the appearance of the Renaissance Platonists: its sun rose higher in the sixteenth and seventeenth centuries so rich in results, and scattered the mists of the Middle Age. Church and Faith were compelled to disappear in the same proportion; and so in the eighteenth century English and French philosophers were able to take up an attitude of direct hostility; until, finally, under Frederick the Great, Kant appeared, and took away from religious belief the support it had previously enjoyed from philosophy: he emancipated the handmaid of theology, and in attacking the question with German thoroughness and patience, gave it an earnest instead of a frivolous tone. The consequence of this is that we see Christianity undermined in the nineteenth century, a serious faith in it almost completely gone; we see it fighting even for bare existence, whilst anxious princes try to set it up a little by artificial means, as a doctor uses a drug on a dying patient. In this connection there is a passage in Condorcet's *"Des Progrès de l'esprit humain"* which looks as if written as a warning to our age: "the religious zeal shown by philosophers and great men was only a political devotion; and every religion which allows itself to be defended as a belief that may usefully be left to the people, can only hope for an agony more or less prolonged." In the whole course of the events which I have indicated, you may always observe that faith and knowledge are related as the two scales of a balance; when the one goes up, the other goes down. So sensitive is the balance that it indicates momentary influences. When, for instance, at the beginning of this century, those inroads of French robbers under the leadership of Bonaparte, and the enormous efforts necessary for driving them out and punishing them, had brought about a temporary neglect of science and consequently a certain decline in the general increase of knowledge, the Church immediately began to raise her head again and Faith began to show fresh signs of life; which, to be sure, in keeping with the times, was partly poetical in its nature. On the other hand, in the more than thirty years of peace which followed, leisure and prosperity furthered the building up of science and the spread of knowledge in an extraordinary degree: the consequence of which is what I have indicated, the dissolution and threatened fall of religion. Perhaps the time is approaching which has so often been prophesied, when religion will take her departure from European humanity, like a nurse which the child has outgrown: the child will now be given over to the instructions of a tutor. For there is no doubt that religious doctrines which are founded merely on authority, miracles and revelations, are only suited to the childhood of humanity. Everyone will admit that a race, the past duration of which on the earth all accounts, physical and historical, agree in placing at not more than some hundred times the life of a man of sixty, is as yet only in its first childhood.

Demopheles. Instead of taking an undisguised pleasure in prophesying the downfall of Christianity, how I wish you would consider what a measureless debt of gratitude European humanity owes to it, how greatly it has benefited by the religion which, after a long interval, followed it from its old home in the East. Europe received from Christianity ideas which were quite new to it, the Knowledge, I mean, of the fundamental truth that life cannot be an end-in-itself, that the true end of our existence lies beyond it. The Greeks and Romans had placed this end altogether in our present life, so that in this sense they may certainly be called blind heathens. And, in keeping with this view of life, all their virtues can be reduced to what is serviceable to the community, to what is useful in fact. Aristotle says quite naively, *Those virtues must necessarily be the greatest which are the most useful to others.* So the ancients thought patriotism the highest virtue, although it is really a very doubtful one, since narrowness, prejudice, vanity and an enlightened self-interest are main elements in it. Just before the passage I quoted, Aristotle enumerates all the virtues, in order to discuss them singly. They are *Justice, Courage, Temperance, Magnificence, Magnanimity, Liberality, Gentleness, Good Sense* and *Wisdom.* How different from the Christian virtues! Plato himself, incomparably the most transcendental philosopher of pre-Christian antiquity, knows no higher virtue than *Justice*; and he alone recommends it unconditionally and for its own sake, whereas the rest make a happy life, *vita beata*, the aim of all virtue, and moral conduct the way to attain it. Christianity freed European humanity from this shallow, crude identification of itself with the hollow, uncertain existence of every day,

> cœlumque tueri
> Jussit, et erectos ad sidera tollere vultus.

Christianity, accordingly, does not preach mere Justice, but *the Love of Mankind, Compassion, Good Works, Forgiveness, Love of your Enemies, Patience, Humility, Resignation, Faith* and *Hope.* It even went a step further, and taught that the world is of evil, and that we need deliverance. It preached despisal of the world, self-denial, chastity, giving up of one's will, that is, turning away from life and its illusory pleasures. It taught the healing power of pain: an instrument of torture is the symbol of Christianity. I am quite ready to admit that this earnest, this only correct view of life was thousands of years previously spread all over Asia in other forms, as it is still, independently of Christianity; but for European humanity it was a new and great revelation. For it is well known that the population of Europe consists of Asiatic races driven out as wanderers from their own homes, and gradually settling down in Europe; on their wanderings these races lost the original religion of their homes, and with it the right view of life: so, under a new sky, they formed religions for themselves, which were rather crude; the worship of Odin, for instance, the Druidic or the Greek religion, the metaphysical content of which was little and shallow. In the meantime the Greeks developed a special, one might almost say, an instinctive sense of beauty, belonging to them alone of all the nations who have ever existed on the earth, peculiar, fine and exact: so that their mythology took, in the mouth of their poets, and in the hands of their artists, an exceedingly beautiful and pleasing shape. On the other hand, the true and deep significance of life was lost to the Greeks and Romans. They lived on like grown-up children, till Christianity came and recalled them to the serious side of existence.

Philalethes. And to see the effects one need only compare antiquity with the Middle Age; the time of Pericles, say, with the fourteenth century. You could scarcely believe you were dealing with the same kind of beings. There, the finest development of humanity, excellent institutions, wise laws, shrewdly apportioned offices, rationally ordered freedom, all the arts, including poetry and philosophy, at their best; the production of works which, after thousands of years, are unparalleled, the creations, as it were, of a higher order of beings, which we can never imitate; life embellished by the noblest fellowship, as portrayed in Xenophen's *Banquet*. Look on the other picture, if you can; a time at which the Church had enslaved the minds, and violence the bodies of men, that knights and priests might lay the whole weight of life upon the common beast of burden, the third estate. There, you have might as right, Feudalism and Fanaticism in close alliance, and in their train abominable ignorance and darkness of mind, a corresponding intolerance, discord of creeds, religious wars, crusades, inquisitions and persecutions; as the form of fellowship, chivalry, compounded of savagery and folly, with its pedantic system of ridiculous false pretences carried to an extreme, its degrading superstition and apish veneration for women. Gallantry is the residue of this veneration, deservedly requited as it is by feminine arrogance; it affords continual food for laughter to all Asiatics, and the Greeks would have joined in it. In the golden Middle Age the practice developed into a regular and methodical service of women; it imposed deeds of heroism, *cours d'amour*, bombastic Troubadour songs, etc.; although it is to be observed that these last buffooneries, which had an intellectual side, were chiefly at home in France; whereas amongst the material sluggish Germans, the knights distinguished themselves rather by drinking and stealing; they were good at boozing and filling their castles with plunder; though in the courts, to be sure, there was no lack of insipid love songs. What caused this utter transformation? Migration and Christianity.

Demopheles. I am glad you reminded me of it. Migration was the source of the evil; Christianity the dam on which it broke. It was chiefly by Christianity that the raw, wild hordes which came flooding in were controlled and tamed. The savage man must first of all learn to kneel, to venerate, to obey; after that he can be civilized. This was done in Ireland by St. Patrick, in Germany by Winifred the Saxon, who was a genuine Boniface. It was migration of peoples, the last advance of Asiatic races towards Europe, followed only by the fruitless attempts of those under Attila, Genghis Khan, and Timur, and as a comic afterpiece, by the gypsies,—it was this movement which swept away the humanity of the ancients. Christianity was precisely the principle which set itself to work against this savagery; just as later, through the whole of the Middle Age, the Church and its hierarchy were most necessary to set limits to the savage barbarism of those masters of violence, the princes and knights: it was what broke up the ice floes in that mighty deluge. Still, the chief aim of Christianity is not so much to make this life pleasant as to render us worthy of a better. It looks away over this span of time, over this fleeting dream, and seeks to lead us to eternal welfare. Its tendency is ethical in the highest sense of the word, a sense unknown in Europe till its advent; as I have shown you, by putting the morality and religion of the ancients side by side with those of Christendom.

Philalethes. You are quite right as regards theory: but look at the practice! In comparison with the ages of Christianity the ancient world was unquestionably less cruel than the Middle Age, with its deaths by exquisite torture, its innumerable burnings at the stake. The ancients, further, were very enduring, laid great stress on justice, frequently sacrificed themselves for their country, showed such traces of every kind of magnanimity, and such genuine manliness, that to this day an acquaintance with their thoughts and actions is called the study of Humanity. The fruits of Christianity were religious wars, butcheries, crusades, inquisitions, extermination of the natives in America, and the introduction of African slaves in their place; and among the ancients there is nothing analogous to this, nothing that can be compared with it; for the slaves of the ancients, the *familia*, the *vernœ*, were a contented race, and faithfully devoted to their masters' service, and as different from the miserable negroes of the sugar plantations, which are a disgrace to humanity, as their two colors are distinct. Those special moral delinquencies for which we reproach the ancients, and which are perhaps less uncommon now-a-days than appears on the surface to be the case, are trifles compared with the Christian enormities I have mentioned. Can you then, all considered, maintain that mankind has been really made morally better by Christianity?

Demopheles. If the results haven't everywhere been in keeping with the purity and truth of the doctrine, it may be because the doctrine has been too noble, too elevated for mankind, that its aim has been placed too high. It was so much easier to come up to the heathen system, or to the Mohammedan. It is precisely what is noble and dignified that is most liable everywhere to misuse and fraud: *abusus optimi pessimus.* Those high doctrines have accordingly now and then served as a pretext for the most abominable proceedings, and for acts of unmitigated wickedness. The downfall of the institutions of the old world, as well as of its arts and sciences, is, as I have said, to be attributed to the inroad of foreign barbarians. The inevitable result of this inroad was that ignorance and savagery got the upper hand; consequently violence and knavery established their dominion, and knights and priests became a burden to mankind. It is partly, however, to be explained by the fact that the new religion made eternal and not temporal welfare the object of desire, taught that simplicity of heart was to be preferred to knowledge, and looked askance at all worldly pleasure. Now the arts and sciences subserve worldly pleasure; but in so far as they could be made serviceable to religion they were promoted, and attained a certain degree of perfection.

Philalethes. In a very narrow sphere. The sciences were suspicious companions, and as such, were placed under restrictions: on the other hand, darling ignorance, that element so necessary to a system of faith, was carefully nourished.

Demopheles. And yet mankind's possessions in the way of knowledge up to that period, which were preserved in the writings of the ancients, were saved from destruction by the clergy, especially by those in the monasteries. How would it have fared if Christianity hadn't come in just before the migration of peoples.

Philalethes. It would really be a most useful inquiry to try and make, with the coldest impartiality, an unprejudiced, careful and accurate comparison of the advantages and disadvantages which may be put down to religion. For that, of course, a much larger knowledge of historical and psychological data than either of us command would be necessary. Academies might make it a subject for a prize essay.

Demopheles. They'll take good care not to do so.

Philalethes. I'm surprised to hear you say that: it's a bad look out for religion. However, there are academies which, in proposing a subject for competition, make it a secret condition that the prize is to go to the man who best interprets their own view. If we could only begin by getting a statistician to tell us how many crimes are prevented every year by religious, and how many by other motives, there would be very few of the former. If a man feels tempted to commit a crime, you may rely upon it that the first consideration which enters his head is the penalty appointed for it, and the chances that it will fall upon him: then comes, as a second consideration, the risk to his reputation. If I am not mistaken, he will ruminate by the hour on these two impediments,

before he ever takes a thought of religious considerations. If he gets
safely over those two first bulwarks against crime, I think religion
alone will very rarely hold him back from it.

Demopheles. I think that it will very often do so, especially when
its influence works through the medium of custom. An atrocious act is
at once felt to be repulsive. What is this but the effect of early
impressions? Think, for instance, how often a man, especially if of
noble birth, will make tremendous sacrifices to perform what he has
promised, motived entirely by the fact that his father has often earnestly
impressed upon him in his childhood that "a man of honor" or "a
gentleman" or a "a cavalier" always keeps his word inviolate.

Philalethes. That's no use unless there is a certain inborn
honorableness. You mustn't ascribe to religion what results from innate
goodness of character, by which compassion for the man who would
suffer by his crime keeps a man from committing it. This is the genuine
moral motive, and as such it is independent of all religions.

Demopheles. But this is a motive which rarely affects the multitude
unless it assumes a religious aspect. The religious aspect at any rate
strengthens its power for good. Yet without any such natural
foundation, religious motives alone are powerful to prevent crime. We
need not be surprised at this in the case of the multitude, when we see
that even people of education pass now and then under the influence,
not indeed of religious motives, which are founded on something which
is at least allegorically true, but of the most absurd superstition, and
allow themselves to be guided by it all their life long; as, for instance,
undertaking nothing on a Friday, refusing to sit down thirteen at a table,
obeying chance omens, and the like. How much more likely is the
multitude to be guided by such things. You can't form any adequate
idea of the narrow limits of the mind in its raw state; it is a place of
absolute darkness, especially when, as often happens, a bad, unjust and
malicious heart is at the bottom of it. People in this condition—and
they form the great bulk of humanity—must be led and controlled as
well as may be, even if it be by really superstitious motives; until such
time as they become susceptible to truer and better ones. As an instance
of the direct working of religion, may be cited the fact, common
enough, in Italy especially, of a thief restoring stolen goods, through
the influence of his confessor, who says he won't absolve him if he
doesn't. Think again of the case of an oath, where religion shows a
most decided influence; whether it be that a man places himself
expressly in the position of a purely *moral being*, and as such looks
upon himself as solemnly appealed to, as seems to be the case in
France, where the formula is simply *je le jure*, and also among the
Quakers, whose solemn *yea* or *nay* is regarded as a substitute for the
oath; or whether it be that a man really believes he is pronouncing
something which may affect his eternal happiness,—a belief which is

presumably only the investiture of the former feeling. At any rate, religious considerations are a means of awakening and calling out a man's moral nature. How often it happens that a man agrees to take a false oath, and then, when it comes to the point, suddenly refuses, and truth and right win the day.

Philalethes. Oftener still false oaths are really taken, and truth and right trampled under foot, though all witnesses of the oath know it well! Still you are quite right to quote the oath as an undeniable example of the practical efficacy of religion. But, in spite of all you've said, I doubt whether the efficacy of religion goes much beyond this. Just think; if a public proclamation were suddenly made announcing the repeal of all the criminal laws; I fancy neither you nor I would have the courage to go home from here under the protection of religious motives. If, in the same way, all religions were declared untrue, we could, under the protection of the laws alone, go on living as before, without any special addition to our apprehensions or our measures of precaution. I will go beyond this, and say that religions have very frequently exercised a decidedly demoralizing influence. One may say generally that duties towards God and duties towards humanity are in inverse ratio. It is easy to let adulation of the Deity make amends for lack of proper behavior towards man. And so we see that in all times and in all countries the great majority of mankind find it much easier to beg their way to heaven by prayers than to deserve to go there by their actions. In every religion it soon comes to be the case that faith, ceremonies, rites and the like, are proclaimed to be more agreeable to the Divine will than moral actions; the former, especially if they are bound up with the emoluments of the clergy, gradually come to be looked upon as a substitute for the latter. Sacrifices in temples, the saying of masses, the founding of chapels, the planting of crosses by the roadside, soon come to be the most meritorious works, so that even great crimes are expiated by them, as also by penance, subjection to priestly authority, confessions, pilgrimages, donations to the temples and the clergy, the building of monasteries and the like. The consequence of all this is that the priests finally appear as middlemen in the corruption of the gods. And if matters don't go quite so far as that, where is the religion whose adherents don't consider prayers, praise and manifold acts of devotion, a substitute, at least in part, for moral conduct? Look at England, where by an audacious piece of priestcraft, the Christian Sunday, introduced by Constantine the Great as a subject for the Jewish Sabbath, is in a mendacious way identified with it, and takes its name,—and this in order that the commands of Jehovah for the Sabbath (that is, the day on which the Almighty had to rest from his six days' labor, so that it is essentially the last day of the week), might be applied to the Christian Sunday, the *dies solis*, the first day of the week which the sun opens in glory, the day of devotion and joy. The consequence of this fraud is that

"Sabbath-breaking," or "the desecration of the Sabbath," that is, the slightest occupation, whether of business or pleasure, all games, music, sewing, worldly books, are on Sundays looked upon as great sins. Surely the ordinary man must believe that if, as his spiritual guides impress upon him, he is only constant in "a strict observance of the holy Sabbath," and is "a regular attendant at Divine Service," that is, if he only invariably idles away his time on Sundays, and doesn't fail to sit two hours in church to hear the same litany for the thousandth time and mutter it in tune with the others, he may reckon on indulgence in regard to those little peccadilloes which he occasionally allows himself. Those devils in human form, the slave owners and slave traders in the Free States of North America (they should be called the Slave States) are, as a rule, orthodox, pious Anglicans who would consider it a grave sin to work on Sundays; and having confidence in this, and their regular attendance at church, they hope for eternal happiness. The demoralizing tendency of religion is less problematical than its moral influence. How great and how certain that moral influence must be to make amends for the enormities which religions, especially the Christian and Mohammedan religions, have produced and spread over the earth! Think of the fanaticism, the endless persecutions, the religious wars, that sanguinary frenzy of which the ancients had no conception! think of the crusades, a butchery lasting two hundred years and inexcusable, its war cry "*It is the will of God*," its object to gain possession of the grave of one who preached love and sufferance! think of the cruel expulsion and extermination of the Moors and Jews from Spain! think of the orgies of blood, the inquisitions, the heretical tribunals, the bloody and terrible conquests of the Mohammedans in three continents, or those of Christianity in America, whose inhabitants were for the most part, and in Cuba entirely, exterminated. According to Las Cases, Christianity murdered twelve millions in forty years, of course all *in majorem Dei gloriam*, and for the propagation of the Gospel, and because what wasn't Christian wasn't even looked upon as human! I have, it is true, touched upon these matters before; but when in our day, we hear of *Latest News from the Kingdom of God* [A missionary paper, of which the 40th annual number appeared in 1856], we shall not be weary of bringing old news to mind. And above all, don't let us forget India, the cradle of the human race, or at least of that part of it to which we belong, where first Mohammedans, and then Christians, were most cruelly infuriated against the adherents of the original faith of mankind. The destruction or disfigurement of the ancient temples and idols, a lamentable, mischievous and barbarous act, still bears witness to the monotheistic fury of the Mohammedans, carried on from Marmud, the Ghaznevid of cursed memory, down to Aureng Zeb, the fratricide, whom the Portuguese Christians have zealously imitated by destruction of temples and the *auto de fé* of the inquisition at Goa. Don't let us forget the chosen people of God, who after they had, by Jehovah's express command, stolen from their old and trusty friends in Egypt the gold and silver vessels which had been lent to them, made a murderous and plundering inroad into "the Promised Land," with the murderer Moses at their head, to tear it from the rightful owners,—again, by the same Jehovah's express and repeated commands, showing no mercy, exterminating the inhabitants, women, children and all (Joshua, ch. 9 and 10). And all this, simply because they weren't circumcised and didn't know Jehovah, which was reason enough to justify every enormity against them; just as for the same reason, in earlier times, the infamous knavery of the patriarch Jacob and his chosen people against Hamor, King of Shalem, and his people, is reported to his glory because the people were unbelievers! (Genesis xxxiii. 18.) Truly, it is the worst side of religions that the believers of one religion have allowed themselves every sin again those of another, and with the utmost ruffianism and cruelty persecuted them; the Mohammedans against the Christians and Hindoos; the Christians against the Hindoos, Mohammedans, American natives, Negroes, Jews, heretics, and others.

Perhaps I go too far in saying *all* religions. For the sake of truth, I must add that the fanatical enormities perpetrated in the name of religion are only to be put down to the adherents of monotheistic creeds, that is, the Jewish faith and its two branches, Christianity and Islamism. We hear of nothing of the kind in the case of Hindoos and Buddhists. Although it is a matter of common knowledge that about the fifth century of our era Buddhism was driven out by the Brahmans from its ancient home in the southernmost part of the Indian peninsula, and afterwards spread over the whole of the rest of Asia, as far as I know, we have no definite account of any crimes of violence, or wars, or cruelties, perpetrated in the course of it.

That may, of course, be attributable to the obscurity which veils the history of those countries; but the exceedingly mild character of their religion, together with their unceasing inculcation of forbearance towards all living things, and the fact that Brahmanism by its caste system properly admits no proselytes, allows one to hope that their adherents may be acquitted of shedding blood on a large scale, and of cruelty in any form. Spence Hardy, in his excellent book on *Eastern Monachism*, praises the extraordinary tolerance of the Buddhists, and adds his assurance that the annals of Buddhism will furnish fewer instances of religious persecution than those of any other religion.

As a matter of fact, it is only to monotheism that intolerance is essential; an only god is by his nature a jealous god, who can allow no other god to exist. Polytheistic gods, on the other hand, are naturally tolerant; they live and let live; their own colleagues are the chief objects of their sufferance, as being gods of the same religion. This toleration is afterwards extended to foreign gods, who are, accordingly, hospitably received, and later on admitted, in some cases, to an equality of rights; the chief example of which is shown by the fact, that the Romans willingly admitted and venerated Phrygian, Egyptian and other gods. Hence it is that monotheistic religions alone furnish the spectacle of religious wars, religious persecutions, heretical tribunals, that breaking of idols and destruction of images of the gods, that razing of Indian temples, and Egyptian colossi, which had looked on the sun three thousand years, just because a jealous god had said, *Thou shalt make no graven image.*

But to return to the chief point. You are certainly right in insisting on the strong metaphysical needs of mankind; but religion appears to me to be not so much a satisfaction as an abuse of those needs. At any rate we have seen that in regard to the furtherance of morality, its utility is, for the most part, problematical, its disadvantages, and especially the atrocities which have followed in its train, are patent to the light of day. Of course it is quite a different matter if we consider the utility of religion as a prop of thrones; for where these are held "by the grace of God," throne and altar are intimately associated; and every wise prince who loves his throne and his family will appear at the head of his people as an exemplar of true religion. Even Machiavelli, in the eighteenth chapter of his book, most earnestly recommended religion to princes. Beyond this, one may say that revealed religions stand to philosophy exactly in the relation of "sovereigns by the grace of God," to "the sovereignty of the people"; so that the two former terms of the parallel are in natural alliance.

Demopheles. Oh, don't take that tone! You're going hand in hand with ochlocracy and anarchy, the arch enemy of all legislative order, all civilization and all humanity.

Philalethes. You are right. It was only a sophism of mine, what the fencing master calls a feint. I retract it. But see how disputing sometimes makes an honest man unjust and malicious. Let us stop.

Demopheles. I can't help regretting that, after all the trouble I've taken, I haven't altered your disposition in regard to religion. On the other hand, I can assure you that everything you have said hasn't shaken my conviction of its high value and necessity.

Philalethes. I fully believe you; for, as we may read in Hudibras—

A man convinced against his will
Is of the same opinion still.

My consolation is that, alike in controversies and in taking mineral waters, the after effects are the true ones.

Demopheles. Well, I hope it'll be beneficial in your case.

Philalethes. It might be so, if I could digest a certain Spanish proverb.

Demopheles. Which is?
Philalethes. Behind the cross stands the devil.
Demopheles. Come, don't let us part with sarcasms. Let us rather admit that religion, like Janus, or better still, like the Brahman god of death, Yama, has two faces, and like him, one friendly, the other sullen. Each of us has kept his eye fixed on one alone.
Philalethes. You are right, old fellow.

A FEW WORDS ON PANTHEISM.

The controversy between Theism and Pantheism might be presented in an allegorical or dramatic form by supposing a dialogue between two persons in the pit of a theatre at Milan during the performance of a piece. One of them, convinced that he is in Girolamo's renowned marionette-theatre, admires the art by which the director gets up the dolls and guides their movements. "Oh, you are quite mistaken," says the other, "we're in the Teatro della Scala; it is the manager and his troupe who are on the stage; they are the persons you see before you; the poet too is taking a part."

The chief objection I have to Pantheism is that it says nothing. To call the world "God" is not to explain it; it is only to enrich our language with a superfluous synonym for the word "world." It comes to the same thing whether you say "the world is God," or "God is the world." But if you start from "God" as something that is given in experience, and has to be explained, and they say, "God is the world," you are affording what is to some extent an explanation, in so far as you are reducing what is unknown to what is partly known (*ignotum per notius*); but it is only a verbal explanation. If, however, you start from what is really given, that is to say, from the world, and say, "the world is God," it is clear that you say nothing, or at least you are explaining what is unknown by what is more unknown.

Hence, Pantheism presupposes Theism; only in so far as you start from a god, that is, in so far as you possess him as something with which you are already familiar, can you end by identifying him with the world; and your purpose in doing so is to put him out of the way in a decent fashion. In other words, you do not start clear from the world as something that requires explanation; you start from God as something that is given, and not knowing what to do with him, you make the world take over his role. This is the origin of Pantheism. Taking an unprejudiced view of the world as it is, no one would dream of regarding it as a god. It must be a very ill-advised god who knows no better way of diverting himself than by turning into such a world as ours, such a mean, shabby world, there to take the form of innumerable millions who live indeed, but are fretted and tormented, and who manage to exist a while together, only by preying on one another; to bear misery, need and death, without measure and without object, in the form, for instance, of millions of negro slaves, or of the three million weavers in Europe who, in hunger and care, lead a miserable existence in damp rooms or the cheerless halls of a factory. What a pastime this for a god, who must, as such, be used to another mode of existence!

We find accordingly that what is described as the great advance from Theism to Pantheism, if looked at seriously, and not simply as a masked negation of the sort indicated above, is a transition from what is unproved and hardly conceivable to what is absolutely absurd. For however obscure, however loose or confused may be the idea which we connect with the word "God," there are two predicates which are inseparable from it, the highest power and the highest wisdom. It is absolutely absurd to think that a being endowed with these qualities should have put himself into the position described above. Theism, on the other hand, is something which is merely unproved; and if it is difficult to look upon the infinite world as the work of a personal, and therefore individual, Being, the like of which we know only from our experience of the animal world, it is nevertheless not an absolutely absurd idea. That a Being, at once almighty and all-good, should create a world of torment is always conceivable; even though we do not know why he does so; and accordingly we find that when people ascribe the height of goodness to this Being, they set up the inscrutable nature of his wisdom as the refuge by which the doctrine escapes the charge of absurdity. Pantheism, however, assumes that the creative God is himself the world of infinite torment, and, in this little world alone, dies every second, and that entirely of his own will; which is absurd. It would be much more correct to identify the world with the devil, as the venerable author of the *Deutsche Theologie* has, in fact, done in a passage of his immortal work, where he says, "*Wherefore the evil spirit and nature are one, and where nature is not overcome, neither is the evil adversary overcome.*"

It is manifest that the Pantheists give the Sansara the name of God. The same name is given by the Mystics to the Nirvana. The latter, however, state more about the Nirvana than they know, which is not done by the Buddhists, whose Nirvana is accordingly a relative nothing. It is only Jews, Christians, and Mohammedans who give its proper and correct meaning to the word "God."

The expression, often heard now-a-days, "the world is an end-in-itself," leaves it uncertain whether Pantheism or a simple Fatalism is to be taken as the explanation of it. But, whichever it be, the expression looks upon the world from a physical point of view only, and leaves out of sight its moral significance, because you cannot assume a moral significance without presenting the world as means to a higher end. The notion that the world has a physical but not a moral meaning, is the most mischievous error sprung from the greatest mental perversity.

ON BOOKS AND READING.

Ignorance is degrading only when found in company with riches. The poor man is restrained by poverty and need: labor occupies his thoughts, and takes the place of knowledge. But rich men who are ignorant live for their lusts only, and are like the beasts of the field; as may be seen every day: and they can also be reproached for not having used wealth and leisure for that which gives them their greatest value.

When we read, another person thinks for us: we merely repeat his mental process. In learning to write, the pupil goes over with his pen what the teacher has outlined in pencil: so in reading; the greater part of the work of thought is already done for us. This is why it relieves us to take up a book after being occupied with our own thoughts. And in reading, the mind is, in fact, only the playground of another's thoughts. So it comes about that if anyone spends almost the whole day in reading, and by way of relaxation devotes the intervals to some thoughtless pastime, he gradually loses the capacity for thinking; just as the man who always rides, at last forgets how to walk. This is the case with many learned persons: they have read themselves stupid. For to occupy every spare moment in reading, and to do nothing but read, is even more paralyzing to the mind than constant manual labor, which at least allows those engaged in it to follow their own thoughts. A spring never free from the pressure of some foreign body at last loses its elasticity; and so does the mind if other people's thoughts are constantly forced upon it. Just as you can ruin the stomach and impair the whole body by taking too much nourishment, so you can overfill and choke the mind by feeding it too much. The more you read, the fewer are the traces left by what you have read: the mind becomes like a tablet crossed over and over with writing. There is no time for ruminating, and in no other way can you assimilate what you have read. If you read on and on without setting your own thoughts to work, what you have read can not strike root, and is generally lost. It is, in fact, just the same with mental as with bodily food: hardly the fifth part of what one takes is assimilated. The rest passes off in evaporation, respiration and the like.

The result of all this is that thoughts put on paper are nothing more than footsteps in the sand: you see the way the man has gone, but to know what he saw on his walk, you want his eyes.

There is no quality of style that can be gained by reading writers who possess it; whether it be persuasiveness, imagination, the gift of drawing comparisons, boldness, bitterness, brevity, grace, ease of expression or wit, unexpected contrasts, a laconic or naive manner, and the like. But if these qualities are already in us, exist, that is to say, potentially, we can call them forth and bring them to consciousness; we can learn the purposes to which they can be put; we can be strengthened in our inclination to use them, or get courage to do so; we can judge by examples the effect of applying them, and so acquire the correct use of them; and of course it is only when we have arrived at that point that we actually possess these qualities. The only way in which reading can form style is by teaching us the use to which we can put our own natural gifts. We must have these gifts before we begin to learn the use of them. Without them, reading teaches us nothing but cold, dead mannerisms and makes us shallow imitators.

The strata of the earth preserve in rows the creatures which lived in former ages; and the array of books on the shelves of a library stores up in like manner the errors of the past and the way in which they have been exposed. Like those creatures, they too were full of life in their time, and made a great deal of noise; but now they are stiff and fossilized, and an object of curiosity to the literary palæontologist alone.

Herodotus relates that Xerxes wept at the sight of his army, which stretched further than the eye could reach, in the thought that of all these, after a hundred years, not one would be alive. And in looking over a huge catalogue of new books, one might weep at thinking that, when ten years have passed, not one of them will be heard of.

It is in literature as in life: wherever you turn, you stumble at once upon the incorrigible mob of humanity, swarming in all directions, crowding and soiling everything, like flies in summer. Hence the number, which no man can count, of bad books, those rank weeds of literature, which draw nourishment from the corn and choke it. The time, money and attention of the public, which rightfully belong to good books and their noble aims, they take for themselves: they are written for the mere purpose of making money or procuring places. So they are not only useless; they do positive mischief. Nine-tenths of the whole of our present literature has no other aim than to get a few shillings out of the pockets of the public; and to this end author, publisher and reviewer are in league.

Let me mention a crafty and wicked trick, albeit a profitable and successful one, practised by littérateurs, hack writers, and voluminous authors. In complete disregard of good taste and the true culture of the period, they have succeeded in getting the whole of the world of fashion into leading strings, so that they are all trained to read in time, and all the same thing, viz., *the newest books*; and that for the purpose of getting food for conversation in the circles in which they move. This is the aim served by bad novels, produced by writers who were once celebrated, as Spindler, Bulwer Lytton, Eugene Sue. What can be more miserable than the lot of a reading public like this, always bound to peruse the latest works of extremely commonplace persons who write for money only, and who are therefore never few in number? and for this advantage they are content to know by name only the works of the few superior minds of all ages and all countries. Literary newspapers, too, are a singularly cunning device for robbing the reading public of the time which, if culture is to be attained, should be devoted to the genuine productions of literature, instead of being occupied by the daily bungling commonplace persons.

Hence, in regard to reading, it is a very important thing to be able to refrain. Skill in doing so consists in not taking into one's hands any book merely because at the time it happens to be extensively read; such as political or religious pamphlets, novels, poetry, and the like, which make a noise, and may even attain to several editions in the first and last year of their existence. Consider, rather, that the man who writes for fools is always sure of a large audience; be careful to limit your time for reading, and devote it exclusively to the works of those great minds of all times and countries, who o'ertop the rest of humanity, those whom the voice of fame points to as such. These alone really educate and instruct. You can never read bad literature too little, nor good literature too much. Bad books are intellectual poison; they destroy the mind. Because people always read what is new instead of the best of all ages, writers remain in the narrow circle of the ideas which happen to prevail in their time; and so the period sinks deeper and deeper into its own mire.

There are at all times two literatures in progress, running side by side, but little known to each other; the one real, the other only apparent. The former grows into permanent literature; it is pursued by those who live *for* science or poetry; its course is sober and quiet, but extremely slow; and it produces in Europe scarcely a dozen works in a century; these, however, are permanent. The other kind is pursued by persons who live *on* science or poetry; it goes at a gallop with much noise and shouting of partisans; and every twelve-month puts a thousand works on the market. But after a few years one asks, Where are they? where is the glory which came so soon and made so much clamor? This kind may be called fleeting, and the other, permanent literature.

In the history of politics, half a century is always a considerable time; the matter which goes to form them is ever on the move; there is always something going on. But in the history of literature there is often a complete standstill for the same period; nothing has happened, for clumsy attempts don't count. You are just where you were fifty years previously.

To explain what I mean, let me compare the advance of knowledge among mankind to the course taken by a planet. The false paths on which humanity usually enters after every important advance are like the epicycles in the Ptolemaic system, and after passing through one of them, the world is just where it was before it entered it. But the great

minds, who really bring the race further on its course do not accompany
it on the epicycles it makes from time to time. This explains why
posthumous fame is often bought at the expense of contemporary
praise, and *vice versa*. An instance of such an epicycle is the
philosophy started by Fichte and Schelling, and crowned by Hegel's
caricature of it. This epicycle was a deviation from the limit to which
philosophy had been ultimately brought by Kant; and at that point I
took it up again afterwards, to carry it further. In the intervening period
the sham philosophers I have mentioned and some others went through
their epicycle, which had just come to an end; so that those who went
with them on their course are conscious of the fact that they are exactly
at the point from which they started.

This circumstance explains why it is that, every thirty years or so,
science, literature, and art, as expressed in the spirit of the time, are
declared bankrupt. The errors which appear from time to time amount
to such a height in that period that the mere weight of their absurdity
makes the fabric fall; whilst the opposition to them has been gathering
force at the same time. So an upset takes place, often followed by an
error in the opposite direction. To exhibit these movements in their
periodical return would be the true practical aim of the history of
literature: little attention, however, is paid to it. And besides, the
comparatively short duration of these periods makes it difficult to
collect the data of epochs long gone by, so that it is most convenient to
observe how the matter stands in one's own generation. An instance of
this tendency, drawn from physical science, is supplied in the
Neptunian geology of Werter.

But let me keep strictly to the example cited above, the nearest we
can take. In German philosophy, the brilliant epoch of Kant was
immediately followed by a period which aimed rather at being
imposing than at convincing. Instead of being thorough and clear, it
tried to be dazzling, hyperbolical, and, in a special degree,
unintelligible: instead of seeking truth, it intrigued. Philosophy could
make no progress in this fashion; and at last the whole school and its
method became bankrupt. For the effrontery of Hegel and his fellows
came to such a pass,—whether because they talked such sophisticated
nonsense, or were so unscrupulously puffed, or because the entire aim
of this pretty piece of work was quite obvious,—that in the end there
was nothing to prevent charlatanry of the whole business from
becoming manifest to everybody: and when, in consequence of certain
disclosures, the favor it had enjoyed in high quarters was withdrawn,
the system was openly ridiculed. This most miserable of all the meagre
philosophies that have ever existed came to grief, and dragged down
with it into the abysm of discredit, the systems of Fichte and Schelling
which had preceded it. And so, as far as Germany is concerned, the
total philosophical incompetence of the first half of the century

following upon Kant is quite plain: and still the Germans boast of their talent for philosophy in comparison with foreigners, especially since an English writer has been so maliciously ironical as to call them "a nation of thinkers."

For an example of the general system of epicycles drawn from the history of art, look at the school of sculpture which flourished in the last century and took its name from Bernini, more especially at the development of it which prevailed in France. The ideal of this school was not antique beauty, but commonplace nature: instead of the simplicity and grace of ancient art, it represented the manners of a French minuet.

This tendency became bankrupt when, under Winkelman's direction, a return was made to the antique school. The history of painting furnishes an illustration in the first quarter of the century, when art was looked upon merely as a means and instrument of mediaeval religious sentiment, and its themes consequently drawn from ecclesiastical subjects alone: these, however, were treated by painters who had none of the true earnestness of faith, and in their delusion they followed Francesco Francia, Pietro Perugino, Angelico da Fiesole and others like them, rating them higher even than the really great masters who followed. It was in view of this terror, and because in poetry an analogous aim had at the same time found favor, that Goethe wrote his parable *Pfaffenspiel*. This school, too, got the reputation of being whimsical, became bankrupt, and was followed by a return to nature, which proclaimed itself in *genre* pictures and scenes of life of every kind, even though it now and then strayed into what was vulgar.

The progress of the human mind in literature is similar. The history of literature is for the most part like the catalogue of a museum of deformities; the spirit in which they keep best is pigskin. The few creatures that have been born in goodly shape need not be looked for there. They are still alive, and are everywhere to be met with in the world, immortal, and with their years ever green. They alone form what I have called real literature; the history of which, poor as it is in persons, we learn from our youth up out of the mouths of all educated people, before compilations recount it for us.

As an antidote to the prevailing monomania for reading literary histories, in order to be able to chatter about everything, without having any real knowledge at all, let me refer to a passage in Lichtenberg's works (vol. II., p. 302), which is well worth perusal.

I believe that the over-minute acquaintance with the history of science and learning, which is such a prevalent feature of our day, is very prejudicial to the advance of knowledge itself. There is pleasure in following up this history; but as a matter of fact, it leaves the mind, not empty indeed, but without any power of its own, just because it makes it so full. Whoever has felt the desire, not to fill up his mind, but to strengthen it, to develop his faculties and aptitudes, and generally, to enlarge his powers, will have found that there is nothing so weakening as intercourse with a so-called littérateur, on a matter of knowledge on which he has not thought at all, though he knows a thousand little facts appertaining to its history and literature. It is like reading a cookery-book when you are hungry. I believe that so-called literary history will never thrive amongst thoughtful people, who are conscious of their own worth and the worth of real knowledge. These people are more given to employing their own reason than to troubling themselves to know how others have employed theirs. The worst of it is that, as you will find, the more knowledge takes the direction of literary research, the less the power of promoting knowledge becomes; the only thing that increases is pride in the possession of it. Such persons believe that they possess knowledge in a greater degree than those who really possess it. It is surely a well-founded remark, that knowledge never makes its possessor proud. Those alone let themselves be blown out with pride, who incapable of extending knowledge in their own persons, occupy themselves with clearing up dark points in its history, or are able to recount what others have done. They are proud, because they consider this occupation, which is mostly of a mechanical nature, the practice of knowledge. I could illustrate what I mean by examples, but it would be an odious task.

Still, I wish some one would attempt a *tragical* history of literature, giving the way in which the writers and artists, who form the proudest possession of the various nations which have given them birth, have been treated by them during their lives. Such a history would exhibit the ceaseless warfare, which what was good and genuine in all times and countries has had to wage with what was bad and perverse. It would tell of the martyrdom of almost all those who truly enlightened humanity, of almost all the great masters of every kind of art: it would show us how, with few exceptions, they were tormented to death, without recognition, without sympathy, without followers; how they lived in poverty and misery, whilst fame, honor, and riches, were the lot of the unworthy; how their fate was that of Esau, who while he was hunting and getting venison for his father, was robbed of the blessing by Jacob, disguised in his brother's clothes, how, in spite of all, they were kept up by the love of their work, until at last the bitter fight of the teacher of humanity is over, until the immortal laurel is held out to him, and the hour strikes when it can be said:

> Der schwere Panzer wird zum Flügelkleide
> Kurz ist der Schmerz, unendlich ist die Freude.

ON PHYSIOGNOMY.

That the outer man is a picture of the inner, and the face an expression and revelation of the whole character, is a presumption likely enough in itself, and therefore a safe one to go by; evidenced as it is by the fact that people are always anxious to see anyone who has made himself famous by good or evil, or as the author of some extraordinary work; or if they cannot get a sight of him, to hear at any rate from others what he looks like. So people go to places where they may expect to see the person who interests them; the press, especially in England, endeavors to give a minute and striking description of his appearance; painters and engravers lose no time in putting him visibly before us; and finally photography, on that very account of such high value, affords the most complete satisfaction of our curiosity. It is also a fact that in private life everyone criticises the physiognomy of those he comes across, first of all secretly trying to discern their intellectual and moral character from their features. This would be a useless proceeding if, as some foolish people fancy, the exterior of a man is a matter of no account; if, as they think, the soul is one thing and the body another, and the body related to the soul merely as the coat to the man himself.

On the contrary, every human face is a hieroglyphic, and a hieroglyphic, too, which admits of being deciphered, the alphabet of which we carry about with us already perfected. As a matter of fact, the face of a man gives us a fuller and more interesting information than his tongue; for his face is the compendium of all he will ever say, as it is the one record of all his thoughts and endeavors. And, moreover, the tongue tells the thought of one man only, whereas the face expresses a thought of nature itself: so that everyone is worth attentive observation, even though everyone may not be worth talking to. And if every individual is worth observation as a single thought of nature, how much more so is beauty, since it is a higher and more general conception of nature, is, in fact, her thought of a species. This is why beauty is so captivating: it is a fundamental thought of nature: whereas the individual is only a by-thought, a corollary.

In private, people always proceed upon the principle that a man is what he looks; and the principle is a right one, only the difficulty lies in its application. For though the art of applying the principle is partly innate and may be partly gained by experience, no one is a master of it, and even the most experienced is not infallible. But for all that, whatever Figaro may say, it is not the face which deceives; it is we who deceive ourselves in reading in it what is not there.

The deciphering of a face is certainly a great and difficult art, and the principles of it can never be learnt in the abstract. The first condition of success is to maintain a purely objective point of view, which is no easy matter. For, as soon as the faintest trace of anything subjective is present, whether dislike or favor, or fear or hope, or even the thought of the impression we ourselves are making upon the object of our attention the characters we are trying to decipher become confused and corrupt. The sound of a language is really appreciated only by one who does not understand it, and that because, in thinking of the signification of a word, we pay no regard to the sign itself. So, in the same way, a physiognomy is correctly gauged only by one to whom it is still strange, who has not grown accustomed to the face by constantly meeting and conversing with the man himself. It is, therefore, strictly speaking, only the first sight of a man which affords that purely objective view which is necessary for deciphering his features. An odor affects us only when we first come in contact with it, and the first glass of wine is the one which gives us its true taste: in the same way, it is only at the first encounter that a face makes its full impression upon us. Consequently the first impression should be carefully attended to and noted, even written down if the subject of it is of personal importance, provided, of course, that one can trust one's own sense of physiognomy. Subsequent acquaintance and intercourse will obliterate the impression, but time will one day prove whether it is true.

Let us, however, not conceal from ourselves the fact that this first impression is for the most part extremely unedifying. How poor most faces are! With the exception of those that are beautiful, good-natured, or intellectual, that is to say, the very few and far between, I believe a person of any fine feeling scarcely ever sees a new face without a sensation akin to a shock, for the reason that it presents a new and surprising combination of unedifying elements. To tell the truth, it is, as a rule, a sorry sight. There are some people whose faces bear the stamp of such artless vulgarity and baseness of character, such an animal limitation of intelligence, that one wonders how they can appear in public with such a countenance, instead of wearing a mask. There are faces, indeed, the very sight of which produces a feeling of pollution. One cannot, therefore, take it amiss of people, whose privileged position admits of it, if they manage to live in retirement and completely free from the painful sensation of "seeing new faces." The metaphysical explanation of this circumstance rests upon the consideration that the individuality of a man is precisely that by the very existence of which he should be reclaimed and corrected. If, on the other hand, a psychological explanation is satisfactory, let any one ask himself what kind of physiognomy he may expect in those who have all their life long, except on the rarest occasions, harbored nothing but petty, base and miserable thoughts, and vulgar, selfish, envious, wicked and malicious desires. Every one of these thoughts and desires has set its mark upon the face during the time it lasted, and by constant repetition, all these marks have in course of time become furrows and blotches, so to speak. Consequently, most people's appearance is such as to produce a shock at first sight; and it is only gradually that one gets accustomed to it, that is to say, becomes so deadened to the impression that it has no more effect on one.

And that the prevailing facial expression is the result of a long process of innumerable, fleeting and characteristic contractions of the features is just the reason why intellectual countenances are of gradual formation. It is, indeed, only in old age that intellectual men attain their sublime expression, whilst portraits of them in their youth show only the first traces of it. But on the other hand, what I have just said about the shock which the first sight of a face generally produces, is in keeping with the remark that it is only at that first sight that it makes its true and full impression. For to get a purely objective and uncorrupted impression of it, we must stand in no kind of relation to the person; if possible, we must not yet have spoken with him. For every conversation places us to some extent upon a friendly footing, establishes a certain *rapport*, a mutual subjective relation, which is at once unfavorable to an objective point of view. And as everyone's endeavor is to win esteem or friendship for himself, the man who is under observation will at once employ all those arts of dissimulation in which he is already versed, and corrupt us with his airs, hypocrisies and flatteries; so that what the first look clearly showed will soon be seen by us no more.

This fact is at the bottom of the saying that "most people gain by further acquaintance"; it ought, however, to run, "delude us by it." It is only when, later on, the bad qualities manifest themselves, that our first judgment as a rule receives its justification and makes good its scornful verdict. It may be that "a further acquaintance" is an unfriendly one, and if that is so, we do not find in this case either that people gain by it. Another reason why people apparently gain on a nearer acquaintance is that the man whose first aspect warns us from him, as soon as we converse with him, no longer shows his own being and character, but also his education; that is, not only what he really is by nature, but also what he has appropriated to himself out of the common wealth of mankind. Three-fourths of what he says belongs not to him, but to the sources from which he obtained it; so that we are often surprised to hear a minotaur speak so humanly. If we make a still closer acquaintance, the animal nature, of which his face gave promise, will manifest itself "in all its splendor." If one is gifted with an acute sense for physiognomy, one should take special note of those verdicts which preceded a closer acquaintance and were therefore genuine. For the face of a man is the exact impression of what he is; and if he deceives us, that is our fault, not his. What a man says, on the other hand, is what he thinks, more often what he has learned, or it may be even, what he pretends to think. And besides this, when we talk to him, or even hear him talking to others, we pay no attention to his physiognomy proper. It is the underlying substance, the fundamental *datum*, and we disregard it; what interests us is its pathognomy, its play of feature during conversation. This, however, is so arranged as to turn the good side upwards.

When Socrates said to a young man who was introduced to him to have his capabilities tested, "Talk in order that I may see you," if indeed by "seeing" he did not simply mean "hearing," he was right, so far as it is only in conversation that the features and especially the eyes become animated, and the intellectual resources and capacities set their mark upon the countenance. This puts us in a position to form a provisional notion of the degree and capacity of intelligence; which was in that case Socrates' aim. But in this connection it is to be observed, firstly, that the rule does not apply to moral qualities, which lie deeper, and in the second place, that what from an objective point of view we gain by the clearer development of the countenance in conversation, we lose from a subjective standpoint on account of the personal relation into which the speaker at once enters in regard to us, and which produces a slight fascination, so that, as explained above, we are not left impartial observers. Consequently from the last point of view we might say with greater accuracy, "Do not speak in order that I may see you."

For to get a pure and fundamental conception of a man's physiognomy, we must observe him when he is alone and left to himself. Society of any kind and conversation throw a reflection upon him which is not his own, generally to his advantage; as he is thereby placed in a state of action and reaction which sets him off. But alone and left to himself, plunged in the depths of his own thoughts and sensations, he is wholly himself, and a penetrating eye for physiognomy can at one glance take a general view of his entire character. For his face, looked at by and in itself, expresses the keynote of all his thoughts and endeavors, the *arrêt irrevocable*, the irrevocable decree of his destiny, the consciousness of which only comes to him when he is alone.

The study of physiognomy is one of the chief means of a knowledge of mankind, because the cast of a man's face is the only sphere in which his arts of dissimulation are of no avail, since these arts extended only to that play of feature which is akin to mimicry. And that is why I recommend such a study to be undertaken when the subject of it is alone and given up to his own thoughts, and before he is spoken to: and this partly for the reason that it is only in such a condition that inspection of the physiognomy pure and simple is possible, because conversation at once lets in a pathognomical element, in which a man can apply the arts of dissimulation which he has learned: partly again because personal contact, even of the very slightest kind, gives a certain bias and so corrupts the judgment of the observer.

And in regard to the study of physiognomy in general, it is further to be observed that intellectual capacity is much easier of discernment than moral character. The former naturally takes a much more outward direction, and expresses itself not only in the face and the play of feature, but also in the gait, down even to the very slightest movement. One could perhaps discriminate from behind between a blockhead, a fool and a man of genius. The blockhead would be discerned by the torpidity and sluggishness of all his movements: folly sets its mark upon every gesture, and so does intellect and a studious nature. Hence that remark of La Bruyère that there is nothing so slight, so simple or imperceptible but that our way of doing it enters in and betrays us: a fool neither comes nor goes, nor sits down, nor gets up, nor holds his tongue, nor moves about in the same way as an intelligent man. (And this is, be it observed by way of parenthesis, the explanation of that sure and certain instinct which, according to Helvetius, ordinary folk possess of discerning people of genius, and of getting out of their way.)

The chief reason for this is that, the larger and more developed the brain, and the thinner, in relation to it, the spine and nerves, the greater is the intellect; and not the intellect alone, but at the same time the mobility and pliancy of all the limbs; because the brain controls them more immediately and resolutely; so that everything hangs more upon a single thread, every movement of which gives a precise expression to its purpose.

This is analogous to, nay, is immediately connected with the fact that the higher an animal stands in the scale of development, the easier it becomes to kill it by wounding a single spot. Take, for example, batrachia: they are slow, cumbrous and sluggish in their movements; they are unintelligent, and, at the same time, extremely tenacious of life; the reason of which is that, with a very small brain, their spine and nerves are very thick. Now gait and movement of the arms are mainly functions of the brain; our limbs receive their motion and every little modification of it from the brain through the medium of the spine.

This is why conscious movements fatigue us: the sensation of fatigue, like that of pain, has its seat in the brain, not, as people commonly suppose, in the limbs themselves; hence motion induces sleep.

On the other hand those motions which are not excited by the brain, that is, the unconscious movements of organic life, of the heart, of the lungs, etc., go on in their course without producing fatigue. And as thought, equally with motion, is a function of the brain, the character of the brain's activity is expressed equally in both, according to the constitution of the individual; stupid people move like lay-figures, while every joint of an intelligent man is eloquent.

But gesture and movement are not nearly so good an index of intellectual qualities as the face, the shape and size of the brain, the contraction and movement of the features, and above all the eye,—from the small, dull, dead-looking eye of a pig up through all gradations to the irradiating, flashing eyes of a genius.

The look of good sense and prudence, even of the best kind, differs from that of genius, in that the former bears the stamp of subjection to the will, while the latter is free from it.

And therefore one can well believe the anecdote told by Squarzafichi in his life of Petrarch, and taken from Joseph Brivius, a contemporary of the poet, how once at the court of the Visconti, when Petrarch and other noblemen and gentlemen were present, Galeazzo Visconti told his son, who was then a mere boy (he was afterwards first Duke of Milan), to pick out the wisest of the company; how the boy looked at them all for a little, and then took Petrarch by the hand and led him up to his father, to the great admiration of all present. For so clearly does nature set the mark of her dignity on the privileged among mankind that even a child can discern it.

Therefore, I should advise my sagacious countrymen, if ever again they wish to trumpet about for thirty years a very commonplace person as a great genius, not to choose for the purpose such a beerhouse-keeper physiognomy as was possessed by that philosopher, upon whose face nature had written, in her clearest characters, the familiar inscription, "commonplace person."

But what applies to intellectual capacity will not apply to moral qualities, to character. It is more difficult to discern its physiognomy, because, being of a metaphysical nature, it lies incomparably deeper.

It is true that moral character is also connected with the constitution, with the organism, but not so immediately or in such direct connection with definite parts of its system as is intellectual capacity.

Hence while everyone makes a show of his intelligence and endeavors to exhibit it at every opportunity, as something with which he is in general quite contented, few expose their moral qualities freely, and most people intentionally cover them up; and long practice makes the concealment perfect. In the meantime, as I explained above, wicked thoughts and worthless efforts gradually set their mask upon the face, especially the eyes. So that, judging by physiognomy, it is easy to warrant that a given man will never produce an immortal work; but not that he will never commit a great crime.

PSYCHOLOGICAL OBSERVATIONS.

For every animal, and more especially for man, a certain conformity and proportion between the will and the intellect is necessary for existing or making any progress in the world. The more precise and correct the proportion which nature establishes, the more easy, safe and agreeable will be the passage through the world. Still, if the right point is only approximately reached, it will be enough to ward off destruction. There are, then, certain limits within which the said proportion may vary, and yet preserve a correct standard of conformity. The normal standard is as follows. The object of the intellect is to light and lead the will on its path, and therefore, the greater the force, impetus and passion, which spurs on the will from within, the more complete and luminous must be the intellect which is attached to it, that the vehement strife of the will, the glow of passion, and the intensity of the emotions, may not lead man astray, or urge him on to ill considered, false or ruinous action; this will, inevitably, be the result, if the will is very violent and the intellect very weak. On the other hand, a phlegmatic character, a weak and languid will, can get on and hold its own with a small amount of intellect; what is naturally moderate needs only moderate support. The general tendency of a want of proportion between the will and the intellect, in other words, of any variation from the normal proportion I have mentioned, is to produce unhappiness, whether it be that the will is greater than the intellect, or the intellect greater than the will. Especially is this the case when the intellect is developed to an abnormal degree of strength and superiority, so as to be out of all proportion to the will, a condition which is the essence of real genius; the intellect is then not only more than enough for the needs and aims of life, it is absolutely prejudicial to them. The result is that, in youth, excessive energy in grasping the objective world, accompanied by a vivid imagination and a total lack of experience, makes the mind susceptible, and an easy prey to extravagant ideas, nay, even to chimeras; and the result is an eccentric and phantastic character. And when, in later years, this state of mind yields and passes away under the teaching of experience, still the genius never feels himself at home in the common world of every day and the ordinary business of life; he will never take his place in it, and accommodate himself to it as accurately as the person of moral intellect; he will be much more likely to make curious mistakes. For the ordinary mind feels itself so completely at home in the narrow circle of its ideas and views of the world that no one can get the better of it in that sphere; its faculties remain true to their original purpose, viz., to promote the service of the will; it devotes itself steadfastly to this end, and abjures extravagant aims. The genius, on the other hand, is at bottom a *monstrum per excessum*; just as, conversely, the passionate, violent and unintelligent man, the brainless barbarian, is a *monstrum per defectum*.

* * * * *

The will to live, which forms the inmost core of every living being, exhibits itself most conspicuously in the higher order of animals, that is, the cleverer ones; and so in them the nature of the will may be seen and examined most clearly. For in the lower orders its activity is not so evident; it has a lower degree of objectivation; whereas, in the class which stands above the higher order of animals, that is, in men, reason enters in; and with reason comes discretion, and with discretion, the capacity of dissimulation, which throws a veil over the operations of the will. And in mankind, consequently, the will appears without its mask only in the affections and the passions. And this is the reason why passion, when it speaks, always wins credence, no matter what the passion may be; and rightly so. For the same reason the passions are the main theme of poets and the stalking horse of actors. The conspicuousness of the will in the lower order of animals explains the delight we take in dogs, apes, cats, etc.; it is the entirely naive way in which they express themselves that gives us so much pleasure.

The sight of any free animal going about its business undisturbed, seeking its food, or looking after its young, or mixing in the company of its kind, all the time being exactly what it ought to be and can be,— what a strange pleasure it gives us! Even if it is only a bird, I can watch it for a long time with delight; or a water rat or a hedgehog; or better still, a weasel, a deer, or a stag. The main reason why we take so much pleasure in looking at animals is that we like to see our own nature in such a simplified form. There is only one mendacious being in the world, and that is man. Every other is true and sincere, and makes no attempt to conceal what it is, expressing its feelings just as they are.

* * * * *

Many things are put down to the force of habit which are rather to be attributed to the constancy and immutability of original, innate character, according to which under like circumstances we always do the same thing: whether it happens for the first or the hundredth time, it is in virtue of the same necessity. Real force of habit, as a matter of fact, rests upon that indolent, passive disposition which seeks to relieve the intellect and the will of a fresh choice, and so makes us do what we did yesterday and have done a hundred times before, and of which we know that it will attain its object.

But the truth of the matter lies deeper, and a more precise explanation of it can be given than appears at first sight. Bodies which may be moved by mechanical means only are subject to the power of inertia; and applied to bodies which may be acted on by motives, this power becomes the force of habit. The actions which we perform by mere habit come about, in fact, without any individual separate motive brought into play for the particular case: hence, in performing them, we really do not think about them. A motive was present only on the first few occasions on which the action happened, which has since become a habit: the secondary after-effect of this motive is the present habit, and it is sufficient to enable the action to continue: just as when a body had been set in motion by a push, it requires no more pushing in order to continue its motion; it will go on to all eternity, if it meets with no friction. It is the same in the case of animals: training is a habit which is forced upon them. The horse goes on drawing his cart quite contentedly, without having to be urged on: the motion is the continued effect of those strokes of the whip, which urged him on at first: by the law of inertia they have become perpetuated as habit. All this is really more than a mere parable: it is the underlying identity of the will at very different degrees of its objectivation, in virtue of which the same law of motion takes such different forms.

* * * * *

Vive muchos años is the ordinary greeting in Spain, and all over the earth it is quite customary to wish people a long life. It is presumably not a knowledge of life which directs such a wish; it is rather knowledge of what man is in his inmost nature, *the will to live.*

The wish which everyone has that he may be remembered after his death,—a wish which rises to the longing for posthumous glory in the case of those whose aims are high,—seems to me to spring from this clinging to life. When the time comes which cuts a man off from every possibility of real existence, he strives after a life which is still attainable, even though it be a shadowy and ideal one.

* * * * *

The deep grief we feel at the loss of a friend arises from the feeling that in every individual there is something which no words can express, something which is peculiarly his own and therefore irreparable. *Omne individuum ineffabile.*

* * * * *

We may come to look upon the death of our enemies and adversaries, even long after it has occurred, with just as much regret as we feel for that of our friends, viz., when we miss them as witnesses of our brilliant success.

* * * * *

That the sudden announcement of a very happy event may easily prove fatal rests upon the fact that happiness and misery depend merely on the proportion which our claims bear to what we get. Accordingly, the good things we possess, or are certain of getting, are not felt to be such; because all pleasure is in fact of a negative nature and effects the relief of pain, while pain or evil is what is really positive; it is the object of immediate sensation. With the possession or certain expectation of good things our demands rises, and increases our capacity for further possession and larger expectations. But if we are depressed by continual misfortune, and our claims reduced to a minimum, the sudden advent of happiness finds no capacity for enjoying it. Neutralized by an absence of pre-existing claims, its effects are apparently positive, and so its whole force is brought into play; hence it may possibly break our feelings, *i.e.*, be fatal to them. And so, as is well known, one must be careful in announcing great happiness. First, one must get the person to hope for it, then open up the prospect of it, then communicate part of it, and at last make it fully known. Every portion of the good news loses its efficacy, because it is anticipated by a demand, and room is left for an increase in it. In view of all this, it may be said that our stomach for good fortune is bottomless, but the entrance to it is narrow. These remarks are not applicable to great misfortunes in the same way. They are more seldom fatal, because hope always sets itself against them. That an analogous part is not played by fear in the case of happiness results from the fact that we are instinctively more inclined to hope than to fear; just as our eyes turn of themselves towards light rather than darkness.

* * * * *

Hope is the result of confusing the desire that something should take place with the probability that it will. Perhaps no man is free from this folly of the heart, which deranges the intellect's correct appreciation of probability to such an extent that, if the chances are a thousand to one against it, yet the event is thought a likely one. Still in spite of this, a sudden misfortune is like a death stroke, whilst a hope that is always disappointed and still never dies, is like death by prolonged torture.

He who has lost all hope has also lost all fear; this is the meaning of the expression "desperate." It is natural to a man to believe what he wishes to be true, and to believe it because he wishes it, If this characteristic of our nature, at once beneficial and assuaging, is rooted out by many hard blows of fate, and a man comes, conversely, to a condition in which he believes a thing must happen because he does not wish it, and what he wishes to happen can never be, just because he wishes it, this is in reality the state described as "desperation."

* * * * *

That we are so often deceived in others is not because our judgment is at fault, but because in general, as Bacon says, *intellectus luminis sicci non est, sed recipit infusionem a voluntate et affectibus*: that is to say, trifles unconsciously bias us for or against a person from the very beginning. It may also be explained by our not abiding by the qualities which we really discover; we go on to conclude the presence of others which we think inseparable from them, or the absence of those which we consider incompatible. For instance, when we perceive generosity, we infer justice; from piety, we infer honesty; from lying, deception; from deception, stealing, etc.; a procedure which opens the door to many false views, partly because human nature is so strange, partly because our standpoint is so one-sided. It is true, indeed, that character always forms a consistent and connected whole; but the roots of all its qualities lie too deep to allow of our concluding from particular data in a given case whether certain qualities can or cannot exist together.

* * * * *

We often happen to say things that may in some way or other be prejudicial to us; but we keep silent about things that might make us look ridiculous; because in this case effect follows very quickly on cause.

* * * * *

The pain of an unfulfilled wish is small in comparison with that of repentance; for the one stands in the presence of the vast open future, whilst the other has the irrevocable past closed behind it.

* * * * *

Geduld, patientia, patience, especially the Spanish *sufrimiento,* is strongly connected with the notion of *suffering.* It is therefore a passive state, just as the opposite is an active state of the mind, with which, when great, patience is incompatible. It is the innate virtue of a phlegmatic, indolent, and spiritless people, as also of women. But that it is nevertheless so very useful and necessary is a sign that the world is very badly constituted.

* * * * *

Money is human happiness in the abstract: he, then, who is no longer capable of enjoying human happiness in the concrete, devotes his heart entirely to money.

* * * * *

Obstinacy is the result of the will forcing itself into the place of the intellect.

* * * * *

If you want to find out your real opinion of anyone, observe the impression made upon you by the first sight of a letter from him.

* * * * *

The course of our individual life and the events in it, as far as their true meaning and connection is concerned, may be compared to a piece of rough mosaic. So long as you stand close in front of it, you cannot get a right view of the objects presented, nor perceive their significance or beauty. Both come in sight only when you stand a little way off. And in the same way you often understand the true connection of important events in your life, not while they are going on, nor soon after they are past, but only a considerable time afterwards.

Is this so, because we require the magnifying effect of imagination? or because we can get a general view only from a distance? or because the school of experience makes our judgment ripe? Perhaps all of these together: but it is certain that we often view in the right light the actions of others, and occasionally even our own, only after the lapse of years. And as it is in one's own life, so it is in history.

* * * * *

Happy circumstances in life are like certain groups of trees. Seen from a distance they look very well: but go up to them and amongst them, and the beauty vanishes; you don't know where it can be; it is only trees you see. And so it is that we often envy the lot of others.

* * * * *

The doctor sees all the weakness of mankind, the lawyer all the wickedness, the theologian all the stupidity.

* * * * *

A person of phlegmatic disposition who is a blockhead, would, with a sanguine nature, be a fool.

* * * * *

Now and then one learns something, but one forgets the whole day long.

Moreover our memory is like a sieve, the holes of which in time get larger and larger: the older we get, the quicker anything entrusted to it slips from the memory, whereas, what was fixed fast in it in early days is there still. The memory of an old man gets clearer and clearer, the further it goes back, and less clear the nearer it approaches the present time; so that his memory, like his eyes, becomes short-sighted.

* * * * *

In the process of learning you may be apprehensive about bewildering and confusing the memory, but not about overloading it, in the strict sense of the word. The faculty for remembering is not diminished in proportion to what one has learnt, just as little as the number of moulds in which you cast sand, lessens its capacity for being cast in new moulds. In this sense the memory is bottomless. And yet the greater and more various any one's knowledge, the longer he takes to find out anything that may suddenly be asked him; because he is like a shopkeeper who has to get the article wanted from a large and multifarious store; or, more strictly speaking, because out of many possible trains of thought he has to recall exactly that one which, as a result of previous training, leads to the matter in question. For the memory is not a repository of things you wish to preserve, but a mere dexterity of the intellectual powers; hence the mind always contains its sum of knowledge only potentially, never actually.

It sometimes happens that my memory will not reproduce some word in a foreign language, or a name, or some artistic expression, although I know it very well. After I have bothered myself in vain about it for a longer or a shorter time, I give up thinking about it altogether. An hour or two afterwards, in rare cases even later still, sometimes only after four or five weeks, the word I was trying to recall occurs to me while I am thinking of something else, as suddenly as if some one had whispered it to me. After noticing this phenomenon with wonder for very many years, I have come to think that the probable explanation of it is as follows. After the troublesome and unsuccessful search, my will retains its craving to know the word, and so sets a watch for it in the intellect. Later on, in the course and play of thought, some word by chance occurs having the same initial letters or some other resemblance to the word which is sought; then the sentinel springs forward and supplies what is wanting to make up the word, seizes it, and suddenly brings it up in triumph, without my knowing where and how he got it; so it seems as if some one had whispered it to me. It is the same process as that adopted by a teacher towards a child who cannot repeat a word; the teacher just suggests the first letter of the word, or even the second too; then the child remembers it. In default of this process, you can end by going methodically through all the letters of the alphabet.

* * * * *

In the ordinary man, injustice rouses a passionate desire for vengeance; and it has often been said that vengeance is sweet. How many sacrifices have been made just to enjoy the feeling of vengeance, without any intention of causing an amount of injury equivalent to what one has suffered. The bitter death of the centaur Nessus was sweetened by the certainty that he had used his last moments to work out an extremely clever vengeance. Walter Scott expresses the same human inclination in language as true as it is strong: "Vengeance is the sweetest morsel to the mouth that ever was cooked in hell!" I shall now attempt a psychological explanation of it.

Suffering which falls to our lot in the course of nature, or by chance, or fate, does not, *ceteris paribus*, seem so painful as suffering which is inflicted on us by the arbitrary will of another. This is because we look upon nature and chance as the fundamental masters of the world; we see that the blow we received from them might just as well have fallen on another. In the case of suffering which springs from this source, we bewail the common lot of humanity rather than our own misfortune. But that it is the arbitrary will of another which inflicts the suffering, is a peculiarly bitter addition to the pain or injury it causes, viz., the consciousness that some one else is superior to us, whether by force or cunning, while we lie helpless. If amends are possible, amends heal the injury; but that bitter addition, "and it was you who did that to me," which is often more painful than the injury itself, is only to be neutralized by vengeance. By inflicting injury on the one who has injured us, whether we do it by force or cunning, is to show our superiority to him, and to annul the proof of his superiority to us. That gives our hearts the satisfaction towards which it yearns. So where there is a great deal of pride and vanity, there also will there be a great desire of vengeance. But as the fulfillment of every wish brings with it more or less of a sense of disappointment, so it is with vengeance. The delight we hope to get from it is mostly embittered by compassion. Vengeance taken will often tear the heart and torment the conscience: the motive to it is no longer active, and what remains is the evidence of our malice.

THE CHRISTIAN SYSTEM.

When the Church says that, in the dogmas of religion, reason is totally incompetent and blind, and its use to be reprehended, it is in reality attesting the fact that these dogmas are allegorical in their nature, and are not to be judged by the standard which reason, taking all things *sensu proprio*, can alone apply. Now the absurdities of a dogma are just the mark and sign of what is allegorical and mythical in it. In the case under consideration, however, the absurdities spring from the fact that two such heterogeneous doctrines as those of the Old and New Testaments had to be combined. The great allegory was of gradual growth. Suggested by external and adventitious circumstances, it was developed by the interpretation put upon them, an interpretation in quiet touch with certain deep-lying truths only half realized. The allegory was finally completed by Augustine, who penetrated deepest into its meaning, and so was able to conceive it as a systematic whole and supply its defects. Hence the Augustinian doctrine, confirmed by Luther, is the complete form of Christianity; and the Protestants of to-day, who take Revelation *sensu proprio* and confine it to a single individual, are in error in looking upon the first beginnings of Christianity as its most perfect expression. But the bad thing about all religions is that, instead of being able to confess their allegorical nature, they have to conceal it; accordingly, they parade their doctrine in all seriousness as true *sensu proprio*, and as absurdities form an essential part of these doctrines, you have the great mischief of a continual fraud. And, what is worse, the day arrives when they are no longer true *sensu proprio*, and then there is an end of them; so that, in that respect, it would be better to admit their allegorical nature at once. But the difficulty is to teach the multitude that something can be both true and untrue at the same time. And as all religions are in a greater or less degree of this nature, we must recognize the fact that mankind cannot get on without a certain amount of absurdity, that absurdity is an element in its existence, and illusion indispensable; as indeed other aspects of life testify.

I have said that the combination of the Old Testament with the New gives rise to absurdities. Among the examples which illustrate what I mean, I may cite the Christian doctrine of Predestination and Grace, as formulated by Augustine and adopted from him by Luther; according to which one man is endowed with grace and another is not.

Grace, then, comes to be a privilege received at birth and brought ready into the world; a privilege, too, in a matter second to none in importance. What is obnoxious and absurd in this doctrine may be traced to the idea contained in the Old Testament, that man is the creation of an external will, which called him into existence out of nothing. It is quite true that genuine moral excellence is really innate; but the meaning of the Christian doctrine is expressed in another and more rational way by the theory of metempsychosis, common to Brahmans and Buddhists. According to this theory, the qualities which distinguish one man from another are received at birth, are brought, that is to say, from another world and a former life; these qualities are not an external gift of grace, but are the fruits of the acts committed in that other world. But Augustine's dogma of Predestination is connected with another dogma, namely, that the mass of humanity is corrupt and doomed to eternal damnation, that very few will be found righteous and attain salvation, and that only in consequence of the gift of grace, and because they are predestined to be saved; whilst the remainder will be overwhelmed by the perdition they have deserved, viz., eternal torment in hell. Taken in its ordinary meaning, the dogma is revolting, for it comes to this: it condemns a man, who may be, perhaps, scarcely twenty years of age, to expiate his errors, or even his unbelief, in everlasting torment; nay, more, it makes this almost universal damnation the natural effect of original sin, and therefore the necessary consequence of the Fall. This is a result which must have been foreseen by him who made mankind, and who, in the first place, made them not better than they are, and secondly, set a trap for them into which he must have known they would fall; for he made the whole world, and nothing is hidden from him. According to this doctrine, then, God created out of nothing a weak race prone to sin, in order to give them over to endless torment. And, as a last characteristic, we are told that this God, who prescribes forbearance and forgiveness of every fault, exercises none himself, but does the exact opposite; for a punishment which comes at the end of all things, when the world is over and done with, cannot have for its object either to improve or deter, and is therefore pure vengeance. So that, on this view, the whole race is actually destined to eternal torture and damnation, and created expressly for this end, the only exception being those few persons who are rescued by election of grace, from what motive one does not know.

Putting these aside, it looks as if the Blessed Lord had created the world for the benefit of the devil! it would have been so much better not to have made it at all. So much, then, for a dogma taken *sensu proprio*. But look at it *sensu allegorico*, and the whole matter becomes capable of a satisfactory interpretation. What is absurd and revolting in this dogma is, in the main, as I said, the simple outcome of Jewish theism, with its "creation out of nothing," and really foolish and paradoxical denial of the doctrine of metempsychosis which is involved in that idea, a doctrine which is natural, to a certain extent self-evident, and, with the exception of the Jews, accepted by nearly the whole human race at all times. To remove the enormous evil arising from Augustine's dogma, and to modify its revolting nature, Pope Gregory I., in the sixth century, very prudently matured the doctrine of *Purgatory*, the essence of which already existed in Origen (cf. Bayle's article on Origen, note B.). The doctrine was regularly incorporated into the faith of the Church, so that the original view was much modified, and a certain substitute provided for the doctrine of metempsychosis; for both the one and the other admit a process of purification. To the same end, the doctrine of "the Restoration of all things" [Greek: apokatastasis] was established, according to which, in the last act of the Human Comedy, the sinners one and all will be reinstated *in integrum*. It is only Protestants, with their obstinate belief in the Bible, who cannot be induced to give up eternal punishment in hell. If one were spiteful, one might say, "much good may it do them," but it is consoling to think that they really do not believe the doctrine; they leave it alone, thinking in their hearts, "It can't be so bad as all that."

The rigid and systematic character of his mind led Augustine, in his austere dogmatism and his resolute definition of doctrines only just indicated in the Bible and, as a matter of fact, resting on very vague grounds, to give hard outlines to these doctrines and to put a harsh construction on Christianity: the result of which is that his views offend us, and just as in his day Pelagianism arose to combat them, so now in our day Rationalism does the same. Take, for example, the case as he states it generally in the *De Civitate Dei*, Bk. xii. ch. 21. It comes to this: God creates a being out of nothing, forbids him some things, and enjoins others upon him; and because these commands are not obeyed, he tortures him to all eternity with every conceivable anguish; and for this purpose, binds soul and body inseparably together, so that, instead, of the torment destroying this being by splitting him up into his elements, and so setting him free, he may live to eternal pain. This poor creature, formed out of nothing! At least, he has a claim on his original nothing: he should be assured, as a matter of right, of this last retreat, which, in any case, cannot be a very evil one: it is what he has inherited. I, at any rate, cannot help sympathizing with him. If you add to this Augustine's remaining doctrines, that all this does not depend on the man's own sins and omissions, but was already predestined to happen, one really is at a loss what to think. Our highly educated Rationalists say, to be sure, "It's all false, it's a mere bugbear; we're in a state of constant progress, step by step raising ourselves to ever greater perfection." Ah! what a pity we didn't begin sooner; we should already have been there.

In the Christian system the devil is a personage of the greatest importance. God is described as absolutely good, wise and powerful; and unless he were counterbalanced by the devil, it would be impossible to see where the innumerable and measureless evils, which predominate in the world, come from, if there were no devil to account for them. And since the Rationalists have done away with the devil, the damage inflicted on the other side has gone on growing, and is becoming more and more palpable; as might have been foreseen, and was foreseen, by the orthodox. The fact is, you cannot take away one pillar from a building without endangering the rest of it. And this confirms the view, which has been established on other grounds, that Jehovah is a transformation of Ormuzd, and Satan of the Ahriman who must be taken in connection with him. Ormuzd himself is a transformation of Indra.

Christianity has this peculiar disadvantage, that, unlike other religions, it is not a pure system of doctrine: its chief and essential feature is that it is a history, a series of events, a collection of facts, a statement of the actions and sufferings of individuals: it is this history which constitutes dogma, and belief in it is salvation. Other religions, Buddhism, for instance, have, it is true, historical appendages, the life, namely, of their founders: this, however, is not part and parcel of the dogma but is taken along with it. For example, the Lalitavistara may be compared with the Gospel so far as it contains the life of Sakya-muni, the Buddha of the present period of the world's history: but this is something which is quite separate and different from the dogma, from the system itself: and for this reason; the lives of former Buddhas were quite other, and those of the future will be quite other, than the life of the Buddha of to-day. The dogma is by no means one with the career of its founder; it does not rest on individual persons or events; it is something universal and equally valid at all times. The Lalitavistara is not, then, a gospel in the Christian sense of the word; it is not the joyful message of an act of redemption; it is the career of him who has shown how each one may redeem himself. The historical constitution of Christianity makes the Chinese laugh at missionaries as story-tellers.

I may mention here another fundamental error of Christianity, an error which cannot be explained away, and the mischievous consequences of which are obvious every day: I mean the unnatural distinction Christianity makes between man and the animal world to which he really belongs. It sets up man as all-important, and looks upon animals as merely things. Brahmanism and Buddhism, on the other hand, true to the facts, recognize in a positive way that man is related generally to the whole of nature, and specially and principally to animal nature; and in their systems man is always represented by the theory of metempsychosis and otherwise, as closely connected with the animal world. The important part played by animals all through Buddhism and

Brahmanism, compared with the total disregard of them in Judaism and Christianity, puts an end to any question as to which system is nearer perfection, however much we in Europe may have become accustomed to the absurdity of the claim. Christianity contains, in fact, a great and essential imperfection in limiting its precepts to man, and in refusing rights to the entire animal world. As religion fails to protect animals against the rough, unfeeling and often more than bestial multitude, the duty falls to the police; and as the police are unequal to the task, societies for the protection of animals are now formed all over Europe and America. In the whole of uncircumcised Asia, such a procedure would be the most superfluous thing in the world, because animals are there sufficiently protected by religion, which even makes them objects of charity. How such charitable feelings bear fruit may be seen, to take an example, in the great hospital for animals at Surat, whither Christians, Mohammedans and Jews can send their sick beasts, which, if cured, are very rightly not restored to their owners. In the same way when a Brahman or a Buddhist has a slice of good luck, a happy issue in any affair, instead of mumbling a *Te Deum*, he goes to the market-place and buys birds and opens their cages at the city gate; a thing which may be frequently seen in Astrachan, where the adherents of every religion meet together: and so on in a hundred similar ways. On the other hand, look at the revolting ruffianism with which our Christian public treats its animals; killing them for no object at all, and laughing over it, or mutilating or torturing them: even its horses, who form its most direct means of livelihood, are strained to the utmost in their old age, and the last strength worked out of their poor bones until they succumb at last under the whip. One might say with truth, Mankind are the devils of the earth, and the animals the souls they torment. But what can you expect from the masses, when there are men of education, zoologists even, who, instead of admitting what is so familiar to them, the essential identity of man and animal, are bigoted and stupid enough to offer a zealous opposition to their honest and rational colleagues, when they class man under the proper head as an animal, or demonstrate the resemblance between him and the chimpanzee or ourang-outang. It is a revolting thing that a writer who is so pious and Christian in his sentiments as Jung Stilling should use a simile like this, in his *Scenen aus dem Geisterreich*. (Bk. II. sc. i., p. 15.) "Suddenly the skeleton shriveled up into an indescribably hideous and dwarf-like form, just as when you bring a large spider into the focus of a burning glass, and watch the purulent blood hiss and bubble in the heat." This man of God then was guilty of such infamy! or looked on quietly when another was committing it! in either case it comes to the same thing here. So little harm did he think of it that he tells us of it in passing, and without a trace of emotion. Such are the effects of the first chapter of Genesis, and, in fact, of the whole of the

Jewish conception of nature. The standard recognized by the Hindus and Buddhists is the Mahavakya (the great word),—"tat-twam-asi" (this is thyself), which may always be spoken of every animal, to keep us in mind of the identity of his inmost being with ours. Perfection of morality, indeed! Nonsense.

The fundamental characteristics of the Jewish religion are realism and optimism, views of the world which are closely allied; they form, in fact, the conditions of theism. For theism looks upon the material world as absolutely real, and regards life as a pleasant gift bestowed upon us. On the other hand, the fundamental characteristics of the Brahman and Buddhist religions are idealism and pessimism, which look upon the existence of the world as in the nature of a dream, and life as the result of our sins. In the doctrines of the Zend-Avesta, from which, as is well known, Judaism sprang, the pessimistic element is represented by Ahriman. In Judaism, Ahriman has as Satan only a subordinate position; but, like Ahriman, he is the lord of snakes, scorpions, and vermin. But the Jewish system forthwith employs Satan to correct its fundamental error of optimism, and in the *Fall* introduces the element of pessimism, a doctrine demanded by the most obvious facts of the world. There is no truer idea in Judaism than this, although it transfers to the course of existence what must be represented as its foundation and antecedent.

The New Testament, on the other hand, must be in some way traceable to an Indian source: its ethical system, its ascetic view of morality, its pessimism, and its Avatar, are all thoroughly Indian. It is its morality which places it in a position of such emphatic and essential antagonism to the Old Testament, so that the story of the Fall is the only possible point of connection between the two. For when the Indian doctrine was imported into the land of promise, two very different things had to be combined: on the one hand the consciousness of the corruption and misery of the world, its need of deliverance and salvation through an Avatar, together with a morality based on self-denial and repentance; on the other hand the Jewish doctrine of Monotheism, with its corollary that "all things are very good" [Greek: panta kala lian]. And the task succeeded as far as it could, as far, that is, as it was possible to combine two such heterogeneous and antagonistic creeds.

As ivy clings for the support and stay it wants to a rough-hewn post, everywhere conforming to its irregularities and showing their outline, but at the same time covering them with life and grace, and changing the former aspect into one that is pleasing to the eye; so the Christian faith, sprung from the wisdom of India, overspreads the old trunk of rude Judaism, a tree of alien growth; the original form must in part remain, but it suffers a complete change and becomes full of life and truth, so that it appears to be the same tree, but is really another.

Judaism had presented the Creator as separated from the world, which he produced out of nothing. Christianity identifies this Creator with the Saviour, and through him, with humanity: he stands as their representative; they are redeemed in him, just as they fell in Adam, and have lain ever since in the bonds of iniquity, corruption, suffering and death. Such is the view taken by Christianity in common with Buddhism; the world can no longer be looked at in the light of Jewish optimism, which found "all things very good": nay, in the Christian scheme, the devil is named as its Prince or Ruler ([Greek: ho archon tou kosmoutoutou.] John 12, 33). The world is no longer an end, but a means: and the realm of everlasting joy lies beyond it and the grave. Resignation in this world and direction of all our hopes to a better, form the spirit of Christianity. The way to this end is opened by the Atonement, that is the Redemption from this world and its ways. And in the moral system, instead of the law of vengeance, there is the command to love your enemy; instead of the promise of innumerable posterity, the assurance of eternal life; instead of visiting the sins of the fathers upon the children to the third and fourth generations, the Holy Spirit governs and overshadows all.

We see, then, that the doctrines of the Old Testament are rectified and their meaning changed by those of the New, so that, in the most important and essential matters, an agreement is brought about between them and the old religions of India. Everything which is true in Christianity may also be found in Brahmanism and Buddhism. But in Hinduism and Buddhism you will look in vain for any parallel to the Jewish doctrines of "a nothing quickened into life," or of "a world made in time," which cannot be humble enough in its thanks and praises to Jehovah for an ephemeral existence full of misery, anguish and need.

Whoever seriously thinks that superhuman beings have ever given our race information as to the aim of its existence and that of the world, is still in his childhood. There is no other revelation than the thoughts of the wise, even though these thoughts, liable to error as is the lot of everything human, are often clothed in strange allegories and myths under the name of religion. So far, then, it is a matter of indifference whether a man lives and dies in reliance on his own or another's thoughts; for it is never more than human thought, human opinion, which he trusts. Still, instead of trusting what their own minds tell them, men have as a rule a weakness for trusting others who pretend to supernatural sources of knowledge. And in view of the enormous intellectual inequality between man and man, it is easy to see that the thoughts of one mind might appear as in some sense a revelation to another.

The Art of Literature.

ON AUTHORSHIP.

There are, first of all, two kinds of authors: those who write for the subject's sake, and those who write for writing's sake. While the one have had thoughts or experiences which seem to them worth communicating, the others want money; and so they write, for money. Their thinking is part of the business of writing. They may be recognized by the way in which they spin out their thoughts to the greatest possible length; then, too, by the very nature of their thoughts, which are only half-true, perverse, forced, vacillating; again, by the aversion they generally show to saying anything straight out, so that they may seem other than they are. Hence their writing is deficient in clearness and definiteness, and it is not long before they betray that their only object in writing at all is to cover paper. This sometimes happens with the best authors; now and then, for example, with Lessing in his *Dramaturgie*, and even in many of Jean Paul's romances. As soon as the reader perceives this, let him throw the book away; for time is precious. The truth is that when an author begins to write for the sake of covering paper, he is cheating the reader; because he writes under the pretext that he has something to say.

Writing for money and reservation of copyright are, at bottom, the ruin of literature. No one writes anything that is worth writing, unless he writes entirely for the sake of his subject. What an inestimable boon it would be, if in every branch of literature there were only a few books, but those excellent! This can never happen, as long as money is to be made by writing. It seems as though the money lay under a curse; for every author degenerates as soon as he begins to put pen to paper in any way for the sake of gain. The best works of the greatest men all come from the time when they had to write for nothing or for very little. And here, too, that Spanish proverb holds good, which declares that honor and money are not to be found in the same purse—*honora y provecho no caben en un saco*. The reason why Literature is in such a bad plight nowadays is simply and solely that people write books to make money. A man who is in want sits down and writes a book, and the public is stupid enough to buy it. The secondary effect of this is the ruin of language.

A great many bad writers make their whole living by that foolish mania of the public for reading nothing but what has just been printed,—journalists, I mean. Truly, a most appropriate name. In plain language it is *journeymen, day-laborers*!

Again, it may be said that there are three kinds of authors. First come those who write without thinking. They write from a full memory, from reminiscences; it may be, even straight out of other people's books. This class is the most numerous. Then come those who do their thinking whilst they are writing. They think in order to write; and there is no lack of them. Last of all come those authors who think before they begin to write. They are rare.

Authors of the second class, who put off their thinking until they come to write, are like a sportsman who goes forth at random and is not likely to bring very much home. On the other hand, when an author of the third or rare class writes, it is like a _battue_. Here the game has been previously captured and shut up within a very small space; from which it is afterwards let out, so many at a time, into another space, also confined. The game cannot possibly escape the sportsman; he has nothing to do but aim and fire—in other words, write down his thoughts. This is a kind of sport from which a man has something to show.

But even though the number of those who really think seriously before they begin to write is small, extremely few of them think about *the subject itself*: the remainder think only about the books that have been written on the subject, and what has been said by others. In order to think at all, such writers need the more direct and powerful stimulus of having other people's thoughts before them. These become their immediate theme; and the result is that they are always under their influence, and so never, in any real sense of the word, are original. But the former are roused to thought by the subject itself, to which their thinking is thus immediately directed. This is the only class that produces writers of abiding fame.

It must, of course, be understood that I am speaking here of writers who treat of great subjects; not of writers on the art of making brandy.

Unless an author takes the material on which he writes out of his own head, that is to say, from his own observation, he is not worth reading. Book-manufacturers, compilers, the common run of history-writers, and many others of the same class, take their material immediately out of books; and the material goes straight to their finger-tips without even paying freight or undergoing examination as it passes through their heads, to say nothing of elaboration or revision. How very learned many a man would be if he knew everything that was in his own books! The consequence of this is that these writers talk in such a loose and vague manner, that the reader puzzles his brain in vain to understand what it is of which they are really thinking. They are thinking of nothing. It may now and then be the case that the book from which they copy has been composed exactly in the same way: so that writing of this sort is like a plaster cast of a cast; and in the end, the bare outline of the face, and that, too, hardly recognizable, is all that is left to your Antinous. Let compilations be read as seldom as possible. It is difficult to avoid them altogether; since compilations also include those text-books which contain in a small space the accumulated knowledge of centuries.

There is no greater mistake than to suppose that the last work is always the more correct; that what is written later on is in every case an improvement on what was written before; and that change always means progress. Real thinkers, men of right judgment, people who are in earnest with their subject,—these are all exceptions only. Vermin is the rule everywhere in the world: it is always on the alert, taking the mature opinions of the thinkers, and industriously seeking to improve upon them (save the mark!) in its own peculiar way.

If the reader wishes to study any subject, let him beware of rushing to the newest books upon it, and confining his attention to them alone, under the notion that science is always advancing, and that the old books have been drawn upon in the writing of the new. They have been drawn upon, it is true; but how? The writer of the new book often does not understand the old books thoroughly, and yet he is unwilling to take their exact words; so he bungles them, and says in his own bad way that which has been said very much better and more clearly by the old writers, who wrote from their own lively knowledge of the subject. The new writer frequently omits the best things they say, their most striking illustrations, their happiest remarks; because he does not see their value or feel how pregnant they are. The only thing that appeals to him is what is shallow and insipid.

It often happens that an old and excellent book is ousted by new and bad ones, which, written for money, appear with an air of great pretension and much puffing on the part of friends. In science a man tries to make his mark by bringing out something fresh. This often means nothing more than that he attacks some received theory which is quite correct, in order to make room for his own false notions. Sometimes the effort is successful for a time; and then a return is made to the old and true theory. These innovators are serious about nothing but their own precious self: it is this that they want to put forward, and the quick way of doing so, as they think, is to start a paradox. Their sterile heads take naturally to the path of negation; so they begin to deny truths that have long been admitted—the vital power, for example, the sympathetic nervous system, *generatio equivoca*, Bichat's distinction between the working of the passions and the working of intelligence; or else they want us to return to crass atomism, and the like. Hence it frequently happens that *the course of science is retrogressive.*

To this class of writers belong those translators who not only translate their author but also correct and revise him; a proceeding which always seems to me impertinent. To such writers I say: Write books yourself which are worth translating, and leave other people's works as they are!

The reader should study, if he can, the real authors, the men who have founded and discovered things; or, at any rate, those who are recognized as the great masters in every branch of knowledge. Let him buy second-hand books rather than read their contents in new ones. To be sure, it is easy to add to any new discovery—*inventis aliquid addere facile est*; and, therefore, the student, after well mastering the rudiments of his subject, will have to make himself acquainted with the more recent additions to the knowledge of it. And, in general, the following rule may be laid down here as elsewhere: if a thing is new, it is seldom good; because if it is good, it is only for a short time new.

What the address is to a letter, the title should be to a book; in other words, its main object should be to bring the book to those amongst the public who will take an interest in its contents. It should, therefore, be expressive; and since by its very nature it must be short, it should be concise, laconic, pregnant, and if possible give the contents in one word. A prolix title is bad; and so is one that says nothing, or is obscure and ambiguous, or even, it may be, false and misleading; this last may possibly involve the book in the same fate as overtakes a wrongly addressed letter. The worst titles of all are those which have been stolen, those, I mean, which have already been borne by other books; for they are in the first place a plagiarism, and secondly the most convincing proof of a total lack of originality in the author. A man who has not enough originality to invent a new title for his book, will be still less able to give it new contents. Akin to these stolen titles are those which have been imitated, that is to say, stolen to the extent of one half; for instance, long after I had produced my treatise *On Will in Nature*, Oersted wrote a book entitled *On Mind in Nature*.

A book can never be anything more than the impress of its author's thoughts; and the value of these will lie either in *the matter about which he has thought*, or in the *form* which his thoughts take, in other words, *what it is that he has thought about it*.

The matter of books is most various; and various also are the several excellences attaching to books on the score of their matter. By matter I mean everything that comes within the domain of actual experience; that is to say, the facts of history and the facts of nature, taken in and by themselves and in their widest sense. Here it is the *thing* treated of, which gives its peculiar character to the book; so that a book can be important, whoever it was that wrote it.

But in regard to the form, the peculiar character of a book depends upon the *person* who wrote it. It may treat of matters which are accessible to everyone and well known; but it is the way in which they are treated, what it is that is thought about them, that gives the book its value; and this comes from its author. If, then, from this point of view a book is excellent and beyond comparison, so is its author. It follows that if a writer is worth reading, his merit rises just in proportion as he owes little to his matter; therefore, the better known and the more hackneyed this is, the greater he will be. The three great tragedians of Greece, for example, all worked at the same subject-matter.

So when a book is celebrated, care should be taken to note whether it is so on account of its matter or its form; and a distinction should be made accordingly.

Books of great importance on account of their matter may proceed from very ordinary and shallow people, by the fact that they alone have had access to this matter; books, for instance, which describe journeys in distant lands, rare natural phenomena, or experiments; or historical occurrences of which the writers were witnesses, or in connection with which they have spent much time and trouble in the research and special study of original documents.

On the other hand, where the matter is accessible to everyone or very well known, everything will depend upon the form; and what it is that is thought about the matter will give the book all the value it possesses. Here only a really distinguished man will be able to produce anything worth reading; for the others will think nothing but what anyone else can think. They will just produce an impress of their own minds; but this is a print of which everyone possesses the original.

However, the public is very much more concerned to have matter than form; and for this very reason it is deficient in any high degree of culture. The public shows its preference in this respect in the most laughable way when it comes to deal with poetry; for there it devotes much trouble to the task of tracking out the actual events or personal circumstances in the life of the poet which served as the occasion of his various works; nay, these events and circumstances come in the end to be of greater importance than the works themselves; and rather than read Goethe himself, people prefer to read what has been written about him, and to study the legend of Faust more industriously than the drama of that name. And when Bürger declared that "people would write learned disquisitions on the question, Who Leonora really was," we find this literally fulfilled in Goethe's case; for we now possess a great many learned disquisitions on Faust and the legend attaching to him. Study of this kind is, and remains, devoted to the material of the drama alone. To give such preference to the matter over the form, is as though a man were to take a fine Etruscan vase, not to admire its shape or coloring, but to make a chemical analysis of the clay and paint of which it is composed.

The attempt to produce an effect by means of the material employed—an attempt which panders to this evil tendency of the public—is most to be condemned in branches of literature where any merit there may be lies expressly in the form; I mean, in poetical work. For all that, it is not rare to find bad dramatists trying to fill the house by means of the matter about which they write. For example, authors of this kind do not shrink from putting on the stage any man who is in any way celebrated, no matter whether his life may have been entirely devoid of dramatic incident; and sometimes, even, they do not wait until the persons immediately connected with him are dead.

The distinction between matter and form to which I am here alluding also holds good of conversation. The chief qualities which enable a man to converse well are intelligence, discernment, wit and vivacity: these supply the form of conversation. But it is not long before attention has to be paid to the matter of which he speaks; in other words, the subjects about which it is possible to converse with him—his knowledge. If this is very small, his conversation will not be worth anything, unless he possesses the above-named formal qualities in a very exceptional degree; for he will have nothing to talk about but those facts of life and nature which everybody knows. It will be just the opposite, however, if a man is deficient in these formal qualities, but has an amount of knowledge which lends value to what he says. This value will then depend entirely upon the matter of his conversation; for, as the Spanish proverb has it, *mas sabe el necio en su casa, que el sabio en la ajena*—a fool knows more of his own business than a wise man does of others.

ON STYLE.

Style is the physiognomy of the mind, and a safer index to character than the face. To imitate another man's style is like wearing a mask, which, be it never so fine, is not long in arousing disgust and abhorrence, because it is lifeless; so that even the ugliest living face is better. Hence those who write in Latin and copy the manner of ancient authors, may be said to speak through a mask; the reader, it is true, hears what they say, but he cannot observe their physiognomy too; he cannot see their *style*. With the Latin works of writers who think for themselves, the case is different, and their style is visible; writers, I mean, who have not condescended to any sort of imitation, such as Scotus Erigena, Petrarch, Bacon, Descartes, Spinoza, and many others. An affectation in style is like making grimaces. Further, the language in which a man writes is the physiognomy of the nation to which he belongs; and here there are many hard and fast differences, beginning from the language of the Greeks, down to that of the Caribbean islanders.

To form a provincial estimate of the value of a writer's productions, it is not directly necessary to know the subject on which he has thought, or what it is that he has said about it; that would imply a perusal of all his works. It will be enough, in the main, to know *how* he has thought. This, which means the essential temper or general quality of his mind, may be precisely determined by his style. A man's style shows the *formal* nature of all his thoughts—the formal nature which can never change, be the subject or the character of his thoughts what it may: it is, as it were, the dough out of which all the contents of his mind are kneaded. When Eulenspiegel was asked how long it would take to walk to the next village, he gave the seemingly incongruous answer: *Walk*. He wanted to find out by the man's pace the distance he would cover in a given time. In the same way, when I have read a few pages of an author, I know fairly well how far he can bring me.

Every mediocre writer tries to mask his own natural style, because in his heart he knows the truth of what I am saying. He is thus forced, at the outset, to give up any attempt at being frank or naïve—a privilege which is thereby reserved for superior minds, conscious of their own worth, and therefore sure of themselves. What I mean is that these everyday writers are absolutely unable to resolve upon writing just as they think; because they have a notion that, were they to do so, their work might possibly look very childish and simple. For all that, it would not be without its value. If they would only go honestly to work, and say, quite simply, the things they have really thought, and just as they have thought them, these writers would be readable and, within their own proper sphere, even instructive.

But instead of that, they try to make the reader believe that their thoughts have gone much further and deeper than is really the case. They say what they have to say in long sentences that wind about in a forced and unnatural way; they coin new words and write prolix periods which go round and round the thought and wrap it up in a sort of disguise. They tremble between the two separate aims of communicating what they want to say and of concealing it. Their object is to dress it up so that it may look learned or deep, in order to give people the impression that there is very much more in it than for the moment meets the eye. They either jot down their thoughts bit by bit, in short, ambiguous, and paradoxical sentences, which apparently mean much more than they say,—of this kind of writing Schelling's treatises on natural philosophy are a splendid instance; or else they hold forth with a deluge of words and the most intolerable diffusiveness, as though no end of fuss were necessary to make the reader understand the deep meaning of their sentences, whereas it is some quite simple if not actually trivial idea,—examples of which may be found in plenty in the popular works of Fichte, and the philosophical manuals of a hundred other miserable dunces not worth mentioning; or, again, they try to write in some particular style which they have been pleased to take up and think very grand, a style, for example, *par excellence* profound and scientific, where the reader is tormented to death by the narcotic effect of long-spun periods without a single idea in them,—such as are furnished in a special measure by those most impudent of all mortals, the Hegelians;[1] or it may be that it is an intellectual style they have striven after, where it seems as though their object were to go crazy altogether; and so on in many other cases. All these endeavors to put off the *nascetur ridiculus mus*—to avoid showing the funny little creature that is born after such mighty throes—often make it difficult to know what it is that they really mean. And then, too, they write down words, nay, even whole sentences, without attaching any meaning to them themselves, but in the hope that someone else will get sense out of them.

And what is at the bottom of all this? Nothing but the untiring effort to sell words for thoughts; a mode of merchandise that is always trying to make fresh openings for itself, and by means of odd expressions, turns of phrase, and combinations of every sort, whether new or used in a new sense, to produce the appearance of intellect in order to make up for the very painfully felt lack of it.

It is amusing to see how writers with this object in view will attempt first one mannerism and then another, as though they were putting on the mask of intellect! This mask may possibly deceive the inexperienced for a while, until it is seen to be a dead thing, with no life in it at all; it is then laughed at and exchanged for another. Such an author will at one moment write in a dithyrambic vein, as though he were tipsy; at another, nay, on the very next page, he will be pompous, severe, profoundly learned and prolix, stumbling on in the most cumbrous way and chopping up everything very small; like the late Christian Wolf, only in a modern dress. Longest of all lasts the mask of unintelligibility; but this is only in Germany, whither it was introduced by Fichte, perfected by Schelling, and carried to its highest pitch in Hegel—always with the best results.

And yet nothing is easier than to write so that no one can understand; just as contrarily, nothing is more difficult than to express deep things in such a way that every one must necessarily grasp them. All the arts and tricks I have been mentioning are rendered superfluous if the author really has any brains; for that allows him to show himself as he is, and confirms to all time Horace's maxim that good sense is the source and origin of good style:

Scribendi recte sapere est et principium et fons.

---

[1] In their Hegel-gazette, commonly known as *Jahrbücher der wissenschaftlichen Literatur.*

But those authors I have named are like certain workers in metal, who try a hundred different compounds to take the place of gold—the only metal which can never have any substitute. Rather than do that, there is nothing against which a writer should be more upon his guard than the manifest endeavor to exhibit more intellect than he really has; because this makes the reader suspect that he possesses very little; since it is always the case that if a man affects anything, whatever it may be, it is just there that he is deficient.

That is why it is praise to an author to say that he is *naïve*; it means that he need not shrink from showing himself as he is. Generally speaking, to be *naïve* is to be attractive; while lack of naturalness is everywhere repulsive. As a matter of fact we find that every really great writer tries to express his thoughts as purely, clearly, definitely and shortly as possible. Simplicity has always been held to be a mark of truth; it is also a mark of genius. Style receives its beauty from the thought it expresses; but with sham-thinkers the thoughts are supposed to be fine because of the style. Style is nothing but the mere silhouette of thought; and an obscure or bad style means a dull or confused brain.

The first rule, then, for a good style is that *the author should have something to say*; nay, this is in itself almost all that is necessary. Ah, how much it means! The neglect of this rule is a fundamental trait in the philosophical writing, and, in fact, in all the reflective literature, of my country, more especially since Fichte. These writers all let it be seen that they want to appear as though they had something to say; whereas they have nothing to say. Writing of this kind was brought in by the pseudo-philosophers at the Universities, and now it is current everywhere, even among the first literary notabilities of the age. It is the mother of that strained and vague style, where there seem to be two or even more meanings in the sentence; also of that prolix and cumbrous manner of expression, called *le stile empesé*; again, of that mere waste of words which consists in pouring them out like a flood; finally, of that trick of concealing the direst poverty of thought under a farrago of never-ending chatter, which clacks away like a windmill and quite stupefies one—stuff which a man may read for hours together without getting hold of a single clearly expressed and definite idea.[2] However, people are easy-going, and they have formed the habit of reading page upon page of all sorts of such verbiage, without having any particular idea of what the author really means. They fancy it is all as it should be, and fail to discover that he is writing simply for writing's sake.

On the other hand, a good author, fertile in ideas, soon wins his

---

[2] Select examples of the art of writing in this style are to be found almost *passim* in the *Jahrbücher* published at Halle, afterwards called the *Deutschen Jahrbücher*.

reader's confidence that, when he writes, he has really and truly *something to say*; and this gives the intelligent reader patience to follow him with attention. Such an author, just because he really has something to say, will never fail to express himself in the simplest and most straightforward manner; because his object is to awake the very same thought in the reader that he has in himself, and no other. So he will be able to affirm with Boileau that his thoughts are everywhere open to the light of the day, and that his verse always says something, whether it says it well or ill:

Ma pensée au grand jour partout s'offre et s'expose,
Et mon vers, bien ou mal, dit toujours quelque chose:

while of the writers previously described it may be asserted, in the words of the same poet, that they talk much and never say anything at all—*qui parlant beaucoup ne disent jamais rien.*

Another characteristic of such writers is that they always avoid a positive assertion wherever they can possibly do so, in order to leave a loophole for escape in case of need. Hence they never fail to choose the more *abstract* way of expressing themselves; whereas intelligent people use the more *concrete*; because the latter brings things more within the range of actual demonstration, which is the source of all evidence.

There are many examples proving this preference for abstract expression; and a particularly ridiculous one is afforded by the use of the verb *to condition* in the sense of *to cause* or *to produce.* People say *to condition something* instead of *to cause it*, because being abstract and indefinite it says less; it affirms that A cannot happen without B, instead of that A is caused by B. A back door is always left open; and this suits people whose secret knowledge of their own incapacity inspires them with a perpetual terror of all positive assertion; while with other people it is merely the effect of that tendency by which everything that is stupid in literature or bad in life is immediately imitated—a fact proved in either case by the rapid way in which it spreads. The Englishman uses his own judgment in what he writes as well as in what he does; but there is no nation of which this eulogy is less true than of the Germans. The consequence of this state of things is that the word *cause* has of late almost disappeared from the language of literature, and people talk only of *condition.* The fact is worth mentioning because it is so characteristically ridiculous.

The very fact that these commonplace authors are never more than half-conscious when they write, would be enough to account for their dullness of mind and the tedious things they produce. I say they are only half-conscious, because they really do not themselves understand the meaning of the words they use: they take words ready-made and commit them to memory. Hence when they write, it is not so much words as whole phrases that they put together—*phrases banales.* This is the explanation of that palpable lack of clearly-expressed thought in what they say. The fact is that they do not possess the die to give this stamp to their writing; clear thought of their own is just what they have not got. And what do we find in its place?—a vague, enigmatical intermixture of words, current phrases, hackneyed terms, and fashionable expressions. The result is that the foggy stuff they write is like a page printed with very old type.

On the other hand, an intelligent author really speaks to us when he writes, and that is why he is able to rouse our interest and commune with us. It is the intelligent author alone who puts individual words together with a full consciousness of their meaning, and chooses them with deliberate design. Consequently, his discourse stands to that of the writer described above, much as a picture that has been really painted, to one that has been produced by the use of a stencil. In the one case, every word, every touch of the brush, has a special purpose; in the other, all is done mechanically. The same distinction may be observed in music. For just as Lichtenberg says that Garrick's soul seemed to be in every muscle in his body, so it is the omnipresence of intellect that always and everywhere characterizes the work of genius.

I have alluded to the tediousness which marks the works of these writers; and in this connection it is to be observed, generally, that tediousness is of two kinds; objective and subjective. A work is objectively tedious when it contains the defect in question; that is to say, when its author has no perfectly clear thought or knowledge to communicate. For if a man has any clear thought or knowledge in him, his aim will be to communicate it, and he will direct his energies to this end; so that the ideas he furnishes are everywhere clearly expressed. The result is that he is neither diffuse, nor unmeaning, nor confused, and consequently not tedious. In such a case, even though the author is at bottom in error, the error is at any rate clearly worked out and well thought over, so that it is at least formally correct; and thus some value always attaches to the work. But for the same reason a work that is objectively tedious is at all times devoid of any value whatever.

The other kind of tediousness is only relative: a reader may find a work dull because he has no interest in the question treated of in it, and this means that his intellect is restricted. The best work may, therefore, be tedious subjectively, tedious, I mean, to this or that particular person; just as, contrarily, the worst work may be subjectively engrossing to this or that particular person who has an interest in the question treated of, or in the writer of the book.

It would generally serve writers in good stead if they would see that, whilst a man should, if possible, think like a great genius, he should talk the same language as everyone else. Authors should use common words to say uncommon things. But they do just the opposite. We find them trying to wrap up trivial ideas in grand words, and to clothe their very ordinary thoughts in the most extraordinary phrases, the most far-fetched, unnatural, and out-of-the-way expressions. Their sentences perpetually stalk about on stilts. They take so much pleasure in bombast, and write in such a high-flown, bloated, affected, hyperbolical and acrobatic style that their prototype is Ancient Pistol, whom his friend Falstaff once impatiently told to say what he had to say *like a man of this world.*[3]

There is no expression in any other language exactly answering to the French *stile empesé*; but the thing itself exists all the more often. When associated with affectation, it is in literature what assumption of dignity, grand airs and primeness are in society; and equally intolerable. Dullness of mind is fond of donning this dress; just as an ordinary life it is stupid people who like being demure and formal.

An author who writes in the prim style resembles a man who dresses himself up in order to avoid being confounded or put on the same level with a mob—a risk never run by the *gentleman*, even in his worst clothes. The plebeian may be known by a certain showiness of attire and a wish to have everything spick and span; and in the same way, the commonplace person is betrayed by his style.

Nevertheless, an author follows a false aim if he tries to write exactly as he speaks. There is no style of writing but should have a certain trace of kinship with the *epigraphic* or *monumental* style, which is, indeed, the ancestor of all styles. For an author to write as he speaks is just as reprehensible as the opposite fault, to speak as he writes; for this gives a pedantic effect to what he says, and at the same time makes him hardly intelligible.

An obscure and vague manner of expression is always and everywhere a very bad sign. In ninety-nine cases out of a hundred it comes from vagueness of thought; and this again almost always means that there is something radically wrong and incongruous about the thought itself—in a word, that it is incorrect. When a right thought springs up in the mind, it strives after expression and is not long in reaching it; for clear thought easily finds words to fit it. If a man is capable of thinking anything at all, he is also always able to express it in clear, intelligible, and unambiguous terms. Those writers who construct difficult, obscure, involved, and equivocal sentences, most certainly do not know aright what it is that they want to say: they have only a dull consciousness of it, which is still in the stage of struggle to shape itself as thought. Often, indeed, their desire is to conceal from themselves and others that they really have nothing at all to say. They

---

[3] *King Henry IV.*, Part II. Act v. Sc. 3.

wish to appear to know what they do not know, to think what they do not think, to say what they do not say. If a man has some real communication to make, which will he choose—an indistinct or a clear way of expressing himself? Even Quintilian remarks that things which are said by a highly educated man are often easier to understand and much clearer; and that the less educated a man is, the more obscurely he will write—*plerumque accidit ut faciliora sint ad intelligendum et lucidiora multo que a doctissimo quoque dicuntur.... Erit ergo etiam obscurior quo quisque deterior.*

An author should avoid enigmatical phrases; he should know whether he wants to say a thing or does not want to say it. It is this indecision of style that makes so many writers insipid. The only case that offers an exception to this rule arises when it is necessary to make a remark that is in some way improper.

As exaggeration generally produces an effect the opposite of that aimed at; so words, it is true, serve to make thought intelligible—but only up to a certain point. If words are heaped up beyond it, the thought becomes more and more obscure again. To find where the point lies is the problem of style, and the business of the critical faculty; for a word too much always defeats its purpose. This is what Voltaire means when he says that *the adjective is the enemy of the substantive.* But, as we have seen, many people try to conceal their poverty of thought under a flood of verbiage.

Accordingly let all redundancy be avoided, all stringing together of remarks which have no meaning and are not worth perusal. A writer must make a sparing use of the reader's time, patience and attention; so as to lead him to believe that his author writes what is worth careful study, and will reward the time spent upon it. It is always better to omit something good than to add that which is not worth saying at all. This is the right application of Hesiod's maxim, [Greek: pleon aemisu pantos][4]—the half is more than the whole. *Le secret pour être ennuyeux, c'est de tout dire.* Therefore, if possible, the quintessence only! mere leading thoughts! nothing that the reader would think for himself. To use many words to communicate few thoughts is everywhere the unmistakable sign of mediocrity. To gather much thought into few words stamps the man of genius.

Truth is most beautiful undraped; and the impression it makes is deep in proportion as its expression has been simple. This is so, partly because it then takes unobstructed possession of the hearer's whole soul, and leaves him no by-thought to distract him; partly, also, because he feels that here he is not being corrupted or cheated by the arts of rhetoric, but that all the effect of what is said comes from the thing

---

[4] *Works and Days*, 40.

itself. For instance, what declamation on the vanity of human existence could ever be more telling than the words of Job? *Man that is born of a woman hath but a short time to live and is full of misery. He cometh up, and is cut down, like a flower; he fleeth as it were a shadow, and never continueth in one stay.*

For the same reason Goethe's naïve poetry is incomparably greater than Schiller's rhetoric. It is this, again, that makes many popular songs so affecting. As in architecture an excess of decoration is to be avoided, so in the art of literature a writer must guard against all rhetorical finery, all useless amplification, and all superfluity of expression in general; in a word, he must strive after *chastity* of style. Every word that can be spared is hurtful if it remains. The law of simplicity and naïveté holds good of all fine art; for it is quite possible to be at once simple and sublime.

True brevity of expression consists in everywhere saying only what is worth saying, and in avoiding tedious detail about things which everyone can supply for himself. This involves correct discrimination between what it necessary and what is superfluous. A writer should never be brief at the expense of being clear, to say nothing of being grammatical. It shows lamentable want of judgment to weaken the expression of a thought, or to stunt the meaning of a period for the sake of using a few words less. But this is the precise endeavor of that false brevity nowadays so much in vogue, which proceeds by leaving out useful words and even by sacrificing grammar and logic. It is not only that such writers spare a word by making a single verb or adjective do duty for several different periods, so that the reader, as it were, has to grope his way through them in the dark; they also practice, in many other respects, an unseemingly economy of speech, in the effort to effect what they foolishly take to be brevity of expression and conciseness of style. By omitting something that might have thrown a light over the whole sentence, they turn it into a conundrum, which the reader tries to solve by going over it again and again.[5]

It is wealth and weight of thought, and nothing else, that gives brevity to style, and makes it concise and pregnant. If a writer's ideas are important, luminous, and generally worth communicating, they will necessarily furnish matter and substance enough to fill out the periods which give them expression, and make these in all their parts both

---

[5] *Translator's Note.*—In the original, Schopenhauer here enters upon a lengthy examination of certain common errors in the writing and speaking of German. His remarks are addressed to his own countrymen, and would lose all point, even if they were intelligible, in an English translation. But for those who practice their German by conversing or corresponding with Germans, let me recommend what he there says as a useful corrective to a slipshod style, such as can easily be contracted if it is assumed that the natives of a country always know their own language perfectly.

grammatically and verbally complete; and so much will this be the case that no one will ever find them hollow, empty or feeble. The diction will everywhere be brief and pregnant, and allow the thought to find intelligible and easy expression, and even unfold and move about with grace.

Therefore instead of contracting his words and forms of speech, let a writer enlarge his thoughts. If a man has been thinned by illness and finds his clothes too big, it is not by cutting them down, but by recovering his usual bodily condition, that he ought to make them fit him again.

Let me here mention an error of style, very prevalent nowadays, and, in the degraded state of literature and the neglect of ancient languages, always on the increase; I mean *subjectivity*. A writer commits this error when he thinks it enough if he himself knows what he means and wants to say, and takes no thought for the reader, who is left to get at the bottom of it as best he can. This is as though the author were holding a monologue; whereas, it ought to be a dialogue; and a dialogue, too, in which he must express himself all the more clearly inasmuch as he cannot hear the questions of his interlocutor.

Style should for this very reason never be subjective, but *objective*; and it will not be objective unless the words are so set down that they directly force the reader to think precisely the same thing as the author thought when he wrote them. Nor will this result be obtained unless the author has always been careful to remember that thought so far follows the law of gravity that it travels from head to paper much more easily than from paper to head; so that he must assist the latter passage by every means in his power. If he does this, a writer's words will have a purely objective effect, like that of a finished picture in oils; whilst the subjective style is not much more certain in its working than spots on the wall, which look like figures only to one whose phantasy has been accidentally aroused by them; other people see nothing but spots and blurs. The difference in question applies to literary method as a whole; but it is often established also in particular instances. For example, in a recently published work I found the following sentence: *I have not written in order to increase the number of existing books.* This means just the opposite of what the writer wanted to say, and is nonsense as well.

He who writes carelessly confesses thereby at the very outset that he does not attach much importance to his own thoughts. For it is only where a man is convinced of the truth and importance of his thoughts, that he feels the enthusiasm necessary for an untiring and assiduous effort to find the clearest, finest, and strongest expression for them,— just as for sacred relics or priceless works of art there are provided silvern or golden receptacles. It was this feeling that led ancient authors, whose thoughts, expressed in their own words, have lived thousands of years, and therefore bear the honored title of _classics_, always to write with care. Plato, indeed, is said to have written the introduction to his _Republic_ seven times over in different ways.[6]

As neglect of dress betrays want of respect for the company a man meets, so a hasty, careless, bad style shows an outrageous lack of regard for the reader, who then rightly punishes it by refusing to read the book. It is especially amusing to see reviewers criticising the works of others in their own most careless style—the style of a hireling. It is as though a judge were to come into court in dressing-gown and slippers! If I see a man badly and dirtily dressed, I feel some hesitation, at first, in entering into conversation with him: and when, on taking up a book, I am struck at once by the negligence of its style, I put it away.

Good writing should be governed by the rule that a man can think only one thing clearly at a time; and, therefore, that he should not be expected to think two or even more things in one and the same moment. But this is what is done when a writer breaks up his principal sentence into little pieces, for the purpose of pushing into the gaps thus made two or three other thoughts by way of parenthesis; thereby unnecessarily and wantonly confusing the reader. And here it is again my own countrymen who are chiefly in fault. That German lends itself to this way of writing, makes the thing possible, but does not justify it. No prose reads more easily or pleasantly than French, because, as a rule, it is free from the error in question. The Frenchman strings his thoughts together, as far as he can, in the most logical and natural order, and so lays them before his reader one after the other for convenient deliberation, so that every one of them may receive undivided attention. The German, on the other hand, weaves them together into a sentence which he twists and crosses, and crosses and twists again; because he wants to say six things all at once, instead of advancing them one by one. His aim should be to attract and hold the reader's attention; but, above and beyond neglect of this aim, he demands from the reader that he shall set the above mentioned rule at defiance, and think three or four different thoughts at one and the same time; or since that is impossible, that his thoughts shall succeed each other as quickly as the vibrations of a cord. In this way an author lays the foundation of his *stile empesé*, which is then carried to perfection by the use of high-flown, pompous expressions to communicate the simplest things, and other artifices of the same kind.

In those long sentences rich in involved parenthesis, like a box of boxes one within another, and padded out like roast geese stuffed with apples, it is really the *memory* that is chiefly taxed; while it is the

---

[6] *Translator's Note.*—It is a fact worth mentioning that the first twelve words of the *Republic* are placed in the exact order which would be natural in English.

understanding and the judgment which should be called into play, instead of having their activity thereby actually hindered and weakened.[7] This kind of sentence furnishes the reader with mere half-phrases, which he is then called upon to collect carefully and store up in his memory, as though they were the pieces of a torn letter, afterwards to be completed and made sense of by the other halves to which they respectively belong. He is expected to go on reading for a little without exercising any thought, nay, exerting only his memory, in the hope that, when he comes to the end of the sentence, he may see its meaning and so receive something to think about; and he is thus given a great deal to learn by heart before obtaining anything to understand. This is manifestly wrong and an abuse of the reader's patience.

The ordinary writer has an unmistakable preference for this style, because it causes the reader to spend time and trouble in understanding that which he would have understood in a moment without it; and this makes it look as though the writer had more depth and intelligence than the reader. This is, indeed, one of those artifices referred to above, by means of which mediocre authors unconsciously, and as it were by instinct, strive to conceal their poverty of thought and give an appearance of the opposite. Their ingenuity in this respect is really astounding.

It is manifestly against all sound reason to put one thought obliquely on top of another, as though both together formed a wooden cross. But this is what is done where a writer interrupts what he has begun to say, for the purpose of inserting some quite alien matter; thus depositing with the reader a meaningless half-sentence, and bidding him keep it until the completion comes. It is much as though a man were to treat his guests by handing them an empty plate, in the hope of something appearing upon it. And commas used for a similar purpose belong to the same family as notes at the foot of the page and parenthesis in the middle of the text; nay, all three differ only in degree. If Demosthenes and Cicero occasionally inserted words by ways of parenthesis, they would have done better to have refrained.

But this style of writing becomes the height of absurdity when the parenthesis are not even fitted into the frame of the sentence, but wedged in so as directly to shatter it. If, for instance, it is an impertinent thing to interrupt another person when he is speaking, it is no less impertinent to interrupt oneself. But all bad, careless, and hasty authors, who scribble with the bread actually before their eyes, use this style of writing six times on a page, and rejoice in it. It consists in—it is

---

[7] *Translator's Note.*—This sentence in the original is obviously meant to illustrate the fault of which it speaks. It does so by the use of a construction very common in German, but happily unknown in English; where, however, the fault itself exists none the less, though in different form.

advisable to give rule and example together, wherever it is possible—breaking up one phrase in order to glue in another. Nor is it merely out of laziness that they write thus. They do it out of stupidity; they think there is a charming *légèreté* about it; that it gives life to what they say. No doubt there are a few rare cases where such a form of sentence may be pardonable.

Few write in the way in which an architect builds; who, before he sets to work, sketches out his plan, and thinks it over down to its smallest details. Nay, most people write only as though they were playing dominoes; and, as in this game, the pieces are arranged half by design, half by chance, so it is with the sequence and connection of their sentences. They only have an idea of what the general shape of their work will be, and of the aim they set before themselves. Many are ignorant even of this, and write as the coral-insects build; period joins to period, and the Lord only knows what the author means.

Life now-a-days goes at a gallop; and the way in which this affects literature is to make it extremely superficial and slovenly.

ON THE STUDY OF LATIN.

The abolition of Latin as the universal language of learned men, together with the rise of that provincialism which attaches to national literatures, has been a real misfortune for the cause of knowledge in Europe. For it was chiefly through the medium of the Latin language that a learned public existed in Europe at all—a public to which every book as it came out directly appealed. The number of minds in the whole of Europe that are capable of thinking and judging is small, as it is; but when the audience is broken up and severed by differences of language, the good these minds can do is very much weakened. This is a great disadvantage; but a second and worse one will follow, namely, that the ancient languages will cease to be taught at all. The neglect of them is rapidly gaining ground both in France and Germany.

If it should really come to this, then farewell, humanity! farewell, noble taste and high thinking! The age of barbarism will return, in spite of railways, telegraphs and balloons. We shall thus in the end lose one more advantage possessed by all our ancestors. For Latin is not only a key to the knowledge of Roman antiquity; its also directly opens up to us the Middle Age in every country in Europe, and modern times as well, down to about the year 1750. Erigena, for example, in the ninth century, John of Salisbury in the twelfth, Raimond Lully in the thirteenth, with a hundred others, speak straight to us in the very language that they naturally adopted in thinking of learned matters. They thus come quite close to us even at this distance of time: we are in direct contact with them, and really come to know them. How would it have been if every one of them spoke in the language that was peculiar to his time and country? We should not understand even the half of what they said. A real intellectual contact with them would be impossible. We should see them like shadows on the farthest horizon, or, may be, through the translator's telescope.

It was with an eye to the advantage of writing in Latin that Bacon, as he himself expressly states, proceeded to translate his *Essays* into that language, under the title *Sermones fideles*; at which work Hobbes assisted him.[8]

Here let me observe, by way of parenthesis, that when patriotism tries to urge its claims in the domain of knowledge, it commits an offence which should not be tolerated. For in those purely human questions which interest all men alike, where truth, insight, beauty, should be of sole account, what can be more impertinent than to let preference for the nation to which a man's precious self happens to belong, affect the balance of judgment, and thus supply a reason for doing violence to truth and being unjust to the great minds of a foreign country in order to make much of the smaller minds of one's own! Still, there are writers in every nation in Europe, who afford examples of this vulgar feeling. It is this which led Yriarte to caricature them in the thirty-third of his charming *Literary Fables*.[9]

In learning a language, the chief difficulty consists in making acquaintance with every idea which it expresses, even though it should use words for which there is no exact equivalent in the mother tongue; and this often happens. In learning a new language a man has, as it were, to mark out in his mind the boundaries of quite new spheres of ideas, with the result that spheres of ideas arise where none were before. Thus he not only learns words, he gains ideas too.

This is nowhere so much the case as in learning ancient languages, for the differences they present in their mode of expression as compared with modern languages is greater than can be found amongst modern languages as compared with one another. This is shown by the fact that in translating into Latin, recourse must be had to quite other

---

[8] Cf. Thomae Hobbes vita: *Carolopoli apud Eleutherium Anglicum*, 1681, p. 22.

[9] *Translator's Note.*—Tomas de Yriarte (1750-91), a Spanish poet, and keeper of archives in the War Office at Madrid. His two best known works are a didactic poem, entitled *La Musica*, and the *Fables* here quoted, which satirize the peculiar foibles of literary men. They have been translated into many languages; into English by Rockliffe (3rd edition, 1866). The fable in question describes how, at a picnic of the animals, a discussion arose as to which of them carried off the palm for superiority of talent. The praises of the ant, the dog, the bee, and the parrot were sung in turn; but at last the ostrich stood up and declared for the dromedary. Whereupon the dromedary stood up and declared for the ostrich. No one could discover the reason for this mutual compliment. Was it because both were such uncouth beasts, or had such long necks, or were neither of them particularly clever or beautiful? or was it because each had a hump? *No!* said the fox, *you are all wrong. Don't you see they are both foreigners*? Cannot the same be said of many men of learning?

turns of phrase than are used in the original. The thought that is to be translated has to be melted down and recast; in other words, it must be analyzed and then recomposed. It is just this process which makes the study of the ancient languages contribute so much to the education of the mind.

It follows from this that a man's thought varies according to the language in which he speaks. His ideas undergo a fresh modification, a different shading, as it were, in the study of every new language. Hence an acquaintance with many languages is not only of much indirect advantage, but it is also a direct means of mental culture, in that it corrects and matures ideas by giving prominence to their many-sided nature and their different varieties of meaning, as also that it increases dexterity of thought; for in the process of learning many languages, ideas become more and more independent of words. The ancient languages effect this to a greater degree than the modern, in virtue of the difference to which I have alluded.

From what I have said, it is obvious that to imitate the style of the ancients in their own language, which is so very much superior to ours in point of grammatical perfection, is the best way of preparing for a skillful and finished expression of thought in the mother-tongue. Nay, if a man wants to be a great writer, he must not omit to do this: just as, in the case of sculpture or painting, the student must educate himself by copying the great masterpieces of the past, before proceeding to original work. It is only by learning to write Latin that a man comes to treat diction as an art. The material in this art is language, which must therefore be handled with the greatest care and delicacy.

The result of such study is that a writer will pay keen attention to the meaning and value of words, their order and connection, their grammatical forms. He will learn how to weigh them with precision, and so become an expert in the use of that precious instrument which is meant not only to express valuable thought, but to preserve it as well. Further, he will learn to feel respect for the language in which he writes and thus be saved from any attempt to remodel it by arbitrary and capricious treatment. Without this schooling, a man's writing may easily degenerate into mere chatter.

To be entirely ignorant of the Latin language is like being in a fine country on a misty day. The horizon is extremely limited. Nothing can be seen clearly except that which is quite close; a few steps beyond, everything is buried in obscurity. But the Latinist has a wide view, embracing modern times, the Middle Age and Antiquity; and his mental horizon is still further enlarged if he studies Greek or even Sanscrit.

If a man knows no Latin, he belongs to the vulgar, even though he be a great virtuoso on the electrical machine and have the base of hydrofluoric acid in his crucible.

There is no better recreation for the mind than the study of the ancient classics. Take any one of them into your hand, be it only for half an hour, and you will feel yourself refreshed, relieved, purified, ennobled, strengthened; just as though you had quenched your thirst at some pure spring. Is this the effect of the old language and its perfect expression, or is it the greatness of the minds whose works remain unharmed and unweakened by the lapse of a thousand years? Perhaps both together. But this I know. If the threatened calamity should ever come, and the ancient languages cease to be taught, a new literature will arise, of such barbarous, shallow and worthless stuff as never was seen before.

ON MEN OF LEARNING.

When one sees the number and variety of institutions which exist for the purposes of education, and the vast throng of scholars and masters, one might fancy the human race to be very much concerned about truth and wisdom. But here, too, appearances are deceptive. The masters teach in order to gain money, and strive, not after wisdom, but the outward show and reputation of it; and the scholars learn, not for the sake of knowledge and insight, but to be able to chatter and give themselves airs. Every thirty years a new race comes into the world—a youngster that knows nothing about anything, and after summarily devouring in all haste the results of human knowledge as they have been accumulated for thousands of years, aspires to be thought cleverer than the whole of the past. For this purpose he goes to the University, and takes to reading books—new books, as being of his own age and standing. Everything he reads must be briefly put, must be new! he is new himself. Then he falls to and criticises. And here I am not taking the slightest account of studies pursued for the sole object of making a living.

Students, and learned persons of all sorts and every age, aim as a rule at acquiring *information* rather than insight. They pique themselves upon knowing about everything—stones, plants, battles, experiments, and all the books in existence. It never occurs to them that information is only a means of insight, and in itself of little or no value; that it is his way of *thinking* that makes a man a philosopher. When I hear of these portents of learning and their imposing erudition, I sometimes say to myself: Ah, how little they must have had to think about, to have been able to read so much! And when I actually find it reported of the elder Pliny that he was continually reading or being read to, at table, on a journey, or in his bath, the question forces itself upon my mind, whether the man was so very lacking in thought of his own that he had to have alien thought incessantly instilled into him; as though he were a consumptive patient taking jellies to keep himself alive. And neither his undiscerning credulity nor his inexpressibly repulsive and barely intelligible style—which seems like of a man taking notes, and very economical of paper—is of a kind to give me a high opinion of his power of independent thought.

We have seen that much reading and learning is prejudicial to thinking for oneself; and, in the same way, through much writing and teaching, a man loses the habit of being quite clear, and therefore thorough, in regard to the things he knows and understands; simply because he has left himself no time to acquire clearness or thoroughness. And so, when clear knowledge fails him in his utterances, he is forced to fill out the gaps with words and phrases. It is this, and not the dryness of the subject-matter, that makes most books such tedious reading. There is a saying that a good cook can make a palatable dish even out of an old shoe; and a good writer can make the dryest things interesting.

With by far the largest number of learned men, knowledge is a means, not an end. That is why they will never achieve any great work; because, to do that, he who pursues knowledge must pursue it as an end, and treat everything else, even existence itself, as only a means. For everything which a man fails to pursue for its own sake is but half-pursued; and true excellence, no matter in what sphere, can be attained only where the work has been produced for its own sake alone, and not as a means to further ends.

And so, too, no one will ever succeed in doing anything really great and original in the way of thought, who does not seek to acquire knowledge for himself, and, making this the immediate object of his studies, decline to trouble himself about the knowledge of others. But the average man of learning studies for the purpose of being able to teach and write. His head is like a stomach and intestines which let the food pass through them undigested. That is just why his teaching and writing is of so little use. For it is not upon undigested refuse that people can be nourished, but solely upon the milk which secretes from the very blood itself.

The wig is the appropriate symbol of the man of learning, pure and simple. It adorns the head with a copious quantity of false hair, in lack of one's own: just as erudition means endowing it with a great mass of alien thought. This, to be sure, does not clothe the head so well and naturally, nor is it so generally useful, nor so suited for all purposes, nor so firmly rooted; nor when alien thought is used up, can it be immediately replaced by more from the same source, as is the case with that which springs from soil of one's own. So we find Sterne, in his *Tristram Shandy*, boldly asserting that *an ounce of a man's own wit is worth a ton of other people's.*

And in fact the most profound erudition is no more akin to genius than a collection of dried plants in like Nature, with its constant flow of new life, ever fresh, ever young, ever changing. There are no two things more opposed than the childish naïveté of an ancient author and the learning of his commentator.

Dilettanti, dilettanti! This is the slighting way in which those who pursue any branch of art or learning for the love and enjoyment of the thing,—*per il loro diletto,* are spoken of by those who have taken it up for the sake of gain, attracted solely by the prospect of money. This contempt of theirs comes from the base belief that no man will seriously devote himself to a subject, unless he is spurred on to it by want, hunger, or else some form of greed. The public is of the same way of thinking; and hence its general respect for professionals and its distrust of *dilettanti.* But the truth is that the *dilettante* treats his subject as an end, whereas the professional, pure and simple, treats it merely as a means. He alone will be really in earnest about a matter, who has a direct interest therein, takes to it because he likes it, and pursues it *con amore.* It is these, and not hirelings, that have always done the greatest work.

In the republic of letters it is as in other republics; favor is shown to the plain man—he who goes his way in silence and does not set up to be cleverer than others. But the abnormal man is looked upon as threatening danger; people band together against him, and have, oh! such a majority on their side.

The condition of this republic is much like that of a small State in America, where every man is intent only upon his own advantage, and seeks reputation and power for himself, quite heedless of the general weal, which then goes to ruin. So it is in the republic of letters; it is himself, and himself alone, that a man puts forward, because he wants to gain fame. The only thing in which all agree is in trying to keep down a really eminent man, if he should chance to show himself, as one who would be a common peril. From this it is easy to see how it fares with knowledge as a whole.

Between professors and independent men of learning there has always been from of old a certain antagonism, which may perhaps be likened to that existing been dogs and wolves. In virtue of their position, professors enjoy great facilities for becoming known to their contemporaries. Contrarily, independent men of learning enjoy, by their position, great facilities for becoming known to posterity; to which it is necessary that, amongst other and much rarer gifts, a man should have a certain leisure and freedom. As mankind takes a long time in finding out on whom to bestow its attention, they may both work together side by side.

He who holds a professorship may be said to receive his food in the stall; and this is the best way with ruminant animals. But he who finds his food for himself at the hands of Nature is better off in the open field.

Of human knowledge as a whole and in every branch of it, by far the largest part exists nowhere but on paper,—I mean, in books, that paper memory of mankind. Only a small part of it is at any given period really active in the minds of particular persons. This is due, in the main, to the brevity and uncertainty of life; but it also comes from the fact that men are lazy and bent on pleasure. Every generation attains, on its hasty passage through existence, just so much of human knowledge as it needs, and then soon disappears. Most men of learning are very superficial. Then follows a new generation, full of hope, but ignorant, and with everything to learn from the beginning. It seizes, in its turn, just so much as it can grasp or find useful on its brief journey and then too goes its way. How badly it would fare with human knowledge if it were not for the art of writing and printing! This it is that makes libraries the only sure and lasting memory of the human race, for its individual members have all of them but a very limited and imperfect one. Hence most men of learning as are loth to have their knowledge examined as merchants to lay bare their books.

Human knowledge extends on all sides farther than the eye can reach; and of that which would be generally worth knowing, no one man can possess even the thousandth part.

All branches of learning have thus been so much enlarged that he who would "do something" has to pursue no more than one subject and disregard all others. In his own subject he will then, it is true, be superior to the vulgar; but in all else he will belong to it. If we add to this that neglect of the ancient languages, which is now-a-days on the increase and is doing away with all general education in the humanities—for a mere smattering of Latin and Greek is of no use—we shall come to have men of learning who outside their own subject display an ignorance truly bovine.

An exclusive specialist of this kind stands on a par with a workman in a factory, whose whole life is spent in making one particular kind of screw, or catch, or handle, for some particular instrument or machine, in which, indeed, he attains incredible dexterity. The specialist may also be likened to a man who lives in his own house and never leaves it. There he is perfectly familiar with everything, every little step, corner, or board; much as Quasimodo in Victor Hugo's *Notre Dame* knows the cathedral; but outside it, all is strange and unknown.

For true culture in the humanities it is absolutely necessary that a man should be many-sided and take large views; and for a man of learning in the higher sense of the word, an extensive acquaintance with history is needful. He, however, who wishes to be a complete philosopher, must gather into his head the remotest ends of human knowledge: for where else could they ever come together?

It is precisely minds of the first order that will never be specialists. For their very nature is to make the whole of existence their problem;

and this is a subject upon which they will every one of them in some form provide mankind with a new revelation. For he alone can deserve the name of genius who takes the All, the Essential, the Universal, for the theme of his achievements; not he who spends his life in explaining some special relation of things one to another.

ON THINKING FOR ONESELF.

A library may be very large; but if it is in disorder, it is not so useful as one that is small but well arranged. In the same way, a man may have a great mass of knowledge, but if he has not worked it up by thinking it over for himself, it has much less value than a far smaller amount which he has thoroughly pondered. For it is only when a man looks at his knowledge from all sides, and combines the things he knows by comparing truth with truth, that he obtains a complete hold over it and gets it into his power. A man cannot turn over anything in his mind unless he knows it; he should, therefore, learn something; but it is only when he has turned it over that he can be said to know it.

Reading and learning are things that anyone can do of his own free will; but not so *thinking*. Thinking must be kindled, like a fire by a draught; it must be sustained by some interest in the matter in hand. This interest may be of purely objective kind, or merely subjective. The latter comes into play only in things that concern us personally. Objective interest is confined to heads that think by nature; to whom thinking is as natural as breathing; and they are very rare. This is why most men of learning show so little of it.

It is incredible what a different effect is produced upon the mind by thinking for oneself, as compared with reading. It carries on and intensifies that original difference in the nature of two minds which leads the one to think and the other to read. What I mean is that reading forces alien thoughts upon the mind—thoughts which are as foreign to the drift and temper in which it may be for the moment, as the seal is to the wax on which it stamps its imprint. The mind is thus entirely under compulsion from without; it is driven to think this or that, though for the moment it may not have the slightest impulse or inclination to do so.

But when a man thinks for himself, he follows the impulse of his own mind, which is determined for him at the time, either by his environment or some particular recollection. The visible world of a man's surroundings does not, as reading does, impress a _single_ definite thought upon his mind, but merely gives the matter and occasion which lead him to think what is appropriate to his nature and present temper. So it is, that much reading deprives the mind of all elasticity; it is like keeping a spring continually under pressure. The safest way of having no thoughts of one's own is to take up a book every moment one has nothing else to do. It is this practice which explains why erudition makes most men more stupid and silly than they are by nature, and prevents their writings obtaining any measure of success. They remain, in Pope's words:

For ever reading, never to be read![10]

Men of learning are those who have done their reading in the pages of a book. Thinkers and men of genius are those who have gone straight to the book of Nature; it is they who have enlightened the world and carried humanity further on its way.

If a man's thoughts are to have truth and life in them, they must, after all, be his own fundamental thoughts; for these are the only ones that he can fully and wholly understand. To read another's thoughts is like taking the leavings of a meal to which we have not been invited, or putting on the clothes which some unknown visitor has laid aside. The thought we read is related to the thought which springs up in ourselves, as the fossil-impress of some prehistoric plant to a plant as it buds forth in spring-time.

Reading is nothing more than a substitute for thought of one's own. It means putting the mind into leading-strings. The multitude of books serves only to show how many false paths there are, and how widely astray a man may wander if he follows any of them. But he who is guided by his genius, he who thinks for himself, who thinks spontaneously and exactly, possesses the only compass by which he can steer aright. A man should read only when his own thoughts stagnate at their source, which will happen often enough even with the best of minds. On the other hand, to take up a book for the purpose of scaring away one's own original thoughts is sin against the Holy Spirit. It is like running away from Nature to look at a museum of dried plants or gaze at a landscape in copperplate.

A man may have discovered some portion of truth or wisdom, after spending a great deal of time and trouble in thinking it over for himself and adding thought to thought; and it may sometimes happen that he could have found it all ready to hand in a book and spared himself the trouble. But even so, it is a hundred times more valuable if he has acquired it by thinking it out for himself. For it is only when we gain our knowledge in this way that it enters as an integral part, a living member, into the whole system of our thought; that it stands in complete and firm relation with what we know; that it is understood with all that underlies it and follows from it; that it wears the color, the precise shade, the distinguishing mark, of our own way of thinking;

---

[10] *Dunciad*, iii, 194.

that it comes exactly at the right time, just as we felt the necessity for it; that it stands fast and cannot be forgotten. This is the perfect application, nay, the interpretation, of Goethe's advice to earn our inheritance for ourselves so that we may really possess it:

> *Was due ererbt von deinen Vätern hast,*
> *Erwirb es, um es zu besitzen.*[11]

The man who thinks for himself, forms his own opinions and learns the authorities for them only later on, when they serve but to strengthen his belief in them and in himself. But the book-philosopher starts from the authorities. He reads other people's books, collects their opinions, and so forms a whole for himself, which resembles an automaton made up of anything but flesh and blood. Contrarily, he who thinks for himself creates a work like a living man as made by Nature. For the work comes into being as a man does; the thinking mind is impregnated from without, and it then forms and bears its child.

Truth that has been merely learned is like an artificial limb, a false tooth, a waxen nose; at best, like a nose made out of another's flesh; it adheres to us only because it is put on. But truth acquired by thinking of our own is like a natural limb; it alone really belongs to us. This is the fundamental difference between the thinker and the mere man of learning. The intellectual attainments of a man who thinks for himself resemble a fine painting, where the light and shade are correct, the tone sustained, the color perfectly harmonized; it is true to life. On the other hand, the intellectual attainments of the mere man of learning are like a large palette, full of all sorts of colors, which at most are systematically arranged, but devoid of harmony, connection and meaning.

Reading is thinking with some one else's head instead of one's own. To think with one's own head is always to aim at developing a coherent whole—a system, even though it be not a strictly complete one; and nothing hinders this so much as too strong a current of others' thoughts, such as comes of continual reading. These thoughts, springing every one of them from different minds, belonging to different systems, and tinged with different colors, never of themselves flow together into an intellectual whole; they never form a unity of knowledge, or insight, or conviction; but, rather, fill the head with a Babylonian confusion of tongues. The mind that is over-loaded with alien thought is thus deprived of all clear insight, and is well-nigh disorganized. This is a state of things observable in many men of learning; and it makes them inferior in sound sense, correct judgment and practical tact, to many illiterate persons, who, after obtaining a

---

[11] *Faust*, I. 329.

little knowledge from without, by means of experience, intercourse with others, and a small amount of reading, have always subordinated it to, and embodied it with, their own thought.

The really scientific *thinker* does the same thing as these illiterate persons, but on a larger scale. Although he has need of much knowledge, and so must read a great deal, his mind is nevertheless strong enough to master it all, to assimilate and incorporate it with the system of his thoughts, and so to make it fit in with the organic unity of his insight, which, though vast, is always growing. And in the process, his own thought, like the bass in an organ, always dominates everything and is never drowned by other tones, as happens with minds which are full of mere antiquarian lore; where shreds of music, as it were, in every key, mingle confusedly, and no fundamental note is heard at all.

Those who have spent their lives in reading, and taken their wisdom from books, are like people who have obtained precise information about a country from the descriptions of many travellers. Such people can tell a great deal about it; but, after all, they have no connected, clear, and profound knowledge of its real condition. But those who have spent their lives in thinking, resemble the travellers themselves; they alone really know what they are talking about; they are acquainted with the actual state of affairs, and are quite at home in the subject.

The thinker stands in the same relation to the ordinary book-philosopher as an eye-witness does to the historian; he speaks from direct knowledge of his own. That is why all those who think for themselves come, at bottom, to much the same conclusion. The differences they present are due to their different points of view; and when these do not affect the matter, they all speak alike. They merely express the result of their own objective perception of things. There are many passages in my works which I have given to the public only after some hesitation, because of their paradoxical nature; and afterwards I have experienced a pleasant surprise in finding the same opinion recorded in the works of great men who lived long ago.

The book-philosopher merely reports what one person has said and another meant, or the objections raised by a third, and so on. He compares different opinions, ponders, criticises, and tries to get at the truth of the matter; herein on a par with the critical historian. For instance, he will set out to inquire whether Leibnitz was not for some time a follower of Spinoza, and questions of a like nature. The curious student of such matters may find conspicuous examples of what I mean in Herbart's *Analytical Elucidation of Morality and Natural Right*, and in the same author's *Letters on Freedom*. Surprise may be felt that a man of the kind should put himself to so much trouble; for, on the face of it, if he would only examine the matter for himself, he would speedily attain his object by the exercise of a little thought. But there is a small difficulty in the way. It does not depend upon his own will. A man can always sit down and read, but not—think. It is with thoughts as with men; they cannot always be summoned at pleasure; we must wait for them to come. Thought about a subject must appear of itself, by a happy and harmonious combination of external stimulus with mental temper and attention; and it is just that which never seems to come to these people.

This truth may be illustrated by what happens in the case of matters affecting our own personal interest. When it is necessary to come to some resolution in a matter of that kind, we cannot well sit down at any given moment and think over the merits of the case and make up our mind; for, if we try to do so, we often find ourselves unable, at that particular moment, to keep our mind fixed upon the subject; it wanders off to other things. Aversion to the matter in question is sometimes to blame for this. In such a case we should not use force, but wait for the proper frame of mind to come of itself. It often comes unexpectedly and returns again and again; and the variety of temper in which we approach it at different moments puts the matter always in a fresh light. It is this long process which is understood by the term *a ripe resolution*. For the work of coming to a resolution must be distributed; and in the process much that is overlooked at one moment occurs to us at another; and the repugnance vanishes when we find, as we usually do, on a closer inspection, that things are not so bad as they seemed.

This rule applies to the life of the intellect as well as to matters of practice. A man must wait for the right moment. Not even the greatest mind is capable of thinking for itself at all times. Hence a great mind does well to spend its leisure in reading, which, as I have said, is a substitute for thought; it brings stuff to the mind by letting another person do the thinking; although that is always done in a manner not our own. Therefore, a man should not read too much, in order that his mind may not become accustomed to the substitute and thereby forget the reality; that it may not form the habit of walking in well-worn paths; nor by following an alien course of thought grow a stranger to its own. Least of all should a man quite withdraw his gaze from the real world for the mere sake of reading; as the impulse and the temper which prompt to thought of one's own come far oftener from the world of reality than from the world of books. The real life that a man sees before him is the natural subject of thought; and in its strength as the primary element of existence, it can more easily than anything else rouse and influence the thinking mind.

After these considerations, it will not be matter for surprise that a man who thinks for himself can easily be distinguished from the book-philosopher by the very way in which he talks, by his marked earnestness, and the originality, directness, and personal conviction that stamp all his thoughts and expressions. The book-philosopher, on the other hand, lets it be seen that everything he has is second-hand; that his ideas are like the number and trash of an old furniture-shop, collected together from all quarters. Mentally, he is dull and pointless—a copy of a copy. His literary style is made up of conventional, nay, vulgar phrases, and terms that happen to be current; in this respect much like a small State where all the money that circulates is foreign, because it has no coinage of its own.

Mere experience can as little as reading supply the place of thought. It stands to thinking in the same relation in which eating stands to digestion and assimilation. When experience boasts that to its discoveries alone is due the advancement of the human race, it is as though the mouth were to claim the whole credit of maintaining the body in health.

The works of all truly capable minds are distinguished by a character of *decision* and *definiteness*, which means they are clear and free from obscurity. A truly capable mind always knows definitely and clearly what it is that it wants to express, whether its medium is prose, verse, or music. Other minds are not decisive and not definite; and by this they may be known for what they are.

The characteristic sign of a mind of the highest order is that it always judges at first hand. Everything it advances is the result of thinking for itself; and this is everywhere evident by the way in which it gives its thoughts utterance. Such a mind is like a Prince. In the realm of intellect its authority is imperial, whereas the authority of minds of a lower order is delegated only; as may be seen in their style, which has no independent stamp of its own.

Every one who really thinks for himself is so far like a monarch. His position is undelegated and supreme. His judgments, like royal decrees, spring from his own sovereign power and proceed directly from himself. He acknowledges authority as little as a monarch admits a command; he subscribes to nothing but what he has himself authorized. The multitude of common minds, laboring under all sorts of current opinions, authorities, prejudices, is like the people, which silently obeys the law and accepts orders from above.

Those who are so zealous and eager to settle debated questions by citing authorities, are really glad when they are able to put the understanding and the insight of others into the field in place of their own, which are wanting. Their number is legion. For, as Seneca says, there is no man but prefers belief to the exercise of judgment— *unusquisque mavult credere quam judicare*. In their controversies such people make a promiscuous use of the weapon of authority, and strike out at one another with it. If any one chances to become involved in such a contest, he will do well not to try reason and argument as a mode of defence; for against a weapon of that kind these people are like Siegfrieds, with a skin of horn, and dipped in the flood of incapacity for thinking and judging. They will meet his attack by bringing up their authorities as a way of abashing him—*argumentum ad verecundiam*, and then cry out that they have won the battle.

In the real world, be it never so fair, favorable and pleasant, we always live subject to the law of gravity which we have to be constantly overcoming. But in the world of intellect we are disembodied spirits, held in bondage to no such law, and free from penury and distress. Thus it is that there exists no happiness on earth like that which, at the auspicious moment, a fine and fruitful mind finds in itself.

The presence of a thought is like the presence of a woman we love. We fancy we shall never forget the thought nor become indifferent to the dear one. But out of sight, out of mind! The finest thought runs the risk of being irrevocably forgotten if we do not write it down, and the darling of being deserted if we do not marry her.

There are plenty of thoughts which are valuable to the man who thinks them; but only few of them which have enough strength to produce repercussive or reflect action—I mean, to win the reader's sympathy after they have been put on paper.

But still it must not be forgotten that a true value attaches only to what a man has thought in the first instance *for his own case*. Thinkers may be classed according as they think chiefly for their own case or for that of others. The former are the genuine independent thinkers; they really think and are really independent; they are the true *philosophers*; they alone are in earnest. The pleasure and the happiness of their existence consists in thinking. The others are the *sophists*; they want to seem that which they are not, and seek their happiness in what they hope to get from the world. They are in earnest about nothing else. To which of these two classes a man belongs may be seen by his whole style and manner. Lichtenberg is an example for the former class; Herder, there can be no doubt, belongs to the second.

When one considers how vast and how close to us is *the problem of existence*—this equivocal, tortured, fleeting, dream-like existence of ours—so vast and so close that a man no sooner discovers it than it overshadows and obscures all other problems and aims; and when one sees how all men, with few and rare exceptions, have no clear consciousness of the problem, nay, seem to be quite unaware of its presence, but busy themselves with everything rather than with this, and live on, taking no thought but for the passing day and the hardly longer span of their own personal future, either expressly discarding the problem or else over-ready to come to terms with it by adopting some system of popular metaphysics and letting it satisfy them; when, I say, one takes all this to heart, one may come to the opinion that man may be said to be *a thinking being* only in a very remote sense, and henceforth feel no special surprise at any trait of human thoughtlessness or folly; but know, rather, that the normal man's intellectual range of vision does indeed extend beyond that of the brute, whose whole existence is, as it were, a continual present, with no consciousness of the past or the future, but not such an immeasurable distance as is generally supposed.

This is, in fact, corroborated by the way in which most men converse; where their thoughts are found to be chopped up fine, like chaff, so that for them to spin out a discourse of any length is impossible.

If this world were peopled by really thinking beings, it could not be that noise of every kind would be allowed such generous limits, as is the case with the most horrible and at the same time aimless form of it.[12] If Nature had meant man to think, she would not have given him ears; or, at any rate, she would have furnished them with airtight flaps, such as are the enviable possession of the bat. But, in truth, man is a poor animal like the rest, and his powers are meant only to maintain him in the struggle for existence; so he must need keep his ears always open, to announce of themselves, by night as by day, the approach of the pursuer.

ON SOME FORMS OF LITERATURE.

In the drama, which is the most perfect reflection of human existence, there are three stages in the presentation of the subject, with a corresponding variety in the design and scope of the piece.

At the first, which is also the most common, stage, the drama is never anything more than merely *interesting*. The persons gain our attention by following their own aims, which resemble ours; the action advances by means of intrigue and the play of character and incident; while wit and raillery season the whole.

At the second stage, the drama becomes *sentimental*. Sympathy is roused with the hero and, indirectly, with ourselves. The action takes a pathetic turn; but the end is peaceful and satisfactory.

The climax is reached with the third stage, which is the most difficult. There the drama aims at being *tragic*. We are brought face to face with great suffering and the storm and stress of existence; and the outcome of it is to show the vanity of all human effort. Deeply moved, we are either directly prompted to disengage our will from the struggle of life, or else a chord is struck in us which echoes a similar feeling.

The beginning, it is said, is always difficult. In the drama it is just

---

[12] *Translator's Note.*—Schopenhauer refers to the cracking of whips. See the Essay *On Noise* in *Studies in Pessimism.*

the contrary; for these the difficulty always lies in the end. This is proved by countless plays which promise very well for the first act or two, and then become muddled, stick or falter—notoriously so in the fourth act—and finally conclude in a way that is either forced or unsatisfactory or else long foreseen by every one. Sometimes, too, the end is positively revolting, as in Lessing's *Emilia Galotti*, which sends the spectators home in a temper.

This difficulty in regard to the end of a play arises partly because it is everywhere easier to get things into a tangle than to get them out again; partly also because at the beginning we give the author *carte blanche* to do as he likes, but, at the end, make certain definite demands upon him. Thus we ask for a conclusion that shall be either quite happy or else quite tragic; whereas human affairs do not easily take so decided a turn; and then we expect that it shall be natural, fit and proper, unlabored, and at the same time foreseen by no one.

These remarks are also applicable to an epic and to a novel; but the more compact nature of the drama makes the difficulty plainer by increasing it.

E nihilo nihil fit. That nothing can come from nothing is a maxim true in fine art as elsewhere. In composing an historical picture, a good artist will use living men as a model, and take the groundwork of the faces from life; and then proceed to idealize them in point of beauty or expression. A similar method, I fancy, is adopted by good novelists. In drawing a character they take a general outline of it from some real person of their acquaintance, and then idealize and complete it to suit their purpose.

A novel will be of a high and noble order, the more it represents of inner, and the less it represents of outer, life; and the ratio between the two will supply a means of judging any novel, of whatever kind, from *Tristram Shandy* down to the crudest and most sensational tale of knight or robber. *Tristram Shandy* has, indeed, as good as no action at all; and there is not much in *La Nouvelle Heloise* and *Wilhelm Meister.* Even *Don Quixote* has relatively little; and what there is, very unimportant, and introduced merely for the sake of fun. And these four are the best of all existing novels.

Consider, further, the wonderful romances of Jean Paul, and how much inner life is shown on the narrowest basis of actual event. Even in Walter Scott's novels there is a great preponderance of inner over outer life, and incident is never brought in except for the purpose of giving play to thought and emotion; whereas, in bad novels, incident is there on its own account. Skill consists in setting the inner life in motion with the smallest possible array of circumstance; for it is this inner life that really excites our interest.

The business of the novelist is not to relate great events, but to make small ones interesting.

History, which I like to think of as the contrary of poetry [Greek: istoroumenon—pepoiaemenon], is for time what geography is for space; and it is no more to be called a science, in any strict sense of the word, than is geography, because it does not deal with universal truths, but only with particular details. History has always been the favorite study of those who wish to learn something, without having to face the effort demanded by any branch of real knowledge, which taxes the intelligence. In our time history is a favorite pursuit; as witness the numerous books upon the subject which appear every year.

If the reader cannot help thinking, with me, that history is merely the constant recurrence of similar things, just as in a kaleidoscope the same bits of glass are represented, but in different combinations, he will not be able to share all this lively interest; nor, however, will he censure it. But there is a ridiculous and absurd claim, made by many people, to regard history as a part of philosophy, nay, as philosophy itself; they imagine that history can take its place.

The preference shown for history by the greater public in all ages may be illustrated by the kind of conversation which is so much in vogue everywhere in society. It generally consists in one person relating something and then another person relating something else; so that in this way everyone is sure of receiving attention. Both here and in the case of history it is plain that the mind is occupied with particular details. But as in science, so also in every worthy conversation, the mind rises to the consideration of some general truth.

This objection does not, however, deprive history of its value. Human life is short and fleeting, and many millions of individuals share in it, who are swallowed by that monster of oblivion which is waiting for them with ever-open jaws. It is thus a very thankworthy task to try to rescue something—the memory of interesting and important events, or the leading features and personages of some epoch—from the general shipwreck of the world.

From another point of view, we might look upon history as the sequel to zoology; for while with all other animals it is enough to observe the species, with man individuals, and therefore individual events have to be studied; because every man possesses a character as an individual. And since individuals and events are without number or end, an essential imperfection attaches to history. In the study of it, all that a man learns never contributes to lessen that which he has still to learn. With any real science, a perfection of knowledge is, at any rate, conceivable.

When we gain access to the histories of China and of India, the endlessness of the subject-matter will reveal to us the defects in the study, and force our historians to see that the object of science is to recognize the many in the one, to perceive the rules in any given example, and to apply to the life of nations a knowledge of mankind;

not to go on counting up facts *ad infinitum.*

There are two kinds of history; the history of politics and the history of literature and art. The one is the history of the will; the other, that of the intellect. The first is a tale of woe, even of terror: it is a record of agony, struggle, fraud, and horrible murder *en masse.* The second is everywhere pleasing and serene, like the intellect when left to itself, even though its path be one of error. Its chief branch is the history of philosophy. This is, in fact, its fundamental bass, and the notes of it are heard even in the other kind of history. These deep tones guide the formation of opinion, and opinion rules the world. Hence philosophy, rightly understood, is a material force of the most powerful kind, though very slow in its working. The philosophy of a period is thus the fundamental bass of its history.

The NEWSPAPER, is the second-hand in the clock of history; and it is not only made of baser metal than those which point to the minute and the hour, but it seldom goes right.

The so-called leading article is the chorus to the drama of passing events.

Exaggeration of every kind is as essential to journalism as it is to the dramatic art; for the object of journalism is to make events go as far as possible. Thus it is that all journalists are, in the very nature of their calling, alarmists; and this is their way of giving interest to what they write. Herein they are like little dogs; if anything stirs, they immediately set up a shrill bark.

Therefore, let us carefully regulate the attention to be paid to this trumpet of danger, so that it may not disturb our digestion. Let us recognize that a newspaper is at best but a magnifying-glass, and very often merely a shadow on the wall.

The *pen* is to thought what the stick is to walking; but you walk most easily when you have no stick, and you think with the greatest perfection when you have no pen in your hand. It is only when a man begins to be old that he likes to use a stick and is glad to take up his pen.

When an *hypothesis* has once come to birth in the mind, or gained a footing there, it leads a life so far comparable with the life of an organism, as that it assimilates matter from the outer world only when it is like in kind with it and beneficial; and when, contrarily, such matter is not like in kind but hurtful, the hypothesis, equally with the organism, throws it off, or, if forced to take it, gets rid of it again entire.

To gain *immortality* an author must possess so many excellences that while it will not be easy to find anyone to understand and appreciate them all, there will be men in every age who are able to recognize and value some of them. In this way the credit of his book will be maintained throughout the long course of centuries, in spite of the fact that human interests are always changing.

An author like this, who has a claim to the continuance of his life even with posterity, can only be a man who, over the wide earth, will seek his like in vain, and offer a palpable contrast with everyone else in virtue of his unmistakable distinction. Nay, more: were he, like the wandering Jew, to live through several generations, he would still remain in the same superior position. If this were not so, it would be difficult to see why his thoughts should not perish like those of other men.

Metaphors and *similes* are of great value, in so far as they explain an unknown relation by a known one. Even the more detailed simile which grows into a parable or an allegory, is nothing more than the exhibition of some relation in its simplest, most visible and palpable form. The growth of ideas rests, at bottom, upon similes; because ideas arise by a process of combining the similarities and neglecting the differences between things. Further, intelligence, in the strict sense of the word, ultimately consists in a seizing of relations; and a clear and pure grasp of relations is all the more often attained when the comparison is made between cases that lie wide apart from one another, and between things of quite different nature. As long as a relation is known to me as existing only in a single case, I have but an *individual* idea of it—in other words, only an intuitive knowledge of it; but as soon as I see the same relation in two different cases, I have a *general* idea of its whole nature, and this is a deeper and more perfect knowledge.

Since, then, similes and metaphors are such a powerful engine of knowledge, it is a sign of great intelligence in a writer if his similes are unusual and, at the same time, to the point. Aristotle also observes that by far the most important thing to a writer is to have this power of metaphor; for it is a gift which cannot be acquired, and it is a mark of genius.

As regards *reading*, to require that a man shall retain everything he has ever read, is like asking him to carry about with him all he has ever eaten. The one kind of food has given him bodily, and the other mental, nourishment; and it is through these two means that he has grown to be what he is. The body assimilates only that which is like it; and so a man retains in his mind only that which interests him, in other words, that which suits his system of thought or his purposes in life.

If a man wants to read good books, he must make a point of avoiding bad ones; for life is short, and time and energy limited.

Repetitio est mater studiorum. Any book that is at all important ought to be at once read through twice; partly because, on a second reading, the connection of the different portions of the book will be better understood, and the beginning comprehended only when the end is known; and partly because we are not in the same temper and disposition on both readings. On the second perusal we get a new view of every passage and a different impression of the whole book, which then appears in another light.

A man's works are the quintessence of his mind, and even though he may possess very great capacity, they will always be incomparably more valuable than his conversation. Nay, in all essential matters his works will not only make up for the lack of personal intercourse with him, but they will far surpass it in solid advantages. The writings even of a man of moderate genius may be edifying, worth reading and instructive, because they are his quintessence—the result and fruit of all his thought and study; whilst conversation with him may be unsatisfactory.

So it is that we can read books by men in whose company we find nothing to please, and that a high degree of culture leads us to seek entertainment almost wholly from books and not from men.

ON CRITICISM.

The following brief remarks on the critical faculty are chiefly intended to show that, for the most part, there is no such thing. It is a *rara avis*; almost as rare, indeed, as the phoenix, which appears only once in five hundred years.

When we speak of *taste*—an expression not chosen with any regard for it—we mean the discovery, or, it may be only the recognition, of what is *right aesthetically*, apart from the guidance of any rule; and this, either because no rule has as yet been extended to the matter in question, or else because, if existing, it is unknown to the artist, or the critic, as the case may be. Instead of *taste*, we might use the expression *aesthetic sense*, if this were not tautological.

The perceptive critical taste is, so to speak, the female analogue to the male quality of productive talent or genius. Not capable of *begetting* great work itself, it consists in a capacity of *reception*, that is to say, of recognizing as such what is right, fit, beautiful, or the reverse; in other words, of discriminating the good from the bad, of discovering and appreciating the one and condemning the other.

In appreciating a genius, criticism should not deal with the errors in his productions or with the poorer of his works, and then proceed to rate him low; it should attend only to the qualities in which he most excels. For in the sphere of intellect, as in other spheres, weakness and perversity cleave so firmly to human nature that even the most brilliant mind is not wholly and at all times free from them. Hence the great errors to be found even in the works of the greatest men; or as Horace puts it, *quandoque bonus dormitat Homerus.*

That which distinguishes genius, and should be the standard for judging it, is the height to which it is able to soar when it is in the proper mood and finds a fitting occasion—a height always out of the reach of ordinary talent. And, in like manner, it is a very dangerous thing to compare two great men of the same class; for instance, two great poets, or musicians, or philosophers, or artists; because injustice to the one or the other, at least for the moment, can hardly be avoided. For in making a comparison of the kind the critic looks to some particular merit of the one and at once discovers that it is absent in the other, who is thereby disparaged. And then if the process is reversed, and the critic begins with the latter and discovers his peculiar merit, which is quite of a different order from that presented by the former, with whom it may be looked for in vain, the result is that both of them suffer undue depreciation.

There are critics who severally think that it rests with each one of them what shall be accounted good, and what bad. They all mistake their own toy-trumpets for the trombones of fame.

A drug does not effect its purpose if the dose is too large; and it is the same with censure and adverse criticism when it exceeds the measure of justice.

The disastrous thing for intellectual merit is that it must wait for those to praise the good who have themselves produced nothing but what is bad; nay, it is a primary misfortune that it has to receive its crown at the hands of the critical power of mankind—a quality of which most men possess only the weak and impotent semblance, so that the reality may be numbered amongst the rarest gifts of nature. Hence La Bruyère's remark is, unhappily, as true as it is neat. *Après l'esprit de discernement*, he says, *ce qu'il y a au monde de plus rare, ce sont les diamans et les perles*. The spirit of discernment! the critical faculty! it is these that are lacking. Men do not know how to distinguish the genuine from the false, the corn from the chaff, gold from copper; or to perceive the wide gulf that separates a genius from an ordinary man. Thus we have that bad state of things described in an old-fashioned verse, which gives it as the lot of the great ones here on earth to be recognized only when they are gone:

Es ist nun das Geschick der Grossen hier auf Erden,
Erst wann sie nicht mehr sind, von uns erkannt zu werden.

When any genuine and excellent work makes its appearance, the chief difficulty in its way is the amount of bad work it finds already in possession of the field, and accepted as though it were good. And then if, after a long time, the new comer really succeeds, by a hard struggle, in vindicating his place for himself and winning reputation, he will soon encounter fresh difficulty from some affected, dull, awkward imitator, whom people drag in, with the object of calmly setting him up on the altar beside the genius; not seeing the difference and really thinking that here they have to do with another great man. This is what

Yriarte means by the first lines of his twenty-eighth Fable, where he
declares that the ignorant rabble always sets equal value on the good
and the bad:

> *Siempre acostumbra hacer el vulgo necio*
> *De lo bueno y lo malo igual aprecio.*

So even Shakespeare's dramas had, immediately after his death, to give
place to those of Ben Jonson, Massinger, Beaumont and Fletcher, and
to yield the supremacy for a hundred years. So Kant's serious
philosophy was crowded out by the nonsense of Fichte, Schelling,
Jacobi, Hegel. And even in a sphere accessible to all, we have seen
unworthy imitators quickly diverting public attention from the
incomparable Walter Scott. For, say what you will, the public has no
sense for excellence, and therefore no notion how very rare it is to find
men really capable of doing anything great in poetry, philosophy, or
art, or that their works are alone worthy of exclusive attention. The
dabblers, whether in verse or in any other high sphere, should be every
day unsparingly reminded that neither gods, nor men, nor booksellers
have pardoned their mediocrity:

> *mediocribus esse poetis*
> *Non homines, non Dî, non concessere columnæ.*[13]

Are they not the weeds that prevent the corn coming up, so that they
may cover all the ground themselves? And then there happens that
which has been well and freshly described by the lamented
Feuchtersleben,[14] who died so young: how people cry out in their haste
that nothing is being done, while all the while great work is quietly
growing to maturity; and then, when it appears, it is not seen or heard
in the clamor, but goes its way silently, in modest grief:

> *"Ist doch,"—rufen sie vermessen—*
> *"Nichts im Werke, nichts gethan!"*
> *Und das Grosse, reift indessen*
> *Still heran.*

---

[13] Horace, *Ars Poetica*, 372.

[14] *Translator's Note.*—Ernst Freiherr von Feuchtersleben (1806-49), an Austrian
physician, philosopher, and poet, and a specialist in medical psychology. The best known
of his songs is that beginning *"Es ist bestimmt in Gottes Rath"* to which Mendelssohn
composed one of his finest melodies.]

Es ersheint nun: niemand sieht es,
Niemand hört es im Geschrei
Mit bescheid'ner Trauer zieht es
Still vorbei.

This lamentable death of the critical faculty is not less obvious in the case of science, as is shown by the tenacious life of false and disproved theories. If they are once accepted, they may go on bidding defiance to truth for fifty or even a hundred years and more, as stable as an iron pier in the midst of the waves. The Ptolemaic system was still held a century after Copernicus had promulgated his theory. Bacon, Descartes and Locke made their way extremely slowly and only after a long time; as the reader may see by d'Alembert's celebrated Preface to the *Encyclopedia*. Newton was not more successful; and this is sufficiently proved by the bitterness and contempt with which Leibnitz attacked his theory of gravitation in the controversy with Clarke.[15] Although Newton lived for almost forty years after the appearance of the *Principia*, his teaching was, when he died, only to some extent accepted in his own country, whilst outside England he counted scarcely twenty adherents; if we may believe the introductory note to Voltaire's exposition of his theory. It was, indeed, chiefly owing to this treatise of Voltaire's that the system became known in France nearly twenty years after Newton's death. Until then a firm, resolute, and patriotic stand was made by the Cartesian *Vortices*; whilst only forty years previously, this same Cartesian philosophy had been forbidden in the French schools; and now in turn d'Agnesseau, the Chancellor, refused Voltaire the *Imprimatur* for his treatise on the Newtonian doctrine. On the other hand, in our day Newton's absurd theory of color still completely holds the field, forty years after the publication of Goethe's. Hume, too, was disregarded up to his fiftieth year, though he began very early and wrote in a thoroughly popular style. And Kant, in spite of having written and talked all his life long, did not become a famous man until he was sixty.

Artists and poets have, to be sure, more chance than thinkers, because their public is at least a hundred times as large. Still, what was thought of Beethoven and Mozart during their lives? what of Dante? what even of Shakespeare? If the latter's contemporaries had in any way recognized his worth, at least one good and accredited portrait of him would have come down to us from an age when the art of painting flourished; whereas we possess only some very doubtful pictures, a bad

---

[15] See especially §§ 35, 113, 118, 120, 122, 128.

copperplate, and a still worse bust on his tomb.[16] And in like manner, if he had been duly honored, specimens of his handwriting would have been preserved to us by the hundred, instead of being confined, as is the case, to the signatures to a few legal documents. The Portuguese are still proud of their only poet Camoëns. He lived, however, on alms collected every evening in the street by a black slave whom he had brought with him from the Indies. In time, no doubt, justice will be done everyone; *tempo è galant' uomo*; but it is as late and slow in arriving as in a court of law, and the secret condition of it is that the recipient shall be no longer alive. The precept of Jesus the son of Sirach is faithfully followed: *Judge none blessed before his death.*[17] He, then, who has produced immortal works, must find comfort by applying to them the words of the Indian myth, that the minutes of life amongst the immortals seem like years of earthly existence; and so, too, that years upon earth are only as the minutes of the immortals.

This lack of critical insight is also shown by the fact that, while in every century the excellent work of earlier time is held in honor, that of its own is misunderstood, and the attention which is its due is given to bad work, such as every decade carries with it only to be the sport of the next. That men are slow to recognize genuine merit when it appears in their own age, also proves that they do not understand or enjoy or really value the long-acknowledged works of genius, which they honor only on the score of authority. The crucial test is the fact that bad work—Fichte's philosophy, for example—if it wins any reputation, also maintains it for one or two generations; and only when its public is very large does its fall follow sooner.

Now, just as the sun cannot shed its light but to the eye that sees it, nor music sound but to the hearing ear, so the value of all masterly work in art and science is conditioned by the kinship and capacity of the mind to which it speaks. It is only such a mind as this that possesses the magic word to stir and call forth the spirits that lie hidden in great work. To the ordinary mind a masterpiece is a sealed cabinet of mystery,—an unfamiliar musical instrument from which the player, however much he may flatter himself, can draw none but confused tones. How different a painting looks when seen in a good light, as compared with some dark corner! Just in the same way, the impression made by a masterpiece varies with the capacity of the mind to understand it.

A fine work, then, requires a mind sensitive to its beauty; a thoughtful work, a mind that can really think, if it is to exist and live at

---

[16] A. Wivell: *An Inquiry into the History, Authenticity, and Characteristics of Shakespeare's Portraits*; with 21 engravings. London, 1836.
[17] *Ecclesiasticus,* xi. 28.

all. But alas! it may happen only too often that he who gives a fine work to the world afterwards feels like a maker of fireworks, who displays with enthusiasm the wonders that have taken him so much time and trouble to prepare, and then learns that he has come to the wrong place, and that the fancied spectators were one and all inmates of an asylum for the blind. Still even that is better than if his public had consisted entirely of men who made fireworks themselves; as in this case, if his display had been extraordinarily good, it might possibly have cost him his head.

The source of all pleasure and delight is the feeling of kinship. Even with the sense of beauty it is unquestionably our own species in the animal world, and then again our own race, that appears to us the fairest. So, too, in intercourse with others, every man shows a decided preference for those who resemble him; and a blockhead will find the society of another blockhead incomparably more pleasant than that of any number of great minds put together. Every man must necessarily take his chief pleasure in his own work, because it is the mirror of his own mind, the echo of his own thought; and next in order will come the work of people like him; that is to say, a dull, shallow and perverse man, a dealer in mere words, will give his sincere and hearty applause only to that which is dull, shallow, perverse or merely verbose. On the other hand, he will allow merit to the work of great minds only on the score of authority, in other words, because he is ashamed to speak his opinion; for in reality they give him no pleasure at all. They do not appeal to him; nay, they repel him; and he will not confess this even to himself. The works of genius cannot be fully enjoyed except by those who are themselves of the privileged order. The first recognition of them, however, when they exist without authority to support them, demands considerable superiority of mind.

When the reader takes all this into consideration, he should be surprised, not that great work is so late in winning reputation, but that it wins it at all. And as a matter of fact, fame comes only by a slow and complex process. The stupid person is by degrees forced, and as it were, tamed, into recognizing the superiority of one who stands immediately above him; this one in his turn bows before some one else; and so it goes on until the weight of the votes gradually prevail over their number; and this is just the condition of all genuine, in other words, deserved fame. But until then, the greatest genius, even after he has passed his time of trial, stands like a king amidst a crowd of his own subjects, who do not know him by sight and therefore will not do his behests; unless, indeed, his chief ministers of state are in his train. For no subordinate official can be the direct recipient of the royal commands, as he knows only the signature of his immediate superior; and this is repeated all the way up into the highest ranks, where the under-secretary attests the minister's signature, and the minister that of the king. There are analogous stages to be passed before a genius can attain widespread fame. This is why his reputation most easily comes to a standstill at the very outset; because the highest authorities, of whom there can be but few, are most frequently not to be found; but the further down he goes in the scale the more numerous are those who take the word from above, so that his fame is no more arrested.

We must console ourselves for this state of things by reflecting that it is really fortunate that the greater number of men do not form a judgment on their own responsibility, but merely take it on authority. For what sort of criticism should we have on Plato and Kant, Homer, Shakespeare and Goethe, if every man were to form his opinion by what he really has and enjoys of these writers, instead of being forced by authority to speak of them in a fit and proper way, however little he may really feel what he says. Unless something of this kind took place, it would be impossible for true merit, in any high sphere, to attain fame at all. At the same time it is also fortunate that every man has just so much critical power of his own as is necessary for recognizing the superiority of those who are placed immediately over him, and for following their lead. This means that the many come in the end to submit to the authority of the few; and there results that hierarchy of critical judgments on which is based the possibility of a steady, and eventually wide-reaching, fame.

The lowest class in the community is quite impervious to the merits of a great genius; and for these people there is nothing left but the monument raised to him, which, by the impression it produces on their senses, awakes in them a dim idea of the man's greatness.

Literary journals should be a dam against the unconscionable scribbling of the age, and the ever-increasing deluge of bad and useless books. Their judgments should be uncorrupted, just and rigorous; and every piece of bad work done by an incapable person; every device by which the empty head tries to come to the assistance of the empty purse, that is to say, about nine-tenths of all existing books, should be mercilessly scourged. Literary journals would then perform their duty, which is to keep down the craving for writing and put a check upon the deception of the public, instead of furthering these evils by a miserable toleration, which plays into the hands of author and publisher, and robs the reader of his time and his money.

If there were such a paper as I mean, every bad writer, every brainless compiler, every plagiarist from other's books, every hollow and incapable place-hunter, every sham-philosopher, every vain and languishing poetaster, would shudder at the prospect of the pillory in which his bad work would inevitably have to stand soon after publication. This would paralyze his twitching fingers, to the true welfare of literature, in which what is bad is not only useless but positively pernicious. Now, most books are bad and ought to have remained unwritten. Consequently praise should be as rare as is now the case with blame, which is withheld under the influence of personal considerations, coupled with the maxim *accedas socius, laudes lauderis ut absens.*

It is quite wrong to try to introduce into literature the same toleration as must necessarily prevail in society towards those stupid, brainless people who everywhere swarm in it. In literature such people are impudent intruders; and to disparage the bad is here duty towards the good; for he who thinks nothing bad will think nothing good either. Politeness, which has its source in social relations, is in literature an alien, and often injurious, element; because it exacts that bad work shall be called good. In this way the very aim of science and art is directly frustrated.

The ideal journal could, to be sure, be written only by people who joined incorruptible honesty with rare knowledge and still rarer power of judgment; so that perhaps there could, at the very most, be one, and even hardly one, in the whole country; but there it would stand, like a just Aeropagus, every member of which would have to be elected by all the others. Under the system that prevails at present, literary journals are carried on by a clique, and secretly perhaps also by booksellers for the good of the trade; and they are often nothing but coalitions of bad heads to prevent the good ones succeeding. As Goethe once remarked to me, nowhere is there so much dishonesty as in literature.

But, above all, anonymity, that shield of all literary rascality, would have to disappear. It was introduced under the pretext of protecting the honest critic, who warned the public, against the resentment of the author and his friends. But where there is one case of this sort, there will be a hundred where it merely serves to take all responsibility from the man who cannot stand by what he has said, or possibly to conceal the shame of one who has been cowardly and base enough to recommend a book to the public for the purpose of putting money into his own pocket. Often enough it is only a cloak for covering the obscurity, incompetence and insignificance of the critic. It is incredible what impudence these fellows will show, and what literary trickery they will venture to commit, as soon as they know they are safe under the shadow of anonymity. Let me recommend a general *Anti-criticism*, a universal medicine or panacea, to put a stop to all anonymous reviewing, whether it praises the bad or blames the good: *Rascal! your name!* For a man to wrap himself up and draw his hat over his face, and then fall upon people who are walking about without any disguise—this is not the part of a gentleman, it is the part of a scoundrel and a knave.

An anonymous review has no more authority than an anonymous letter; and one should be received with the same mistrust as the other. Or shall we take the name of the man who consents to preside over what is, in the strict sense of the word, *une société anonyme* as a guarantee for the veracity of his colleagues?

Even Rousseau, in the preface to the *Nouvelle Heloïse,* declares *tout honnête homme doit avouer les livres qu'il public*; which in plain language means that every honorable man ought to sign his articles, and that no one is honorable who does not do so. How much truer this is of polemical writing, which is the general character of reviews! Riemer was quite right in the opinion he gives in his *Reminiscences of Goethe:*[18] *An overt enemy,* he says, *an enemy who meets you face to face, is an honorable man, who will treat you fairly, and with whom you can come to terms and be reconciled: but an enemy who conceals himself is a base, cowardly scoundrel, who has not courage enough to avow his own judgment; it is not his opinion that he cares about, but only the secret pleasures of wreaking his anger without being found out or punished.* This will also have been Goethe's opinion, as he was generally the source from which Riemer drew his observations. And, indeed, Rousseau's maxim applies to every line that is printed. Would a man in a mask ever be allowed to harangue a mob, or speak in any assembly; and that, too, when he was going to attack others and overwhelm them with abuse?

Anonymity is the refuge for all literary and journalistic rascality. It is a practice which must be completely stopped. Every article, even in a newspaper, should be accompanied by the name of its author; and the editor should be made strictly responsible for the accuracy of the signature. The freedom of the press should be thus far restricted; so that when a man publicly proclaims through the far-sounding trumpet of the newspaper, he should be answerable for it, at any rate with his honor, if he has any; and if he has none, let his name neutralize the effect of his words. And since even the most insignificant person is known in his own circle, the result of such a measure would be to put an end to two-thirds of the newspaper lies, and to restrain the audacity of many a poisonous tongue.

ON REPUTATION.

Writers may be classified as meteors, planets and fixed stars. A meteor makes a striking effect for a moment. You look up and cry *There!* and it is gone for ever. Planets and wandering stars last a much longer time. They often outshine the fixed stars and are confounded with them by the inexperienced; but this only because they are near. It is not long before they must yield their place; nay, the light they give is reflected only, and the sphere of their influence is confined to their own

---

[18] Preface, p. xxix.

orbit—their contemporaries. Their path is one of change and movement, and with the circuit of a few years their tale is told. Fixed stars are the only ones that are constant; their position in the firmament is secure; they shine with a light of their own; their effect to-day is the same as it was yesterday, because, having no parallax, their appearance does not alter with a difference in our standpoint. They belong not to *one* system, *one* nation only, but to the universe. And just because they are so very far away, it is usually many years before their light is visible to the inhabitants of this earth.

We have seen in the previous chapter that where a man's merits are of a high order, it is difficult for him to win reputation, because the public is uncritical and lacks discernment. But another and no less serious hindrance to fame comes from the envy it has to encounter. For even in the lowest kinds of work, envy balks even the beginnings of a reputation, and never ceases to cleave to it up to the last. How great a part is played by envy in the wicked ways of the world! Ariosto is right in saying that the dark side of our mortal life predominates, so full it is of this evil:

> *questa assai più oscura che serena*
> *Vita mortal, tutta d'invidia piena.*

For envy is the moving spirit of that secret and informal, though flourishing, alliance everywhere made by mediocrity against individual eminence, no matter of what kind. In his own sphere of work no one will allow another to be distinguished: he is an intruder who cannot be tolerated. *Si quelq'un excelle parmi nous, qu'il aille exceller ailleurs!* this is the universal password of the second-rate. In addition, then, to the rarity of true merit and the difficulty it has in being understood and recognized, there is the envy of thousands to be reckoned with, all of them bent on suppressing, nay, on smothering it altogether. No one is taken for what he is, but for what others make of him; and this is the handle used by mediocrity to keep down distinction, by not letting it come up as long as that can possibly be prevented.

There are two ways of behaving in regard to merit: either to have some of one's own, or to refuse any to others. The latter method is more convenient, and so it is generally adopted. As envy is a mere sign of deficiency, so to envy merit argues the lack of it. My excellent Balthazar Gracian has given a very fine account of this relation between envy and merit in a lengthy fable, which may be found in his *Discreto* under the heading *Hombre de ostentacion*. He describes all the birds as meeting together and conspiring against the peacock, because of his magnificent feathers. *If*, said the magpie, *we could only manage to put a stop to the cursed parading of his tail, there would soon be an end of his beauty; for what is not seen is as good as what does not exist.*

This explains how modesty came to be a virtue. It was invented only as a protection against envy. That there have always been rascals to urge this virtue, and to rejoice heartily over the bashfulness of a man of merit, has been shown at length in my chief work.[19] In Lichtenberg's *Miscellaneous Writings* I find this sentence quoted: *Modesty should be the virtue of those who possess no other.* Goethe has a well-known saying, which offends many people: *It is only knaves who are modest!—Nur die Lumpen sind bescheiden!* but it has its prototype in Cervantes, who includes in his *Journey up Parnassus* certain rules of conduct for poets, and amongst them the following: *Everyone whose verse shows him to be a poet should have a high opinion of himself, relying on the proverb that he is a knave who thinks himself one.* And Shakespeare, in many of his Sonnets, which gave him the only opportunity he had of speaking of himself, declares, with a confidence equal to his ingenuousness, that what he writes is immortal.[20]

A method of underrating good work often used by envy—in reality, however, only the obverse side of it—consists in the dishonorable and unscrupulous laudation of the bad; for no sooner does bad work gain currency than it draws attention from the good. But however effective this method may be for a while, especially if it is applied on a large scale, the day of reckoning comes at last, and the fleeting credit given to bad work is paid off by the lasting discredit which overtakes those who abjectly praised it. Hence these critics prefer to remain anonymous.

A like fate threatens, though more remotely, those who depreciate and censure good work; and consequently many are too prudent to attempt it. But there is another way; and when a man of eminent merit appears, the first effect he produces is often only to pique all his rivals, just as the peacock's tail offended the birds. This reduces them to a deep silence; and their silence is so unanimous that it savors of preconcertion. Their tongues are all paralyzed. It is the *silentium livoris* described by Seneca. This malicious silence, which is technically known as *ignoring*, may for a long time interfere with the growth of reputation; if, as happens in the higher walks of learning, where a man's immediate audience is wholly composed of rival workers and professed students, who then form the channel of his fame, the greater

---

[19] *Welt als Wille*, Vol. II. c. 37.

[20] Collier, one of his critical editors, in his Introduction to the Sonettes, remarks upon this point: "In many of them are to be found most remarkable indications of self-confidence and of assurance in the immortality of his verses, and in this respect the author's opinion was constant and uniform. He never scruples to express it, ... and perhaps there is no writer of ancient or modern times who, for the quantity of such writings left behind him, has so frequently or so strongly declared that what he had produced in this department of poetry 'the world would not willingly let die.'"

public is obliged to use its suffrage without being able to examine the matter for itself. And if, in the end, that malicious silence is broken in upon by the voice of praise, it will be but seldom that this happens entirely apart from some ulterior aim, pursued by those who thus manipulate justice. For, as Goethe says in the *West-östlicher Divan*, a man can get no recognition, either from many persons or from only one, unless it is to publish abroad the critic's own discernment:

> *Denn es ist kein Anerkenen,*
> *Weder Vieler, noch des Einen,*
> *Wenn es nicht am Tage fördert,*
> *Wo man selbst was möchte scheinen.*

The credit you allow to another man engaged in work similar to your own or akin to it, must at bottom be withdrawn from yourself; and you can praise him only at the expense of your own claims.

Accordingly, mankind is in itself not at all inclined to award praise and reputation; it is more disposed to blame and find fault, whereby it indirectly praises itself. If, notwithstanding this, praise is won from mankind, some extraneous motive must prevail. I am not here referring to the disgraceful way in which mutual friends will puff one another into a reputation; outside of that, an effectual motive is supplied by the feeling that next to the merit of doing something oneself, comes that of correctly appreciating and recognizing what others have done. This accords with the threefold division of heads drawn up by Hesiod[21] and afterwards by Machiavelli[22] *There are*, says the latter, *in the capacities of mankind, three varieties: one man will understand a thing by himself; another so far as it is explained to him; a third, neither of himself nor when it is put clearly before him.* He, then, who abandons hope of making good his claims to the first class, will be glad to seize the opportunity of taking a place in the second. It is almost wholly owing to this state of things that merit may always rest assured of ultimately meeting with recognition.

To this also is due the fact that when the value of a work has once been recognized and may no longer be concealed or denied, all men vie in praising and honoring it; simply because they are conscious of thereby doing themselves an honor. They act in the spirit of Xenophon's remark: *he must be a wise man who knows what is wise.* So when they see that the prize of original merit is for ever out of their reach, they hasten to possess themselves of that which comes second best—the correct appreciation of it. Here it happens as with an army

---

[21] *Works and Days*, 293.
[22] *The Prince*, ch. 22.

which has been forced to yield; when, just as previously every man wanted to be foremost in the fight, so now every man tries to be foremost in running away. They all hurry forward to offer their applause to one who is now recognized to be worthy of praise, in virtue of a recognition, as a rule unconscious, of that law of homogeneity which I mentioned in the last chapter; so that it may seem as though their way of thinking and looking at things were homogeneous with that of the celebrated man, and that they may at least save the honor of their literary taste, since nothing else is left them.

From this it is plain that, whereas it is very difficult to win fame, it is not hard to keep it when once attained; and also that a reputation which comes quickly does not last very long; for here too, *quod cito fit, cito perit*. It is obvious that if the ordinary average man can easily recognize, and the rival workers willingly acknowledge, the value of any performance, it will not stand very much above the capacity of either of them to achieve it for themselves. *Tantum quisque laudat, quantum se posse sperat imitari*—a man will praise a thing only so far as he hopes to be able to imitate it himself. Further, it is a suspicious sign if a reputation comes quickly; for an application of the laws of homogeneity will show that such a reputation is nothing but the direct applause of the multitude. What this means may be seen by a remark once made by Phocion, when he was interrupted in a speech by the loud cheers of the mob. Turning to his friends who were standing close by, he asked: *Have I made a mistake and said something stupid?*[23]

Contrarily, a reputation that is to last a long time must be slow in maturing, and the centuries of its duration have generally to be bought at the cost of contemporary praise. For that which is to keep its position so long, must be of a perfection difficult to attain; and even to recognize this perfection requires men who are not always to be found, and never in numbers sufficiently great to make themselves heard; whereas envy is always on the watch and doing its best to smother their voice. But with moderate talent, which soon meets with recognition, there is the danger that those who possess it will outlive both it and themselves; so that a youth of fame may be followed by an old age of obscurity. In the case of great merit, on the other hand, a man may remain unknown for many years, but make up for it later on by attaining a brilliant reputation. And if it should be that this comes only after he is no more, well! he is to be reckoned amongst those of whom Jean Paul says that extreme unction is their baptism. He may console himself by thinking of the Saints, who also are canonized only after they are dead.

---

[23] Plutarch, *Apophthegms.*

Thus what Mahlmann[24] has said so well in *Herodes* holds good; in this world truly great work never pleases at once, and the god set up by the multitude keeps his place on the altar but a short time:

> *Ich denke, das wahre Grosse in der Welt*
> *Ist immer nur Das was nicht gleich gefällt*
> *Und wen der Pöbel zum Gotte weiht,*
> *Der steht auf dem Altar nur kurze Zeit.*

It is worth mention that this rule is most directly confirmed in the case of pictures, where, as connoisseurs well know, the greatest masterpieces are not the first to attract attention. If they make a deep impression, it is not after one, but only after repeated, inspection; but then they excite more and more admiration every time they are seen.

Moreover, the chances that any given work will be quickly and rightly appreciated, depend upon two conditions: firstly, the character of the work, whether high or low, in other words, easy or difficult to understand; and, secondly, the kind of public it attracts, whether large or small. This latter condition is, no doubt, in most instances a corollary of the former; but it also partly depends upon whether the work in question admits, like books and musical compositions, of being produced in great numbers. By the compound action of these two conditions, achievements which serve no materially useful end—and these alone are under consideration here—will vary in regard to the chances they have of meeting with timely recognition and due appreciation; and the order of precedence, beginning with those who have the greatest chance, will be somewhat as follows: acrobats, circus riders, ballet-dancers, jugglers, actors, singers, musicians, composers, poets (both the last on account of the multiplication of their works), architects, painters, sculptors, philosophers.

The last place of all is unquestionably taken by philosophers because their works are meant not for entertainment, but for instruction, and because they presume some knowledge on the part of the reader, and require him to make an effort of his own to understand them. This makes their public extremely small, and causes their fame to be more remarkable for its length than for its breadth. And, in general, it may be said that the possibility of a man's fame lasting a long time, stands in almost inverse ratio with the chance that it will be early in making its appearance; so that, as regards length of fame, the above order of precedence may be reversed. But, then, the poet and the composer will come in the end to stand on the same level as the philosopher; since,

---

[24] *Translator's Note.*—August Mahlmann (1771-1826), journalist, poet and story-writer. His *Herodes vor Bethlehem* is a parody of Kotzebue's *Hussiten vor Naumburg*.

when once a work is committed to writing, it is possible to preserve it to all time. However, the first place still belongs by right to the philosopher, because of the much greater scarcity of good work in this sphere, and the high importance of it; and also because of the possibility it offers of an almost perfect translation into any language. Sometimes, indeed, it happens that a philosopher's fame outlives even his works themselves; as has happened with Thales, Empedocles, Heraclitus, Democritus, Parmenides, Epicurus and many others.

My remarks are, as I have said, confined to achievements that are not of any material use. Work that serves some practical end, or ministers directly to some pleasure of the senses, will never have any difficulty in being duly appreciated. No first-rate pastry-cook could long remain obscure in any town, to say nothing of having to appeal to posterity.

Under fame of rapid growth is also to be reckoned fame of a false and artificial kind; where, for instance, a book is worked into a reputation by means of unjust praise, the help of friends, corrupt criticism, prompting from above and collusion from below. All this tells upon the multitude, which is rightly presumed to have no power of judging for itself. This sort of fame is like a swimming bladder, by its aid a heavy body may keep afloat. It bears up for a certain time, long or short according as the bladder is well sewed up and blown; but still the air comes out gradually, and the body sinks. This is the inevitable fate of all works which are famous by reason of something outside of themselves. False praise dies away; collusion comes to an end; critics declare the reputation ungrounded; it vanishes, and is replaced by so much the greater contempt. Contrarily, a genuine work, which, having the source of its fame in itself, can kindle admiration afresh in every age, resembles a body of low specific gravity, which always keeps up of its own accord, and so goes floating down the stream of time.

Men of great genius, whether their work be in poetry, philosophy or art, stand in all ages like isolated heroes, keeping up single-handed a desperate struggling against the onslaught of an army of opponents.[25] Is not this characteristic of the miserable nature of mankind? The dullness, grossness, perversity, silliness and brutality of by far the greater part of the race, are always an obstacle to the efforts of the genius, whatever be the method of his art; they so form that hostile army to which at last he has to succumb. Let the isolated champion achieve what he may: it is slow to be acknowledged; it is late in being

---

[25] *Translator's Note.*—At this point Schopenhauer interrupts the thread of his discourse to speak at length upon an example of false fame. Those who are at all acquainted with the philosopher's views will not be surprised to find that the writer thus held up to scorn is Hegel; and readers of the other volumes in this series will, with the translator, have had by now quite enough of the subject. The passage is therefore omitted.

appreciated, and then only on the score of authority; it may easily fall into neglect again, at any rate for a while. Ever afresh it finds itself opposed by false, shallow, and insipid ideas, which are better suited to that large majority, that so generally hold the field. Though the critic may step forth and say, like Hamlet when he held up the two portraits to his wretched mother, _Have you eyes? Have you eyes_? alas! they have none. When I watch the behavior of a crowd of people in the presence of some great master's work, and mark the manner of their applause, they often remind me of trained monkeys in a show. The monkey's gestures are, no doubt, much like those of men; but now and again they betray that the real inward spirit of these gestures is not in them. Their irrational nature peeps out.

It is often said of a man that *he is in advance of his age*; and it follows from the above remarks that this must be taken to mean that he is in advance of humanity in general. Just because of this fact, a genius makes no direct appeal except to those who are too rare to allow of their ever forming a numerous body at any one period. If he is in this respect not particularly favored by fortune, he will be *misunderstood by his own age*; in other words, he will remain unaccepted until time gradually brings together the voices of those few persons who are capable of judging a work of such high character. Then posterity will say: *This man was in advance of his age*, instead of *in advance of humanity*; because humanity will be glad to lay the burden of its own faults upon a single epoch.

Hence, if a man has been superior to his own age, he would also have been superior to any other; provided that, in that age, by some rare and happy chance, a few just men, capable of judging in the sphere of his achievements, had been born at the same time with him; just as when, according to a beautiful Indian myth, Vischnu becomes incarnate as a hero, so, too, Brahma at the same time appears as the singer of his deeds; and hence Valmiki, Vyasa and Kalidasa are incarnations of Brahma.

In this sense, then, it may be said that every immortal work puts its age to the proof, whether or no it will be able to recognize the merit of it. As a rule, the men of any age stand such a test no better than the neighbors of Philemon and Baucis, who expelled the deities they failed to recognize. Accordingly, the right standard for judging the intellectual worth of any generation is supplied, not by the great minds that make their appearance in it—for their capacities are the work of Nature, and the possibility of cultivating them a matter of chance circumstance—but by the way in which contemporaries receive their works; whether, I mean, they give their applause soon and with a will, or late and in niggardly fashion, or leave it to be bestowed altogether by posterity.

This last fate will be especially reserved for works of a high character. For the happy chance mentioned above will be all the more certain not to come, in proportion as there are few to appreciate the kind of work done by great minds. Herein lies the immeasurable advantage possessed by poets in respect of reputation; because their work is accessible to almost everyone. If it had been possible for Sir Walter Scott to be read and criticised by only some hundred persons, perhaps in his life-time any common scribbler would have been preferred to him; and afterwards, when he had taken his proper place, it would also have been said in his honor that he was _in advance of his age_. But if envy, dishonesty and the pursuit of personal aims are added to the incapacity of those hundred persons who, in the name of their generation, are called upon to pass judgment on a work, then indeed it meets with the same sad fate as attends a suitor who pleads before a tribunal of judges one and all corrupt.

In corroboration of this, we find that the history of literature generally shows all those who made knowledge and insight their goal to have remained unrecognized and neglected, whilst those who paraded with the vain show of it received the admiration of their contemporaries, together with the emoluments.

The effectiveness of an author turns chiefly upon his getting the reputation that he should be read. But by practicing various arts, by the operation of chance, and by certain natural affinities, this reputation is quickly won by a hundred worthless people: while a worthy writer may come by it very slowly and tardily. The former possess friends to help them; for the rabble is always a numerous body which holds well together. The latter has nothing but enemies; because intellectual superiority is everywhere and under all circumstances the most hateful thing in the world, and especially to bunglers in the same line of work, who want to pass for something themselves.[26]

This being so, it is a prime condition for doing any great work— any work which is to outlive its own age, that a man pay no heed to his contemporaries, their views and opinions, and the praise or blame which they bestow. This condition is, however, fulfilled of itself when a man really does anything great, and it is fortunate that it is so. For if, in producing such a work, he were to look to the general opinion or the judgment of his colleagues, they would lead him astray at every step. Hence, if a man wants to go down to posterity, he must withdraw from the influence of his own age. This will, of course, generally mean that he must also renounce any influence upon it, and be ready to buy centuries of fame by foregoing the applause of his contemporaries.

For when any new and wide-reaching truth comes into the world—

---

[26] If the professors of philosophy should chance to think that I am here hinting at them and the tactics they have for more than thirty years pursued toward my works, they have hit the nail upon the head.

and if it is new, it must be paradoxical—an obstinate stand will be made against it as long as possible; nay, people will continue to deny it even after they slacken their opposition and are almost convinced of its truth. Meanwhile it goes on quietly working its way, and, like an acid, undermining everything around it. From time to time a crash is heard; the old error comes tottering to the ground, and suddenly the new fabric of thought stands revealed, as though it were a monument just uncovered. Everyone recognizes and admires it. To be sure, this all comes to pass for the most part very slowly. As a rule, people discover a man to be worth listening to only after he is gone; their *hear*, *hear*, resounds when the orator has left the platform.

Works of the ordinary type meet with a better fate. Arising as they do in the course of, and in connection with, the general advance in contemporary culture, they are in close alliance with the spirit of their age—in other words, just those opinions which happen to be prevalent at the time. They aim at suiting the needs of the moment. If they have any merit, it is soon recognized; and they gain currency as books which reflect the latest ideas. Justice, nay, more than justice, is done to them. They afford little scope for envy; since, as was said above, a man will praise a thing only so far as he hopes to be able to imitate it himself.

But those rare works which are destined to become the property of all mankind and to live for centuries, are, at their origin, too far in advance of the point at which culture happens to stand, and on that very account foreign to it and the spirit of their own time. They neither belong to it nor are they in any connection with it, and hence they excite no interest in those who are dominated by it. They belong to another, a higher stage of culture, and a time that is still far off. Their course is related to that of ordinary works as the orbit of Uranus to the orbit of Mercury. For the moment they get no justice done to them. People are at a loss how to treat them; so they leave them alone, and go their own snail's pace for themselves. Does the worm see the eagle as it soars aloft?

Of the number of books written in any language about one in 100,000 forms a part of its real and permanent literature. What a fate this one book has to endure before it outstrips those 100,000 and gains its due place of honor! Such a book is the work of an extraordinary and eminent mind, and therefore it is specifically different from the others; a fact which sooner or later becomes manifest.

Let no one fancy that things will ever improve in this respect. No! the miserable constitution of humanity never changes, though it may, to be sure, take somewhat varying forms with every generation. A distinguished mind seldom has its full effect in the life-time of its possessor; because, at bottom, it is completely and properly understood only by minds already akin to it.

As it is a rare thing for even one man out of many millions to tread the path that leads to immortality, he must of necessity be very lonely. The journey to posterity lies through a horribly dreary region, like the Lybian desert, of which, as is well known, no one has any idea who has not seen it for himself. Meanwhile let me before all things recommend the traveler to take light baggage with him; otherwise he will have to throw away too much on the road. Let him never forget the words of Balthazar Gracian: *lo bueno si breve, dos vezes bueno*—good work is doubly good if it is short. This advice is specially applicable to my own countrymen.

Compared with the short span of time they live, men of great intellect are like huge buildings, standing on a small plot of ground. The size of the building cannot be seen by anyone, just in front of it; nor, for an analogous reason, can the greatness of a genius be estimated while he lives. But when a century has passed, the world recognizes it and wishes him back again.

If the perishable son of time has produced an imperishable work, how short his own life seems compared with that of his child! He is like Semela or Maia—a mortal mother who gave birth to an immortal son; or, contrarily, he is like Achilles in regard to Thetis. What a contrast there is between what is fleeting and what is permanent! The short span of a man's life, his necessitous, afflicted, unstable existence, will seldom allow of his seeing even the beginning of his immortal child's brilliant career; nor will the father himself be taken for that which he really is. It may be said, indeed, that a man whose fame comes after him is the reverse of a nobleman, who is preceded by it.

However, the only difference that it ultimately makes to a man to receive his fame at the hands of contemporaries rather than from posterity is that, in the former case, his admirers are separated from him by space, and in the latter by time. For even in the case of contemporary fame, a man does not, as a rule, see his admirers actually before him. Reverence cannot endure close proximity; it almost always dwells at some distance from its object; and in the presence of the person revered it melts like butter in the sun. Accordingly, if a man is celebrated with his contemporaries, nine-tenths of those amongst whom he lives will let their esteem be guided by his rank and fortune; and the remaining tenth may perhaps have a dull consciousness of his high qualities, because they have heard about him from remote quarters. There is a fine Latin letter of Petrarch's on this incompatibility between reverence and the presence of the person, and between fame and life. It comes second in his *Epistolæ familiares?*[27] and it is addressed to Thomas Messanensis. He there observes, amongst other things, that the learned men of his age all made it a rule to think little of a man's

---

[27] In the Venetian edition of 1492.

writings if they had even once seen him.

Since distance, then, is essential if a famous man is to be recognized and revered, it does not matter whether it is distance of space or of time. It is true that he may sometimes hear of his fame in the one case, but never in the other; but still, genuine and great merit may make up for this by confidently anticipating its posthumous fame. Nay, he who produces some really great thought is conscious of his connection with coming generations at the very moment he conceives it; so that he feels the extension of his existence through centuries and thus lives *with* posterity as well as *for* it. And when, after enjoying a great man's work, we are seized with admiration for him, and wish him back, so that we might see and speak with him, and have him in our possession, this desire of ours is not unrequited; for he, too, has had his longing for that posterity which will grant the recognition, honor, gratitude and love denied by envious contemporaries.

If intellectual works of the highest order are not allowed their due until they come before the tribunal of posterity, a contrary fate is prepared for certain brilliant errors which proceed from men of talent, and appear with an air of being well grounded. These errors are defended with so much acumen and learning that they actually become famous with their own age, and maintain their position at least during their author's lifetime. Of this sort are many false theories and wrong criticisms; also poems and works of art, which exhibit some false taste or mannerism favored by contemporary prejudice. They gain reputation and currency simply because no one is yet forthcoming who knows how to refute them or otherwise prove their falsity; and when he appears, as he usually does, in the next generation, the glory of these works is brought to an end. Posthumous judges, be their decision favorable to the appellant or not, form the proper court for quashing the verdict of contemporaries. That is why it is so difficult and so rare to be victorious alike in both tribunals.

The unfailing tendency of time to correct knowledge and judgment should always be kept in view as a means of allaying anxiety, whenever any grievous error appears, whether in art, or science, or practical life, and gains ground; or when some false and thoroughly perverse policy of movement is undertaken and receives applause at the hands of men. No one should be angry, or, still less, despondent; but simply imagine that the world has already abandoned the error in question, and now only requires time and experience to recognize of its own accord that which a clear vision detected at the first glance.

When the facts themselves are eloquent of a truth, there is no need to rush to its aid with words: for time will give it a thousand tongues. How long it may be before they speak, will of course depend upon the difficulty of the subject and the plausibility of the error; but come they will, and often it would be of no avail to try to anticipate them. In the worst cases it will happen with theories as it happens with affairs in practical life; where sham and deception, emboldened by success, advance to greater and greater lengths, until discovery is made almost inevitable. It is just so with theories; through the blind confidence of the blockheads who broach them, their absurdity reaches such a pitch that at last it is obvious even to the dullest eye. We may thus say to such people: *the wilder your statements, the better.*

There is also some comfort to be found in reflecting upon all the whims and crotchets which had their day and have now utterly vanished. In style, in grammar, in spelling, there are false notions of this sort which last only three or four years. But when the errors are on a large scale, while we lament the brevity of human life, we shall in any case, do well to lag behind our own age when we see it on a downward path. For there are two ways of not keeping on a level with the times. A man may be below it; or he may be above it.

ON GENIUS.

No difference of rank, position, or birth, is so great as the gulf that separates the countless millions who use their head only in the service of their belly, in other words, look upon it as an instrument of the will, and those very few and rare persons who have the courage to say: No! it is too good for that; my head shall be active only in its own service; it shall try to comprehend the wondrous and varied spectacle of this world, and then reproduce it in some form, whether as art or as literature, that may answer to my character as an individual. These are the truly noble, the real *noblesse* of the world. The others are serfs and go with the soil—*glebæ adscripti.* Of course, I am here referring to those who have not only the courage, but also the call, and therefore the right, to order the head to quit the service of the will; with a result that proves the sacrifice to have been worth the making. In the case of those to whom all this can only partially apply, the gulf is not so wide; but even though their talent be small, so long as it is real, there will always be a sharp line of demarcation between them and the millions.[28]

The works of fine art, poetry and philosophy produced by a nation are the outcome of the superfluous intellect existing in it.

For him who can understand aright—*cum grano salis*—the relation between the genius and the normal man may, perhaps, be best

---

[28] The correct scale for adjusting the hierarchy of intelligences is furnished by the degree in which the mind takes merely individual or approaches universal views of things. The brute recognizes only the individual as such: its comprehension does not extend beyond the limits of the individual. But man reduces the individual to the general; herein lies the exercise of his reason; and the higher his intelligence reaches, the nearer do his general ideas approach the point at which they become universal.

expressed as follows: A genius has a double intellect, one for himself and the service of his will; the other for the world, of which he becomes the mirror, in virtue of his purely objective attitude towards it. The work of art or poetry or philosophy produced by the genius is simply the result, or quintessence, of this contemplative attitude, elaborated according to certain technical rules.

The normal man, on the other hand, has only a single intellect, which may be called *subjective* by contrast with the *objective* intellect of genius. However acute this subjective intellect may be—and it exists in very various degrees of perfection—it is never on the same level with the double intellect of genius; just as the open chest notes of the human voice, however high, are essentially different from the falsetto notes. These, like the two upper octaves of the flute and the harmonics of the violin, are produced by the column of air dividing itself into two vibrating halves, with a node between them; while the open chest notes of the human voice and the lower octave of the flute are produced by the undivided column of air vibrating as a whole. This illustration may help the reader to understand that specific peculiarity of genius which is unmistakably stamped on the works, and even on the physiognomy, of him who is gifted with it. At the same time it is obvious that a double intellect like this must, as a rule, obstruct the service of the will; and this explains the poor capacity often shown by genius in the conduct of life. And what specially characterizes genius is that it has none of that sobriety of temper which is always to be found in the ordinary simple intellect, be it acute or dull.

The brain may be likened to a parasite which is nourished as a part of the human frame without contributing directly to its inner economy; it is securely housed in the topmost story, and there leads a self-sufficient and independent life. In the same way it may be said that a man endowed with great mental gifts leads, apart from the individual life common to all, a second life, purely of the intellect. He devotes himself to the constant increase, rectification and extension, not of mere learning, but of real systematic knowledge and insight; and remains untouched by the fate that overtakes him personally, so long as it does not disturb him in his work. It is thus a life which raises a man and sets him above fate and its changes. Always thinking, learning, experimenting, practicing his knowledge, the man soon comes to look upon this second life as the chief mode of existence, and his merely personal life as something subordinate, serving only to advance ends higher than itself.

An example of this independent, separate existence is furnished by Goethe. During the war in the Champagne, and amid all the bustle of the camp, he made observations for his theory of color; and as soon as the numberless calamities of that war allowed of his retiring for a short time to the fortress of Luxembourg, he took up the manuscript of his

Farbenlehre. This is an example which we, the salt of the earth, should endeavor to follow, by never letting anything disturb us in the pursuit of our intellectual life, however much the storm of the world may invade and agitate our personal environment; always remembering that we are the sons, not of the bondwoman, but of the free. As our emblem and coat of arms, I propose a tree mightily shaken by the wind, but still bearing its ruddy fruit on every branch; with the motto *Dum convellor mitescunt*, or *Conquassata sed ferax.*

That purely intellectual life of the individual has its counterpart in humanity as a whole. For there, too, the real life is the life of the *will*, both in the empirical and in the transcendental meaning of the word. The purely intellectual life of humanity lies in its effort to increase knowledge by means of the sciences, and its desire to perfect the arts. Both science and art thus advance slowly from one generation to another, and grow with the centuries, every race as it hurries by furnishing its contribution. This intellectual life, like some gift from heaven, hovers over the stir and movement of the world; or it is, as it were, a sweet-scented air developed out of the ferment itself—the real life of mankind, dominated by will; and side by side with the history of nations, the history of philosophy, science and art takes its innocent and bloodless way.

The difference between the genius and the ordinary man is, no doubt, a *quantitative* one, in so far as it is a difference of degree; but I am tempted to regard it also as *qualitative*, in view of the fact that ordinary minds, notwithstanding individual variation, have a certain tendency to think alike. Thus on similar occasions their thoughts at once all take a similar direction, and run on the same lines; and this explains why their judgments constantly agree—not, however, because they are based on truth. To such lengths does this go that certain fundamental views obtain amongst mankind at all times, and are always being repeated and brought forward anew, whilst the great minds of all ages are in open or secret opposition to them.

A genius is a man in whose mind the world is presented as an object is presented in a mirror, but with a degree more of clearness and a greater distinction of outline than is attained by ordinary people. It is from him that humanity may look for most instruction; for the deepest insight into the most important matters is to be acquired, not by an observant attention to detail, but by a close study of things as a whole. And if his mind reaches maturity, the instruction he gives will be conveyed now in one form, now in another. Thus genius may be defined as an eminently clear consciousness of things in general, and therefore, also of that which is opposed to them, namely, one's own self.

The world looks up to a man thus endowed, and expects to learn something about life and its real nature. But several highly favorable circumstances must combine to produce genius, and this is a very rare event. It happens only now and then, let us say once in a century, that a man is born whose intellect so perceptibly surpasses the normal measure as to amount to that second faculty which seems to be accidental, as it is out of all relation to the will. He may remain a long time without being recognized or appreciated, stupidity preventing the one and envy the other. But should this once come to pass, mankind will crowd round him and his works, in the hope that he may be able to enlighten some of the darkness of their existence or inform them about it. His message is, to some extent, a revelation, and he himself a higher being, even though he may be but little above the ordinary standard.

Like the ordinary man, the genius is what he is chiefly for himself. This is essential to his nature: a fact which can neither be avoided nor altered, he may be for others remains a matter of chance and of secondary importance. In no case can people receive from his mind more than a reflection, and then only when he joins with them in the attempt to get his thought into their heads; where, however, it is never anything but an exotic plant, stunted and frail.

In order to have original, uncommon, and perhaps even immortal thoughts, it is enough to estrange oneself so fully from the world of things for a few moments, that the most ordinary objects and events appear quite new and unfamiliar. In this way their true nature is disclosed. What is here demanded cannot, perhaps, be said to be difficult; it is not in our power at all, but is just the province of genius.

By itself, genius can produce original thoughts just as little as a woman by herself can bear children. Outward circumstances must come to fructify genius, and be, as it were, a father to its progeny.

The mind of genius is among other minds what the carbuncle is among precious stones: it sends forth light of its own, while the others reflect only that which they have received. The relation of the genius to the ordinary mind may also be described as that of an idio-electrical body to one which merely is a conductor of electricity.

The mere man of learning, who spends his life in teaching what he has learned, is not strictly to be called a man of genius; just as idio-electrical bodies are not conductors. Nay, genius stands to mere learning as the words to the music in a song. A man of learning is a man who has learned a great deal; a man of genius, one from whom we learn something which the genius has learned from nobody. Great minds, of which there is scarcely one in a hundred millions, are thus the lighthouses of humanity; and without them mankind would lose itself in the boundless sea of monstrous error and bewilderment.

And so the simple man of learning, in the strict sense of the word—the ordinary professor, for instance—looks upon the genius much as we look upon a hare, which is good to eat after it has been killed and dressed up. So long as it is alive, it is only good to shoot at.

He who wishes to experience gratitude from his contemporaries, must adjust his pace to theirs. But great things are never produced in this way. And he who wants to do great things must direct his gaze to posterity, and in firm confidence elaborate his work for coming generations. No doubt, the result may be that he will remain quite unknown to his contemporaries, and comparable to a man who, compelled to spend his life upon a lonely island, with great effort sets up a monument there, to transmit to future sea-farers the knowledge of his existence. If he thinks it a hard fate, let him console himself with the reflection that the ordinary man who lives for practical aims only, often suffers a like fate, without having any compensation to hope for; inasmuch as he may, under favorable conditions, spend a life of material production, earning, buying, building, fertilizing, laying out, founding, establishing, beautifying with daily effort and unflagging zeal, and all the time think that he is working for himself; and yet in the end it is his descendants who reap the benefit of it all, and sometimes not even his descendants. It is the same with the man of genius; he, too, hopes for his reward and for honor at least; and at last finds that he has worked for posterity alone. Both, to be sure, have inherited a great deal from their ancestors.

The compensation I have mentioned as the privilege of genius lies, not in what it is to others, but in what it is to itself. What man has in any real sense lived more than he whose moments of thought make their echoes heard through the tumult of centuries? Perhaps, after all, it would be the best thing for a genius to attain undisturbed possession of himself, by spending his life in enjoying the pleasure of his own thoughts, his own works, and by admitting the world only as the heir of his ample existence. Then the world would find the mark of his existence only after his death, as it finds that of the Ichnolith.[29]

It is not only in the activity of his highest powers that the genius surpasses ordinary people. A man who is unusually well-knit, supple and agile, will perform all his movements with exceptional ease, even with comfort, because he takes a direct pleasure in an activity for which he is particularly well-equipped, and therefore often exercises it without any object. Further, if he is an acrobat or a dancer, not only does he take leaps which other people cannot execute, but he also betrays rare elasticity and agility in those easier steps which others can also perform, and even in ordinary walking. In the same way a man of superior mind will not only produce thoughts and works which could never have come from another; it will not be here alone that he will show his greatness; but as knowledge and thought form a mode of

---

[29] *Translator's Note.*—For an illustration of this feeling in poetry, Schopenhauer refers the reader to Byron's *Prophecy of Dante*: introd. to C. 4.

activity natural and easy to him, he will also delight himself in them at all times, and so apprehend small matters which are within the range of other minds, more easily, quickly and correctly than they. Thus he will take a direct and lively pleasure in every increase of Knowledge, every problem solved, every witty thought, whether of his own or another's; and so his mind will have no further aim than to be constantly active. This will be an inexhaustible spring of delight; and boredom, that spectre which haunts the ordinary man, can never come near him.

Then, too, the masterpieces of past and contemporary men of genius exist in their fullness for him alone. If a great product of genius is recommended to the ordinary, simple mind, it will take as much pleasure in it as the victim of gout receives in being invited to a ball. The one goes for the sake of formality, and the other reads the book so as not to be in arrear. For La Bruyère was quite right when he said: *All the wit in the world is lost upon him who has none.* The whole range of thought of a man of talent, or of a genius, compared with the thoughts of the common man, is, even when directed to objects essentially the same, like a brilliant oil-painting, full of life, compared with a mere outline or a weak sketch in water-color.

All this is part of the reward of genius, and compensates him for a lonely existence in a world with which he has nothing in common and no sympathies. But since size is relative, it comes to the same thing whether I say, Caius was a great man, or Caius has to live amongst wretchedly small people: for Brobdingnack and Lilliput vary only in the point from which they start. However great, then, however admirable or instructive, a long posterity may think the author of immortal works, during his lifetime he will appear to his contemporaries small, wretched, and insipid in proportion. This is what I mean by saying that as there are three hundred degrees from the base of a tower to the summit, so there are exactly three hundred from the summit to the base. Great minds thus owe little ones some indulgence; for it is only in virtue of these little minds that they themselves are great.

Let us, then, not be surprised if we find men of genius generally unsociable and repellent. It is not their want of sociability that is to blame. Their path through the world is like that of a man who goes for a walk on a bright summer morning. He gazes with delight on the beauty and freshness of nature, but he has to rely wholly on that for entertainment; for he can find no society but the peasants as they bend over the earth and cultivate the soil. It is often the case that a great mind prefers soliloquy to the dialogue he may have in this world. If he condescends to it now and then, the hollowness of it may possibly drive him back to his soliloquy; for in forgetfulness of his interlocutor, or caring little whether he understands or not, he talks to him as a child talks to a doll.

Modesty in a great mind would, no doubt, be pleasing to the world; but, unluckily, it is a *contradictio in adjecto.* It would compel a genius to give the thoughts and opinions, nay, even the method and style, of the million preference over his own; to set a higher value upon them; and, wide apart as they are, to bring his views into harmony with theirs, or even suppress them altogether, so as to let the others hold the field. In that case, however, he would either produce nothing at all, or else his achievements would be just upon a level with theirs. Great, genuine and extraordinary work can be done only in so far as its author disregards the method, the thoughts, the opinions of his contemporaries, and quietly works on, in spite of their criticism, on his side despising what they praise. No one becomes great without arrogance of this sort. Should his life and work fall upon a time which cannot recognize and appreciate him, he is at any rate true to himself; like some noble traveler forced to pass the night in a miserable inn; when morning comes, he contentedly goes his way.

A poet or philosopher should have no fault to find with his age if it only permits him to do his work undisturbed in his own corner; nor with his fate if the corner granted him allows of his following his vocation without having to think about other people.

For the brain to be a mere laborer in the service of the belly, is indeed the common lot of almost all those who do not live on the work of their hands; and they are far from being discontented with their lot. But it strikes despair into a man of great mind, whose brain-power goes beyond the measure necessary for the service of the will; and he prefers, if need be, to live in the narrowest circumstances, so long as they afford him the free use of his time for the development and application of his faculties; in other words, if they give him the leisure which is invaluable to him.

It is otherwise with ordinary people: for them leisure has no value in itself, nor is it, indeed, without its dangers, as these people seem to know. The technical work of our time, which is done to an unprecedented perfection, has, by increasing and multiplying objects of luxury, given the favorites of fortune a choice between more leisure and culture upon the one side, and additional luxury and good living, but with increased activity, upon the other; and, true to their character, they choose the latter, and prefer champagne to freedom. And they are consistent in their choice; for, to them, every exertion of the mind which does not serve the aims of the will is folly. Intellectual effort for its own sake, they call eccentricity. Therefore, persistence in the aims of the will and the belly will be concentricity; and, to be sure, the will is the centre, the kernel of the world.

But in general it is very seldom that any such alternative is presented. For as with money, most men have no superfluity, but only just enough for their needs, so with intelligence; they possess just what will suffice for the service of the will, that is, for the carrying on of their business. Having made their fortune, they are content to gape or to indulge in sensual pleasures or childish amusements, cards or dice; or they will talk in the dullest way, or dress up and make obeisance to one another. And how few are those who have even a little superfluity of intellectual power! Like the others they too make themselves a pleasure; but it is a pleasure of the intellect. Either they will pursue some liberal study which brings them in nothing, or they will practice some art; and in general, they will be capable of taking an objective interest in things, so that it will be possible to converse with them. But with the others it is better not to enter into any relations at all; for, except when they tell the results of their own experience or give an account of their special vocation, or at any rate impart what they have learned from some one else, their conversation will not be worth listening to; and if anything is said to them, they will rarely grasp or understand it aright, and it will in most cases be opposed to their own opinions. Balthazar Gracian describes them very strikingly as men who are not men—*hombres che non lo son.* And Giordano Bruno *says* the same thing: *What a difference there is in having to do with men compared with those who are only made in their image and likeness!*[30] And how wonderfully this passage agrees with that remark in the Kurral: *The common people look like men but I have never seen anything quite like them.* If the reader will consider the extent to which these ideas agree in thought and even in expression, and in the wide difference between them in point of date and nationality, he cannot doubt but that they are at one with the facts of life. It was certainly not under the influence of those passages that, about twenty years ago, I tried to get a snuff-box made, the lid of which should have two fine chestnuts represented upon it, if possible in mosaic; together with a leaf which was to show that they were horse-chestnuts. This symbol was meant to keep the thought constantly before my mind. If anyone wishes for entertainment, such as will prevent him feeling solitary even when he is alone, let me recommend the company of dogs, whose moral and intellectual qualities may almost afford delight and gratification.

Still, we should always be careful to avoid being unjust. I am often surprised by the cleverness, and now and again by the stupidity of my dog; and I have similar experiences with mankind. Countless times, in indignation at their incapacity, their total lack of discernment, their bestiality, I have been forced to echo the old complaint that folly is the mother and the nurse of the human race:

---

[30] *Opera*: ed. Wagner, 1. 224.

*Humani generis mater nutrixque profecto
Stultitia est.*

But at other times I have been astounded that from such a race there could have gone forth so many arts and sciences, abounding in so much use and beauty, even though it has always been the few that produce them. Yet these arts and sciences have struck root, established and perfected themselves: and the race has with persistent fidelity preserved Homer, Plato, Horace and others for thousands of years, by copying and treasuring their writings, thus saving them from oblivion, in spite of all the evils and atrocities that have happened in the world. Thus the race has proved that it appreciates the value of these things, and at the same time it can form a correct view of special achievements or estimate signs of judgment and intelligence. When this takes place amongst those who belong to the great multitude, it is by a kind of inspiration. Sometimes a correct opinion will be formed by the multitude itself; but this is only when the chorus of praise has grown full and complete. It is then like the sound of untrained voices; where there are enough of them, it is always harmonious.

Those who emerge from the multitude, those who are called men of genius, are merely the *lucida intervalla* of the whole human race. They achieve that which others could not possibly achieve. Their originality is so great that not only is their divergence from others obvious, but their individuality is expressed with such force, that all the men of genius who have ever existed show, every one of them, peculiarities of character and mind; so that the gift of his works is one which he alone of all men could ever have presented to the world. This is what makes that simile of Ariosto's so true and so justly celebrated: *Natura lo fece e poi ruppe lo stampo*. After Nature stamps a man of genius, she breaks the die.

But there is always a limit to human capacity; and no one can be a great genius without having some decidedly weak side, it may even be, some intellectual narrowness. In other words, there will foe some faculty in which he is now and then inferior to men of moderate endowments. It will be a faculty which, if strong, might have been an obstacle to the exercise of the qualities in which he excels. What this weak point is, it will always be hard to define with any accuracy even in a given case. It may be better expressed indirectly; thus Plato's weak point is exactly that in which Aristotle is strong, and *vice versa*; and so, too, Kant is deficient just where Goethe is great.

Now, mankind is fond of venerating something; but its veneration is generally directed to the wrong object, and it remains so directed until posterity comes to set it right. But the educated public is no sooner set right in this, than the honor which is due to genius degenerates; just as the honor which the faithful pay to their saints easily passes into a frivolous worship of relics. Thousands of Christians adore the relics of a saint whose life and doctrine are unknown to them; and the religion of thousands of Buddhists lies more in veneration of the Holy Tooth or some such object, or the vessel that contains it, or the Holy Bowl, or the fossil footstep, or the Holy Tree which Buddha planted, than in the thorough knowledge and faithful practice of his high teaching. Petrarch's house in Arqua; Tasso's supposed prison in Ferrara; Shakespeare's house in Stratford, with his chair; Goethe's house in Weimar, with its furniture; Kant's old hat; the autographs of great men; these things are gaped at with interest and awe by many who have never read their works. They cannot do anything more than just gape.

The intelligent amongst them are moved by the wish to see the objects which the great man habitually had before his eyes; and by a strange illusion, these produce the mistaken notion that with the objects they are bringing back the man himself, or that something of him must cling to them. Akin to such people are those who earnestly strive to acquaint themselves with the subject-matter of a poet's works, or to unravel the personal circumstances and events in his life which have suggested particular passages. This is as though the audience in a theatre were to admire a fine scene and then rush upon the stage to look at the scaffolding that supports it. There are in our day enough instances of these critical investigators, and they prove the truth of the saying that mankind is interested, not in the *form* of a work, that is, in its manner of treatment, but in its actual matter. All it cares for is the theme. To read a philosopher's biography, instead of studying his thoughts, is like neglecting a picture and attending only to the style of its frame, debating whether it is carved well or ill, and how much it cost to gild it.

This is all very well. However, there is another class of persons whose interest is also directed to material and personal considerations, but they go much further and carry it to a point where it becomes absolutely futile. Because a great man has opened up to them the treasures of his inmost being, and, by a supreme effort of his faculties, produced works which not only redound to their elevation and enlightenment, but will also benefit their posterity to the tenth and twentieth generation; because he has presented mankind with a matchless gift, these varlets think themselves justified in sitting in judgment upon his personal morality, and trying if they cannot discover here or there some spot in him which will soothe the pain they feel at the sight of so great a mind, compared with the overwhelming feeling of their own nothingness.

This is the real source of all those prolix discussions, carried on in countless books and reviews, on the moral aspect of Goethe's life, and whether he ought not to have married one or other of the girls with whom he fell in love in his young days; whether, again, instead of honestly devoting himself to the service of his master, he should not have been a man of the people, a German patriot, worthy of a seat in the *Paulskirche*, and so on. Such crying ingratitude and malicious detraction prove that these self-constituted judges are as great knaves morally as they are intellectually, which is saying a great deal.

A man of talent will strive for money and reputation; but the spring that moves genius to the production of its works is not as easy to name. Wealth is seldom its reward. Nor is it reputation or glory; only a Frenchman could mean that. Glory is such an uncertain thing, and, if you look at it closely, of so little value. Besides it never corresponds to the effort you have made:

Responsura tuo nunquam est par fama labori.

Nor, again, is it exactly the pleasure it gives you; for this is almost outweighed by the greatness of the effort. It is rather a peculiar kind of instinct, which drives the man of genius to give permanent form to what he sees and feels, without being conscious of any further motive. It works, in the main, by a necessity similar to that which makes a tree bear its fruit; and no external condition is needed but the ground upon which it is to thrive.

On a closer examination, it seems as though, in the case of a genius, the will to live, which is the spirit of the human species, were conscious of having, by some rare chance, and for a brief period, attained a greater clearness of vision, and were now trying to secure it, or at least the outcome of it, for the whole species, to which the individual genius in his inmost being belongs; so that the light which he sheds about him may pierce the darkness and dullness of ordinary human consciousness and there produce some good effect.

Arising in some such way, this instinct drives the genius to carry his work to completion, without thinking of reward or applause or sympathy; to leave all care for his own personal welfare; to make his life one of industrious solitude, and to strain his faculties to the utmost. He thus comes to think more about posterity than about contemporaries; because, while the latter can only lead him astray, posterity forms the majority of the species, and time will gradually bring the discerning few who can appreciate him. Meanwhile it is with him as with the artist described by Goethe; he has no princely patron to prize his talents, no friend to rejoice with him:

Ein Fürst der die Talente schätzte,
Ein Freund, der sich mit mir ergötzte,
Die haben leider mir gefehlt.

His work is, as it were, a sacred object and the true fruit of his life, and his aim in storing it away for a more discerning posterity will be to make it the property of mankind. An aim like this far surpasses all others, and for it he wears the crown of thorns which is one day to bloom into a wreath of laurel. All his powers are concentrated in the effort to complete and secure his work; just as the insect, in the last stage of its development, uses its whole strength on behalf of a brood it will never live to see; it puts its eggs in some place of safety, where, as it well knows, the young will one day find life and nourishment, and then dies in confidence.

Studies in Pessimism.

ON THE SUFFERINGS OF THE WORLD.

Unless *suffering* is the direct and immediate object of life, our existence must entirely fail of its aim. It is absurd to look upon the enormous amount of pain that abounds everywhere in the world, and originates in needs and necessities inseparable from life itself, as serving no purpose at all and the result of mere chance. Each separate misfortune, as it comes, seems, no doubt, to be something exceptional; but misfortune in general is the rule.

I know of no greater absurdity than that propounded by most systems of philosophy in declaring evil to be negative in its character. Evil is just what is positive; it makes its own existence felt. Leibnitz is particularly concerned to defend this absurdity; and he seeks to strengthen his position by using a palpable and paltry sophism.[31] It is the good which is negative; in other words, happiness and satisfaction always imply some desire fulfilled, some state of pain brought to an end.

This explains the fact that we generally find pleasure to be not nearly so pleasant as we expected, and pain very much more painful.

The pleasure in this world, it has been said, outweighs the pain; or, at any rate, there is an even balance between the two. If the reader wishes to see shortly whether this statement is true, let him compare the respective feelings of two animals, one of which is engaged in eating the other.

---

[31] *Translator's Note,* cf. *Thèod,* §153.—Leibnitz argued that evil is a negative quality—*i.e.,* the absence of good; and that its active and seemingly positive character is an incidental and not an essential part of its nature. Cold, he said, is only the absence of the power of heat, and the active power of expansion in freezing water is an incidental and not an essential part of the nature of cold. The fact is, that the power of expansion in freezing water is really an increase of repulsion amongst its molecules; and Schopenhauer is quite right in calling the whole argument a sophism.

The best consolation in misfortune or affliction of any kind will be the thought of other people who are in a still worse plight than yourself; and this is a form of consolation open to every one. But what an awful fate this means for mankind as a whole!

We are like lambs in a field, disporting themselves under the eye of the butcher, who chooses out first one and then another for his prey. So it is that in our good days we are all unconscious of the evil Fate may have presently in store for us—sickness, poverty, mutilation, loss of sight or reason.

No little part of the torment of existence lies in this, that Time is continually pressing upon us, never letting us take breath, but always coming after us, like a taskmaster with a whip. If at any moment Time stays his hand, it is only when we are delivered over to the misery of boredom.

But misfortune has its uses; for, as our bodily frame would burst asunder if the pressure of the atmosphere was removed, so, if the lives of men were relieved of all need, hardship and adversity; if everything they took in hand were successful, they would be so swollen with arrogance that, though they might not burst, they would present the spectacle of unbridled folly—nay, they would go mad. And I may say, further, that a certain amount of care or pain or trouble is necessary for every man at all times. A ship without ballast is unstable and will not go straight.

Certain it is that *work, worry, labor* and *trouble*, form the lot of almost all men their whole life long. But if all wishes were fulfilled as soon as they arose, how would men occupy their lives? what would they do with their time? If the world were a paradise of luxury and ease, a land flowing with milk and honey, where every Jack obtained his Jill at once and without any difficulty, men would either die of boredom or hang themselves; or there would be wars, massacres, and murders; so that in the end mankind would inflict more suffering on itself than it has now to accept at the hands of Nature.

In early youth, as we contemplate our coming life, we are like children in a theatre before the curtain is raised, sitting there in high spirits and eagerly waiting for the play to begin. It is a blessing that we do not know what is really going to happen. Could we foresee it, there are times when children might seem like innocent prisoners, condemned, not to death, but to life, and as yet all unconscious of what their sentence means. Nevertheless, every man desires to reach old age; in other words, a state of life of which it may be said: "It is bad to-day, and it will be worse to-morrow; and so on till the worst of all."

If you try to imagine, as nearly as you can, what an amount of misery, pain and suffering of every kind the sun shines upon in its course, you will admit that it would be much better if, on the earth as little as on the moon, the sun were able to call forth the phenomena of

life; and if, here as there, the surface were still in a crystalline state.

Again, you may look upon life as an unprofitable episode, disturbing the blessed calm of non-existence. And, in any case, even though things have gone with you tolerably well, the longer you live the more clearly you will feel that, on the whole, life is *a disappointment, nay, a cheat.*

If two men who were friends in their youth meet again when they are old, after being separated for a life-time, the chief feeling they will have at the sight of each other will be one of complete disappointment at life as a whole; because their thoughts will be carried back to that earlier time when life seemed so fair as it lay spread out before them in the rosy light of dawn, promised so much—and then performed so little. This feeling will so completely predominate over every other that they will not even consider it necessary to give it words; but on either side it will be silently assumed, and form the ground-work of all they have to talk about.

He who lives to see two or three generations is like a man who sits some time in the conjurer's booth at a fair, and witnesses the performance twice or thrice in succession. The tricks were meant to be seen only once; and when they are no longer a novelty and cease to deceive, their effect is gone.

While no man is much to be envied for his lot, there are countless numbers whose fate is to be deplored.

Life is a task to be done. It is a fine thing to say *defunctus est*; it means that the man has done his task.

If children were brought into the world by an act of pure reason alone, would the human race continue to exist? Would not a man rather have so much sympathy with the coming generation as to spare it the burden of existence? or at any rate not take it upon himself to impose that burden upon it in cold blood.

I shall be told, I suppose, that my philosophy is comfortless—because I speak the truth; and people prefer to be assured that everything the Lord has made is good. Go to the priests, then, and leave philosophers in peace! At any rate, do not ask us to accommodate our doctrines to the lessons you have been taught. That is what those rascals of sham philosophers will do for you. Ask them for any doctrine you please, and you will get it. Your University professors are bound to preach optimism; and it is an easy and agreeable task to upset their theories.

I have reminded the reader that every state of welfare, every feeling of satisfaction, is negative in its character; that is to say, it consists in freedom from pain, which is the positive element of existence. It follows, therefore, that the happiness of any given life is to be measured, not by its joys and pleasures, but by the extent to which it has been free from suffering—from positive evil. If this is the true

standpoint, the lower animals appear to enjoy a happier destiny than man. Let us examine the matter a little more closely.

However varied the forms that human happiness and misery may take, leading a man to seek the one and shun the other, the material basis of it all is bodily pleasure or bodily pain. This basis is very restricted: it is simply health, food, protection from wet and cold, the satisfaction of the sexual instinct; or else the absence of these things. Consequently, as far as real physical pleasure is concerned, the man is not better off than the brute, except in so far as the higher possibilities of his nervous system make him more sensitive to every kind of pleasure, but also, it must be remembered, to every kind of pain. But then compared with the brute, how much stronger are the passions aroused in him! what an immeasurable difference there is in the depth and vehemence of his emotions!—and yet, in the one case, as in the other, all to produce the same result in the end: namely, health, food, clothing, and so on.

The chief source of all this passion is that thought for what is absent and future, which, with man, exercises such a powerful influence upon all he does. It is this that is the real origin of his cares, his hopes, his fears—emotions which affect him much more deeply than could ever be the case with those present joys and sufferings to which the brute is confined. In his powers of reflection, memory and foresight, man possesses, as it were, a machine for condensing and storing up his pleasures and his sorrows. But the brute has nothing of the kind; whenever it is in pain, it is as though it were suffering for the first time, even though the same thing should have previously happened to it times out of number. It has no power of summing up its feelings. Hence its careless and placid temper: how much it is to be envied! But in man reflection comes in, with all the emotions to which it gives rise; and taking up the same elements of pleasure and pain which are common to him and the brute, it develops his susceptibility to happiness and misery to such a degree that, at one moment the man is brought in an instant to a state of delight that may even prove fatal, at another to the depths of despair and suicide.

If we carry our analysis a step farther, we shall find that, in order to increase his pleasures, man has intentionally added to the number and pressure of his needs, which in their original state were not much more difficult to satisfy than those of the brute. Hence luxury in all its forms; delicate food, the use of tobacco and opium, spirituous liquors, fine clothes, and the thousand and one things than he considers necessary to his existence.

And above and beyond all this, there is a separate and peculiar source of pleasure, and consequently of pain, which man has established for himself, also as the result of using his powers of reflection; and this occupies him out of all proportion to its value, nay,

almost more than all his other interests put together—I mean ambition and the feeling of honor and shame; in plain words, what he thinks about the opinion other people have of him. Taking a thousand forms, often very strange ones, this becomes the goal of almost all the efforts he makes that are not rooted in physical pleasure or pain. It is true that besides the sources of pleasure which he has in common with the brute, man has the pleasures of the mind as well. These admit of many gradations, from the most innocent trifling or the merest talk up to the highest intellectual achievements; but there is the accompanying boredom to be set against them on the side of suffering. Boredom is a form of suffering unknown to brutes, at any rate in their natural state; it is only the very cleverest of them who show faint traces of it when they are domesticated; whereas in the case of man it has become a downright scourge. The crowd of miserable wretches whose one aim in life is to fill their purses but never to put anything into their heads, offers a singular instance of this torment of boredom. Their wealth becomes a punishment by delivering them up to misery of having nothing to do; for, to escape it, they will rush about in all directions, traveling here, there and everywhere. No sooner do they arrive in a place than they are anxious to know what amusements it affords; just as though they were beggars asking where they could receive a dole! Of a truth, need and boredom are the two poles of human life. Finally, I may mention that as regards the sexual relation, a man is committed to a peculiar arrangement which drives him obstinately to choose one person. This feeling grows, now and then, into a more or less passionate love,[32] which is the source of little pleasure and much suffering.

It is, however, a wonderful thing that the mere addition of thought should serve to raise such a vast and lofty structure of human happiness and misery; resting, too, on the same narrow basis of joy and sorrow as man holds in common with the brute, and exposing him to such violent emotions, to so many storms of passion, so much convulsion of feeling, that what he has suffered stands written and may be read in the lines on his face. And yet, when all is told, he has been struggling ultimately for the very same things as the brute has attained, and with an incomparably smaller expenditure of passion and pain.

But all this contributes to increase the measures of suffering in human life out of all proportion to its pleasures; and the pains of life are made much worse for man by the fact that death is something very real to him. The brute flies from death instinctively without really knowing what it is, and therefore without ever contemplating it in the way

---

[32] I have treated this subject at length in a special chapter of the second volume of my chief work.

natural to a man, who has this prospect always before his eyes. So that even if only a few brutes die a natural death, and most of them live only just long enough to transmit their species, and then, if not earlier, become the prey of some other animal,—whilst man, on the other hand, manages to make so-called natural death the rule, to which, however, there are a good many exceptions,—the advantage is on the side of the brute, for the reason stated above. But the fact is that man attains the natural term of years just as seldom as the brute; because the unnatural way in which he lives, and the strain of work and emotion, lead to a degeneration of the race; and so his goal is not often reached.

The brute is much more content with mere existence than man; the plant is wholly so; and man finds satisfaction in it just in proportion as he is dull and obtuse. Accordingly, the life of the brute carries less of sorrow with it, but also less of joy, when compared with the life of man; and while this may be traced, on the one side, to freedom from the torment of *care* and *anxiety*, it is also due to the fact that *hope*, in any real sense, is unknown to the brute. It is thus deprived of any share in that which gives us the most and best of our joys and pleasures, the mental anticipation of a happy future, and the inspiriting play of phantasy, both of which we owe to our power of imagination. If the brute is free from care, it is also, in this sense, without hope; in either case, because its consciousness is limited to the present moment, to what it can actually see before it. The brute is an embodiment of present impulses, and hence what elements of fear and hope exist in its nature—and they do not go very far—arise only in relation to objects that lie before it and within reach of those impulses: whereas a man's range of vision embraces the whole of his life, and extends far into the past and future.

Following upon this, there is one respect in which brutes show real wisdom when compared with us—I mean, their quiet, placid enjoyment of the present moment. The tranquillity of mind which this seems to give them often puts us to shame for the many times we allow our thoughts and our cares to make us restless and discontented. And, in fact, those pleasures of hope and anticipation which I have been mentioning are not to be had for nothing. The delight which a man has in hoping for and looking forward to some special satisfaction is a part of the real pleasure attaching to it enjoyed in advance. This is afterwards deducted; for the more we look forward to anything, the less satisfaction we find in it when it comes. But the brute's enjoyment is not anticipated, and therefore, suffers no deduction; so that the actual pleasure of the moment comes to it whole and unimpaired. In the same way, too, evil presses upon the brute only with its own intrinsic weight; whereas with us the fear of its coming often makes its burden ten times more grievous.

It is just this characteristic way in which the brute gives itself up

entirely to the present moment that contributes so much to the delight we take in our domestic pets. They are the present moment personified, and in some respects they make us feel the value of every hour that is free from trouble and annoyance, which we, with our thoughts and preoccupations, mostly disregard. But man, that selfish and heartless creature, misuses this quality of the brute to be more content than we are with mere existence, and often works it to such an extent that he allows the brute absolutely nothing more than mere, bare life. The bird which was made so that it might rove over half of the world, he shuts up into the space of a cubic foot, there to die a slow death in longing and crying for freedom; for in a cage it does not sing for the pleasure of it. And when I see how man misuses the dog, his best friend; how he ties up this intelligent animal with a chain, I feel the deepest sympathy with the brute and burning indignation against its master.

We shall see later that by taking a very high standpoint it is possible to justify the sufferings of mankind. But this justification cannot apply to animals, whose sufferings, while in a great measure brought about by men, are often considerable even apart from their agency.[33] And so we are forced to ask, Why and for what purpose does all this torment and agony exist? There is nothing here to give the will pause; it is not free to deny itself and so obtain redemption. There is only one consideration that may serve to explain the sufferings of animals. It is this: that the will to live, which underlies the whole world of phenomena, must, in their case satisfy its cravings by feeding upon itself. This it does by forming a gradation of phenomena, every one of which exists at the expense of another. I have shown, however, that the capacity for suffering is less in animals than in man. Any further explanation that may be given of their fate will be in the nature of hypothesis, if not actually mythical in its character; and I may leave the reader to speculate upon the matter for himself.

Brahma is said to have produced the world by a kind of fall or mistake; and in order to atone for his folly, he is bound to remain in it himself until he works out his redemption. As an account of the origin of things, that is admirable! According to the doctrines of *Buddhism*, the world came into being as the result of some inexplicable disturbance in the heavenly calm of Nirvana, that blessed state obtained by expiation, which had endured so long a time—the change taking place by a kind of fatality. This explanation must be understood as having at bottom some moral bearing; although it is illustrated by an exactly parallel theory in the domain of physical science, which places the origin of the sun in a primitive streak of mist, formed one knows not how. Subsequently, by a series of moral errors, the world became

---

[33] Cf. *Welt als Wille und Vorstellung*, vol. ii. p. 404.

gradually worse and worse—true of the physical orders as well—until
it assumed the dismal aspect it wears to-day. Excellent! The *Greeks*
looked upon the world and the gods as the work of an inscrutable
necessity. A passable explanation: we may be content with it until we
can get a better. Again, *Ormuzd* and *Ahriman* are rival powers,
continually at war. That is not bad. But that a God like Jehovah should
have created this world of misery and woe, out of pure caprice, and
because he enjoyed doing it, and should then have clapped his hands in
praise of his own work, and declared everything to be very good—that
will not do at all! In its explanation of the origin of the world, Judaism
is inferior to any other form of religious doctrine professed by a
civilized nation; and it is quite in keeping with this that it is the only
one which presents no trace whatever of any belief in the immortality
of the soul.[34]

Even though Leibnitz' contention, that this is the best of all
possible worlds, were correct, that would not justify God in having
created it. For he is the Creator not of the world only, but of possibility
itself; and, therefore, he ought to have so ordered possibility as that it
would admit of something better.

There are two things which make it impossible to believe that this
world is the successful work of an all-wise, all-good, and, at the same
time, all-powerful Being; firstly, the misery which abounds in it
everywhere; and secondly, the obvious imperfection of its highest
product, man, who is a burlesque of what he should be. These things
cannot be reconciled with any such belief. On the contrary, they are just
the facts which support what I have been saying; they are our authority
for viewing the world as the outcome of our own misdeeds, and
therefore, as something that had better not have been. Whilst, under the
former hypothesis, they amount to a bitter accusation against the
Creator, and supply material for sarcasm; under the latter they form an
indictment against our own nature, our own will, and teach us a lesson
of humility. They lead us to see that, like the children of a libertine, we
come into the world with the burden of sin upon us; and that it is only
through having continually to atone for this sin that our existence is so
miserable, and that its end is death.

There is nothing more certain than the general truth that it is the
grievous *sin of the world* which has produced the grievous *suffering of
the world*. I am not referring here to the physical connection between
these two things lying in the realm of experience; my meaning is
metaphysical. Accordingly, the sole thing that reconciles me to the Old
Testament is the story of the Fall. In my eyes, it is the only
metaphysical truth in that book, even though it appears in the form of

---

[34] See *Parerga*, vol. i. pp. 139 *et seq.*

an allegory. There seems to me no better explanation of our existence than that it is the result of some false step, some sin of which we are paying the penalty. I cannot refrain from recommending the thoughtful reader a popular, but at the same time, profound treatise on this subject by Claudius[35] which exhibits the essentially pessimistic spirit of Christianity. It is entitled: *Cursed is the ground for thy sake.*

Between the ethics of the Greeks and the ethics of the Hindoos, there is a glaring contrast. In the one case (with the exception, it must be confessed, of Plato), the object of ethics is to enable a man to lead a happy life; in the other, it is to free and redeem him from life altogether—as is directly stated in the very first words of the *Sankhya Karika.*

Allied with this is the contrast between the Greek and the Christian idea of death. It is strikingly presented in a visible form on a fine antique sarcophagus in the gallery of Florence, which exhibits, in relief, the whole series of ceremonies attending a wedding in ancient times, from the formal offer to the evening when Hymen's torch lights the happy couple home. Compare with that the Christian coffin, draped in mournful black and surmounted with a crucifix! How much significance there is in these two ways of finding comfort in death. They are opposed to each other, but each is right. The one points to the *affirmation* of the will to live, which remains sure of life for all time, however rapidly its forms may change. The other, in the symbol of suffering and death, points to the *denial* of the will to live, to redemption from this world, the domain of death and devil. And in the question between the affirmation and the denial of the will to live, Christianity is in the last resort right.

The contrast which the New Testament presents when compared with the Old, according to the ecclesiastical view of the matter, is just that existing between my ethical system and the moral philosophy of Europe. The Old Testament represents man as under the dominion of Law, in which, however, there is no redemption. The New Testament declares Law to have failed, frees man from its dominion,[36] and in its stead preaches the kingdom of grace, to be won by faith, love of neighbor and entire sacrifice of self. This is the path of redemption from the evil of the world. The spirit of the New Testament is undoubtedly asceticism, however your protestants and rationalists may twist it to suit their purpose. Asceticism is the denial of the will to live; and the transition from the Old Testament to the New, from the

---

[35] *Translator's Note.*—Matthias Claudius (1740-1815), a popular poet, and friend of Klopstock, Herder and Leasing. He edited the *Wandsbecker Bote*, in the fourth part of which appeared the treatise mentioned above. He generally wrote under the pseudonym of *Asmus*, and Schopenhauer often refers to him by this name.

[36] Cf. Romans vii; Galatians ii, iii.

dominion of Law to that of Faith, from justification by works to redemption through the Mediator, from the domain of sin and death to eternal life in Christ, means, when taken in its real sense, the transition from the merely moral virtues to the denial of the will to live. My philosophy shows the metaphysical foundation of justice and the love of mankind, and points to the goal to which these virtues necessarily lead, if they are practised in perfection. At the same time it is candid in confessing that a man must turn his back upon the world, and that the denial of the will to live is the way of redemption. It is therefore really at one with the spirit of the New Testament, whilst all other systems are couched in the spirit of the Old; that is to say, theoretically as well as practically, their result is Judaism—mere despotic theism. In this sense, then, my doctrine might be called the only true Christian philosophy— however paradoxical a statement this may seem to people who take superficial views instead of penetrating to the heart of the matter.

If you want a safe compass to guide you through life, and to banish all doubt as to the right way of looking at it, you cannot do better than accustom yourself to regard this world as a penitentiary, a sort of a penal colony, or [Greek: ergastaerion] as the earliest philosopher called it.[37] Amongst the Christian Fathers, Origen, with praiseworthy courage, took this view,[38] which is further justified by certain objective theories of life. I refer, not to my own philosophy alone, but to the wisdom of all ages, as expressed in Brahmanism and Buddhism, and in the sayings of Greek philosophers like Empedocles and Pythagoras; as also by Cicero, in his remark that the wise men of old used to teach that we come into this world to pay the penalty of crime committed in another state of existence—a doctrine which formed part of the initiation into the mysteries.[39] And Vanini—whom his contemporaries burned, finding that an easier task than to confute him—puts the same thing in a very forcible way. *Man,* he says, *is so full of every kind of misery that, were it not repugnant to the Christian religion, I should venture to affirm that if evil spirits exist at all, they have posed into human form and are now atoning for their crimes.*[40] And true Christianity—using the word in its right sense—also regards our existence as the consequence of sin and error.

If you accustom yourself to this view of life you will regulate your expectations accordingly, and cease to look upon all its disagreeable incidents, great and small, its sufferings, its worries, its misery, as anything unusual or irregular; nay, you will find that everything is as it should be, in a world where each of us pays the penalty of existence in

---

[37] Cf. Clem. Alex. Strom. L. iii, c, 3, p. 399.
[38] Augustine *de civitate Dei.,* L. xi. c. 23.
[39] Cf. *Fragmenta de philosophia.*
[40] *De admirandis naturæ arcanis*; dial L. p. 35.

his own peculiar way. Amongst the evils of a penal colony is the society of those who form it; and if the reader is worthy of better company, he will need no words from me to remind him of what he has to put up with at present. If he has a soul above the common, or if he is a man of genius, he will occasionally feel like some noble prisoner of state, condemned to work in the galleys with common criminals; and he will follow his example and try to isolate himself.

In general, however, it should be said that this view of life will enable us to contemplate the so-called imperfections of the great majority of men, their moral and intellectual deficiencies and the resulting base type of countenance, without any surprise, to say nothing of indignation; for we shall never cease to reflect where we are, and that the men about us are beings conceived and born in sin, and living to atone for it. That is what Christianity means in speaking of the sinful nature of man.

Pardon's the word to all![41] Whatever folly men commit, be their shortcomings or their vices what they may, let us exercise forbearance; remembering that when these faults appear in others, it is our follies and vices that we behold. They are the shortcomings of humanity, to which we belong; whose faults, one and all, we share; yes, even those very faults at which we now wax so indignant, merely because they have not yet appeared in ourselves. They are faults that do not lie on the surface. But they exist down there in the depths of our nature; and should anything call them forth, they will come and show themselves, just as we now see them in others. One man, it is true, may have faults that are absent in his fellow; and it is undeniable that the sum total of bad qualities is in some cases very large; for the difference of individuality between man and man passes all measure.

In fact, the conviction that the world and man is something that had better not have been, is of a kind to fill us with indulgence towards one another. Nay, from this point of view, we might well consider the proper form of address to be, not *Monsieur, Sir, mein Herr,* but *my fellow-sufferer, Socî malorum, compagnon de miseres!* This may perhaps sound strange, but it is in keeping with the facts; it puts others in a right light; and it reminds us of that which is after all the most necessary thing in life—the tolerance, patience, regard, and love of neighbor, of which everyone stands in need, and which, therefore, every man owes to his fellow.

---

[41] "Cymbeline," Act v. Sc. 5.

THE VANITY OF EXISTENCE.

This vanity finds expression in the whole way in which things exist; in the infinite nature of Time and Space, as opposed to the finite nature of the individual in both; in the ever-passing present moment as the only mode of actual existence; in the interdependence and relativity of all things; in continual Becoming without ever Being; in constant wishing and never being satisfied; in the long battle which forms the history of life, where every effort is checked by difficulties, and stopped until they are overcome. Time is that in which all things pass away; it is merely the form under which the will to live—the thing-in-itself and therefore imperishable—has revealed to it that its efforts are in vain; it is that agent by which at every moment all things in our hands become as nothing, and lose any real value they possess.

That which *has been* exists no more; it exists as little as that which has *never* been. But of everything that exists you must say, in the next moment, that it has been. Hence something of great importance now past is inferior to something of little importance now present, in that the latter is a *reality*, and related to the former as something to nothing.

A man finds himself, to his great astonishment, suddenly existing, after thousands and thousands of years of non-existence: he lives for a little while; and then, again, comes an equally long period when he must exist no more. The heart rebels against this, and feels that it cannot be true. The crudest intellect cannot speculate on such a subject without having a presentiment that Time is something ideal in its nature. This ideality of Time and Space is the key to every true system of metaphysics; because it provides for quite another order of things than is to be met with in the domain of nature. This is why Kant is so great.

Of every event in our life we can say only for one moment that it *is*; for ever after, that it *was*. Every evening we are poorer by a day. It might, perhaps, make us mad to see how rapidly our short span of time ebbs away; if it were not that in the furthest depths of our being we are secretly conscious of our share in the exhaustible spring of eternity, so that we can always hope to find life in it again.

Consideration of the kind, touched on above, might, indeed, lead us to embrace the belief that the greatest *wisdom* is to make the enjoyment of the present the supreme object of life; because that is the only reality, all else being merely the play of thought. On the other hand, such a course might just as well be called the greatest *folly*: for that which in the next moment exists no more, and vanishes utterly, like a dream, can never be worth a serious effort.

The whole foundation on which our existence rests is the present—the ever-fleeting present. It lies, then, in the very nature of our existence to take the form of constant motion, and to offer no possibility of our ever attaining the rest for which we are always striving. We are like a man running downhill, who cannot keep on his legs unless he runs on, and will inevitably fall if he stops; or, again, like a pole balanced on the tip of one's finger; or like a planet, which would fall into its sun the moment it ceased to hurry forward on its way. Unrest is the mark of existence.

In a world where all is unstable, and nought can endure, but is swept onwards at once in the hurrying whirlpool of change; where a man, if he is to keep erect at all, must always be advancing and moving, like an acrobat on a rope—in such a world, happiness in inconceivable. How can it dwell where, as Plato says, *continual Becoming and never Being* is the sole form of existence? In the first place, a man never is happy, but spends his whole life in striving after something which he thinks will make him so; he seldom attains his goal, and when he does, it is only to be disappointed; he is mostly shipwrecked in the end, and comes into harbor with masts and rigging gone. And then, it is all one whether he has been happy or miserable; for his life was never anything more than a present moment always vanishing; and now it is over.

At the same time it is a wonderful thing that, in the world of human beings as in that of animals in general, this manifold restless motion is produced and kept up by the agency of two simple impulses—hunger and the sexual instinct; aided a little, perhaps, by the influence of boredom, but by nothing else; and that, in the theatre of life, these suffice to form the *primum mobile* of how complicated a machinery, setting in motion how strange and varied a scene!

On looking a little closer, we find that inorganic matter presents a constant conflict between chemical forces, which eventually works dissolution; and on the other hand, that organic life is impossible without continual change of matter, and cannot exist if it does not receive perpetual help from without. This is the realm of *finality*; and its opposite would be *an infinite existence*, exposed to no attack from without, and needing nothing to support it; [Greek: haei hosautos dn], the realm of eternal peace; [Greek: oute giguomenon oute apollumenon], some timeless, changeless state, one and undiversified; the negative knowledge of which forms the dominant note of the Platonic philosophy. It is to some such state as this that the denial of the will to live opens up the way.

The scenes of our life are like pictures done in rough mosaic. Looked at close, they produce no effect. There is nothing beautiful to be found in them, unless you stand some distance off. So, to gain anything we have longed for is only to discover how vain and empty it is; and even though we are always living in expectation of better things, at the same time we often repent and long to have the past back again. We look upon the present as something to be put up with while it lasts, and serving only as the way towards our goal. Hence most people, if they glance back when they come to the end of life, will find that all along they have been living *ad interim*: they will be surprised to find that the very thing they disregarded and let slip by unenjoyed, was just the life in the expectation of which they passed all their time. Of how many a man may it not be said that hope made a fool of him until he danced into the arms of death!

Then again, how insatiable a creature is man! Every satisfaction he attains lays the seeds of some new desire, so that there is no end to the wishes of each individual will. And why is this? The real reason is simply that, taken in itself, Will is the lord of all worlds: everything belongs to it, and therefore no one single thing can ever give it satisfaction, but only the whole, which is endless. For all that, it must rouse our sympathy to think how very little the Will, this lord of the world, really gets when it takes the form of an individual; usually only just enough to keep the body together. This is why man is so very miserable.

Life presents itself chiefly as a task—the task, I mean, of subsisting at all, *gagner sa vie*. If this is accomplished, life is a burden, and then there comes the second task of doing something with that which has been won—of warding off boredom, which, like a bird of prey, hovers over us, ready to fall wherever it sees a life secure from need. The first task is to win something; the second, to banish the feeling that it has been won; otherwise it is a burden.

Human life must be some kind of mistake. The truth of this will be sufficiently obvious if we only remember that man is a compound of needs and necessities hard to satisfy; and that even when they are satisfied, all he obtains is a state of painlessness, where nothing remains to him but abandonment to boredom. This is direct proof that existence has no real value in itself; for what is boredom but the feeling of the emptiness of life? If life—the craving for which is the very essence of our being—were possessed of any positive intrinsic value, there would be no such thing as boredom at all: mere existence would satisfy us in itself, and we should want for nothing. But as it is, we take no delight in existence except when we are struggling for something; and then distance and difficulties to be overcome make our goal look as though it would satisfy us—an illusion which vanishes when we reach it; or else when we are occupied with some purely intellectual interest—when in reality we have stepped forth from life to look upon it from the outside, much after the manner of spectators at a play. And even sensual pleasure itself means nothing but a struggle and aspiration, ceasing the moment its aim is attained. Whenever we are not occupied in one of these ways, but cast upon existence itself, its vain and worthless nature is brought home to us; and this is what we mean by boredom. The hankering after what is strange and uncommon—an innate and ineradicable tendency of human nature—shows how glad we are at any interruption of that natural course of affairs which is so very tedious.

That this most perfect manifestation of the will to live, the human organism, with the cunning and complex working of its machinery, must fall to dust and yield up itself and all its strivings to extinction—this is the naïve way in which Nature, who is always so true and sincere in what she says, proclaims the whole struggle of this will as in its very essence barren and unprofitable. Were it of any value in itself, anything unconditioned and absolute, it could not thus end in mere nothing.

If we turn from contemplating the world as a whole, and, in particular, the generations of men as they live their little hour of mock-existence and then are swept away in rapid succession; if we turn from this, and look at life in its small details, as presented, say, in a comedy, how ridiculous it all seems! It is like a drop of water seen through a microscope, a single drop teeming with *infusoria*; or a speck of cheese full of mites invisible to the naked eye. How we laugh as they bustle about so eagerly, and struggle with one another in so tiny a space! And whether here, or in the little span of human life, this terrible activity produces a comic effect.

It is only in the microscope that our life looks so big. It is an indivisible point, drawn out and magnified by the powerful lenses of Time and Space.

ON SUICIDE.

As far as I know, none but the votaries of monotheistic, that is to say, Jewish religions, look upon suicide as a crime. This is all the more striking, inasmuch as neither in the Old nor in the New Testament is there to be found any prohibition or positive disapproval of it; so that religious teachers are forced to base their condemnation of suicide on philosophical grounds of their own invention. These are so very bad that writers of this kind endeavor to make up for the weakness of their arguments by the strong terms in which they express their abhorrence of the practice; in other words, they declaim against it. They tell us that suicide is the greatest piece of cowardice; that only a madman could be guilty of it; and other insipidities of the same kind; or else they make the nonsensical remark that suicide is *wrong*; when it is quite obvious that there is nothing in the world to which every mail has a more unassailable title than to his own life and person.

Suicide, as I have said, is actually accounted a crime; and a crime which, especially under the vulgar bigotry that prevails in England, is followed by an ignominious burial and the seizure of the man's property; and for that reason, in a case of suicide, the jury almost always brings in a verdict of insanity. Now let the reader's own moral feelings decide as to whether or not suicide is a criminal act. Think of the impression that would be made upon you by the news that some one you know had committed the crime, say, of murder or theft, or been guilty of some act of cruelty or deception; and compare it with your feelings when you hear that he has met a voluntary death. While in the one case a lively sense of indignation and extreme resentment will be aroused, and you will call loudly for punishment or revenge, in the other you will be moved to grief and sympathy; and mingled with your thoughts will be admiration for his courage, rather than the moral disapproval which follows upon a wicked action. Who has not had acquaintances, friends, relations, who of their own free will have left this world; and are these to be thought of with horror as criminals? Most emphatically, No! I am rather of opinion that the clergy should be challenged to explain what right they have to go into the pulpit, or take up their pens, and stamp as a crime an action which many men whom we hold in affection and honor have committed; and to refuse an honorable burial to those who relinquish this world voluntarily. They have no Biblical authority to boast of, as justifying their condemnation of suicide; nay, not even any philosophical arguments that will hold water; and it must be understood that it is arguments we want, and that we will not be put off with mere phrases or words of abuse. If the criminal law forbids suicide, that is not an argument valid in the Church; and besides, the prohibition is ridiculous; for what penalty can frighten a man who is not afraid of death itself? If the law punishes people for trying to commit suicide, it is punishing the want of skill that makes the attempt a failure.

The ancients, moreover, were very far from regarding the matter in that light. Pliny says: *Life is not so desirable a thing as to be protracted at any cost. Whoever you are, you are sure to die, even though your life has been full of abomination and crime. The chief of all remedies for a troubled mind is the feeling that among the blessings which Nature gives to man, there is none greater than an opportune death; and the best of it is that every one can avail himself of it.*[42] And elsewhere the same writer declares: *Not even to God are all things possible; for he could not compass his own death, if he willed to die, and yet in all the miseries of our earthly life, this is the best of his gifts to man.*[43] Nay, in Massilia and on the isle of Ceos, the man who could give valid reasons for relinquishing his life, was handed the cup of hemlock by the magistrate; and that, too, in public.[44] And in ancient times, how many

---

[42] Hist. Nat. Lib. xxviii., 1.

[43] Loc. cit. Lib. ii. c. 7.

[44] 3 Valerius Maximus; hist. Lib. ii., c. 6, § 7 et 8. Heraclides Ponticus; fragmenta de rebus publicis, ix. Aeliani variæ historiæ, iii., 37. Strabo; Lib. x., c. 5, 6.

heroes and wise men died a voluntary death. Aristotle,[45] it is true, declared suicide to be an offence against the State, although not against the person; but in Stobæus' exposition of the Peripatetic philosophy there is the following remark: *The good man should flee life when his misfortunes become too great; the bad man, also, when he is too prosperous.* And similarly: *So he will marry and beget children and take part in the affairs of the State, and, generally, practice virtue and continue to live; and then, again, if need be, and at any time necessity compels him, he will depart to his place of refuge in the tomb.*[46] And we find that the Stoics actually praised suicide as a noble and heroic action, as hundreds of passages show; above all in the works of Seneca, who expresses the strongest approval of it. As is well known, the Hindoos look upon suicide as a religious act, especially when it takes the form of self-immolation by widows; but also when it consists in casting oneself under the wheels of the chariot of the god at Juggernaut, or being eaten by crocodiles in the Ganges, or being drowned in the holy tanks in the temples, and so on. The same thing occurs on the stage—that mirror of life. For example, in *L'Orphelin de la Chine*[47] a celebrated Chinese play, almost all the noble characters end by suicide; without the slightest hint anywhere, or any impression being produced on the spectator, that they are committing a crime. And in our own theatre it is much the same—Palmira, for instance, in *Mahomet*, or Mortimer in *Maria Stuart*, Othello, Countess Terzky.[48] Is Hamlet's monologue the meditation of a criminal? He merely declares that if we had any certainty of being annihilated by it, death would be infinitely preferable to the world as it is. But *there lies the rub!*

The reasons advanced against suicide by the clergy of monotheistic, that is to say, Jewish religions, and by those philosophers who adapt themselves thereto, are weak sophisms which can easily be refuted.[49] The most thorough-going refutation of them is given by Hume in his *Essay on Suicide*. This did not appeal until after his death, when it was immediately suppressed, owing to the scandalous bigotry and outrageous ecclesiastical tyranny that prevailed in England; and hence only a very few copies of it were sold under cover of secrecy and at a high price. This and another treatise by that great man have come to us from Basle, and we may be thankful for the reprint.[50] It is a great

---

[45] *Eth. Nichom.*, v. 15.

[46] Stobæus. *Ecl. Eth.*. ii., c. 7, pp. 286, 312.

[47] Traduit par St. Julien, 1834.

[48] *Translator's Note.*—Palmira: a female slave in Goethe's play of *Mahomet*. Mortimer: a would-be lover and rescuer of Mary in Schiller's *Maria Stuart*. Countess Terzky: a leading character in Schiller's *Wallenstein's Tod.*

[49] See my treatise on the *Foundation of Morals*, § 5.

[50] *Essays on Suicide* and the *Immortality of the Soul*, by the late David Hume, Basle, 1799, sold by James Decker.

disgrace to the English nation that a purely philosophical treatise, which, proceeding from one of the first thinkers and writers in England, aimed at refuting the current arguments against suicide by the light of cold reason, should be forced to sneak about in that country, as though it were some rascally production, until at last it found refuge on the Continent. At the same time it shows what a good conscience the Church has in such matters.

In my chief work I have explained the only valid reason existing against suicide on the score of mortality. It is this: that suicide thwarts the attainment of the highest moral aim by the fact that, for a real release from this world of misery, it substitutes one that is merely apparent. But from a *mistake* to a *crime* is a far cry; and it is as a crime that the clergy of Christendom wish us to regard suicide.

The inmost kernel of Christianity is the truth that suffering—*the Cross*—is the real end and object of life. Hence Christianity condemns suicide as thwarting this end; whilst the ancient world, taking a lower point of view, held it in approval, nay, in honor.[51] But if that is to be accounted a valid reason against suicide, it involves the recognition of asceticism; that is to say, it is valid only from a much higher ethical standpoint than has ever been adopted by moral philosophers in Europe. If we abandon that high standpoint, there is no tenable reason left, on the score of morality, for condemning suicide. The extraordinary energy and zeal with which the clergy of monotheistic religions attack suicide is not supported either by any passages in the Bible or by any considerations of weight; so that it looks as though they must have some secret reason for their contention. May it not be this— that the voluntary surrender of life is a bad compliment for him who said that *all things were very good?* If this is so, it offers another instance of the crass optimism of these religions,—denouncing suicide to escape being denounced by it.

It will generally be found that, as soon as the terrors of life reach the point at which they outweigh the terrors of death, a man will put an end to his life. But the terrors of death offer considerable resistance; they stand like a sentinel at the gate leading out of this world. Perhaps there is no man alive who would not have already put an end to his life, if this end had been of a purely negative character, a sudden stoppage

---

[51] *Translator's Note.*—Schopenhauer refers to *Die Welt als Wille und Vorstellung*, vol. i., § 69, where the reader may find the same argument stated at somewhat greater length. According to Schopenhauer, moral freedom—the highest ethical aim—is to be obtained only by a denial of the will to live. Far from being a denial, suicide is an emphatic assertion of this will. For it is in fleeing from the pleasures, not from the sufferings of life, that this denial consists. When a man destroys his existence as an individual, he is not by any means destroying his will to live. On the contrary, he would like to live if he could do so with satisfaction to himself; if he could assert his will against the power of circumstance; but circumstance is too strong for him.

of existence. There is something positive about it; it is the destruction of the body; and a man shrinks from that, because his body is the manifestation of the will to live.

However, the struggle with that sentinel is, as a rule, not so hard as it may seem from a long way off, mainly in consequence of the antagonism between the ills of the body and the ills of the mind. If we are in great bodily pain, or the pain lasts a long time, we become indifferent to other troubles; all we think about is to get well. In the same way great mental suffering makes us insensible to bodily pain; we despise it; nay, if it should outweigh the other, it distracts our thoughts, and we welcome it as a pause in mental suffering. It is this feeling that makes suicide easy; for the bodily pain that accompanies it loses all significance in the eyes of one who is tortured by an excess of mental suffering. This is especially evident in the case of those who are driven to suicide by some purely morbid and exaggerated ill-humor. No special effort to overcome their feelings is necessary, nor do such people require to be worked up in order to take the step; but as soon as the keeper into whose charge they are given leaves them for a couple of minutes, they quickly bring their life to an end.

When, in some dreadful and ghastly dream, we reach the moment of greatest horror, it awakes us; thereby banishing all the hideous shapes that were born of the night. And life is a dream: when the moment of greatest horror compels us to break it off, the same thing happens.

Suicide may also be regarded as an experiment—a question which man puts to Nature, trying to force her to an answer. The question is this: What change will death produce in a man's existence and in his insight into the nature of things? It is a clumsy experiment to make; for it involves the destruction of the very consciousness which puts the question and awaits the answer.

IMMORTALITY:[52] A DIALOGUE.

THRASYMACHOS—PHILALETHES.

Thrasymachos. Tell me now, in one word, what shall I be after my death? And mind you be clear and precise.

Philalethes. All and nothing!

Thrasymachos. I thought so! I gave you a problem, and you solve it by a contradiction. That's a very stale trick.

Philalethes. Yes, but you raise transcendental questions, and you expect me to answer them in language that is only made for immanent knowledge. It's no wonder that a contradiction ensues.

Thrasymachos. What do you mean by transcendental questions and immanent knowledge? I've heard these expressions before, of course; they are not new to me. The Professor was fond of using them, but only as predicates of the Deity, and he never talked of anything else; which was all quite right and proper. He argued thus: if the Deity was in the world itself, he was immanent; if he was somewhere outside it, he was transcendent. Nothing could be clearer and more obvious! You knew where you were. But this Kantian rigmarole won't do any more: it's antiquated and no longer applicable to modern ideas. Why, we've had a whole row of eminent men in the metropolis of German learning—

Philalethes. (Aside.) German humbug, he means.

Thrasymachos. The mighty Schleiermacher, for instance, and that gigantic intellect, Hegel; and at this time of day we've abandoned that nonsense. I should rather say we're so far beyond it that we can't put up with it any more. What's the use of it then? What does it all mean?

Philalethes. Transcendental knowledge is knowledge which passes beyond the bounds of possible experience, and strives to determine the nature of things as they are in themselves. Immanent knowledge, on the other hand, is knowledge which confines itself entirely with those bounds; so that it cannot apply to anything but actual phenomena. As far as you are an individual, death will be the end of you. But your individuality is not your true and inmost being: it is only the outward manifestation of it. It is not the *thing-in-itself*, but only the phenomenon

---

[52] *Translator's Note.*—The word immortality—*Unsterblichkeit*—does not occur in the original; nor would it, in its usual application, find a place in Schopenhauer's vocabulary. The word he uses is *Unzerstörbarkeit—indestructibility.* But I have preferred *immortality*, because that word is commonly associated with the subject touched upon in this little debate. If any critic doubts the wisdom of this preference, let me ask him to try his hand at a short, concise, and, at the same time, popularly intelligible rendering of the German original, which runs thus: *Zur Lehre von der Unzerstörbarkeit unseres wahren Wesens durch den Tod: Meine dialogische Schlussbelustigung.*

presented in the form of time; and therefore with a beginning and an end. But your real being knows neither time, nor beginning, nor end, nor yet the limits of any given individual. It is everywhere present in every individual; and no individual can exist apart from it. So when death comes, on the one hand you are annihilated as an individual; on the other, you are and remain everything. That is what I meant when I said that after your death you would be all and nothing. It is difficult to find a more precise answer to your question and at the same time be brief. The answer is contradictory, I admit; but it is so simply because your life is in time, and the immortal part of you in eternity. You may put the matter thus: Your immortal part is something that does not last in time and yet is indestructible; but there you have another contradiction! You see what happens by trying to bring the transcendental within the limits of immanent knowledge. It is in some sort doing violence to the latter by misusing it for ends it was never meant to serve.

Thrasymachos. Look here, I shan't give two-pence for your immortality unless I'm to remain an individual.

Philalethes. Well, perhaps I may be able to satisfy you on this point. Suppose I guarantee that after death you shall remain an individual, but only on condition that you first spend three months of complete unconsciousness.

Thrasymachos. I shall have no objection to that.

Philalethes. But remember, if people are completely unconscious, they take no account of time. So, when you are dead, it's all the same to you whether three months pass in the world of consciousness, or ten thousand years. In the one case as in the other, it is simply a matter of believing what is told you when you awake. So far, then, you can afford to be indifferent whether it is three months or ten thousand years that pass before you recover your individuality.

Thrasymachos. Yes, if it comes to that, I suppose you're right.

Philalethes. And if by chance, after those ten thousand years have gone by, no one ever thinks of awakening you, I fancy it would be no great misfortune. You would have become quite accustomed to non-existence after so long a spell of it—following upon such a very few years of life. At any rate you may be sure you would be perfectly ignorant of the whole thing. Further, if you knew that the mysterious power which keeps you in your present state of life had never once ceased in those ten thousand years to bring forth other phenomena like yourself, and to endow them with life, it would fully console you.

Thrasymachos. Indeed! So you think you're quietly going to do me out of my individuality with all this fine talk. But I'm up to your tricks. I tell you I won't exist unless I can have my individuality. I'm not going to be put off with 'mysterious powers,' and what you call 'phenomena.' I can't do without my individuality, and I won't give it up.

Philalethes. You mean, I suppose, that your individuality is such a delightful thing, so splendid, so perfect, and beyond compare—that you can't imagine anything better. Aren't you ready to exchange your present state for one which, if we can judge by what is told us, may possibly be superior and more endurable?

Thrasymachos. Don't you see that my individuality, be it what it may, is my very self? To me it is the most important thing in the world.

For God is God and I am I.

I want to exist, *I, I*. That's the main thing. I don't care about an existence which has to be proved to be mine, before I can believe it.

Philalethes. Think what you're doing! When you say *I, I, I* want to exist, it is not you alone that says this. Everything says it, absolutely everything that has the faintest trace of consciousness. It follows, then, that this desire of yours is just the part of you that is *not individual*— the part that is common to all things without distinction. It is the cry, not of the individual, but of existence itself; it is the intrinsic element in everything that exists, nay, it is the cause of anything existing at all. This desire craves for, and so is satisfied with, nothing less than existence in general—not any definite individual existence. No! that is not its aim. It seems to be so only because this desire—this *Will*— attains consciousness only in the individual, and therefore looks as though it were concerned with nothing but the individual. There lies the illusion—an illusion, it is true, in which the individual is held fast: but, if he reflects, he can break the fetters and set himself free. It is only indirectly, I say, that the individual has this violent craving for existence. It is *the Will to Live* which is the real and direct aspirant— alike and identical in all things. Since, then, existence is the free work, nay, the mere reflection of the will, where existence is, there, too, must be will; and for the moment the will finds its satisfaction in existence itself; so far, I mean, as that which never rests, but presses forward eternally, can ever find any satisfaction at all. The will is careless of the individual: the individual is not its business; although, as I have said, this seems to be the case, because the individual has no direct consciousness of will except in himself. The effect of this is to make the individual careful to maintain his own existence; and if this were not so, there would be no surety for the preservation of the species. From all this it is clear that individuality is not a form of perfection, but rather of limitation; and so to be freed from it is not loss but gain. Trouble yourself no more about the matter. Once thoroughly recognize what you are, what your existence really is, namely, the universal will to live, and the whole question will seem to you childish, and most ridiculous!

Thrasymachos. You're childish yourself and most ridiculous, like all philosophers! and if a man of my age lets himself in for a quarter-of-an-hour's talk with such fools, it is only because it amuses me and passes the time. I've more important business to attend to, so Good-bye.

PSYCHOLOGICAL OBSERVATIONS.

There is an unconscious propriety in the way in which, in all European languages, the word *person* is commonly used to denote a human being. The real meaning of *persona* is *a mask*, such as actors were accustomed to wear on the ancient stage; and it is quite true that no one shows himself as he is, but wears his mask and plays his part. Indeed, the whole of our social arrangements may be likened to a perpetual comedy; and this is why a man who is worth anything finds society so insipid, while a blockhead is quite at home in it.

* * * * *

Reason deserves to be called a prophet; for in showing us the consequence and effect of our actions in the present, does it not tell us what the future will be? This is precisely why reason is such an excellent power of restraint in moments when we are possessed by some base passion, some fit of anger, some covetous desire, that will lead us to do things whereof we must presently repent.

* * * * *

Hatred comes from the heart; *contempt* from the head; and neither feeling is quite within our control. For we cannot alter our heart; its basis is determined by motives; and our head deals with objective facts, and applies to them rules which are immutable. Any given individual is the union of a particular heart with a particular head.

Hatred and contempt are diametrically opposed and mutually exclusive. There are even not a few cases where hatred of a person is rooted in nothing but forced esteem for his qualities. And besides, if a man sets out to hate all the miserable creatures he meets, he will not have much energy left for anything else; whereas he can despise them, one and all, with the greatest ease. True, genuine contempt is just the reverse of true, genuine pride; it keeps quite quiet and gives no sign of its existence. For if a man shows that he despises you, he signifies at least this much regard for you, that he wants to let you know how little he appreciates you; and his wish is dictated by hatred, which cannot exist with real contempt. On the contrary, if it is genuine, it is simply the conviction that the object of it is a man of no value at all. Contempt is not incompatible with indulgent and kindly treatment, and for the sake of one's own peace and safety, this should not be omitted; it will prevent irritation; and there is no one who cannot do harm if he is roused to it. But if this pure, cold, sincere contempt ever shows itself, it will be met with the most truculent hatred; for the despised person is not in a position to fight contempt with its own weapons.

* * * * *

Melancholy is a very different thing from bad humor, and of the two, it is not nearly so far removed from a gay and happy temperament. Melancholy attracts, while bad humor repels.

Hypochondria is a species of torment which not only makes us unreasonably cross with the things of the present; not only fills us with groundless anxiety on the score of future misfortunes entirely of our own manufacture; but also leads to unmerited self-reproach for what we have done in the past.

Hypochondria shows itself in a perpetual hunting after things that vex and annoy, and then brooding over them. The cause of it is an inward morbid discontent, often co-existing with a naturally restless temperament. In their extreme form, this discontent and this unrest lead to suicide.

* * * * *

Any incident, however trivial, that rouses disagreeable emotion, leaves an after-effect in our mind, which for the time it lasts, prevents our taking a clear objective view of the things about us, and tinges all our thoughts: just as a small object held close to the eye limits and distorts our field of vision.

* * * * *

What makes people *hard-hearted* is this, that each man has, or fancies he has, as much as he can bear in his own troubles. Hence, if a man suddenly finds himself in an unusually happy position, it will in most cases result in his being sympathetic and kind. But if he has never been in any other than a happy position, or this becomes his permanent state, the effect of it is often just the contrary: it so far removes him from suffering that he is incapable of feeling any more sympathy with it. So it is that the poor often show themselves more ready to help than the rich.

* * * * *

At times it seems as though we both wanted and did not want the same thing, and felt at once glad and sorry about it. For instance, if on some fixed date we are going to be put to a decisive test about anything in which it would be a great advantage to us to come off victorious, we shall be anxious for it to take place at once, and at the same time we shall tremble at the thought of its approach. And if, in the meantime, we hear that, for once in a way, the date has been postponed, we shall experience a feeling both of pleasure and of annoyance; for the news is disappointing, but nevertheless it affords us momentary relief. It is just the same thing if we are expecting some important letter carrying a definite decision, and it fails to arrive.

In such cases there are really two different motives at work in us; the stronger but more distant of the two being the desire to stand the test and to have the decision given in our favor; and the weaker, which touches us more nearly, the wish to be left for the present in peace and quiet, and accordingly in further enjoyment of the advantage which at any rate attaches to a state of hopeful uncertainty, compared with the possibility that the issue may be unfavorable.

* * * * *

In my head there is a permanent opposition-party; and whenever I take any step or come to any decision—though I may have given the matter mature consideration—it afterwards attacks what I have done, without, however, being each time necessarily in the right. This is, I suppose, only a form of rectification on the part of the spirit of scrutiny; but it often reproaches me when I do not deserve it. The same thing, no doubt, happens to many others as well; for where is the man who can help thinking that, after all, it were better not to have done something that he did with great deliberation:

> *Quid tam dextro pede concipis ut te*
> *Conatus non poeniteat votique peracti?*

* * * * *

Why is it that *common* is an expression of contempt? and that *uncommon, extraordinary, distinguished,* denote approbation? Why is everything that is common contemptible?

Common in its original meaning denotes that which is peculiar to all men, *i.e.,* shared equally by the whole species, and therefore an inherent part of its nature. Accordingly, if an individual possesses no qualities beyond those which attach to mankind in general, he is a *common man. Ordinary* is a much milder word, and refers rather to intellectual character; whereas *common* has more of a moral application.

What value can a creature have that is not a whit different from millions of its kind? Millions, do I say? nay, an infiniture of creatures which, century after century, in never-ending flow, Nature sends bubbling up from her inexhaustible springs; as generous with them as the smith with the useless sparks that fly around his anvil.

It is obviously quite right that a creature which has no qualities except those of the species, should have to confine its claim to an existence entirely within the limits of the species, and live a life conditioned by those limits.

In various passages of my works,[53] I have argued that whilst a lower animal possesses nothing more than the generic character of its species, man is the only being which can lay claim to possess an individual character. But in most men this individual character comes to very little in reality; and they may be almost all ranged under certain classes: *ce sont des espèces.* Their thoughts and desires, like their faces, are those of the species, or, at any rate, those of the class to which they belong; and accordingly, they are of a trivial, every-day, common character, and exist by the thousand. You can usually tell beforehand what they are likely to do and say. They have no special stamp or mark to distinguish them; they are like manufactured goods, all of a piece.

If, then, their nature is merged in that of the species, how shall their existence go beyond it? The curse of vulgarity puts men on a par with the lower animals, by allowing them none but a generic nature, a generic form of existence. Anything that is high or great or noble, must then, as a mater of course, and by its very nature, stand alone in a world where no better expression can be found to denote what is base and contemptible than that which I have mentioned as in general use, namely, *common.*

* * * * *

Will, as the *thing-in-itself,* is the foundation of all being; it is part and parcel of every creature, and the permanent element in everything. Will, then, is that which we possess in common with all men, nay, with all animals, and even with lower forms of existence; and in so far we are akin to everything—so far, that is, as everything is filled to overflowing with will. On the other hand, that which places one being over another, and sets differences between man and man, is intellect and knowledge; therefore in every manifestation of self we should, as far as possible, give play to the intellect alone; for, as we have seen, the will is the *common* part of us. Every violent exhibition of will is

---

[53] *Grundprobleme der Ethik,* p. 48; *Welt als Wille und Vorstellung,* vol. i. p. 338.

common and vulgar; in other words, it reduces us to the level of the species, and makes us a mere type and example of it; in that it is just the character of the species that we are showing. So every fit of anger is something *common*—every unrestrained display of joy, or of hate, or fear—in short, every form of emotion; in other words, every movement of the will, if it's so strong as decidedly to outweigh the intellectual element in consciousness, and to make the man appear as a being that *wills* rather than *knows*.

In giving way to emotion of this violent kind, the greatest genius puts himself on a level with the commonest son of earth. Contrarily, if a man desires to be absolutely uncommon, in other words, great, he should never allow his consciousness to be taken possession of and dominated by the movement of his will, however much he may be solicited thereto. For example, he must be able to observe that other people are badly disposed towards him, without feeling any hatred towards them himself; nay, there is no surer sign of a great mind than that it refuses to notice annoying and insulting expressions, but straightway ascribes them, as it ascribes countless other mistakes, to the defective knowledge of the speaker, and so merely observes without feeling them. This is the meaning of that remark of Gracian, that nothing is more unworthy of a man than to let it be seen that he is one—*el mayor desdoro de un hombre es dar muestras de que es hombre.*

And even in the drama, which is the peculiar province of the passions and emotions, it is easy for them to appear common and vulgar. And this is specially observable in the works of the French tragic writers, who set no other aim before themselves but the delineation of the passions; and by indulging at one moment in a vaporous kind of pathos which makes them ridiculous, at another in epigrammatic witticisms, endeavor to conceal the vulgarity of their subject. I remember seeing the celebrated Mademoiselle Rachel as Maria Stuart: and when she burst out in fury against Elizabeth—though she did it very well—I could not help thinking of a washerwoman. She played the final parting in such a way as to deprive it of all true tragic feeling, of which, indeed, the French have no notion at all. The same part was incomparably better played by the Italian Ristori; and, in fact, the Italian nature, though in many respects very different from the German, shares its appreciation for what is deep, serious, and true in Art; herein opposed to the French, which everywhere betrays that it possesses none of this feeling whatever.

The noble, in other words, the uncommon, element in the drama—nay, what is sublime in it—is not reached until the intellect is set to work, as opposed to the will; until it takes a free flight over all those passionate movements of the will, and makes them subject of its contemplation. Shakespeare, in particular, shows that this is his general method, more especially in Hamlet. And only when intellect rises to the point where the vanity of all effort is manifest, and the will proceeds to an act of self-annulment, is the drama tragic in the true sense of the word; it is then that it reaches its highest aim in becoming really sublime.

* * * * *

Every man takes the limits of his own field of vision for the limits of the world. This is an error of the intellect as inevitable as that error of the eye which lets us fancy that on the horizon heaven and earth meet. This explains many things, and among them the fact that everyone measures us with his own standard—generally about as long as a tailor's tape, and we have to put up with it: as also that no one will allow us to be taller than himself—a supposition which is once for all taken for granted.

* * * * *

There is no doubt that many a man owes his good fortune in life solely to the circumstance that he has a pleasant way of smiling, and so wins the heart in his favor.

However, the heart would do better to be careful, and to remember what Hamlet put down in his tablets—*that one may smile, and smile, and be a villain.*

* * * * *

Everything that is really fundamental in a man, and therefore genuine works, as such, unconsciously; in this respect like the power of nature. That which has passed through the domain of consciousness is thereby transformed into an idea or picture; and so if it comes to be uttered, it is only an idea or picture which passes from one person to another.

Accordingly, any quality of mind or character that is genuine and lasting, is originally unconscious; and it is only when unconsciously brought into play that it makes a profound impression. If any like quality is consciously exercised, it means that it has been worked up; it becomes intentional, and therefore matter of affectation, in other words, of deception.

If a man does a thing unconsciously, it costs him no trouble; but if he tries to do it by taking trouble, he fails. This applies to the origin of those fundamental ideas which form the pith and marrow of all genuine work. Only that which is innate is genuine and will hold water; and every man who wants to achieve something, whether in practical life, in literature, or in art, must *follow the rules without knowing them.*

* * * * *

Men of very great capacity, will as a rule, find the company of very stupid people preferable to that of the common run; for the same reason that the tyrant and the mob, the grandfather and the grandchildren, are natural allies.

* * * * *

That line of Ovid's,

Pronaque cum spectent animalia cetera terram,

can be applied in its true physical sense to the lower animals alone; but in a metaphorical and spiritual sense it is, alas! true of nearly all men as well. All their plans and projects are merged in the desire of physical enjoyment, physical well-being. They may, indeed, have personal interests, often embracing a very varied sphere; but still these latter receive their importance entirely from the relation in which they stand to the former. This is not only proved by their manner of life and the things they say, but it even shows itself in the way they look, the expression of their physiognomy, their gait and gesticulations. Everything about them cries out; *in terram prona!*

It is not to them, it is only to the nobler and more highly endowed natures—men who really think and look about them in the world, and form exceptional specimens of humanity—that the next lines are applicable;

Os homini sublime dedit coelumque tueri
Jussit et erectos ad sidera tollere vultus.

* * * * *

No one knows what capacities for doing and suffering he has in himself, until something comes to rouse them to activity: just as in a pond of still water, lying there like a mirror, there is no sign of the roar and thunder with which it can leap from the precipice, and yet remain what it is; or again, rise high in the air as a fountain. When water is as cold as ice, you can have no idea of the latent warmth contained in it.

* * * * *

Why is it that, in spite of all the mirrors in the world, no one really knows what he looks like?

A man may call to mind the face of his friend, but not his own. Here, then, is an initial difficulty in the way of applying the maxim, *Know thyself.*

This is partly, no doubt, to be explained by the fact that it is physically impossible for a man to see himself in the glass except with face turned straight towards it and perfectly motionless; where the expression of the eye, which counts for so much, and really gives its whole character to the face, is to a great extent lost. But co-existing with this physical impossibility, there seems to me to be an ethical impossibility of an analogous nature, and producing the same effect. A man cannot look upon his own reflection as though the person presented there were *a stranger* to him; and yet this is necessary if he is to take *an objective view.* In the last resort, an objective view means a deep-rooted feeling on the part of the individual, as a moral being, that that which he is contemplating is *not himself*;[54] and unless he can take this point of view, he will not see things in a really true light, which is possible only if he is alive to their actual defects, exactly as they are. Instead of that, when a man sees himself in the glass, something out of his own egotistic nature whispers to him to take care to remember that *it is no stranger, but himself, that he is looking at*; and this operates as a *noli me tangere*, and prevents him taking an objective view. It seems, indeed, as if, without the leaven of a grain of malice, such a view were impossible.

* * * * *

According as a man's mental energy is exerted or relaxed, will life appear to him either so short, and petty, and fleeting, that nothing can possibly happen over which it is worth his while to spend emotion; that nothing really matters, whether it is pleasure or riches, or even fame, and that in whatever way a man may have failed, he cannot have lost much—or, on the other hand, life will seem so long, so important, so all in all, so momentous and so full of difficulty that we have to plunge into it with our whole soul if we are to obtain a share of its goods, make sure of its prizes, and carry out our plans. This latter is the immanent and common view of life; it is what Gracian means when he speaks of the serious way of looking at things—*tomar muy de veras el vivir.* The former is the transcendental view, which is well expressed in Ovid's *non est tanti*—it is not worth so much trouble; still better, however, by Plato's remark that nothing in human affairs is worth any great

---

[54] Cf. *Grundprobleme der Ethik*, p. 275.

anxiety—[Greek: oute ti ton anthropinon axion esti megalaes spoudaes.] This condition of mind is due to the intellect having got the upper hand in the domain of consciousness, where, freed from the mere service of the will, it looks upon the phenomena of life objectively, and so cannot fail to gain a clear insight into its vain and futile character. But in the other condition of mind, will predominates; and the intellect exists only to light it on its way to the attainment of its desires.

A man is great or small according as he leans to the one or the other of these views of life.

* * * * *

People of very brilliant ability think little of admitting their errors and weaknesses, or of letting others see them. They look upon them as something for which they have duly paid; and instead of fancying that these weaknesses are a disgrace to them, they consider they are doing them an honor. This is especially the case when the errors are of the kind that hang together with their qualities—*conditiones sine quibus non*—or, as George Sand said, *les défauts de ses vertus.*

Contrarily, there are people of good character and irreproachable intellectual capacity, who, far from admitting the few little weaknesses they have, conceal them with care, and show themselves very sensitive to any suggestion of their existence; and this, just because their whole merit consists in being free from error and infirmity. If these people are found to have done anything wrong, their reputation immediately suffers.

* * * * *

With people of only moderate ability, modesty is mere honesty; but with those who possess great talent, it is hypocrisy. Hence, it is just as becoming in the latter to make no secret of the respect they bear themselves and no disguise of the fact that they are conscious of unusual power, as it is in the former to be modest. Valerius Maximus gives some very neat examples of this in his chapter on self-confidence, *de fiducia sui.*

* * * * *

Not to go to the theatre is like making one's toilet without a mirror. But it is still worse to take a decision without consulting a friend. For a man may have the most excellent judgment in all other matters, and yet go wrong in those which concern himself; because here the will comes in and deranges the intellect at once. Therefore let a man take counsel of a friend. A doctor can cure everyone but himself; if he falls ill, he sends for a colleague.

* * * * *

In all that we do, we wish, more or less, to come to the end; we are impatient to finish and glad to be done. But the last scene of all, the general end, is something that, as a rule, we wish as far off as may be.

* * * * *

Every parting gives a foretaste of death; every coming together again a foretaste of the resurrection. This is why even people who were indifferent to each other, rejoice so much if they come together again after twenty or thirty years' separation.

* * * * *

Intellects differ from one another in a very real and fundamental way: but no comparison can well be made by merely general observations. It is necessary to come close, and to go into details; for the difference that exists cannot be seen from afar; and it is not easy to judge by outward appearances, as in the several cases of education, leisure and occupation. But even judging by these alone, it must be admitted that many a man has *a degree of existence* at least ten times as high as another—in other words, exists ten times as much.

I am not speaking here of savages whose life is often only one degree above that of the apes in their woods. Consider, for instance, a porter in Naples or Venice (in the north of Europe solicitude for the winter months makes people more thoughtful and therefore reflective); look at the life he leads, from its beginning to its end:—driven by poverty; living on his physical strength; meeting the needs of every day, nay, of every hour, by hard work, great effort, constant tumult, want in all its forms, no care for the morrow; his only comfort rest after exhaustion; continuous quarreling; not a moment free for reflection; such sensual delights as a mild climate and only just sufficient food will permit of; and then, finally, as the metaphysical element, the crass superstition of his church; the whole forming a manner of life with only a low degree of consciousness, where a man hustles, or rather is hustled, through his existence. This restless and confused dream forms the life of how many millions!

Such men *think* only just so much as is necessary to carry out their will for the moment. They never reflect upon their life as a connected whole, let alone, then, upon existence in general; to a certain extent they may be said to exist without really knowing it. The existence of the mobsman or the slave who lives on in this unthinking way, stands very much nearer than ours to that of the brute, which is confined entirely to the present moment; but, for that very reason, it has also less of pain in it than ours. Nay, since all pleasure is in its nature negative, that is to say, consists in freedom from some form of misery or need, the constant and rapid interchange between setting about something and getting it done, which is the permanent accompaniment of the work they do, and then again the augmented form which this takes when they go from work to rest and the satisfaction of their needs—all this gives them a constant source of enjoyment; and the fact that it is much commoner to see happy faces amongst the poor than amongst the rich, is a sure proof that it is used to good advantage.

Passing from this kind of man, consider, next, the sober, sensible merchant, who leads a life of speculation, thinks long over his plans and carries them out with great care, founds a house, and provides for his wife, his children and descendants; takes his share, too, in the life of a community. It is obvious that a man like this has a much higher degree of consciousness than the former, and so his existence has a higher degree of reality.

Then look at the man of learning, who investigates, it may be, the history of the past. He will have reached the point at which a man becomes conscious of existence as a whole, sees beyond the period of his own life, beyond his own personal interests, thinking over the whole course of the world's history.

Then, finally, look at the poet or the philosopher, in whom reflection has reached such a height, that, instead of being drawn on to investigate any one particular phenomenon of existence, he stands in amazement *before existence itself,* this great sphinx, and makes it his problem. In him consciousness has reached the degree of clearness at which it embraces the world itself: his intellect has completely abandoned its function as the servant of his will, and now holds the world before him; and the world calls upon him much more to examine and consider it, than to play a part in it himself. If, then, the degree of consciousness is the degree of reality, such a man will be said to exist most of all, and there will be sense and significance in so describing him.

Between the two extremes here sketched, and the intervening stages, everyone will be able to find the place at which he himself stands.

* * * * *

We know that man is in general superior to all other animals, and this is also the case in his capacity for being trained. Mohammedans are trained to pray with their faces turned towards Mecca, five times a day; and they never fail to do it. Christians are trained to cross themselves on certain occasions, to bow, and so on. Indeed, it may be said that religion is the *chef d'oeuvre* of the art of training, because it trains people in the way they shall think: and, as is well known, you cannot begin the process too early. There is no absurdity so palpable but that it may be firmly planted in the human head if you only begin to inculcate it before the age of five, by constantly repeating it with an air of great solemnity. For as in the case of animals, so in that of men, training is successful only when you begin in early youth.

Noblemen and gentlemen are trained to hold nothing sacred but their word of honor—to maintain a zealous, rigid, and unshaken belief in the ridiculous code of chivalry; and if they are called upon to do so, to seal their belief by dying for it, and seriously to regard a king as a being of a higher order.

Again, our expressions of politeness, the compliments we make, in particular, the respectful attentions we pay to ladies, are a matter of training; as also our esteem for good birth, rank, titles, and so on. Of the same character is the resentment we feel at any insult directed against us; and the measure of this resentment may be exactly determined by the nature of the insult. An Englishman, for instance, thinks it a deadly insult to be told that he is no gentleman, or, still worse, that he is a liar; a Frenchman has the same feeling if you call him a coward, and a German if you say he is stupid.

There are many persons who are trained to be strictly honorable in regard to one particular matter, while they have little honor to boast of in anything else. Many a man, for instance, will not steal your money; but he will lay hands on everything of yours that he can enjoy without having to pay for it. A man of business will often deceive you without the slightest scruple, but he will absolutely refuse to commit a theft.

Imagination is strong in a man when that particular function of the brain which enables him to observe is roused to activity without any necessary excitement of the senses. Accordingly, we find that imagination is active just in proportion as our senses are not excited by external objects. A long period of solitude, whether in prison or in a sick room; quiet, twilight, darkness—these are the things that promote its activity; and under their influence it comes into play of itself. On the other hand, when a great deal of material is presented to our faculties of observation, as happens on a journey, or in the hurly-burly of the world, or, again, in broad daylight, the imagination is idle, and, even though call may be made upon it, refuses to become active, as though it understood that that was not its proper time.

However, if the imagination is to yield any real product, it must have received a great deal of material from the external world. This is the only way in which its storehouse can be filled. The phantasy is nourished much in the same way as the body, which is least capable of any work and enjoys doing nothing just in the very moment when it receives its food which it has to digest. And yet it is to this very food that it owes the power which it afterwards puts forth at the right time.

* * * * *

Opinion is like a pendulum and obeys the same law. If it goes past the centre of gravity on one side, it must go a like distance on the other; and it is only after a certain time that it finds the true point at which it can remain at rest.

* * * * *

By a process of contradiction, distance in space makes things look small, and therefore free from defect. This is why a landscape looks so much better in a contracting mirror or in a *camera obscura*, than it is in reality. The same effect is produced by distance in time. The scenes and events of long ago, and the persons who took part in them, wear a charming aspect to the eye of memory, which sees only the outlines and takes no note of disagreeable details. The present enjoys no such advantage, and so it always seems defective.

And again, as regards space, small objects close to us look big, and if they are very close, we may be able to see nothing else, but when we go a little way off, they become minute and invisible. It is the same again as regards time. The little incidents and accidents of every day fill us with emotion, anxiety, annoyance, passion, as long as they are close to us, when they appear so big, so important, so serious; but as soon as they are borne down the restless stream of time, they lose what significance they had; we think no more of them and soon forget them altogether. They were big only because they were near.

* * * * *

Joy and *sorrow* are not ideas of the mind, but affections of the will, and so they do not lie in the domain of memory. We cannot recall our joys and sorrows; by which I mean that we cannot renew them. We can recall only the *ideas* that accompanied them; and, in particular, the things we were led to say; and these form a gauge of our feelings at the time. Hence our memory of joys and sorrows is always imperfect, and they become a matter of indifference to us as soon as they are over. This explains the vanity of the attempt, which we sometimes make, to revive the pleasures and the pains of the past. Pleasure and pain are essentially an affair of the will; and the will, as such, is not possessed of memory, which is a function of the intellect; and this in its turn gives out and takes in nothing but thoughts and ideas, which are not here in question.

It is a curious fact that in bad days we can very vividly recall the good time that is now no more; but that in good days, we have only a very cold and imperfect memory of the bad.

* * * * *

We have a much better memory of actual objects or pictures than for mere ideas. Hence a good imagination makes it easier to learn languages; for by its aid, the new word is at once united with the actual object to which it refers; whereas, if there is no imagination, it is simply put on a parallel with the equivalent word in the mother tongue.

Mnemonics should not only mean the art of keeping something indirectly in the memory by the use of some direct pun or witticism; it should, rather, be applied to a systematic theory of memory, and explain its several attributes by reference both to its real nature, and to the relation in which these attributes stand to one another.

* * * * *

There are moments in life when our senses obtain a higher and rarer degree of clearness, apart from any particular occasion for it in the nature of our surroundings; and explicable, rather, on physiological grounds alone, as the result of some enhanced state of susceptibility, working from within outwards. Such moments remain indelibly impressed upon the memory, and preserve themselves in their individuality entire. We can assign no reason for it, nor explain why this among so many thousand moments like it should be specially remembered. It seems as much a matter of chance as when single specimens of a whole race of animals now extinct are discovered in the layers of a rock; or when, on opening a book, we light upon an insect accidentally crushed within the leaves. Memories of this kind are always sweet and pleasant.

* * * * *

It occasionally happens that, for no particular reason, long-forgotten scenes suddenly start up in the memory. This may in many cases be due to the action of some hardly perceptible odor, which accompanied those scenes and now recurs exactly same as before. For it is well known that the sense of smell is specially effective in awakening memories, and that in general it does not require much to rouse a train of ideas. And I may say, in passing, that the sense of sight is connected with the understanding,[55] the sense of hearing with the reason,[56] and, as we see in the present case, the sense of smell with the memory. Touch and Taste are more material and dependent upon contact. They have no ideal side.

* * * * *

It must also be reckoned among the peculiar attributes of memory that a slight state of intoxication often so greatly enhances the recollection of past times and scenes, that all the circumstances connected with them come back much more clearly than would be possible in a state of sobriety; but that, on the other hand, the recollection of what one said or did while the intoxication lasted, is more than usually imperfect; nay, that if one has been absolutely tipsy, it is gone altogether. We may say, then, that whilst intoxication enhances the memory for what is past, it allows it to remember little of the present.

* * * * *

Men need some kind of external activity, because they are inactive within. Contrarily, if they are active within, they do not care to be dragged out of themselves; it disturbs and impedes their thoughts in a way that is often most ruinous to them.

* * * * *

I am not surprised that some people are bored when they find themselves alone; for they cannot laugh if they are quite by themselves. The very idea of it seems folly to them.

Are we, then, to look upon laughter as merely O signal for others—a mere sign, like a word? What makes it impossible for people to laugh when they are alone is nothing but want of imagination, dullness of mind generally—[Greek: anaisthaesia kai bradutaes psuchaes], as Theophrastus has it.[57] The lower animals never laugh, either alone or in company. Myson, the misanthropist, was once surprised by one of these people as he was laughing to himself. *Why do you laugh?* he asked; *there is no one with you. That is just why I am laughing*, said Myson.

---

[55] *Wierfache Wurzel* § 21.
[56] *Parerga* vol. ii, § 311.
[57] *Characters*, c. 27.

* * * * *

Natural *gesticulation*, such as commonly accompanies any lively talk, is a language of its own, more widespread, even, than the language of words—so far, I mean, as it is independent of words and alike in all nations. It is true that nations make use of it in proportion as they are vivacious, and that in particular cases, amongst the Italians, for instance, it is supplemented by certain peculiar gestures which are merely conventional, and therefore possessed of nothing more than a local value.

In the universal use made of it, gesticulation has some analogy with logic and grammar, in that it has to do with the form, rather than with the matter of conversation; but on the other hand it is distinguishable from them by the fact that it has more of a moral than of an intellectual bearing; in other words, it reflects the movements of the will. As an accompaniment of conversation it is like the bass of a melody; and if, as in music, it keeps true to the progress of the treble, it serves to heighten the effect.

In a conversation, the gesture depends upon the form in which the subject-matter is conveyed; and it is interesting to observe that, whatever that subject-matter may be, with a recurrence of the form, the very same gesture is repeated. So if I happen to see—from my window, say—two persons carrying on a lively conversation, without my being able to catch a word, I can, nevertheless, understand the general nature of it perfectly well; I mean, the kind of thing that is being said and the form it takes. There is no mistake about it. The speaker is arguing about something, advancing his reasons, then limiting their application, then driving them home and drawing the conclusion in triumph; or he is recounting his experiences, proving, perhaps, beyond the shadow of a doubt, how much he has been injured, but bringing the clearest and most damning evidence to show that his opponents were foolish and obstinate people who would not be convinced; or else he is telling of the splendid plan he laid, and how he carried it to a successful issue, or perhaps failed because the luck was against him; or, it may be, he is saying that he was completely at a loss to know what to do, or that he was quick in seeing some traps set for him, and that by insisting on his rights or by applying a little force, he succeeded in frustrating and punishing his enemies; and so on in hundreds of cases of a similar kind.

Strictly speaking, however, what I get from gesticulation alone is an abstract notion of the essential drift of what is being said, and that, too, whether I judge from a moral or an intellectual point of view. It is the quintessence, the true substance of the conversation, and this remains identical, no matter what may have given rise to the conversation, or what it may be about; the relation between the two being that of a general idea or class-name to the individuals which it covers.

As I have said, the most interesting and amusing part of the matter is the complete identity and solidarity of the gestures used to denote the same set of circumstances, even though by people of very different temperament; so that the gestures become exactly like words of a language, alike for every one, and subject only to such small modifications as depend upon variety of accent and education. And yet there can be no doubt but that these standing gestures, which every one uses, are the result of no convention or collusion. They are original and innate—a true language of nature; consolidated, it may be, by imitation and the influence of custom.

It is well known that it is part of an actor's duty to make a careful study of gesture; and the same thing is true, to a somewhat smaller degree, of a public speaker. This study must consist chiefly in watching others and imitating their movements, for there are no abstract rules fairly applicable to the matter, with the exception of some very general leading principles, such as—to take an example—that the gesture must not follow the word, but rather come immediately before it, by way of announcing its approach and attracting the hearer's attention.

Englishmen entertain a peculiar contempt for gesticulation, and look upon it as something vulgar and undignified. This seems to me a silly prejudice on their part, and the outcome of their general prudery. For here we have a language which nature has given to every one, and which every one understands; and to do away with and forbid it for no better reason than that it is opposed to that much-lauded thing, gentlemanly feeling, is a very questionable proceeding.

ON EDUCATION.

The human intellect is said to be so constituted that *general ideas* arise by abstraction from *particular observations*, and therefore come after them in point of time. If this is what actually occurs, as happens in the case of a man who has to depend solely upon his own experience for what he learns—who has no teacher and no book,—such a man knows quite well which of his particular observations belong to and are represented by each of his general ideas. He has a perfect acquaintance with both sides of his experience, and accordingly, he treats everything that comes in his way from a right standpoint. This might be called the *natural* method of education.

Contrarily, the *artificial* method is to hear what other people say, to learn and to read, and so to get your head crammed full of general ideas before you have any sort of extended acquaintance with the world as it is, and as you may see it for yourself. You will be told that the particular observations which go to make these general ideas will come to you later on in the course of experience; but until that time arrives, you apply your general ideas wrongly, you judge men and things from a wrong standpoint, you see them in a wrong light, and treat them in a wrong way. So it is that education perverts the mind.

This explains why it so frequently happens that, after a long course of learning and reading, we enter upon the world in our youth, partly with an artless ignorance of things, partly with wrong notions about them; so that our demeanor savors at one moment of a nervous anxiety, at another of a mistaken confidence. The reason of this is simply that our head is full of general ideas which we are now trying to turn to some use, but which we hardly ever apply rightly. This is the result of acting in direct opposition to the natural development of the mind by obtaining general ideas first, and particular observations last: it is putting the cart before the horse. Instead of developing the child's own faculties of discernment, and teaching it to judge and think for itself, the teacher uses all his energies to stuff its head full of the ready-made thoughts of other people. The mistaken views of life, which spring from a false application of general ideas, have afterwards to be corrected by long years of experience; and it is seldom that they are wholly corrected. This is why so few men of learning are possessed of common-sense, such as is often to be met with in people who have had no instruction at all.

To acquire a knowledge of the world might be defined as the aim of all education; and it follows from what I have said that special stress should be laid upon beginning to acquire this knowledge *at the right end.* As I have shown, this means, in the main, that the particular observation of a thing shall precede the general idea of it; further, that narrow and circumscribed ideas shall come before ideas of a wide range. It means, therefore, that the whole system of education shall follow in the steps that must have been taken by the ideas themselves in the course of their formation. But whenever any of these steps are skipped or left out, the instruction is defective, and the ideas obtained are false; and finally, a distorted view of the world arises, peculiar to the individual himself—a view such as almost everyone entertains for some time, and most men for as long as they live. No one can look into his own mind without seeing that it was only after reaching a very mature age, and in some cases when he least expected it, that he came to a right understanding or a clear view of many matters in his life, that, after all, were not very difficult or complicated. Up till then, they were points in his knowledge of the world which were still obscure, due to his having skipped some particular lesson in those early days of his education, whatever it may have been like—whether artificial and conventional, or of that natural kind which is based upon individual experience.

It follows that an attempt should be made to find out the strictly natural course of knowledge, so that education may proceed methodically by keeping to it; and that children may become acquainted with the ways of the world, without getting wrong ideas into their heads, which very often cannot be got out again. If this plan were adopted, special care would have to be taken to prevent children from using words without clearly understanding their meaning and application. The fatal tendency to be satisfied with words instead of trying to understand things—to learn phrases by heart, so that they may prove a refuge in time of need, exists, as a rule, even in children; and the tendency lasts on into manhood, making the knowledge of many learned persons to consist in mere verbiage.

However, the main endeavor must always be to let particular observations precede general ideas, and not *vice versa*, as is usually and unfortunately the case; as though a child should come feet foremost into the world, or a verse be begun by writing down the rhyme! The ordinary method is to imprint ideas and opinions, in the strict sense of the word, *prejudices*, on the mind of the child, before it has had any but a very few particular observations. It is thus that he afterwards comes to view the world and gather experience through the medium of those ready-made ideas, rather than to let his ideas be formed for him out of his own experience of life, as they ought to be.

A man sees a great many things when he looks at the world for himself, and he sees them from many sides; but this method of learning is not nearly so short or so quick as the method which employs abstract ideas and makes hasty generalizations about everything. Experience, therefore, will be a long time in correcting preconceived ideas, or perhaps never bring its task to an end; for wherever a man finds that the aspect of things seems to contradict the general ideas he has formed, he will begin by rejecting the evidence it offers as partial and one-sided; nay, he will shut his eyes to it altogether and deny that it stands in any contradiction at all with his preconceived notions, in order that he may thus preserve them uninjured. So it is that many a man carries about a burden of wrong notions all his life long—crotchets, whims, fancies, prejudices, which at last become fixed ideas. The fact is that he has never tried to form his fundamental ideas for himself out of his own experience of life, his own way of looking at the world, because he has taken over his ideas ready-made from other people; and this it is that makes him—as it makes how many others!—so shallow and superficial.

Instead of that method of instruction, care should be taken to educate children on the natural lines. No idea should ever be established in a child's mind otherwise than by what the child can see for itself, or at any rate it should be verified by the same means; and the result of this would be that the child's ideas, if few, would be well-grounded and accurate. It would learn how to measure things by its own standard rather than by another's; and so it would escape a thousand strange fancies and prejudices, and not need to have them eradicated by the lessons it will subsequently be taught in the school of life. The child would, in this way, have its mind once for all habituated to clear views and thorough-going knowledge; it would use its own judgment and take an unbiased estimate of things.

And, in general, children should not form their notions of what life is like from the copy before they have learned it from the original, to whatever aspect of it their attention may be directed. Instead, therefore, of hastening to place *books*, and books alone, in their hands, let them be made acquainted, step by step, with *things*—with the actual circumstances of human life. And above all let care be taken to bring them to a clear and objective view of the world as it is, to educate them always to derive their ideas directly from real life, and to shape them in conformity with it—not to fetch them from other sources, such as books, fairy tales, or what people say—then to apply them ready-made to real life. For this will mean that their heads are full of wrong notions, and that they will either see things in a false light or try in vain to *remodel the world* to suit their views, and so enter upon false paths; and that, too, whether they are only constructing theories of life or engaged in the actual business of it. It is incredible how much harm is done when the seeds of wrong notions are laid in the mind in those early years, later on to bear a crop of prejudice; for the subsequent lessons, which are learned from real life in the world have to be devoted mainly to their extirpation. *To unlearn the evil* was the answer, according to Diogenes Laertius,[58] Antisthenes gave, when he was asked what branch of knowledge was most necessary; and we can see what he meant.

No child under the age of fifteen should receive instruction in subjects which may possibly be the vehicle of serious error, such as philosophy, religion, or any other branch of knowledge where it is necessary to take large views; because wrong notions imbibed early can seldom be rooted out, and of all the intellectual faculties, judgment is the last to arrive at maturity. The child should give its attention either to subjects where no error is possible at all, such as mathematics, or to those in which there is no particular danger in making a mistake, such as languages, natural science, history and so on. And in general, the branches of knowledge which are to be studied at any period of life should be such as the mind is equal to at that period and can perfectly understand. Childhood and youth form the time for collecting materials, for getting a special and thorough knowledge of the individual and particular things. In those years it is too early to form views on a large scale; and ultimate explanations must be put off to a later date. The

---

[58] vi. 7.

faculty of judgment, which cannot come into play without mature experience, should be left to itself; and care should be taken not to anticipate its action by inculcating prejudice, which will paralyze it for ever.

On the other hand, the memory should be specially taxed in youth, since it is then that it is strongest and most tenacious. But in choosing the things that should be committed to memory the utmost care and forethought must be exercised; as lessons well learnt in youth are never forgotten. This precious soil must therefore be cultivated so as to bear as much fruit as possible. If you think how deeply rooted in your memory are those persons whom you knew in the first twelve years of your life, how indelible the impression made upon you by the events of those years, how clear your recollection of most of the things that happened to you then, most of what was told or taught you, it will seem a natural thing to take the susceptibility and tenacity of the mind at that period as the ground-work of education. This may be done by a strict observance of method, and a systematic regulation of the impressions which the mind is to receive.

But the years of youth allotted to a man are short, and memory is, in general, bound within narrow limits; still more so, the memory of any one individual. Since this is the case, it is all-important to fill the memory with what is essential and material in any branch of knowledge, to the exclusion of everything else. The decision as to what is essential and material should rest with the masterminds in every department of thought; their choice should be made after the most mature deliberation, and the outcome of it fixed and determined. Such a choice would have to proceed by sifting the things which it is necessary and important for a man to know in general, and then, necessary and important for him to know in any particular business or calling. Knowledge of the first kind would have to be classified, after an encyclopedic fashion, in graduated courses, adapted to the degree of general culture which a man may be expected to have in the circumstances in which he is placed; beginning with a course limited to the necessary requirements of primary education, and extending upwards to the subjects treated of in all the branches of philosophical thought. The regulation of the second kind of knowledge would be left to those who had shown genuine mastery in the several departments into which it is divided; and the whole system would provide an elaborate rule or canon for intellectual education, which would, of course, have to be revised every ten years. Some such arrangement as this would employ the youthful power of the memory to best advantage, and supply excellent working material to the faculty of judgment, when it made its appearance later on.

A man's knowledge may be said to be mature, in other words, it has reached the most complete state of perfection to which he, as an individual, is capable of bringing it, when an exact correspondence is established between the whole of his abstract ideas and the things he has actually perceived for himself. This will mean that each of his abstract ideas rests, directly or indirectly, upon a basis of observation, which alone endows it with any real value; and also that he is able to place every observation he makes under the right abstract idea which belongs to it. Maturity is the work of experience alone; and therefore it requires time. The knowledge we derive from our own observation is usually distinct from that which we acquire through the medium of abstract ideas; the one coming to us in the natural way, the other by what people tell us, and the course of instruction we receive, whether it is good or bad. The result is, that in youth there is generally very little agreement or correspondence between our abstract ideas, which are merely phrases in the mind, and that real knowledge which we have obtained by our own observation. It is only later on that a gradual approach takes place between these two kinds of knowledge, accompanied by a mutual correction of error; and knowledge is not mature until this coalition is accomplished. This maturity or perfection of knowledge is something quite independent of another kind of perfection, which may be of a high or a low order—the perfection, I mean, to which a man may bring his own individual faculties; which is measured, not by any correspondence between the two kinds of knowledge, but by the degree of intensity which each kind attains.

For the practical man the most needful thing is to acquire an accurate and profound knowledge of *the ways of the world.* But this, though the most needful, is also the most wearisome of all studies, as a man may reach a great age without coming to the end of his task; whereas, in the domain of the sciences, he masters the more important facts when he is still young. In acquiring that knowledge of the world, it is while he is a novice, namely, in boyhood and in youth, that the first and hardest lessons are put before him; but it often happens that even in later years there is still a great deal to be learned.

The study is difficult enough in itself; but the difficulty is doubled by *novels*, which represent a state of things in life and the world, such as, in fact, does not exist. Youth is credulous, and accepts these views of life, which then become part and parcel of the mind; so that, instead of a merely negative condition of ignorance, you have positive error—a whole tissue of false notions to start with; and at a later date these actually spoil the schooling of experience, and put a wrong construction on the lessons it teaches. If, before this, the youth had no light at all to guide him, he is now misled by a will-o'-the-wisp; still more often is this the case with a girl. They have both had a false view of things foisted on them by reading novels; and expectations have been aroused which can never be fulfilled. This generally exercises a baneful influence on their whole life. In this respect those whose youth has allowed them no time or opportunity for reading novels—those who work with their hands and the like—are in a position of decided advantage. There are a few novels to which this reproach cannot be addressed—nay, which have an effect the contrary of bad. First and foremost, to give an example, *Gil Blas*, and the other works of Le Sage (or rather their Spanish originals); further, *The Vicar of Wakefield*, and, to some extent Sir Walter Scott's novels. *Don Quixote* may be regarded as a satirical exhibition of the error to which I am referring.

OF WOMEN.

Schiller's poem in honor of women, *Würde der Frauen*, is the result of much careful thought, and it appeals to the reader by its antithetic style and its use of contrast; but as an expression of the true praise which should be accorded to them, it is, I think, inferior to these few words of Jouy's: *Without women, the beginning of our life would be helpless; the middle, devoid of pleasure; and the end, of consolation.* The same thing is more feelingly expressed by Byron in *Sardanapalus*:

> *The very first of human life must spring from woman's breast,*
> *Your first small words are taught you from her lips,*
> *Your first tears quench'd by her, and your last sighs*
> *Too often breathed out in a woman's hearing,*
> *When men have shrunk from the ignoble care*
> *Of watching the last hour of him who led them.*

(Act I Scene 2.)

These two passages indicate the right standpoint for the appreciation of women.

You need only look at the way in which she is formed, to see that woman is not meant to undergo great labor, whether of the mind or of the body. She pays the debt of life not by what she does, but by what she suffers; by the pains of child-bearing and care for the child, and by submission to her husband, to whom she should be a patient and cheering companion. The keenest sorrows and joys are not for her, nor is she called upon to display a great deal of strength. The current of her life should be more gentle, peaceful and trivial than man's, without being essentially happier or unhappier.

Women are directly fitted for acting as the nurses and teachers of our early childhood by the fact that they are themselves childish, frivolous and short-sighted; in a word, they are big children all their life long—a kind of intermediate stage between the child and the full-grown man, who is man in the strict sense of the word. See how a girl will fondle a child for days together, dance with it and sing to it; and then think what a man, with the best will in the world, could do if he were put in her place.

With young girls Nature seems to have had in view what, in the language of the drama, is called *a striking effect*; as for a few years she dowers them with a wealth of beauty and is lavish in her gift of charm, at the expense of all the rest of their life; so that during those years they may capture the fantasy of some man to such a degree that he is hurried away into undertaking the honorable care of them, in some form or other, as long as they live—a step for which there would not appear to be any sufficient warranty if reason only directed his thoughts. Accordingly, Nature has equipped woman, as she does all her creatures, with the weapons and implements requisite for the safeguarding of her existence, and for just as long as it is necessary for her to have them. Here, as elsewhere, Nature proceeds with her usual economy; for just as the female ant, after fecundation, loses her wings, which are then superfluous, nay, actually a danger to the business of breeding; so, after giving birth to one or two children, a woman generally loses her beauty; probably, indeed, for similar reasons.

And so we find that young girls, in their hearts, look upon domestic affairs or work of any kind as of secondary importance, if not actually as a mere jest. The only business that really claims their earnest attention is love, making conquests, and everything connected with this—dress, dancing, and so on.

The nobler and more perfect a thing is, the later and slower it is in arriving at maturity. A man reaches the maturity of his reasoning powers and mental faculties hardly before the age of twenty-eight; a woman at eighteen. And then, too, in the case of woman, it is only reason of a sort—very niggard in its dimensions. That is why women remain children their whole life long; never seeing anything but what is quite close to them, cleaving to the present moment, taking appearance for reality, and preferring trifles to matters of the first importance. For it is by virtue of his reasoning faculty that man does not live in the present only, like the brute, but looks about him and considers the past and the future; and this is the origin of prudence, as well as of that care and anxiety which so many people exhibit. Both the advantages and the disadvantages which this involves, are shared in by the woman to a smaller extent because of her weaker power of reasoning. She may, in fact, be described as intellectually short-sighted, because, while she has an intuitive understanding of what lies quite close to her, her field of vision is narrow and does not reach to what is remote; so that things which are absent, or past, or to come, have much less effect upon women than upon men. This is the reason why women are more often inclined to be extravagant, and sometimes carry their inclination to a length that borders upon madness. In their hearts, women think that it is men's business to earn money and theirs to spend it—if possible during their husband's life, but, at any rate, after his death. The very fact that their husband hands them over his earnings for purposes of housekeeping, strengthens them in this belief.

However many disadvantages all this may involve, there is at least this to be said in its favor; that the woman lives more in the present than the man, and that, if the present is at all tolerable, she enjoys it more eagerly. This is the source of that cheerfulness which is peculiar to women, fitting her to amuse man in his hours of recreation, and, in case of need, to console him when he is borne down by the weight of his cares.

It is by no means a bad plan to consult women in matters of difficulty, as the Germans used to do in ancient times; for their way of looking at things is quite different from ours, chiefly in the fact that they like to take the shortest way to their goal, and, in general, manage to fix their eyes upon what lies before them; while we, as a rule, see far beyond it, just because it is in front of our noses. In cases like this, we need to be brought back to the right standpoint, so as to recover the near and simple view.

Then, again, women are decidedly more sober in their judgment than we are, so that they do not see more in things than is really there; whilst, if our passions are aroused, we are apt to see things in an exaggerated way, or imagine what does not exist.

The weakness of their reasoning faculty also explains why it is that women show more sympathy for the unfortunate than men do, and so treat them with more kindness and interest; and why it is that, on the contrary, they are inferior to men in point of justice, and less honorable and conscientious. For it is just because their reasoning power is weak that present circumstances have such a hold over them, and those concrete things, which lie directly before their eyes, exercise a power which is seldom counteracted to any extent by abstract principles of thought, by fixed rules of conduct, firm resolutions, or, in general, by consideration for the past and the future, or regard for what is absent and remote. Accordingly, they possess the first and main elements that go to make a virtuous character, but they are deficient in those secondary qualities which are often a necessary instrument in the formation of it.[59]

Hence, it will be found that the fundamental fault of the female character is that it has *no sense of justice*. This is mainly due to the fact, already mentioned, that women are defective in the powers of reasoning and deliberation; but it is also traceable to the position which

---

[59] In this respect they may be compared to an animal organism which contains a liver but no gall-bladder. Here let me refer to what I have said in my treatise on *The Foundation of Morals*, § 17.

Nature has assigned to them as the weaker sex. They are dependent, not upon strength, but upon craft; and hence their instinctive capacity for cunning, and their ineradicable tendency to say what is not true. For as lions are provided with claws and teeth, and elephants and boars with tusks, bulls with horns, and cuttle fish with its clouds of inky fluid, so Nature has equipped woman, for her defence and protection, with the arts of dissimulation; and all the power which Nature has conferred upon man in the shape of physical strength and reason, has been bestowed upon women in this form. Hence, dissimulation is innate in woman, and almost as much a quality of the stupid as of the clever. It is as natural for them to make use of it on every occasion as it is for those animals to employ their means of defence when they are attacked; they have a feeling that in doing so they are only within their rights. Therefore a woman who is perfectly truthful and not given to dissimulation is perhaps an impossibility, and for this very reason they are so quick at seeing through dissimulation in others that it is not a wise thing to attempt it with them. But this fundamental defect which I have stated, with all that it entails, gives rise to falsity, faithlessness, treachery, ingratitude, and so on. Perjury in a court of justice is more often committed by women than by men. It may, indeed, be generally questioned whether women ought to be sworn in at all. From time to time one finds repeated cases everywhere of ladies, who want for nothing, taking things from shop-counters when no one is looking, and making off with them.

Nature has appointed that the propagation of the species shall be the business of men who are young, strong and handsome; so that the race may not degenerate. This is the firm will and purpose of Nature in regard to the species, and it finds its expression in the passions of women. There is no law that is older or more powerful than this. Woe, then, to the man who sets up claims and interests that will conflict with it; whatever he may say and do, they will be unmercifully crushed at the first serious encounter. For the innate rule that governs women's conduct, though it is secret and unformulated, nay, unconscious in its working, is this: *We are justified in deceiving those who think they have acquired rights over the species by paying little attention to the individual, that is, to us. The constitution and, therefore, the welfare of the species have been placed in our hands and committed to our care, through the control we obtain over the next generation, which proceeds from us; let us discharge our duties conscientiously.* But women have no abstract knowledge of this leading principle; they are conscious of it only as a concrete fact; and they have no other method of giving expression to it than the way in which they act when the opportunity arrives. And then their conscience does not trouble them so much as we fancy; for in the darkest recesses of their heart, they are aware that in committing a breach of their duty towards the individual, they have all the better fulfilled their duty towards the species, which is infinitely greater.[60]

And since women exist in the main solely for the propagation of the species, and are not destined for anything else, they live, as a rule, more for the species than for the individual, and in their hearts take the affairs of the species more seriously than those of the individual. This gives their whole life and being a certain levity; the general bent of their character is in a direction fundamentally different from that of man; and it is this to which produces that discord in married life which is so frequent, and almost the normal state.

The natural feeling between men is mere indifference, but between women it is actual enmity. The reason of this is that trade-jealousy— *odium figulinum*—which, in the case of men does not go beyond the confines of their own particular pursuit; but, with women, embraces the whole sex; since they have only one kind of business. Even when they meet in the street, women look at one another like Guelphs and Ghibellines. And it is a patent fact that when two women make first acquaintance with each other, they behave with more constraint and dissimulation than two men would show in a like case; and hence it is that an exchange of compliments between two women is a much more ridiculous proceeding than between two men. Further, whilst a man will, as a general rule, always preserve a certain amount of consideration and humanity in speaking to others, even to those who are in a very inferior position, it is intolerable to see how proudly and disdainfully a fine lady will generally behave towards one who is in a lower social rank (I do not mean a woman who is in her service), whenever she speaks to her. The reason of this may be that, with women, differences of rank are much more precarious than with us; because, while a hundred considerations carry weight in our case, in theirs there is only one, namely, with which man they have found favor; as also that they stand in much nearer relations with one another than men do, in consequence of the one-sided nature of their calling. This makes them endeavor to lay stress upon differences of rank.

It is only the man whose intellect is clouded by his sexual impulses that could give the name of *the fair sex* to that under-sized, narrow-shouldered, broad-hipped, and short-legged race; for the whole beauty of the sex is bound up with this impulse. Instead of calling them beautiful, there would be more warrant for describing women as the un-aesthetic sex. Neither for music, nor for poetry, nor for fine art, have they really and truly any sense or susceptibility; it is a mere mockery if they make a pretence of it in order to assist their endeavor to please.

---

[60] A more detailed discussion of the matter in question may be found in my chief work, *Die Welt als Wille und Vorstellung*, vol. ii, ch. 44.

Hence, as a result of this, they are incapable of taking a *purely objective interest* in anything; and the reason of it seems to me to be as follows. A man tries to acquire *direct* mastery over things, either by understanding them, or by forcing them to do his will. But a woman is always and everywhere reduced to obtaining this mastery *indirectly*, namely, through a man; and whatever direct mastery she may have is entirely confined to him. And so it lies in woman's nature to look upon everything only as a means for conquering man; and if she takes an interest in anything else, it is simulated—a mere roundabout way of gaining her ends by coquetry, and feigning what she does not feel. Hence, even Rousseau declared: *Women have, in general, no love for any art; they have no proper knowledge of any; and they have no genius.*[61]

No one who sees at all below the surface can have failed to remark the same thing. You need only observe the kind of attention women bestow upon a concert, an opera, or a play—the childish simplicity, for example, with which they keep on chattering during the finest passages in the greatest masterpieces. If it is true that the Greeks excluded women from their theatres they were quite right in what they did; at any rate you would have been able to hear what was said upon the stage. In our day, besides, or in lieu of saying, *Let a woman keep silence in the church*, it would be much to the point to say *Let a woman keep silence in the theatre*. This might, perhaps, be put up in big letters on the curtain.

And you cannot expect anything else of women if you consider that the most distinguished intellects among the whole sex have never managed to produce a single achievement in the fine arts that is really great, genuine, and original; or given to the world any work of permanent value in any sphere. This is most strikingly shown in regard to painting, where mastery of technique is at least as much within their power as within ours—and hence they are diligent in cultivating it; but still, they have not a single great painting to boast of, just because they are deficient in that objectivity of mind which is so directly indispensable in painting. They never get beyond a subjective point of view. It is quite in keeping with this that ordinary women have no real susceptibility for art at all; for Nature proceeds in strict sequence—*non facit saltum*. And Huarte[62] in his *Examen de ingenios para las scienzias*—a book which has been famous for three hundred years— denies women the possession of all the higher faculties. The case is not altered by particular and partial exceptions; taken as a whole, women

---

[61] Lettre à d'Alembert, Note xx.

[62] *Translator's Note.*—Juan Huarte (1520?-1590) practised as a physician at Madrid. The work cited by Schopenhauer is known, and has been translated into many languages.

are, and remain, thorough-going Philistines, and quite incurable. Hence, with that absurd arrangement which allows them to share the rank and title of their husbands they are a constant stimulus to his ignoble ambitions. And, further, it is just because they are Philistines that modern society, where they take the lead and set the tone, is in such a bad way. Napoleon's saying—that *women have no rank*—should be adopted as the right standpoint in determining their position in society; and as regards their other qualities Chamfort[63] makes the very true remark: *They are made to trade with our own weaknesses and our follies, but not with our reason. The sympathies that exist between them and men are skin-deep only, and do not touch the mind or the feelings or the character.* They form the *sexus sequior*—the second sex, inferior in every respect to the first; their infirmities should be treated with consideration; but to show them great reverence is extremely ridiculous, and lowers us in their eyes. When Nature made two divisions of the human race, she did not draw the line exactly through the middle. These divisions are polar and opposed to each other, it is true; but the difference between them is not qualitative merely, it is also quantitative.

This is just the view which the ancients took of woman, and the view which people in the East take now; and their judgment as to her proper position is much more correct than ours, with our old French notions of gallantry and our preposterous system of reverence—that highest product of Teutonico-Christian stupidity. These notions have served only to make women more arrogant and overbearing; so that one is occasionally reminded of the holy apes in Benares, who in the consciousness of their sanctity and inviolable position, think they can do exactly as they please.

But in the West, the woman, and especially the *lady*, finds herself in a false position; for woman, rightly called by the ancients, *sexus sequior*, is by no means fit to be the object of our honor and veneration, or to hold her head higher than man and be on equal terms with him. The consequences of this false position are sufficiently obvious. Accordingly, it would be a very desirable thing if this Number-Two of the human race were in Europe also relegated to her natural place, and an end put to that lady nuisance, which not only moves all Asia to laughter, but would have been ridiculed by Greece and Rome as well. It is impossible to calculate the good effects which such a change would bring about in our social, civil and political arrangements. There would be no necessity for the Salic law: it would be a superfluous truism. In Europe the *lady*, strictly so-called, is a being who should not exist at all; she should be either a housewife or a girl who hopes to become

---

[63] *Translator's Note.*—See *Counsels and Maxims*, p. 12, Note.

one; and she should be brought up, not to be arrogant, but to be thrifty and submissive. It is just because there are such people as *ladies* in Europe that the women of the lower classes, that is to say, the great majority of the sex, are much more unhappy than they are in the East. And even Lord Byron says: *Thought of the state of women under the ancient Greeks—convenient enough. Present state, a remnant of the barbarism of the chivalric and the feudal ages—artificial and unnatural. They ought to mind home—and be well fed and clothed—but not mixed in society. Well educated, too, in religion—but to read neither poetry nor politics—nothing but books of piety and cookery. Music—drawing—dancing—also a little gardening and ploughing now and then. I have seen them mending the roads in Epirus with good success. Why not, as well as hay-making and milking?*

The laws of marriage prevailing in Europe consider the woman as the equivalent of the man—start, that is to say, from a wrong position. In our part of the world where monogamy is the rule, to marry means to halve one's rights and double one's duties. Now, when the laws gave women equal rights with man, they ought to have also endowed her with a masculine intellect. But the fact is, that just in proportion as the honors and privileges which the laws accord to women, exceed the amount which nature gives, is there a diminution in the number of women who really participate in these privileges; and all the remainder are deprived of their natural rights by just so much as is given to the others over and above their share. For the institution of monogamy, and the laws of marriage which it entails, bestow upon the woman an unnatural position of privilege, by considering her throughout as the full equivalent of the man, which is by no means the case; and seeing this, men who are shrewd and prudent very often scruple to make so great a sacrifice and to acquiesce in so unfair an arrangement.

Consequently, whilst among polygamous nations every woman is provided for, where monogamy prevails the number of married women is limited; and there remains over a large number of women without stay or support, who, in the upper classes, vegetate as useless old maids, and in the lower succumb to hard work for which they are not suited; or else become *filles de joie*, whose life is as destitute of joy as it is of honor. But under the circumstances they become a necessity; and their position is openly recognized as serving the special end of warding off temptation from those women favored by fate, who have found, or may hope to find, husbands. In London alone there are 80,000 prostitutes. What are they but the women, who, under the institution of monogamy have come off worse? Theirs is a dreadful fate: they are human sacrifices offered up on the altar of monogamy. The women whose wretched position is here described are the inevitable set-off to the European lady with her arrogance and pretension. Polygamy is therefore a real benefit to the female sex if it is taken as a whole. And, from another point of view, there is no true reason why a man whose wife suffers from chronic illness, or remains barren, or has gradually become too old for him, should not take a second. The motives which induce so many people to become converts to Mormonism[64] appear to be just those which militate against the unnatural institution of monogamy.

Moreover, the bestowal of unnatural rights upon women has imposed upon them unnatural duties, and, nevertheless, a breach of these duties makes them unhappy. Let me explain. A man may often think that his social or financial position will suffer if he marries, unless he makes some brilliant alliance. His desire will then be to win a woman of his own choice under conditions other than those of marriage, such as will secure her position and that of the children. However fair, reasonable, fit and proper these conditions may be, and the woman consents by foregoing that undue amount of privilege which marriage alone can bestow, she to some extent loses her honor, because marriage is the basis of civic society; and she will lead an unhappy life, since human nature is so constituted that we pay an attention to the opinion of other people which is out of all proportion to its value. On the other hand, if she does not consent, she runs the risk either of having to be given in marriage to a man whom she does not like, or of being landed high and dry as an old maid; for the period during which she has a chance of being settled for life is very short. And in view of this aspect of the institution of monogamy, Thomasius' profoundly learned treatise, *de Concubinatu*, is well worth reading; for it shows that, amongst all nations and in all ages, down to the Lutheran Reformation, concubinage was permitted; nay, that it was an institution which was to a certain extent actually recognized by law, and attended with no dishonor. It was only the Lutheran Reformation that degraded it from this position. It was seen to be a further justification for the marriage of the clergy; and then, after that, the Catholic Church did not dare to remain behind-hand in the matter.

There is no use arguing about polygamy; it must be taken as *de facto* existing everywhere, and the only question is as to how it shall be regulated. Where are there, then, any real monogamists? We all live, at any rate, for a time, and most of us, always, in polygamy. And so, since every man needs many women, there is nothing fairer than to allow him, nay, to make it incumbent upon him, to provide for many women. This will reduce woman to her true and natural position as a subordinate being; and the *lady*—that monster of European civilization and Teutonico-Christian stupidity—will disappear from the world,

---

[64] *Translator's Note.*—The Mormons have recently given up polygamy, and received the American franchise in its stead.

leaving only *women*, but no more *unhappy women*, of whom Europe is now full.

In India, no woman is ever independent, but in accordance with the law of Manu,[65] she stands under the control of her father, her husband, her brother or her son. It is, to be sure, a revolting thing that a widow should immolate herself upon her husband's funeral pyre; but it is also revolting that she should spend her husband's money with her paramours—the money for which he toiled his whole life long, in the consoling belief that he was providing for his children. Happy are those who have kept the middle course—*medium tenuere beati.*

The first love of a mother for her child is, with the lower animals as with men, of a purely *instinctive* character, and so it ceases when the child is no longer in a physically helpless condition. After that, the first love should give way to one that is based on habit and reason; but this often fails to make its appearance, especially where the mother did not love the father. The love of a father for his child is of a different order, and more likely to last; because it has its foundation in the fact that in the child he recognizes his own inner self; that is to say, his love for it is metaphysical in its origin.

In almost all nations, whether of the ancient or the modern world, even amongst the Hottentots,[66] property is inherited by the male descendants alone; it is only in Europe that a departure has taken place; but not amongst the nobility, however. That the property which has cost men long years of toil and effort, and been won with so much difficulty, should afterwards come into the hands of women, who then, in their lack of reason, squander it in a short time, or otherwise fool it away, is a grievance and a wrong as serious as it is common, which should be prevented by limiting the right of women to inherit. In my opinion, the best arrangement would be that by which women, whether widows or daughters, should never receive anything beyond the interest for life on property secured by mortgage, and in no case the property itself, or the capital, except where all male descendants fail. The people who make money are men, not women; and it follows from this that women are neither justified in having unconditional possession of it, nor fit persons to be entrusted with its administration. When wealth, in any true sense of the word, that is to say, funds, houses or land, is to go to them as an inheritance they should never be allowed the free disposition of it. In their case a guardian should always be appointed; and hence they should never be given the free control of their own children, wherever it can be avoided. The vanity of women, even

---

[65] Ch. V., v. 148.

[66] Leroy, *Lettres philosophiques sur l'intelligence et la perfectibilité des animaux, avec quelques lettres sur l'homme*, p. 298, Paris, 1802.

though it should not prove to be greater than that of men, has this much danger in it, that it takes an entirely material direction. They are vain, I mean, of their personal beauty, and then of finery, show and magnificence. That is just why they are so much in their element in society. It is this, too, which makes them so inclined to be extravagant, all the more as their reasoning power is low. Accordingly we find an ancient writer describing woman as in general of an extravagant nature—[Greek: Gynae to synolon esti dapanaeron Physei][67] But with men vanity often takes the direction of non-material advantages, such as intellect, learning, courage.

In the *Politics*[68] Aristotle explains the great disadvantage which accrued to the Spartans from the fact that they conceded too much to their women, by giving them the right of inheritance and dower, and a great amount of independence; and he shows how much this contributed to Sparta's fall. May it not be the case in France that the influence of women, which went on increasing steadily from the time of Louis XIII., was to blame for that gradual corruption of the Court and the Government, which brought about the Revolution of 1789, of which all subsequent disturbances have been the fruit? However that may be, the false position which women occupy, demonstrated as it is, in the most glaring way, by the institution of the *lady*, is a fundamental defect in our social scheme, and this defect, proceeding from the very heart of it, must spread its baneful influence in all directions.

* * * * *

That woman is by nature meant to obey may be seen by the fact that every woman who is placed in the unnatural position of complete independence, immediately attaches herself to some man, by whom she allows herself to be guided and ruled. It is because she needs a lord and master. If she is young, it will be a lover; if she is old, a priest.

ON NOISE.

Kant wrote a treatise on *The Vital Powers*. I should prefer to write a dirge for them. The superabundant display of vitality, which takes the form of knocking, hammering, and tumbling things about, has proved a daily torment to me all my life long. There are people, it is true—nay, a great many people—who smile at such things, because they are not sensitive to noise; but they are just the very people who are also not sensitive to argument, or thought, or poetry, or art, in a word, to any

---

[67] Brunck's *Gnomici poetæ graeci*, v. 115.
[68] Bk. I, ch. 9.

kind of intellectual influence. The reason of it is that the tissue of their brains is of a very rough and coarse quality. On the other hand, noise is a torture to intellectual people. In the biographies of almost all great writers, or wherever else their personal utterances are recorded, I find complaints about it; in the case of Kant, for instance, Goethe, Lichtenberg, Jean Paul; and if it should happen that any writer has omitted to express himself on the matter, it is only for want of an opportunity.

This aversion to noise I should explain as follows: If you cut up a large diamond into little bits, it will entirely lose the value it had as a whole; and an army divided up into small bodies of soldiers, loses all its strength. So a great intellect sinks to the level of an ordinary one, as soon as it is interrupted and disturbed, its attention distracted and drawn off from the matter in hand; for its superiority depends upon its power of concentration—of bringing all its strength to bear upon one theme, in the same way as a concave mirror collects into one point all the rays of light that strike upon it. Noisy interruption is a hindrance to this concentration. That is why distinguished minds have always shown such an extreme dislike to disturbance in any form, as something that breaks in upon and distracts their thoughts. Above all have they been averse to that violent interruption that comes from noise. Ordinary people are not much put out by anything of the sort. The most sensible and intelligent of all nations in Europe lays down the rule, *Never Interrupt!* as the eleventh commandment. Noise is the most impertinent of all forms of interruption. It is not only an interruption, but also a disruption of thought. Of course, where there is nothing to interrupt, noise will not be so particularly painful. Occasionally it happens that some slight but constant noise continues to bother and distract me for a time before I become distinctly conscious of it. All I feel is a steady increase in the labor of thinking—just as though I were trying to walk with a weight on my foot. At last I find out what it is.

Let me now, however, pass from genus to species. The most inexcusable and disgraceful of all noises is the cracking of whips—a truly infernal thing when it is done in the narrow resounding streets of a town. I denounce it as making a peaceful life impossible; it puts an end to all quiet thought. That this cracking of whips should be allowed at all seems to me to show in the clearest way how senseless and thoughtless is the nature of mankind. No one with anything like an idea in his head can avoid a feeling of actual pain at this sudden, sharp crack, which paralyzes the brain, rends the thread of reflection, and murders thought. Every time this noise is made, it must disturb a hundred people who are applying their minds to business of some sort, no matter how trivial it may be; while on the thinker its effect is woeful and disastrous, cutting his thoughts asunder, much as the executioner's axe severs the head from the body. No sound, be it ever so shrill, cuts so sharply into the brain as this cursed cracking of whips; you feel the sting of the lash right inside your head; and it affects the brain in the same way as touch affects a sensitive plant, and for the same length of time.

With all due respect for the most holy doctrine of utility, I really cannot see why a fellow who is taking away a wagon-load of gravel or dung should thereby obtain the right to kill in the bud the thoughts which may happen to be springing up in ten thousand heads—the number he will disturb one after another in half an hour's drive through the town. Hammering, the barking of dogs, and the crying of children are horrible to hear; but your only genuine assassin of thought is the crack of a whip; it exists for the purpose of destroying every pleasant moment of quiet thought that any one may now and then enjoy. If the driver had no other way of urging on his horse than by making this most abominable of all noises, it would be excusable; but quite the contrary is the case. This cursed cracking of whips is not only unnecessary, but even useless. Its aim is to produce an effect upon the intelligence of the horse; but through the constant abuse of it, the animal becomes habituated to the sound, which falls upon blunted feelings and produces no effect at all. The horse does not go any faster for it. You have a remarkable example of this in the ceaseless cracking of his whip on the part of a cab-driver, while he is proceeding at a slow pace on the lookout for a fare. If he were to give his horse the slightest touch with the whip, it would have much more effect. Supposing, however, that it were absolutely necessary to crack the whip in order to keep the horse constantly in mind of its presence, it would be enough to make the hundredth part of the noise. For it is a well-known fact that, in regard to sight and hearing, animals are sensitive to even the faintest indications; they are alive to things that we can scarcely perceive. The most surprising instances of this are furnished by trained dogs and canary birds.

It is obvious, therefore, that here we have to do with an act of pure wantonness; nay, with an impudent defiance offered to those members of the community who work with their heads by those who work with their hands. That such infamy should be tolerated in a town is a piece of barbarity and iniquity, all the more as it could easily be remedied by a police-notice to the effect that every lash shall have a knot at the end of it. There can be no harm in drawing the attention of the mob to the fact that the classes above them work with their heads, for any kind of headwork is mortal anguish to the man in the street. A fellow who rides through the narrow alleys of a populous town with unemployed post-horses or cart-horses, and keeps on cracking a whip several yards long with all his might, deserves there and then to stand down and receive five really good blows with a stick.

All the philanthropists in the world, and all the legislators, meeting to advocate and decree the total abolition of corporal punishment, will never persuade me to the contrary! There is something even more disgraceful than what I have just mentioned. Often enough you may see a carter walking along the street, quite alone, without any horses, and still cracking away incessantly; so accustomed has the wretch become to it in consequence of the unwarrantable toleration of this practice. A man's body and the needs of his body are now everywhere treated with a tender indulgence. Is the thinking mind then, to be the only thing that is never to obtain the slightest measure of consideration or protection, to say nothing of respect? Carters, porters, messengers—these are the beasts of burden amongst mankind; by all means let them be treated justly, fairly, indulgently, and with forethought; but they must not be permitted to stand in the way of the higher endeavors of humanity by wantonly making a noise. How many great and splendid thoughts, I should like to know, have been lost to the world by the crack of a whip? If I had the upper hand, I should soon produce in the heads of these people an indissoluble association of ideas between cracking a whip and getting a whipping.

Let us hope that the more intelligent and refined among the nations will make a beginning in this matter, and then that the Germans may take example by it and follow suit.[69] Meanwhile, I may quote what Thomas Hood says of them:[70] *For a musical nation, they are the most noisy I ever met with.* That they are so is due to the fact, not that they are more fond of making a noise than other people—they would deny it if you asked them—but that their senses are obtuse; consequently, when they hear a noise, it does not affect them much. It does not disturb them in reading or thinking, simply because they do not think; they only smoke, which is their substitute for thought. The general toleration of unnecessary noise—the slamming of doors, for instance, a very unmannerly and ill-bred thing—is direct evidence that the prevailing habit of mind is dullness and lack of thought. In Germany it seems as though care were taken that no one should ever think for mere noise—to mention one form of it, the way in which drumming goes on for no purpose at all.

Finally, as regards the literature of the subject treated of in this chapter, I have only one work to recommend, but it is a good one. I refer to a poetical epistle in *terzo rimo* by the famous painter Bronzino, entitled *De' Romori: a Messer Luca Martini.* It gives a detailed description of the torture to which people are put by the various noises of a small Italian town. Written in a tragicomic style, it is very amusing. The epistle may be found in *Opere burlesche del Berni,*

---

[69] According to a notice issued by the Society for the Protection of Animals in Munich, the superfluous whipping and the cracking of whips were, in December, 1858, positively forbidden in Nuremberg.

[70] In *Up the Rhine.*

Aretino ed altri, Vol. II., p. 258; apparently published in Utrecht in 1771.

A FEW PARABLES.

In a field of ripening corn I came to a place which had been trampled down by some ruthless foot; and as I glanced amongst the countless stalks, every one of them alike, standing there so erect and bearing the full weight of the ear, I saw a multitude of different flowers, red and blue and violet. How pretty they looked as they grew there so naturally with their little foliage! But, thought I, they are quite useless; they bear no fruit; they are mere weeds, suffered to remain only because there is no getting rid of them. And yet, but for these flowers, there would be nothing to charm the eye in that wilderness of stalks. They are emblematic of poetry and art, which, in civic life—so severe, but still useful and not without its fruit—play the same part as flowers in the corn.

* * * * *

There are some really beautifully landscapes in the world, but the human figures in them are poor, and you had not better look at them.

* * * * *

The fly should be used as the symbol of impertinence and audacity; for whilst all other animals shun man more than anything else, and run away even before he comes near them, the fly lights upon his very nose.

* * * * *

Two Chinamen traveling in Europe went to the theatre for the first time. One of them did nothing but study the machinery, and he succeeded in finding out how it was worked. The other tried to get at the meaning of the piece in spite of his ignorance of the language. Here you have the Astronomer and the Philosopher.

* * * * *

Wisdom which is only theoretical and never put into practice, is like a double rose; its color and perfume are delightful, but it withers away and leaves no seed.

No rose without a thorn. Yes, but many a thorn without a rose.

* * * * *

A wide-spreading apple-tree stood in full bloom, and behind it a straight fir raised its dark and tapering head. *Look at the thousands of gay blossoms which cover me everywhere,* said the apple-tree; *what have you to show in comparison? Dark-green needles! That is true,* replied the fir, *but when winter comes, you will be bared of your glory; and I shall be as I am now.*

* * * * *

Once, as I was botanizing under an oak, I found amongst a number of other plants of similar height one that was dark in color, with tightly closed leaves and a stalk that was very straight and stiff. When I touched it, it said to me in firm tones: *Let me alone; I am not for your collection, like these plants to which Nature has given only a single year of life. I am a little oak.*

So it is with a man whose influence is to last for hundreds of years. As a child, as a youth, often even as a full-grown man, nay, his whole life long, he goes about among his fellows, looking like them and seemingly as unimportant. But let him alone; he will not die. Time will come and bring those who know how to value him.

* * * * *

The man who goes up in a balloon does not feel as though he were ascending; he only sees the earth sinking deeper under him.

There is a mystery which only those will understand who feel the truth of it.

* * * * *

Your estimation of a man's size will be affected by the distance at which you stand from him, but in two entirely opposite ways according as it is his physical or his mental stature that you are considering. The one will seem smaller, the farther off you move; the other, greater.

* * * * *

Nature covers all her works with a varnish of beauty, like the tender bloom that is breathed, as it were, on the surface of a peach or a plum. Painters and poets lay themselves out to take off this varnish, to store it up, and give it us to be enjoyed at our leisure. We drink deep of this beauty long before we enter upon life itself; and when afterwards we come to see the works of Nature for ourselves, the varnish is gone: the artists have used it up and we have enjoyed it in advance. Thus it is that the world so often appears harsh and devoid of charm, nay, actually repulsive. It were better to leave us to discover the varnish for ourselves. This would mean that we should not enjoy it all at once and in large quantities; we should have no finished pictures, no perfect poems; but we should look at all things in that genial and pleasing light in which even now a child of Nature sometimes sees them—some one who has not anticipated his aesthetic pleasures by the help of art, or taken the charms of life too early.

* * * * *

The Cathedral in Mayence is so shut in by the houses that are built round about it, that there is no one spot from which you can see it as a whole. This is symbolic of everything great or beautiful in the world. It ought to exist for its own sake alone, but before very long it is misused to serve alien ends. People come from all directions wanting to find in it support and maintenance for themselves; they stand in the way and spoil its effect. To be sure, there is nothing surprising in this, for in a world of need and imperfection everything is seized upon which can be used to satisfy want. Nothing is exempt from this service, no, not even those very things which arise only when need and want are for a moment lost sight of—the beautiful and the true, sought for their own sakes.

This is especially illustrated and corroborated in the case of institutions—whether great or small, wealthy or poor, founded, no matter in what century or in what land, to maintain and advance human knowledge, and generally to afford help to those intellectual efforts which ennoble the race. Wherever these institutions may be, it is not long before people sneak up to them under the pretence of wishing to further those special ends, while they are really led on by the desire to secure the emoluments which have been left for their furtherance, and thus to satisfy certain coarse and brutal instincts of their own. Thus it is that we come to have so many charlatans in every branch of knowledge. The charlatan takes very different shapes according to circumstances; but at bottom he is a man who cares nothing about knowledge for its own sake, and only strives to gain the semblance of it that he may use it for his own personal ends, which are always selfish and material.

* * * * *

Every hero is a Samson. The strong man succumbs to the intrigues of the weak and the many; and if in the end he loses all patience he crushes both them and himself. Or he is like Gulliver at Lilliput, overwhelmed by an enormous number of little men.

* * * * *

A mother gave her children Aesop's fables to read, in the hope of educating and improving their minds; but they very soon brought the book back, and the eldest, wise beyond his years, delivered himself as follows: *This is no book for us; it's much too childish and stupid. You can't make us believe that foxes and wolves and ravens are able to talk; we've got beyond stories of that kind!*

In these young hopefuls you have the enlightened Rationalists of the future.

* * * * *

A number of porcupines huddled together for warmth on a cold day in winter; but, as they began to prick one another with their quills, they were obliged to disperse. However the cold drove them together again, when just the same thing happened. At last, after many turns of huddling and dispersing, they discovered that they would be best off by remaining at a little distance from one another. In the same way the need of society drives the human porcupines together, only to be mutually repelled by the many prickly and disagreeable qualities of their nature. The moderate distance which they at last discover to be the only tolerable condition of intercourse, is the code of politeness and fine manners; and those who transgress it are roughly told—in the English phrase—*to keep their distance.* By this arrangement the mutual need of warmth is only very moderately satisfied; but then people do not get pricked. A man who has some heat in himself prefers to remain outside, where he will neither prick other people nor get pricked himself.

The Art of Controversy.

PRELIMINARY: LOGIC AND DIALECTIC.

By the ancients, Logic and Dialectic were used as synonymous terms; although [Greek: logizesthai], "to think over, to consider, to calculate," and [Greek: dialegesthai], "to converse," are two very different things.

The name Dialectic was, as we are informed by Diogenes Laertius, first used by Plato; and in the *Phædrus, Sophist, Republic*, bk. vii., and elsewhere, we find that by Dialectic he means the regular employment of the reason, and skill in the practice of it. Aristotle also uses the word in this sense; but, according to Laurentius Valla, he was the first to use Logic too in a similar way.[71] Dialectic, therefore, seems to be an older word than Logic. Cicero and Quintilian use the words in the same general signification.[72]

This use of the words and synonymous terms lasted through the Middle Ages into modern times; in fact, until the present day. But more recently, and in particular by Kant, Dialectic has often been employed in a bad sense, as meaning "the art of sophistical controversy"; and hence Logic has been preferred, as of the two the more innocent designation. Nevertheless, both originally meant the same thing; and in the last few years they have again been recognised as synonymous.

It is a pity that the words have thus been used from of old, and that I am not quite at liberty to distinguish their meanings. Otherwise, I should have preferred to define *Logic* (from [Greek: logos], "word" and "reason," which are inseparable) as "the science of the laws of thought, that is, of the method of reason"; and *Dialectic* (from [Greek: dialegesthai], "to converse"—and every conversation communicates either facts or opinions, that is to say, it is historical or deliberative) as "the art of disputation," in the modern sense of the word. It is clear, then, that Logic deals with a subject of a purely *à priori* character, separable in definition from experience, namely, the laws of thought, the process of reason or the [Greek: logos], the laws, that is, which reason follows when it is left to itself and not hindered, as in the case of solitary thought on the part of a rational being who is in no way misled. Dialectic, on the other hand, would treat of the intercourse between two rational beings who, because they are rational, ought to think in common, but who, as soon as they cease to agree like two clocks keeping exactly the same time, create a disputation, or intellectual contest. Regarded as purely rational beings, the individuals would, I say, necessarily be in agreement, and their variation springs from the difference essential to individuality; in other words, it is drawn from experience.

Logic, therefore, as the science of thought, or the science of the process of pure reason, should be capable of being constructed *à priori*.

---

[71] He speaks of [Greek: dyscherelai logicai], that is, "difficult points," [Greek: protasis logicae aporia logicae]

[72] Cic. *in Lucullo*: *Dialecticam inventam esse, veri et falsi quasi disceptatricem.* *Topica*, c. 2: *Stoici enim judicandi vias diligenter persecuti sunt, ea scientia, quam* Dialecticen *appellant.* Quint., lib. ii., 12: *Itaque hæc pars dialecticae, sive illam disputatricem dicere malimus*; and with him this latter word appears to be the Latin equivalent for Dialectic. (So far according to "Petri Rami dialectica, Audomari Talaei praelectionibus illustrata." 1569.)

Dialectic, for the most part, can be constructed only *à posteriori*; that is to say, we may learn its rules by an experiential knowledge of the disturbance which pure thought suffers through the difference of individuality manifested in the intercourse between two rational beings, and also by acquaintance with the means which disputants adopt in order to make good against one another their own individual thought, and to show that it is pure and objective. For human nature is such that if A. and B. are engaged in thinking in common, and are communicating their opinions to one another on any subject, so long as it is not a mere fact of history, and A. perceives that B.'s thoughts on one and the same subject are not the same as his own, he does not begin by revising his own process of thinking, so as to discover any mistake which he may have made, but he assumes that the mistake has occurred in B.'s. In other words, man is naturally obstinate; and this quality in him is attended with certain results, treated of in the branch of knowledge which I should like to call Dialectic, but which, in order to avoid misunderstanding, I shall call Controversial or Eristical Dialectic. Accordingly, it is the branch of knowledge which treats of the obstinacy natural to man. Eristic is only a harsher name for the same thing.

Controversial Dialectic is the art of disputing, and of disputing in such a way as to hold one's own, whether one is in the right or the wrong—*per fas et nefas.*[73] A man may be objectively in the right, and nevertheless in the eyes of bystanders, and sometimes in his own, he may come off worst. For example, I may advance a proof of some assertion, and my adversary may refute the proof, and thus appear to have refuted the assertion, for which there may, nevertheless, be other

---

[73] According to Diogenes Laertius, v., 28, Aristotle put Rhetoric and Dialectic together, as aiming at persuasion, [Greek: to pithanon]; and Analytic and Philosophy as aiming at truth. Aristotle does, indeed, distinguish between (1) *Logic*, or Analytic, as the theory or method of arriving at true or apodeictic conclusions; and (2) *Dialectic* as the method of arriving at conclusions that are accepted or pass current as true, [Greek: endoxa] *probabilia*; conclusions in regard to which it is not taken for granted that they are false, and also not taken for granted that they are true in themselves, since that is not the point. What is this but the art of being in the right, whether one has any reason for being so or not, in other words, the art of attaining the appearance of truth, regardless of its substance? That is, then, as I put it above.

Aristotle divides all conclusions into logical and dialectical, in the manner described, and then into eristical. (3) *Eristic* is the method by which the form of the conclusion is correct, but the premisses, the materials from which it is drawn, are not true, but only appear to be true. Finally (4) *Sophistic* is the method in which the form of the conclusion is false, although it seems correct. These three last properly belong to the art of Controversial Dialectic, as they have no objective truth in view, but only the appearance of it, and pay no regard to truth itself; that is to say, they aim at victory. Aristotle's book on *Sophistic Conclusions* was edited apart from the others, and at a later date. It was the last book of his *Dialectic*.

proofs. In this case, of course, my adversary and I change places: he comes off best, although, as a matter of fact, he is in the wrong.

If the reader asks how this is, I reply that it is simply the natural baseness of human nature. If human nature were not base, but thoroughly honourable, we should in every debate have no other aim than the discovery of truth; we should not in the least care whether the truth proved to be in favour of the opinion which we had begun by expressing, or of the opinion of our adversary. That we should regard as a matter of no moment, or, at any rate, of very secondary consequence; but, as things are, it is the main concern. Our innate vanity, which is particularly sensitive in reference to our intellectual powers, will not suffer us to allow that our first position was wrong and our adversary's right. The way out of this difficulty would be simply to take the trouble always to form a correct judgment. For this a man would have to think before he spoke. But, with most men, innate vanity is accompanied by loquacity and innate dishonesty. They speak before they think; and even though they may afterwards perceive that they are wrong, and that what they assert is false, they want it to seem the contrary. The interest in truth, which may be presumed to have been their only motive when they stated the proposition alleged to be true, now gives way to the interests of vanity: and so, for the sake of vanity, what is true must seem false, and what is false must seem true.

However, this very dishonesty, this persistence in a proposition which seems false even to ourselves, has something to be said for it. It often happens that we begin with the firm conviction of the truth of our statement; but our opponent's argument appears to refute it. Should we abandon our position at once, we may discover later on that we were right after all; the proof we offered was false, but nevertheless there was a proof for our statement which was true. The argument which would have been our salvation did not occur to us at the moment. Hence we make it a rule to attack a counter-argument, even though to all appearances it is true and forcible, in the belief that its truth is only superficial, and that in the course of the dispute another argument will occur to us by which we may upset it, or succeed in confirming the truth of our statement. In this way we are almost compelled to become dishonest; or, at any rate, the temptation to do so is very great. Thus it is that the weakness of our intellect and the perversity of our will lend each other mutual support; and that, generally, a disputant fights not for truth, but for his proposition, as though it were a battle *pro aris et focis*. He sets to work *per fas et nefas*; nay, as we have seen, he cannot easily do otherwise. As a rule, then, every man will insist on maintaining whatever he has said, even though for the moment he may consider it false or doubtful.[74]

To some extent every man is armed against such a procedure by his own cunning and villainy. He learns by daily experience, and thus comes to have his own *natural Dialectic*, just as he has his own *natural Logic*. But his Dialectic is by no means as safe a guide as his Logic. It is not so easy for any one to think or draw an inference contrary to the laws of Logic; false judgments are frequent, false conclusions very rare. A man cannot easily be deficient in natural Logic, but he may very easily be deficient in natural Dialectic, which is a gift apportioned in unequal measure. In so far natural Dialectic resembles the faculty of judgment, which differs in degree with every man; while reason, strictly speaking, is the same. For it often happens that in a matter in which a man is really in the right, he is confounded or refuted by merely superficial arguments; and if he emerges victorious from a contest, he owes it very often not so much to the correctness of his judgment in stating his proposition, as to the cunning and address with which he defended it.

Here, as in all other cases, the best gifts are born with a man; nevertheless, much may be done to make him a master of this art by practice, and also by a consideration of the tactics which may be used to defeat an opponent, or which he uses himself for a similar purpose. Therefore, even though Logic may be of no very real, practical use, Dialectic may certainly be so; and Aristotle, too, seems to me to have drawn up his Logic proper, or Analytic, as a foundation and preparation for his Dialectic, and to have made this his chief business. Logic is concerned with the mere form of propositions; Dialectic, with their contents or matter—in a word, with their substance. It was proper, therefore, to consider the general form of all propositions before proceeding to particulars.

Aristotle does not define the object of Dialectic as exactly as I have done it here; for while he allows that its principal object is disputation, he declares at the same time that it is also the discovery of truth.[75]

---

[74] Machiavelli recommends his Prince to make use of every moment that his neighbour is weak, in order to attack him; as otherwise his neighbour may do the same. If honour and fidelity prevailed in the world, it would be a different matter; but as these are qualities not to be expected, a man must not practise them himself, because he will meet with a bad return. It is just the same in a dispute: if I allow that my opponent is right as soon as he seems to be so, it is scarcely probable that he will do the same when the position is reversed; and as he acts wrongly, I am compelled to act wrongly too. It is easy to say that we must yield to truth, without any prepossession in favour of our own statements; but we cannot assume that our opponent will do it, and therefore we cannot do it either. Nay, if I were to abandon the position on which I had previously bestowed much thought, as soon as it appeared that he was right, it might easily happen that I might be misled by a momentary impression, and give up the truth in order to accept an error.

[75] *Topica*, bk. i., 2.

Again, he says, later on, that if, from the philosophical point of view, propositions are dealt with according to their truth, Dialectic regards them according to their plausibility, or the measure in which they will win the approval and assent of others.[76] He is aware that the objective truth of a proposition must be distinguished and separated from the way in which it is pressed home, and approbation won for it; but he fails to draw a sufficiently sharp distinction between these two aspects of the matter, so as to reserve Dialectic for the latter alone.[77] The rules which he often gives for Dialectic contain some of those which properly belong to Logic; and hence it appears to me that he has not provided a clear solution of the problem.

We must always keep the subject of one branch of knowledge quite distinct from that of any other. To form a clear idea of the province of Dialectic, we must pay no attention to objective truth, which is an affair of Logic; we must regard it simply as *the art of getting the best of it in a dispute*, which, as we have seen, is all the easier if we are actually in the right. In itself Dialectic has nothing to do but to show how a man may defend himself against attacks of every

---

[76] *Ib.*, 12.

[77] On the other hand, in his book *De Sophisticis Elenchis*, he takes too much trouble to separate *Dialectic* from *Sophistic* and *Eristic*, where the distinction is said to consist in this, that dialectical conclusions are true in their form and their contents, while sophistical and eristical conclusions are false.

Eristic so far differs from Sophistic that, while the master of Eristic aims at mere victory, the Sophist looks to the reputation, and with it, the monetary rewards which he will gain. But whether a proposition is true in respect of its contents is far too uncertain a matter to form the foundation of the distinction in question; and it is a matter on which the disputant least of all can arrive at certainty; nor is it disclosed in any very sure form even by the result of the disputation. Therefore, when Aristotle speaks of *Dialectic*, we must include in it Sophistic, Eristic, and Peirastic, and define it as "the art of getting the best of it in a dispute," in which, unquestionably, the safest plan is to be in the right to begin with; but this in itself is not enough in the existing disposition of mankind, and, on the other hand, with the weakness of the human intellect, it is not altogether necessary. Other expedients are required, which, just because they are unnecessary to the attainment of objective truth, may also be used when a man is objectively in the wrong; and whether or not this is the case, is hardly ever a matter of complete certainty.

I am of opinion, therefore, that a sharper distinction should be drawn between Dialectic and Logic than Aristotle has given us; that to Logic we should assign objective truth as far as it is merely formal, and that Dialectic should be confined to the art of gaining one's point, and contrarily, that Sophistic and Eristic should not be distinguished from Dialectic in Aristotle's fashion, since the difference which he draws rests on objective and material truth; and in regard to what this is, we cannot attain any clear certainty before discussion; but we are compelled, with Pilate, to ask, *What is truth?* For truth is in the depths, [Greek: en butho hae halaetheia] (a saying of Democritus, *Diog. Laert.*, ix., 72). Two men often engage in a warm dispute, and then return to their homes each of the other's opinion, which he has exchanged for his own. It is easy to say that in every dispute we should have no other aim than the advancement of truth; but before dispute no one knows where it is, and through his opponent's arguments and his own a man is misled.

kind, and especially against dishonest attacks; and, in the same fashion, how he may attack another man's statement without contradicting himself, or generally without being defeated. The discovery of objective truth must be separated from the art of winning acceptance for propositions; for objective truth is an entirely different matter: it is the business of sound judgment, reflection and experience, for which there is no special art.

Such, then, is the aim of Dialectic. It has been defined as the Logic of appearance; but the definition is a wrong one, as in that case it could only be used to repel false propositions. But even when a man has the right on his side, he needs Dialectic in order to defend and maintain it; he must know what the dishonest tricks are, in order to meet them; nay, he must often make use of them himself, so as to beat the enemy with his own weapons.

Accordingly, in a dialectical contest we must put objective truth aside, or, rather, we must regard it as an accidental circumstance, and look only to the defence of our own position and the refutation of our opponent's.

In following out the rules to this end, no respect should be paid to objective truth, because we usually do not know where the truth lies. As I have said, a man often does not himself know whether he is in the right or not; he often believes it, and is mistaken: both sides often believe it. Truth is in the depths. At the beginning of a contest each man believes, as a rule, that right is on his side; in the course of it, both become doubtful, and the truth is not determined or confirmed until the close.

Dialectic, then, need have nothing to do with truth, as little as the fencing master considers who is in the right when a dispute leads to a duel. Thrust and parry is the whole business. Dialectic is the art of intellectual fencing; and it is only when we so regard it that we can erect it into a branch of knowledge. For if we take purely objective truth as our aim, we are reduced to mere Logic; if we take the maintenance of false propositions, it is mere Sophistic; and in either case it would have to be assumed that we were aware of what was true and what was false; and it is seldom that we have any clear idea of the truth beforehand. The true conception of Dialectic is, then, that which we have formed: it is the art of intellectual fencing used for the purpose of getting the best of it in a dispute; and, although the name *Eristic* would be more suitable, it is more correct to call it controversial Dialectic, *Dialectica eristica*.

Dialectic in this sense of the word has no other aim but to reduce to a regular system and collect and exhibit the arts which most men employ when they observe, in a dispute, that truth is not on their side, and still attempt to gain the day. Hence, it would be very inexpedient to pay any regard to objective truth or its advancement in a science of

Dialectic; since this is not done in that original and natural Dialectic innate in men, where they strive for nothing but victory. The science of Dialectic, in one sense of the word, is mainly concerned to tabulate and analyse dishonest stratagems, in order that in a real debate they may be at once recognised and defeated. It is for this very reason that Dialectic must admittedly take victory, and not objective truth, for its aim and purpose.

I am not aware that anything has been done in this direction, although I have made inquiries far and wide.[78] It is, therefore, an uncultivated soil. To accomplish our purpose, we must draw from our experience; we must observe how in the debates which often arise in our intercourse with our fellow-men this or that stratagem is employed by one side or the other. By finding out the common elements in tricks repeated in different forms, we shall be enabled to exhibit certain general stratagems which may be advantageous, as well for our own use, as for frustrating others if they use them.

What follows is to be regarded as a first attempt.

THE BASIS OF ALL DIALECTIC.

First of all, we must consider the essential nature of every dispute: what it is that really takes place in it.

Our opponent has stated a thesis, or we ourselves,—it is all one. There are two modes of refuting it, and two courses that we may pursue.

I. The modes are (1) *ad rem*, (2) *ad hominem* or *ex concessis*. That is to say: We may show either that the proposition is not in accordance with the nature of things, i.e., with absolute, objective truth; or that it is inconsistent with other statements or admissions of our opponent, i.e., with truth as it appears to him. The latter mode of arguing a question produces only a relative conviction, and makes no difference whatever to the objective truth of the matter.

II. The two courses that we may pursue are (1) the direct, and (2) the indirect refutation. The direct attacks the reason for the thesis; the indirect, its results. The direct refutation shows that the thesis is not true; the indirect, that it cannot be true.

The direct course admits of a twofold procedure. Either we may show that the reasons for the statement are false (*nego majorem, minorem*); or we may admit the reasons or premises, but show that the statement does not follow from them (*nego consequentiam*)_; that is,

---

[78] Diogenes Laertes tells us that among the numerous writings on Rhetoric by Theophrastus, all of which have been lost, there was one entitled [Greek: Agonistikon taes peri tous eristikous gogous theorias.] That would have been just what we want.

we attack the conclusion or form of the syllogism.

The direct refutation makes use either of the *diversion* or of the *instance*.

(a) The *diversion.*—We accept our opponent's proposition as true, and then show what follows from it when we bring it into connection with some other proposition acknowledged to be true. We use the two propositions as the premises of a syllogism giving a conclusion which is manifestly false, as contradicting either the nature of things,[79] or other statements of our opponent himself; that is to say, the conclusion is false either *ad rem* or *ad hominem.*[80] Consequently, our opponent's proposition must have been false; for, while true premises can give only a true conclusion, false premises need not always give a false one.

(b) The instance, or the example to the contrary.—This consists in refuting the general proposition by direct reference to particular cases which are included in it in the way in which it is stated, but to which it does not apply, and by which it is therefore shown to be necessarily false.

Such is the framework or skeleton of all forms of disputation; for to this every kind of controversy may be ultimately reduced. The whole of a controversy may, however, actually proceed in the manner described, or only appear to do so; and it may be supported by genuine or spurious arguments. It is just because it is not easy to make out the truth in regard to this matter, that debates are so long and so obstinate.

Nor can we, in ordering the argument, separate actual from apparent truth, since even the disputants are not certain about it beforehand. Therefore I shall describe the various tricks or stratagems without regard to questions of objective truth or falsity; for that is a matter on which we have no assurance, and which cannot be determined previously. Moreover, in every disputation or argument on any subject we must agree about something; and by this, as a principle, we must be willing to judge the matter in question. We cannot argue with those who deny principles: *Contra negantem principia non est disputandum.*

---

[79] If it is in direct contradiction with a perfectly undoubted, truth, we have reduced our opponent's position *ad absurdum.*

[80] Socrates, in *Hippia Maj. et alias.*

STRATAGEMS.

I.

The *Extension.*—This consists in carrying your opponent's proposition beyond its natural limits; in giving it as general a signification and as wide a sense as possible, so as to exaggerate it; and, on the other hand, in giving your own proposition as restricted a sense and as narrow limits as you can, because the more general a statement becomes, the more numerous are the objections to which it is open. The defence consists in an accurate statement of the point or essential question at issue.

Example 1.—I asserted that the English were supreme in drama. My opponent attempted _to_ give an instance to the contrary, and replied that it was a well-known fact that in music, and consequently in opera, they could do nothing at all. I repelled the attack by reminding him that music was not included in dramatic art, which covered tragedy and comedy alone. This he knew very well. What he had done was to try to generalise my proposition, so that it would apply to all theatrical representations, and, consequently, to opera and then to music, in order to make certain of defeating me. Contrarily, we may save our proposition by reducing it within narrower limits than we had first intended, if our way of expressing it favours this expedient.

Example 2.—A. declares that the Peace of 1814 gave back their independence to all the German towns of the Hanseatic League. B. gives an instance to the contrary by reciting the fact that Dantzig, which received its independence from Buonaparte, lost it by that Peace. A. saves himself thus: "I said 'all German towns,' and Dantzig was in Poland."

This trick was mentioned by Aristotle in the *Topica* (bk. viii., cc. 11, 12).

Example 3.—Lamarck, in his *Philosophic Zoologique* (vol. i., p. 208), states that the polype has no feeling, because it has no nerves. It is certain, however, that it has some sort of perception; for it advances towards light by moving in an ingenious fashion from branch to branch, and it seizes its prey. Hence it has been assumed that its nervous system is spread over the whole of its body in equal measure, as though it were blended with it; for it is obvious that the polype possesses some faculty of perception without having any separate organs of sense. Since this assumption refutes Lamarck's position, he argues thus: "In that case all parts of its body must be capable of every kind of feeling, and also of motion, of will, of thought. The polype would have all the organs of the most perfect animal in every point of its body; every point could see, smell, taste, hear, and so on; nay, it could think, judge, and draw conclusions; every particle of its body would be a perfect animal and it would stand higher than man, as every part of it would possess all the faculties which man possesses only in the whole of him. Further, there would be no reason for not extending what is true of the polype to all monads, the most imperfect of all creatures, and ultimately to the plants, which are also alive, etc., etc." By using dialectical tricks of this kind a writer betrays that he is secretly conscious of being in the wrong. Because it was said that the creature's whole body is sensitive to light, and is therefore possessed of nerves, he makes out that its whole body is capable of thought.

II.

The *Homonymy.*—This trick is to extend a proposition to something which has little or nothing in common with the matter in question but the similarity of the word; then to refute it triumphantly, and so claim credit for having refuted the original statement.

It may be noted here that synonyms are two words for the same conception; homonyms, two conceptions which are covered by the same word. (See Aristotle, *Topica*, bk. i., c. 13.) "Deep," "cutting," "high," used at one moment of bodies at another of tones, are homonyms; "honourable" and "honest" are synonyms.

This is a trick which may be regarded as identical with the sophism *ex homonymia*; although, if the sophism is obvious, it will deceive no one.

> *Every light can be extinguished.*
> *The intellect is a light.*
> *Therefore it can be extinguished.*

Here it is at once clear that there are four terms in the syllogism, "light" being used both in a real and in a metaphorical sense. But if the sophism takes a subtle form, it is, of course, apt to mislead, especially where the conceptions which are covered by the same word are related, and inclined to be interchangeable. It is never subtle enough to deceive, if it is used intentionally; and therefore cases of it must be collected from actual and individual experience.

It would be a very good thing if every trick could receive some short and obviously appropriate name, so that when a man used this or that particular trick, he could be at once reproached for it.

I will give two examples of the homonymy.

Example 1.—A.: "You are not yet initiated into the mysteries of the Kantian philosophy."

B.: "Oh, if it's mysteries you're talking of, I'll have nothing to do with them."

Example 2.—I condemned the principle involved in the word *honour* as a foolish one; for, according to it, a man loses his honour by receiving an insult, which he cannot wipe out unless he replies with a still greater insult, or by shedding his adversary's blood or his own. I contended that a man's true honour cannot be outraged by what he suffers, but only and alone by what he does; for there is no saying what may befall any one of us. My opponent immediately attacked the reason I had given, and triumphantly proved to me that when a tradesman was falsely accused of misrepresentation, dishonesty, or neglect in his business, it was an attack upon his honour, which in this case was outraged solely by what he suffered, and that he could only retrieve it by punishing his aggressor and making him retract.

Here, by a homonymy, he was foisting *civic honour*, which is otherwise called *good name*, and which may be outraged by libel and slander, on to the conception of *knightly honour*, also called *point d'honneur*, which may be outraged by insult. And since an attack on the former cannot be disregarded, but must be repelled by public disproof, so, with the same justification, an attack on the latter must not be disregarded either, but it must be defeated by still greater insult and a duel. Here we have a confusion of two essentially different things through the homonymy in the word *honour*, and a consequent alteration of the point in dispute.

III.

Another trick is to take a proposition which is laid down relatively, and in reference to some particular matter, as though it were uttered with a general or absolute application; or, at least, to take it in some quite different sense, and then refute it. Aristotle's example is as follows:

A Moor is black; but in regard to his teeth he is white; therefore, he is black and not black at the same moment. This is an obvious sophism, which will deceive no one. Let us contrast it with one drawn from actual experience.

In talking of philosophy, I admitted that my system upheld the Quietists, and commended them. Shortly afterwards the conversation turned upon Hegel, and I maintained that his writings were mostly nonsense; or, at any rate, that there were many passages in them where the author wrote the words, and it was left to the reader to find a meaning for them. My opponent did not attempt to refute this assertion *ad rem*, but contented himself by advancing the *argumentum ad hominem*, and telling me that I had just been praising the Quietists, and that they had written a good deal of nonsense too.

This I admitted; but, by way of correcting him, I said that I had praised the Quietists, not as philosophers and writers, that is to say, for their achievements in the sphere of *theory*, but only as men, and for their conduct in mere matters of *practice*; and that in Hegel's case we were talking of theories. In this way I parried the attack.

The first three tricks are of a kindred character. They have this in common, that something different is attacked from that which was asserted. It would therefore be an *ignoratio elenchi* to allow oneself to be disposed of in such a manner.

For in all the examples that I have given, what the opponent says is true, but it stands in apparent and not in real contradiction with the thesis. All that the man whom he is attacking has to do is to deny the validity of his syllogism; to deny, namely, the conclusion which he draws, that because his proposition is true, ours is false. In this way his refutation is itself directly refuted by a denial of his conclusion, *per negationem consequentiae*. Another trick is to refuse to admit true premises because of a foreseen conclusion. There are two ways of defeating it, incorporated in the next two sections.

IV.

If you want to draw a conclusion, you must not let it be foreseen, but you must get the premises admitted one by one, unobserved, mingling them here and there in your talk; otherwise, your opponent will attempt all sorts of chicanery. Or, if it is doubtful whether your opponent will admit them, you must advance the premises of these premises; that is to say, you must draw up pro-syllogisms, and get the premises of several of them admitted in no definite order. In this way you conceal your game until you have obtained all the admissions that are necessary, and so reach your goal by making a circuit. These rules are given by Aristotle in his *Topica*, bk. viii., c. 1. It is a trick which needs no illustration.

V.

To prove the truth of a proposition, you may also employ previous propositions that are not true, should your opponent refuse to admit the true ones, either because he fails to perceive their truth, or because he sees that the thesis immediately follows from them. In that case the plan is to take propositions which are false in themselves but true for your opponent, and argue from the way in which he thinks, that is to say, *ex concessis*. For a true conclusion may follow from false premises, but not *vice versâ*. In the same fashion your opponent's false propositions may be refuted by other false propositions, which he, however, takes to be true; for it is with him that you have to do, and you must use the thoughts that he uses. For instance, if he is a member of some sect to which you do not belong, you may employ the declared, opinions of this sect against him, as principles.[81]

VI.

Another plan is to beg the question in disguise by postulating what has to be proved, either (1) under another name; for instance, "good repute" instead of "honour"; "virtue" instead of "virginity," etc.; or by using such convertible terms as "red-blooded animals" and "vertebrates"; or (2) by making a general assumption covering the particular point in dispute; for instance, maintaining the uncertainty of medicine by postulating the uncertainty of all human knowledge. (3) If, *vice versâ*, two things follow one from the other, and one is to be proved, you may postulate the other. (4) If a general proposition is to be proved, you may get your opponent to admit every one of the particulars. This is the converse of the second.[82]

VII.

Should the disputation be conducted on somewhat strict and formal lines, and there be a desire to arrive at a very clear understanding, he who states the proposition and wants to prove it may proceed against his opponent by question, in order to show the truth of the statement from his admissions. The erotematic, or Socratic, method was especially in use among the ancients; and this and some of the tricks following later on are akin to it.[83]

The plan is to ask a great many wide-reaching questions at once, so as to hide what you want to get admitted, and, on the other hand, quickly propound the argument resulting from the admissions; for those who are slow of understanding cannot follow accurately, and do not notice any mistakes or gaps there may be in the demonstration.

VIII.

This trick consists in making your opponent angry; for when he is angry he is incapable of judging aright, and perceiving where his advantage lies. You can make him angry by doing him repeated injustice, or practising some kind of chicanery, and being generally insolent.

---

[81] Aristotle, *Topica* bk. viii., chap. 2.

[82] *Idem*, chap. 11. The last chapter of this work contains some good rules for the practice of Dialectics.

[83] They are all a free version of chap. 15 of Aristotle's *De Sophistici Elenchis.*

IX.

Or you may put questions in an order different from that which the conclusion to be drawn from them requires, and transpose them, so as not to let him know at what you are aiming. He can then take no precautions. You may also use his answers for different or even opposite conclusions, according to their character. This is akin to the trick of masking your procedure.

X.

If you observe that your opponent designedly returns a negative answer to the questions which, for the sake of your proposition, you want him to answer in the affirmative, you must ask the converse of the proposition, as though it were that which you were anxious to see affirmed; or, at any rate, you may give him his choice of both, so that he may not perceive which of them you are asking him to affirm.

XL.

If you make an induction, and your opponent grants you the particular cases by which it is to be supported, you must refrain from asking him if he also admits the general truth which issues from the particulars, but introduce it afterwards as a settled and admitted fact; for, in the meanwhile, he will himself come to believe that he has admitted it, and the same impression will be received by the audience, because they will remember the many questions as to the particulars, and suppose that they must, of course, have attained their end.

XII.

If the conversation turns upon some general conception which has no particular name, but requires some figurative or metaphorical designation, you must begin by choosing a metaphor that is favourable to your proposition. For instance, the names used to denote the two political parties in Spain, *Serviles* and *Liberates*, are obviously chosen by the latter. The name *Protestants* is chosen by themselves, and also the name *Evangelicals*; but the Catholics call them *heretics*. Similarly, in regard to the names of things which admit of a more exact and definite meaning: for example, if your opponent proposes an *alteration*, you can call it an *innovation*, as this is an invidious word. If you yourself make the proposal, it will be the converse. In the first case, you can call the antagonistic principle "the existing order," in the second, "antiquated prejudice." What an impartial man with no further purpose to serve would call "public worship" or a "system of religion," is described by an adherent as "piety," "godliness": and by an opponent as "bigotry," "superstition." This is, at bottom, a subtle *petitio principii.* What is sought to be proved is, first of all, inserted in the definition, whence it is then taken by mere analysis. What one man calls "placing in safe custody," another calls "throwing into prison." A speaker often betrays his purpose beforehand by the names which he gives to things. One man talks of "the clergy"; another, of "the priests."

Of all the tricks of controversy, this is the most frequent, and it is used instinctively. You hear of "religious zeal," or "fanaticism"; a *"faux pas"* a "piece of gallantry," or "adultery"; an "equivocal," or a "bawdy" story; "embarrassment," or "bankruptcy"; "through influence and connection," or by "bribery and nepotism"; "sincere gratitude," or "good pay."

XIII.

To make your opponent accept a proposition, you must give him the counter-proposition as well, leaving him his choice of the two; and you must render the contrast as glaring as you can, so that to avoid being paradoxical he will accept the proposition, which is thus made to look quite probable. For instance, if you want to make him admit that a boy must do everything that his father tells him to do, ask him "whether in all things we must obey or disobey our parents." Or, if a thing is said to occur "often," ask whether by "often" you are to understand few or many cases; and he will say "many." It is as though you were to put grey next black, and call it white; or next white, and call it black.

XIV.

This, which is an impudent trick, is played as follows: When your opponent has answered several of your questions without the answers turning out favourable to the conclusion at which you are aiming, advance the desired conclusion,—although it does not in the least follow,—as though it had been proved, and proclaim it in a tone of triumph. If your opponent is shy or stupid, and you yourself possess a great deal of impudence and a good voice, the trick may easily succeed. It is akin to the fallacy *non causae ut causae.*

XV.

If you have advanced a paradoxical proposition and find a difficulty in proving it, you may submit for your opponent's acceptance or rejection some true proposition, the truth of which, however, is not quite palpable, as though you wished to draw your proof from it.

Should he reject it because he suspects a trick, you can obtain your triumph by showing how absurd he is; should he accept it, you have got reason on your side for the moment, and must now look about you; or else you can employ the previous trick as well, and maintain that your paradox is proved by the proposition which he has accepted. For this an extreme degree of impudence is required; but experience shows cases of it, and there are people who practise it by instinct.

XVI.

Another trick is to use arguments *ad hominem*, or *ex concessis*[84] When your opponent makes a proposition, you must try to see whether it is not in some way—if needs be, only apparently—inconsistent with some other proposition which he has made or admitted, or with the principles of a school or sect which he has commended and approved, or with the actions of those who support the sect, or else of those who give it only an apparent and spurious support, or with his own actions or want of action. For example, should he defend suicide, you may at once exclaim, "Why don't you hang yourself?" Should he maintain that Berlin is an unpleasant place to live in, you may say, "Why don't you leave by the first train?" Some such claptrap is always possible.

XVII.

If your opponent presses you with a counter-proof, you will often be able to save yourself by advancing some subtle distinction, which, it is true, had not previously occurred to you; that is, if the matter admits of a double application, or of being taken in any ambiguous sense.

---

[84] The truth from which I draw my proof may he either (1) of an objective and universally valid character; in that case my proof is veracious, *secundum veritatem*; and it is such proof alone that has any genuine validity. Or (2) it may be valid only for the person to whom I wish to prove my proposition, and with whom I am disputing. He has, that is to say, either taken up some position once for all as a prejudice, or hastily admitted it in the course of the dispute; and on this I ground my proof. In that case, it is a proof valid only for this particular man, *ad hominem*. *I* compel my opponent to grant my proposition, but I fail to establish it as a truth of universal validity. My proof avails for my opponent alone, but for no one else. For example, if my opponent is a devotee of Kant's, and I ground my proof on some utterance of that philosopher, it is a proof which in itself is only *ad hominem*. If he is a Mohammedan, I may prove my point by reference to a passage in the Koran, and that is sufficient for him; but here it is only a proof *ad hominem*.

XVIII.

If you observe that your opponent has taken up a line of argument which will end in your defeat, you must not allow him to carry it to its conclusion, but interrupt the course of the dispute in time, or break it off altogether, or lead him away from the subject, and bring him to others. In short, you must effect the trick which will be noticed later on, the *mutatio controversiae*. (See § xxix.)

XIX.

Should your opponent expressly challenge you to produce any objection to some definite point in his argument, and you have nothing much to say, you must try to give the matter a general turn, and then talk against that. If you are called upon to say why a particular physical hypothesis cannot be accepted, you may speak of the fallibility of human knowledge, and give various illustrations of it.

XX.

When you have elicited all your premisses, and your opponent has admitted them, you must refrain from asking him for the conclusion, but draw it at once for yourself; nay, even though one or other of the premisses should be lacking, you may take it as though it too had been admitted, and draw the conclusion. This trick is an application of the fallacy *non causae ut causae*.

XXI.

When your opponent uses a merely superficial or sophistical argument and you see through it, you can, it is true, refute it by setting forth its captious and superficial character; but it is better to meet him with a counter-argument which is just as superficial and sophistical, and so dispose of him; for it is with victory that you are concerned, and not with truth. If, for example, he adopts an *argumentum ad hominem*, it is sufficient to take the force out of it by a counter *argumentum ad hominem* or *argumentum ex concessis*; and, in general, instead of setting forth the true state of the case at equal length, it is shorter to take this course if it lies open to you.

XXII.

If your opponent requires you to admit something from which the point in dispute will immediately follow, you must refuse to do so, declaring that it is a *petitio principii* For he and the audience will regard a proposition which is near akin to the point in dispute as identical with it, and in this way you deprive him of his best argument.

XXIII.

Contradiction and contention irritate a man into exaggerating his statement. By contradicting your opponent you may drive him into extending beyond its proper limits a statement which, at all events within those limits and in itself, is true; and when you refute this exaggerated form of it, you look as though you had also refuted his original statement. Contrarily, you must take care not to allow yourself to be misled by contradictions into exaggerating or extending a statement of your own. It will often happen that your opponent will himself directly try to extend your statement further than you meant it; here you must at once stop him, and bring him back to the limits which you set up; "That's what I said, and no more."

XXIV.

This trick consists in stating a false syllogism. Your opponent makes a proposition, and by false inference and distortion of his ideas you force from it other propositions which it does not contain and he does not in the least mean; nay, which are absurd or dangerous. It then looks as if his proposition gave rise to others which are inconsistent either with themselves or with some acknowledged truth, and so it appears to be indirectly refuted. This is the *diversion*, and it is another application of the fallacy *non causae ut causae.*

XXV.

This is a case of the *diversion* by means of an *instance to the contrary*. With an induction ([Greek: epagogae]), a great number of particular instances are required in order to establish it as a universal proposition; but with the *diversion* ([Greek: apagogae]) a single instance, to which the proposition does not apply, is all that is necessary to overthrow it. This is a controversial method known as the *instance—instantia*, [Greek: enstasis]. For example, "all ruminants are horned" is a proposition which may be upset by the single instance of the camel. The *instance* is a case in which a universal truth is sought to be applied, and something is inserted in the fundamental definition of it which is not universally true, and by which it is upset. But there is room for mistake; and when this trick is employed by your opponent, you must observe (1) whether the example which he gives is really true; for there are problems of which the only true solution is that the case in point is not true—for example, many miracles, ghost stories, and so on; and (2) whether it really comes under the conception of the truth thus stated; for it may only appear to do so, and the matter is one to be settled by precise distinctions; and (3) whether it is really inconsistent with this conception; for this again may be only an apparent inconsistency.

XXVI.

A brilliant move is the *retorsio argumenti*, or turning of the tables, by which your opponent's argument is turned against himself. He declares, for instance, "So-and-so is a child, you must make allowance for him." You retort, "Just because he is a child, I must correct him; otherwise he will persist in his bad habits."

XXVII.

Should your opponent surprise you by becoming particularly angry at an argument, you must urge it with all the more zeal; not only because it is a good thing to make him angry, but because it may be presumed that you have here put your finger on the weak side of his case, and that just here he is more open to attack than even for the moment you perceive.

XXVIII.

This is chiefly practicable in a dispute between scholars in the presence of the unlearned. If you have no argument *ad rem*, and none either *ad hominem*, you can make one *ad auditores*; that is to say, you can start some invalid objection, which, however, only an expert sees to be invalid. Now your opponent is an expert, but those who form your audience are not, and accordingly in their eyes he is defeated; particularly if the objection which you make places him in any ridiculous light. People are ready to laugh, and you have the laughers on your side. To show that your objection is an idle one, would require a long explanation on the part of your opponent, and a reference to the principles of the branch of knowledge in question, or to the elements of the matter which you are discussing; and people are not disposed to listen to it.

For example, your opponent states that in the original formation of a mountain-range the granite and other elements in its composition were, by reason of their high temperature, in a fluid or molten state; that the temperature must have amounted to some 480° Fahrenheit; and that when the mass took shape it was covered by the sea. You reply, by an argument *ad auditores*, that at that temperature—nay, indeed, long before it had been reached, namely, at 212° Fahrenheit—the sea would have been boiled away, and spread through the air in the form of steam. At this the audience laughs. To refute the objection, your opponent would have to show that the boiling-point depends not only on the degree of warmth, but also on the atmospheric pressure; and that as soon as about half the sea-water had gone off in the shape of steam, this pressure would be so greatly increased that the rest of it would fail to boil even at a temperature of 480°. He is debarred from giving this explanation, as it would require a treatise to demonstrate the matter to those who had no acquaintance with physics.

XXIX.[85]

If you find that you are being worsted, you can make a *diversion*— that is, you can suddenly begin to talk of something else, as though it had a bearing on the matter in dispute, and afforded an argument against your opponent. This may be done without presumption if the diversion has, in fact, some general bearing on the matter; but it is a piece of impudence if it has nothing to do with the case, and is only brought in by way of attacking your opponent.

For example, I praised the system prevailing in China, where there is no such thing as hereditary nobility, and offices are bestowed only on those who succeed in competitive examinations. My opponent maintained that learning, as little as the privilege of birth (of which he had a high opinion) fits a man for office. We argued, and he got the worst of it. Then he made a diversion, and declared that in China all ranks were punished with the bastinado, which he connected with the immoderate indulgence in tea, and proceeded to make both of them a subject of reproach to the Chinese. To follow him into all this would have been to allow oneself to be drawn into a surrender of the victory which had already been won.

The diversion is mere impudence if it completely abandons the point in dispute, and raises, for instance, some such objection as "Yes, and you also said just now," and so on. For then the argument becomes to some extent personal; of the kind which will be treated of in the last section. Strictly speaking, it is half-way between the *argumentum ad personam*, which will there be discussed, and the *argumentum ad*

---

[85] See § xviii.

hominem.

How very innate this trick is, may be seen in every quarrel between common people. If one of the parties makes some personal reproach against the other, the latter, instead of answering it by refuting it, allows it to stand,—as it were, admits it; and replies by reproaching his antagonist on some other ground. This is a stratagem like that pursued by Scipio when he attacked the Carthaginians, not in Italy, but in Africa. In war, diversions of this kind may be profitable; but in a quarrel they are poor expedients, because the reproaches remain, and those who look on hear the worst that can be said of both parties. It is a trick that should be used only *faute de mieux.*

XXX.

This is the *argumentum ad verecundiam.* It consists in making an appeal to authority rather than reason, and in using such an authority as may suit the degree of knowledge possessed by your opponent.

Every man prefers belief to the exercise of judgment, says Seneca; and it is therefore an easy matter if you have an authority on your side which your opponent respects. The more limited his capacity and knowledge, the greater is the number of the authorities who weigh with him. But if his capacity and knowledge are of a high order, there are very few; indeed, hardly any at all. He may, perhaps, admit the authority of professional men versed in a science or an art or a handicraft of which he knows little or nothing; but even so he will regard it with suspicion. Contrarily, ordinary folk have a deep respect for professional men of every kind. They are unaware that a man who makes a profession of a thing loves it not for the thing itself, but for the money he makes by it; or that it is rare for a man who teaches to know his subject thoroughly; for if he studies it as he ought, he has in most cases no time left in which to teach it.

But there are very many authorities who find respect with the mob, and if you have none that is quite suitable, you can take one that appears to be so; you may quote what some said in another sense or in other circumstances. Authorities which your opponent fails to understand are those of which he generally thinks the most. The unlearned entertain a peculiar respect for a Greek or a Latin flourish. You may also, should it be necessary, not only twist your authorities, but actually falsify them, or quote something which you have invented entirely yourself. As a rule, your opponent has no books at hand, and could not use them if he had. The finest illustration of this is furnished by the French *curé,* who, to avoid being compelled, like other citizens, to pave the street in front of his house, quoted a saying which he described as biblical: *paveant illi, ego non pavebo.* That was quite enough for the municipal officers.

A universal prejudice may also be used as an authority; for most people think with Aristotle that that may be said to exist which many believe. There is no opinion, however absurd, which men will not readily embrace as soon as they can be brought to the conviction that it is generally adopted. Example affects their thought just as it affects their action. They are like sheep following the bell-wether just as he leads them. They would sooner die than think. It is very curious that the universality of an opinion should have so much weight with people, as their own experience might tell them that its acceptance is an entirely thoughtless and merely imitative process. But it tells them nothing of the kind, because they possess no self-knowledge whatever. It is only the elect Who Say with Plato: [Greek: tois pollois polla dokei] which means that the public has a good many bees in its bonnet, and that it would be a long business to get at them.

But to speak seriously, the universality of an opinion is no proof, nay, it is not even a probability, that the opinion is right. Those who maintain that it is so must assume (1) that length of time deprives a universal opinion of its demonstrative force, as otherwise all the old errors which were once universally held to be true would have to be recalled; for instance, the Ptolemaic system would have to be restored, or Catholicism re-established in all Protestant countries. They must assume (2) that distance of space has the same effect; otherwise the respective universality of opinion among the adherents of Buddhism, Christianity, and Islam will put them in a difficulty.

When we come to look into the matter, so-called universal opinion is the opinion of two or three persons; and we should be persuaded of this if we could see the way in which it really arises.

We should find that it is two or three persons who, in the first instance, accepted it, or advanced and maintained it; and of whom people were so good as to believe that they had thoroughly tested it. Then a few other persons, persuaded beforehand that the first were men of the requisite capacity, also accepted the opinion. These, again, were trusted by many others, whose laziness suggested to them that it was better to believe at once, than to go through the troublesome task of testing the matter for themselves. Thus the number of these lazy and credulous adherents grew from day to day; for the opinion had no sooner obtained a fair measure of support than its further supporters attributed this to the fact that the opinion could only have obtained it by the cogency of its arguments. The remainder were then compelled to grant what was universally granted, so as not to pass for unruly persons who resisted opinions which every one accepted, or pert fellows who thought themselves cleverer than any one else.

When opinion reaches this stage, adhesion becomes a duty; and henceforward the few who are capable of forming a judgment hold their peace. Those who venture to speak are such as are entirely incapable of forming any opinions or any judgment of their own, being merely the echo of others' opinions; and, nevertheless, they defend them with all the greater zeal and intolerance. For what they hate in people who think differently is not so much the different opinions which they profess, as the presumption of wanting to form their own judgment; a presumption of which they themselves are never guilty, as they are very well aware. In short, there are very few who can think, but every man wants to have an opinion; and what remains but to take it ready-made from others, instead of forming opinions for himself?

Since this is what happens, where is the value of the opinion even of a hundred millions? It is no more established than an historical fact reported by a hundred chroniclers who can be proved to have plagiarised it from one another; the opinion in the end being traceable to a single individual.[86] It is all what I say, what you say, and, finally, what he says; and the whole of it is nothing but a series of assertions:

Dico ego, tu dicis, sed denique dixit et ille;
Dictaque post toties, nil nisi dicta vides.

Nevertheless, in a dispute with ordinary people, we may employ universal opinion as an authority. For it will generally be found that when two of them are fighting, that is the weapon which both of them choose as a means of attack. If a man of the better sort has to deal with them, it is most advisable for him to condescend to the use of this weapon too, and to select such authorities as will make an impression on his opponent's weak side. For, *ex hypoihesi*, he is as insensible to all rational argument as a horny-hided Siegfried, dipped in the flood of incapacity, and unable to think or judge.

Before a tribunal the dispute is one between authorities alone,— such authoritative statements, I mean, as are laid down by legal experts; and here the exercise of judgment consists in discovering what law or authority applies to the case in question. There is, however, plenty of room for Dialectic; for should the case in question and the law not really fit each other, they can, if necessary, be twisted until they appear to do so, or *vice versa*.

XXXI.

If you know that you have no reply to the arguments which your opponent advances, you may, by a fine stroke of irony, declare yourself to be an incompetent judge: "What you now say passes my poor powers of comprehension; it may be all very true, but I can't

---

[86] See Bayle's *Pensées sur les Comètes*, i., p. 10.

understand it, and I refrain from any expression of opinion on it." In this way you insinuate to the bystanders, with whom you are in good repute, that what your opponent says is nonsense. Thus, when Kant's *Kritik* appeared, or, rather, when it began to make a noise in the world, many professors of the old ecclectic school declared that they failed to understand it, in the belief that their failure settled the business. But when the adherents of the new school proved to them that they were quite right, and had really failed to understand it, they were in a very bad humour.

This is a trick which may be used only when you are quite sure that the audience thinks much better of you that of your opponent. A professor, for instance may try it on a student.

Strictly, it is a case of the preceding trick: it is a particularly malicious assertion of one's own authority, instead of giving reasons. The counter-trick is to say: "I beg your pardon; but, with your penetrating intellect, it must be very easy for you to understand anything; and it can only be my poor statement of the matter that is at fault"; and then go on to rub it into him until he understands it *nolens volens*, and sees for himself that it was really his own fault alone. In this way you parry his attack. With the greatest politeness he wanted to insinuate that you were talking nonsense; and you, with equal courtesy, prove to him that he is a fool.

XXXII.

If you are confronted with an assertion, there is a short way of getting rid of it, or, at any rate, of throwing suspicion on it, by putting it into some odious category; even though the connection is only apparent, or else of a loose character. You can say, for instance, "That is Manichæism," or "It is Arianism," or "Pelagianism," or "Idealism," or "Spinozism," or "Pantheism," or "Brownianism," or "Naturalism," or "Atheism," or "Rationalism," "Spiritualism," "Mysticism," and so on. In making an objection of this kind, you take it for granted (1) that the assertion in question is identical with, or is at least contained in, the category cited—that is to say, you cry out, "Oh, I have heard that before"; and (2) that the system referred to has been entirely refuted, and does not contain a word of truth.

XXXIII.

"That's all very well in theory, but it won't do in practice." In this sophism you admit the premises but deny the conclusion, in contradiction with a well-known rule of logic. The assertion is based upon an impossibility: what is right in theory _must_ work in practice; and if it does not, there is a mistake in the theory; something has been overlooked and not allowed for; and, consequently, what is wrong in practice is wrong in theory too.

XXXIV.

When you state a question or an argument, and your opponent gives you no direct answer or reply, but evades it by a counter-question or an indirect answer, or some assertion which has no bearing on the matter, and, generally, tries to turn the subject, it is a sure sign that you have touched a weak spot, sometimes without knowing it. You have, as it were, reduced him to silence. You must, therefore, urge the point all the more, and not let your opponent evade it, even when you do not know where the weakness which you have hit upon really lies.

XXXV.

There is another trick which, as soon as it is practicable, makes all others unnecessary. Instead of working on your opponent's intellect by argument, work on his will by motive; and he, and also the audience if they have similar interests, will at once be won over to your opinion, even though you got it out of a lunatic asylum; for, as a general rule, half an ounce of will is more effective than a hundredweight of insight and intelligence. This, it is true, can be done only under peculiar circumstances. If you succeed in making your opponent feel that his opinion, should it prove true, will be distinctly prejudicial to his interest, he will let it drop like a hot potato, and feel that it was very imprudent to take it up.

A clergyman, for instance, is defending some philosophical dogma; you make him sensible of the fact that it is in immediate contradiction with one of the fundamental doctrines of his Church, and he abandons it.

A landed proprietor maintains that the use of machinery in agricultural operations, as practised in England, is an excellent institution, since an engine does the work of many men. You give him to understand that it will not be very long before carriages are also worked by steam, and that the value of his large stud will be greatly depreciated; and you will see what he will say.

In such cases every man feels how thoughtless it is to sanction a law unjust to himself—*quam temere in nosmet legem sancimus iniquam*! Nor is it otherwise if the bystanders, but not your opponent, belong to the same sect, guild, industry, club, etc., as yourself. Let his thesis be never so true, as soon as you hint that it is prejudicial to the common interests of the said society, all the bystanders will find that your opponent's arguments, however excellent they be, are weak and contemptible; and that yours, on the other hand, though they were random conjecture, are correct and to the point; you will have a chorus of loud approval on your side, and your opponent will be driven out of the field with ignominy. Nay, the bystanders will believe, as a rule, that they have agreed with you out of pure conviction. For what is not to our interest mostly seems absurd to us; our intellect being no *siccum lumen*. This trick might be called "taking the tree by its root"; its usual name is the *argumentum ab utili.*

XXXVI.

You may also puzzle and bewilder your opponent by mere bombast; and the trick is possible, because a man generally supposes that there must be some meaning in words:

> *Gewöhnlich glaubt der Mensch, wenn er nur Worte hört,*
> *Es müsse sich dabei doch auch was denken lassen.*

If he is secretly conscious of his own weakness, and accustomed to hear much that he does not understand, and to make as though he did, you can easily impose upon him by some serious fooling that sounds very deep or learned, and deprives him of hearing, sight, and thought; and by giving out that it is the most indisputable proof of what you assert. It is a well-known fact that in recent times some philosophers have practised this trick on the whole of the public with the most brilliant success. But since present examples are odious, we may refer to *The Vicar of Wakefield* for an old one.

XXXVII.

Should your opponent be in the right, but, luckily for your contention, choose a faulty proof, you can easily manage to refute it, and then claim that you have thus refuted his whole position. This is a trick which ought to be one of the first; it is, at bottom, an expedient by which an *argumentum ad hominem* is put forward as an *argumentum ad rem*. If no accurate proof occurs to him or to the bystanders, you have won the day. For example, if a man advances the ontological argument by way of proving God's existence, you can get the best of him, for the ontological argument may easily be refuted. This is the way in which bad advocates lose a good case, by trying to justify it by an authority which does not fit it, when no fitting one occurs to them.

XXXVIII.

A last trick is to become personal, insulting, rude, as soon as you perceive that your opponent has the upper hand, and that you are going to come off worst. It consists in passing from the subject of dispute, as from a lost game, to the disputant himself, and in some way attacking his person. It may be called the *argumentum ad personam*, to distinguish it from the *argumentum ad hominem*, which passes from the objective discussion of the subject pure and simple to the statements or admissions which your opponent has made in regard to it. But in becoming personal you leave the subject altogether, and turn your attack to his person, by remarks of an offensive and spiteful character. It is an appeal from the virtues of the intellect to the virtues of the body, or to mere animalism. This is a very popular trick, because every one is able to carry it into effect; and so it is of frequent application. Now the question is, What counter-trick avails for the other party? for if he has recourse to the same rule, there will be blows, or a duel, or an action for slander.

It would be a great mistake to suppose that it is sufficient not to become personal yourself. For by showing a man quite quietly that he is wrong, and that what he says and thinks is incorrect—a process which occurs in every dialectical victory—you embitter him more than if you used some rude or insulting expression. Why is this? Because, as Hobbes observes,[87] all mental pleasure consists in being able to compare oneself with others to one's own advantage. Nothing is of greater moment to a man than the gratification of his vanity, and no wound is more painful than that which is inflicted on it. Hence such phrases as "Death before dishonour," and so on. The gratification of vanity arises mainly by comparison of oneself with others, in every respect, but chiefly in respect of one's intellectual powers; and so the most effective and the strongest gratification of it is to be found in controversy. Hence the embitterment of defeat, apart from any question of injustice; and hence recourse to that last weapon, that last trick, which you cannot evade by mere politeness. A cool demeanour may, however, help you here, if, as soon as your opponent becomes personal, you quietly reply, "That has no bearing on the point in dispute," and immediately bring the conversation back to it, and continue to show him that he is wrong, without taking any notice of his insults. Say, as Themistocles said to Eurybiades—*Strike, but hear me.* But such demeanour is not given to every one.

As a sharpening of wits, controversy is often, indeed, of mutual

---

[87] *Elementa philosophica de Cive.*

advantage, in order to correct one's thoughts and awaken new views. But in learning and in mental power both disputants must be tolerably equal. If one of them lacks learning, he will fail to understand the other, as he is not on the same level with his antagonist. If he lacks mental power, he will be embittered, and led into dishonest tricks, and end by being rude.

The only safe rule, therefore, is that which Aristotle mentions in the last chapter of his *Topica*: not to dispute with the first person you meet, but only with those of your acquaintance of whom you know that they possess sufficient intelligence and self-respect not to advance absurdities; to appeal to reason and not to authority, and to listen to reason and yield to it; and, finally, to cherish truth, to be willing to accept reason even from an opponent, and to be just enough to bear being proved to be in the wrong, should truth lie with him. From this it follows that scarcely one man in a hundred is worth your disputing with him. You may let the remainder say what they please, for every one is at liberty to be a fool—*desipere est jus gentium*. Remember what Voltaire says: *La paix vaut encore mieux que la vérité.* Remember also an Arabian proverb which tells us that *on the tree of silence there hangs its fruit, which is peace.*

ON THE COMPARATIVE PLACE OF INTEREST AND BEAUTY IN WORKS OF ART.

In the productions of poetic genius, especially of the epic and dramatic kind, there is, apart from Beauty, another quality which is attractive: I mean Interest.

The beauty of a work of art consists in the fact that it holds up a clear mirror to certain *ideas* inherent in the world in general; the beauty of a work of poetic art in particular is that it renders the ideas inherent in mankind, and thereby leads it to a knowledge of these ideas. The means which poetry uses for this end are the exhibition of significant characters and the invention of circumstances which will bring about significant situations, giving occasion to the characters to unfold their peculiarities and show what is in them; so that by some such representation a clearer and fuller knowledge of the many-sided idea of humanity may be attained. Beauty, however, in its general aspect, is the inseparable characteristic of the idea when it has become known. In other words, everything is beautiful in which an idea is revealed; for to be beautiful means no more than clearly to express an idea.

Thus we perceive that beauty is always an affair of *knowledge*, and that it appeals to *the knowing subject*, and not to *the will*; nay, it is a fact that the apprehension of beauty on the part of the subject involves a complete suppression of the will.

On the other hand, we call drama or descriptive poetry interesting when it represents events and actions of a kind which necessarily arouse concern or sympathy, like that which we feel in real events involving our own person. The fate of the person represented in them is felt in just the same fashion as our own: we await the development of events with anxiety; we eagerly follow their course; our hearts quicken when the hero is threatened; our pulse falters as the danger reaches its acme, and throbs again when he is suddenly rescued. Until we reach the end of the story we cannot put the book aside; we lie away far into the night sympathising with our hero's troubles as though they were our own. Nay, instead of finding pleasure and recreation in such representations, we should feel all the pain which real life often inflicts upon us, or at least the kind which pursues us in our uneasy dreams, if in the act of reading or looking at the stage we had not the firm ground of reality always beneath our feet. As it is, in the stress of a too violent feeling, we can find relief from the illusion of the moment, and then give way to it again at will. Moreover, we can gain this relief without any such violent transition as occurs in a dream, when we rid ourselves of its terrors only by the act of awaking.

It is obvious that what is affected by poetry of this character is our *will*, and not merely our intellectual powers pure and simple. The word *interest* means, therefore, that which arouses the concern of the individual will, *quod nostrâ interest*; and here it is that beauty is clearly distinguished from interest. The one is an affair of the intellect, and that, too, of the purest and simplest kind. The other works upon the will. Beauty, then, consists in an apprehension of ideas; and knowledge of this character is beyond the range of the principle that nothing happens without a cause. Interest, on the other hand, has its origin nowhere but in the course of events; that is to say, in the complexities which are possible only through the action of this principle in its different forms.

We have now obtained a clear conception of the essential difference between the beauty and the interest of a work of art. We have recognised that beauty is the true end of every art, and therefore, also, of the poetic art. It now remains to raise the question whether the interest of a work of art is a second end, or a means to the exhibition of its beauty; or whether the interest of it is produced by its beauty as an essential concomitant, and comes of itself as soon as it is beautiful; or whether interest is at any rate compatible with the main end of art; or, finally, whether it is a hindrance to it.

In the first place, it is to be observed that the interest of a work of art is confined to works of poetic art. It does not exist in the case of fine art, or of music or architecture. Nay, with these forms of art it is not even conceivable, unless, indeed, the interest be of an entirely personal character, and confined to one or two spectators; as, for example, where a picture is a portrait of some one whom we love or hate; the building, my house or my prison; the music, my wedding dance, or the tune to which I marched to the war. Interest of this kind is clearly quite foreign to the essence and purpose of art; it disturbs our judgment in so far as it makes the purely artistic attitude impossible. It may be, indeed, that to a smaller extent this is true of all interest.

Now, since the interest of a work of art lies in the fact that we have the same kind of sympathy with a poetic representation as with reality, it is obvious that the representation must deceive us for the moment; and this it can do only by its truth. But truth is an element in perfect art. A picture, a poem, should be as true as nature itself; but at the same time it should lay stress on whatever forms the unique character of its subject by drawing out all its essential manifestations, and by rejecting everything that is unessential and accidental. The picture or the poem will thus emphasize its *idea*, and give us that *ideal truth* which is superior to nature.

Truth, then, forms the point that is common both to interest and beauty in a work of art, as it is its truth which produces the illusion. The fact that the truth of which I speak is *ideal truth* might, indeed, be detrimental to the illusion, since it is just here that we have the general difference between poetry and reality, art and nature. But since it is possible for reality to coincide with the ideal, it is not actually necessary that this difference should destroy the illusion. In the case of fine arts there is, in the range of the means which art adopts, a certain limit, and beyond it illusion is impossible. Sculpture, that is to say, gives us mere colourless form; its figures are without eyes and without movement; and painting provides us with no more than a single view, enclosed within strict limits, which separate the picture from the adjacent reality. Here, then, there is no room for illusion, and consequently none for that interest or sympathy which resembles the interest we have in reality; the will is at once excluded, and the object alone is presented to us in a manner that frees it from any personal concern.

It is a highly remarkable fact that a spurious kind of fine art oversteps these limits, produces an illusion of reality, and arouses our interest; but at the same time it destroys the effect which fine art produces, and serves as nothing but a mere means of exhibiting the beautiful, that is, of communicating a knowledge of the ideas which it embodies. I refer to *waxwork*. Here, we might say, is the dividing line which separates it from the province of fine art. When waxwork is properly executed, it produces a perfect illusion; but for that very reason we approach a wax figure as we approach a real man, who, as such, is for the moment an object presented to our will. That is to say, he is an object of interest; he arouses the will, and consequently stills the intellect. We come up to a wax figure with the same reserve and caution as a real man would inspire in us: our will is excited; it waits to see whether he is going to be friendly to us, or the reverse, fly from us, or attack us; in a word, it expects some action of him. But as the figure, nevertheless, shows no sign of life, it produces the impression which is so very disagreeable, namely, of a corpse. This is a case where the interest is of the most complete kind, and yet where there is no work of art at all. In other words, interest is not in itself a real end of art.

The same truth is illustrated by the fact that even in poetry it is only the dramatic and descriptive kind to which interest attaches; for if interest were, with beauty, the aim of art, poetry of the lyrical kind would, for that very reason, not take half so great a position as the other two.

In the second place, if interest were a means in the production of beauty, every interesting work would also be beautiful. That, however, is by no means the case. A drama or a novel may often attract us by its interest, and yet be so utterly deficient in any kind of beauty that we are afterwards ashamed of having wasted our time on it. This applies to many a drama which gives no true picture of the real life of man; which contains characters very superficially drawn, or so distorted as to be actual monstrosities, such as are not to be found in nature; but the course of events and the play of the action are so intricate, and we feel so much for the hero in the situation in which he is placed, that we are not content until we see the knot untangled and the hero rescued. The action is so cleverly governed and guided in its course that we remain in a state of constant curiosity as to what is going to happen, and we are utterly unable to form a guess; so that between eagerness and surprise our interest is kept active; and as we are pleasantly entertained, we do not notice the lapse of time. Most of Kotzebue's plays are of this character. For the mob this is the right thing: it looks for amusement, something to pass the time, not for intellectual perception. Beauty is an affair of such perception; hence sensibility to beauty varies as much as the intellectual faculties themselves. For the inner truth of a representation, and its correspondence with the real nature of humanity, the mob has no sense at all. What is flat and superficial it can grasp, but the depths of human nature are opened to it in vain.

It is also to be observed that dramatic representations which depend for their value on their interest lose by repetition, because they are no longer able to arouse curiosity as to their course, since it is already known. To see them often, makes them stale and tedious. On the other hand, works of which the value lies in their beauty gain by repetition, as they are then more and more understood.

Most novels are on the same footing as dramatic representations of this character. They are creatures of the same sort of imagination as we see in the story-teller of Venice and Naples, who lays a hat on the ground and waits until an audience is assembled. Then he spins a tale which so captivates his hearers that, when he gets to the catastrophe, he makes a round of the crowd, hat in hand, for contributions, without the least fear that his hearers will slip away. Similar story-tellers ply their trade in this country, though in a less direct fashion. They do it through the agency of publishers and circulating libraries. Thus they can avoid going about in rags, like their colleagues elsewhere; they can offer the children of their imagination to the public under the title of novels, short stories, romantic poems, fairy tales, and so on; and the public, in a dressing-gown by the fireside, sits down more at its ease, but also with a greater amount of patience, to the enjoyment of the interest which they provide.

How very little aesthetic value there generally is in productions of this sort is well known; and yet it cannot be denied that many of them are interesting; or else how could they be so popular?

We see, then, in reply to our second question, that interest does not necessarily involve beauty; and, conversely, it is true that beauty does not necessarily involve interest. Significant characters may be represented, that open up the depths of human nature, and it may all be expressed in actions and sufferings of an exceptional kind, so that the real nature of humanity and the world may stand forth in the picture in the clearest and most forcible lines; and yet no high degree of interest may be excited in the course of events by the continued progress of the action, or by the complexity and unexpected solution of the plot. The immortal masterpieces of Shakespeare contain little that excites interest; the action does not go forward in one straight line, but falters, as in *Hamlet*, all through the play; or else it spreads out in breadth, as in *The Merchant of Venice*, whereas length is the proper dimension of interest; or the scenes hang loosely together, as in *Henry IV*. Thus it is that Shakespeare's dramas produce no appreciable effect on the mob.

The dramatic requirement stated by Aristotle, and more particularly the unity of action, have in view the interest of the piece rather than its artistic beauty. It may be said, generally, that these requirements are drawn up in accordance with the principle of sufficient reason to which I have referred above. We know, however, that the *idea*, and, consequently, the beauty of a work of art, exist only for the perceptive intelligence which has freed itself from the domination of that principle. It is just here that we find the distinction between interest and beauty; as it is obvious that interest is part and parcel of the mental attitude which is governed by the principle, whereas beauty is always beyond its range. The best and most striking refutation of the Aristotelian unities is Manzoni's. It may be found in the preface to his dramas.

What is true of Shakespeare's dramatic works is true also of Goethe's. Even *Egmont* makes little effect on the public, because it contains scarcely any complication or development; and if *Egmont* fails, what are we to say of *Tasso* or *Iphigenia*? That the Greek tragedians did not look to interest as a means of working upon the public, is clear from the fact that the material of their masterpieces was almost always known to every one: they selected events which had often been treated dramatically before. This shows us how sensitive was the Greek public to the beautiful, as it did not require the interest of unexpected events and new stories to season its enjoyment.

Neither does the quality of interest often attach to masterpieces of descriptive poetry. Father Homer lays the world and humanity before us in its true nature, but he takes no trouble to attract our sympathy by a complexity of circumstance, or to surprise us by unexpected entanglements. His pace is lingering; he stops at every scene; he puts one picture after another tranquilly before us, elaborating it with care. We experience no passionate emotion in reading him; our demeanour is one of pure perceptive intelligence; he does not arouse our will, but sings it to rest; and it costs us no effort to break off in our reading, for we are not in condition of eager curiosity. This is all still more true of Dante, whose work is not, in the proper sense of the word, an epic, but a descriptive poem. The same thing may be said of the four immortal romances: *Don Quixote, Tristram Shandy, La Nouvelle Heloïse*, and *Wilhelm Meister*. To arouse our interest is by no means the chief aim of these works; in *Tristram Shandy* the hero, even at the end of the book, is only eight years of age.

On the other hand, we must not venture to assert that the quality of interest is not to be found in masterpieces of literature. We have it in Schiller's dramas in an appreciable degree, and consequently they are popular; also in the *Œdipus Rex* of Sophocles. Amongst masterpieces of description, we find it in Ariosto's *Orlando Furioso*; nay, an example of a high degree of interest, bound up with the beautiful, is afforded in an excellent novel by Walter Scott—*The Heart of Midlothian*. This is the most interesting work of fiction that I know, where all the effects due to interest, as I have given them generally in the preceding remarks, may be most clearly observed. At the same time it is a very beautiful romance throughout; it shows the most varied pictures of life, drawn with striking truth; and it exhibits highly different characters with great justice and fidelity.

Interest, then, is certainly compatible with beauty. That was our third question. Nevertheless, a comparatively small admixture of the element of interest may well be found to be most advantageous as far as beauty is concerned; for beauty is and remains the end of art. Beauty is in twofold opposition with interest; firstly, because it lies in the perception of the idea, and such perception takes its object entirely out of the range of the forms enunciated by the principle of sufficient reason; whereas interest has its sphere mainly in circumstance, and it is out of this principle that the complexity of circumstance arises. Secondly, interest works by exciting the will; whereas beauty exists only for the pure perceptive intelligence, which has no will. However, with dramatic and descriptive literature an admixture of interest is necessary, just as a volatile and gaseous substance requires a material basis if it is to be preserved and transferred. The admixture is necessary, partly, indeed, because interest is itself created by the events which have to be devised in order to set the characters in motion; partly because our minds would be weary of watching scene after scene if they had no concern for us, or of passing from one significant picture to another if we were not drawn on by some secret thread. It is this that we call interest; it is the sympathy which the event in itself forces us to feel, and which, by riveting our attention, makes the mind obedient to the poet, and able to follow him into all the parts of his story.

If the interest of a work of art is sufficient to achieve this result, it does all that can be required of it; for its only service is to connect the pictures by which the poet desires to communicate a knowledge of the idea, as if they were pearls, and interest were the thread that holds them together, and makes an ornament out of the whole. But interest is prejudicial to beauty as soon as it oversteps this limit; and this is the case if we are so led away by the interest of a work that whenever we come to any detailed description in a novel, or any lengthy reflection on the part of a character in a drama, we grow impatient and want to put spurs to our author, so that we may follow the development of events with greater speed. Epic and dramatic writings, where beauty and interest are both present in a high degree, may be compared to the working of a watch, where interest is the spring which keeps all the wheels in motion. If it worked unhindered, the watch would run down in a few minutes. Beauty, holding us in the spell of description and reflection, is like the barrel which checks its movement.

Or we may say that interest is the body of a poetic work, and beauty the soul. In the epic and the drama, interest, as a necessary quality of the action, is the matter; and beauty, the form that requires the matter in order to be visible.

PSYCHOLOGICAL OBSERVATIONS.

In the moment when a great affliction overtakes us, we are hurt to find that the world about us is unconcerned and goes its own way. As Goethe says in *Tasso*, how easily it leaves us helpless and alone, and continues its course like the sun and the moon and the other gods:

> *... die Welt, wie sie so leicht,*
> *Uns hülflos, einsam lässt, und ihren Weg,*
> *Wie Sonn' und Mond und andre Götter geht.*

Nay more! it is something intolerable that even we ourselves have to go on with the mechanical round of our daily business, and that thousands of our own actions are and must be unaffected by the pain that throbs within us. And so, to restore the harmony between our outward doings and our inward feelings, we storm and shout, and tear our hair, and stamp with pain or rage.

Our temperament is so *despotic* that we are not satisfied unless we draw everything into our own life, and force all the world to sympathise with us. The only way of achieving this would be to win the love of others, so that the afflictions which oppress our own hearts might oppress theirs as well. Since that is attended with some difficulty, we often choose the shorter way, and blab out our burden of woe to people who do not care, and listen with curiosity, but without sympathy, and much oftener with satisfaction.

Speech and the communication of thought, which, in their mutual relations, are always attended by a slight impulse on the part of the will, are almost a physical necessity. Sometimes, however, the lower animals entertain me much more than the average man. For, in the first place, what can such a man say? It is only conceptions, that is, the driest of ideas, that can be communicated by means of words; and what sort of conceptions has the average man to communicate, if he does not merely tell a story or give a report, neither of which makes conversation? The greatest charm of conversation is the mimetic part of it,—the character that is manifested, be it never so little. Take the best of men; how little he can *say* of what goes on within him, since it is only conceptions that are communicable; and yet a conversation with a clever man is one of the greatest of pleasures.

It is not only that ordinary men have little to say, but what intellect they have puts them in the way of concealing and distorting it; and it is the necessity of practising this concealment that gives them such a pitiable character; so that what they exhibit is not even the little that they have, but a mask and disguise. The lower animals, which have no reason, can conceal nothing; they are altogether *naïve*, and therefore very entertaining, if we have only an eye for the kind of communications which they make. They speak not with words, but with shape and structure, and manner of life, and the things they set about; they express themselves, to an intelligent observer, in a very pleasing and entertaining fashion. It is a varied life that is presented to him, and one that in its manifestation is very different from his own; and yet essentially it is the same. He sees it in its simple form, when reflection is excluded; for with the lower animals life is lived wholly in and for the present moment: it is the present that the animal grasps; it has no care, or at least no conscious care, for the morrow, and no fear of death; and so it is wholly taken up with life and living.

* * * * *

The conversation among ordinary people, when it does not relate to any special matter of fact, but takes a more general character, mostly consists in hackneyed commonplaces, which they alternately repeat to each other with the utmost complacency.[88]

* * * * *

Some men can despise any blessing as soon as they cease to possess it; others only when they have obtained it. The latter are the more unhappy, and the nobler, of the two.

* * * * *

When the aching heart grieves no more over any particular object, but is oppressed by life as a whole, it withdraws, as it were, into itself. There is here a retreat and gradual extinction of the will, whereby the body, which is the manifestation of the will, is slowly but surely undermined; and the individual experiences a steady dissolution of his bonds,—a quiet presentiment of death. Hence the heart which aches has a secret joy of its own; and it is this, I fancy, which the English call "the joy of grief."

The pain that extends to life as a whole, and loosens our hold on it, is the only pain that is really *tragic*. That which attaches to particular objects is a will that is broken, but not resigned; it exhibits the struggle and inner contradiction of the will and of life itself; and it is comic, be it never so violent. It is like the pain of the miser at the loss of his hoard. Even though pain of the tragic kind proceeds from a single definite object, it does not remain there; it takes the separate affliction only as a *symbol* of life as a whole, and transfers it thither.

* * * * *

Vexation is the attitude of the individual as intelligence towards the check imposed upon a strong manifestation of the individual as will. There are two ways of avoiding it: either by repressing the violence of the will—in other words, by virtue; or by keeping the intelligence from dwelling upon the check—in other words, by Stoicism.

* * * * *

---

[88] *Translator's Note.*—This observation is in Schopenhauer's own English.

To win the favour of a very beautiful woman by one's personality alone is perhaps a greater satisfaction to one's vanity than to anything else; for it is an assurance that one's personality is an equivalent for the person that is treasured and desired and defied above all others. Hence it is that despised love is so great a pang, especially when it is associated with well-founded jealousy.

With this joy and this pain, it is probable that vanity is more largely concerned than the senses, because it is only the things of the mind, and not mere sensuality, that produce such violent convulsions. The lower animals are familiar with lust, but not with the passionate pleasures and pains of love.

* * * * *

To be suddenly placed in a strange town or country where the manner of life, possibly even the language, is very different from our own, is, at the first moment, like stepping into cold water. We are brought into sudden contact with a new temperature, and we feel a powerful and superior influence from without which affects us uncomfortably. We find ourselves in a strange element, where we cannot move with ease; and, over and above that, we have the feeling that while everything strikes us as strange, we ourselves strike others in the same way. But as soon as we are a little composed and reconciled to our surroundings, as soon as we have appropriated some of its temperature, we feel an extraordinary sense of satisfaction, as in bathing in cool water; we assimilate ourselves to the new element, and cease to have any necessary pre-occupation with our person. We devote our attention undisturbed to our environment, to which we now feel ourselves superior by being able to view it in an objective and disinterested fashion, instead of being oppressed by it, as before.

* * * * *

When we are on a journey, and all kinds of remarkable objects press themselves on our attention, the intellectual food which we receive is often so large in amount that we have no time for digestion; and we regret that the impressions which succeed one another so quickly leave no permanent trace. But at bottom it is the same with travelling as with reading. How often do we complain that we cannot remember one thousandth part of what we read! In both cases, however, we may console ourselves with the reflection that the things we see and read make an impression on the mind before they are forgotten, and so contribute to its formation and nurture; while that which we only remember does no more than stuff it and puff it out, filling up its hollows with matter that will always be strange to it, and leaving it in itself a blank.

* * * * *

It is the very many and varied forms in which human life is presented to us on our travels that make them entertaining. But we never see more than its outside, such as is everywhere open to public view and accessible to strangers. On the other hand, human life on its inside, the heart and centre, where it lives and moves and shows its character, and in particular that part of the inner side which could be seen at home amongst our relatives, is not seen; we have exchanged it for the outer side. This is why on our travels we see the world like a painted landscape, with a very wide horizon, but no foreground; and why, in time, we get tired of it.

* * * * *

One man is more concerned with the impression which he makes upon the rest of mankind; another, with the impression which the rest of mankind makes upon him. The disposition of the one is subjective; of the other, objective; the one is, in the whole of his existence, more in the nature of an idea which is merely presented; the other, more of the being who presents it.

* * * * *

A woman (with certain exceptions which need not be mentioned) will not take the first step with a man; for in spite of all the beauty she may have, she risks a refusal. A man may be ill in mind or body, or busy, or gloomy, and so not care for advances; and a refusal would be a blow to her vanity. But as soon as he takes the first step, and helps her over this danger, he stands on a footing of equality with her, and will generally find her quite tractable.

* * * * *

The praise with which many men speak of their wives is really given to their own judgment in selecting them. This arises, perhaps, from a feeling of the truth of the saying, that a man shows what he is by the way in which he dies, and by the choice of his wife.

* * * * *

If education or warning were of any avail, how could Seneca's pupil be a Nero?

* * * * *

The Pythagorean[89] principle that *like is known only by like* is in many respects a true one. It explains how it is that every man understands his fellow only in so far as he resembles him, or, at least, is of a similar character. What one man is quite sure of perceiving in another is that which is common to all, namely, the vulgar, petty or mean elements of our nature; here every man has a perfect understanding of his fellows; but the advantage which one man has over another does not exist for the other, who, be the talents in question as extraordinary as they may, will never see anything beyond what he possesses himself, for the very good reason that this is all he wants to see. If there is anything on which he is in doubt, it will give him a vague sense of fear, mixed with pique; because it passes his comprehension, and therefore is uncongenial to him.

This is why it is mind alone that understands mind; why works of genius are wholly understood and valued only by a man of genius, and why it must necessarily be a long time before they indirectly attract attention at the hands of the crowd, for whom they will never, in any true sense, exist. This, too, is why one man will look another in the face, with the impudent assurance that he will never see anything but a miserable resemblance of himself; and this is just what he will see, as he cannot grasp anything beyond it. Hence the bold way in which one man will contradict another. Finally, it is for the same reason that great superiority of mind isolates a man, and that those of high gifts keep themselves aloof from the vulgar (and that means every one); for if they mingle with the crowd, they can communicate only such parts of them as they share with the crowd, and so make themselves *common*. Nay, even though they possess some well-founded and authoritative reputation amongst the crowd, they are not long in losing it, together with any personal weight it may give them, since all are blind to the qualities on which it is based, but have their eyes open to anything that is vulgar and common to themselves. They soon discover the truth of the Arabian proverb: *Joke with a slave, and he'll show you his heels.*

It also follows that a man of high gifts, in his intercourse with others, must always reflect that the best part of him is out of sight in the clouds; so that if he desires to know accurately how much he can be to any one else, he has only to consider how much the man in question is to him. This, as a rule, is precious little; and therefore he is as

---

[89] See Porphyry, *de Vita Pythagorae.*

uncongenial to the other, as the other to him.

* * * * *

Goethe says somewhere that man is not without a vein of veneration. To satisfy this impulse to venerate, even in those who have no sense for what is really worthy, substitutes are provided in the shape of princes and princely families, nobles, titles, orders, and money-bags.

* * * * *

Vague longing and boredom are close akin.

* * * * *

When a man is dead, we envy him no more; and we only half envy him when he is old.

* * * * *

Misanthropy and love of solitude are convertible ideas.

* * * * *

In chess, the object of the game, namely, to checkmate one's opponent, is of arbitrary adoption; of the possible means of attaining it, there is a great number; and according as we make a prudent use of them, we arrive at our goal. We enter on the game of our own choice.

Nor is it otherwise with human life, only that here the entrance is not of our choosing, but is forced on us; and the object, which is to live and exist, seems, indeed, at times as though it were of arbitrary adoption, and that we could, if necessary, relinquish it. Nevertheless it is, in the strict sense of the word, a natural object; that is to say, we cannot relinquish it without giving up existence itself. If we regard our existence as the work of some arbitrary power outside us, we must, indeed, admire the cunning by which that creative mind has succeeded in making us place so much value on an object which is only momentary and must of necessity be laid aside very soon, and which we see, moreover, on reflection, to be altogether vanity—in making, I say, this object so dear to us that we eagerly exert all our strength in working at it; although we knew that as soon as the game is over, the object will exist for us no longer, and that, on the whole, we cannot say what it is that makes it so attractive. Nay, it seems to be an object as arbitrarily adopted as that of checkmating our opponent's king; and, nevertheless, we are always intent on the means of attaining it, and think and brood over nothing else. It is clear that the reason of it is that our intellect is only capable of looking outside, and has no power at all of looking within; and, since this is so, we have come to the conclusion that we must make the best of it.

ON THE WISDOM OF LIFE: APHORISMS

The simple Philistine believes that life is something infinite and unconditioned, and tries to look upon it and live it as though it left nothing to be desired. By method and principle the learned Philistine does the same: he believes that his methods and his principles are unconditionally perfect and objectively valid; so that as soon as he has found them, he has nothing to do but apply them to circumstances, and then approve or condemn. But happiness and truth are not to be seized in this fashion. It is phantoms of them alone that are sent to us here, to stir us to action; the average man pursues the shadow of happiness with unwearied labour; and the thinker, the shadow of truth; and both, though phantoms are all they have, possess in them as much as they can grasp. Life is a language in which certain truths are conveyed to us; could we learn them in some other way, we should not live. Thus it is that wise sayings and prudential maxims will never make up for the lack of experience, or be a substitute for life itself. Still they are not to be despised; for they, too, are a part of life; nay, they should be highly esteemed and regarded as the loose pages which others have copied from the book of truth as it is imparted by the spirit of the world. But they are pages which must needs be imperfect, and can never replace the real living voice. Still less can this be so when we reflect that life, or the book of truth, speaks differently to us all; like the apostles who preached at Pentecost, and instructed the multitude, appearing to each man to speak in his own tongue.

* * * * *

Recognise the truth in yourself, recognise yourself in the truth; and in the same moment you will find, to your astonishment, that the home which you have long been looking for in vain, which has filled your most ardent dreams, is there in its entirety, with every detail of it true, in the very place where you stand. It is there that your heaven touches your earth.

* * * * *

What makes us almost inevitably ridiculous is our serious way of treating the passing moment, as though it necessarily had all the importance which it seems to have. It is only a few great minds that are above this weakness, and, instead of being laughed at, have come to laugh themselves.

* * * * *

The bright and good moments of our life ought to teach us how to act aright when we are melancholy and dull and stupid, by preserving the memory of their results; and the melancholy, dull, and stupid moments should teach us to be modest when we are bright. For we generally value ourselves according to our best and brightest moments; and those in which we are weak and dull and miserable, we regard as no proper part of us. To remember them will teach us to be modest, humble, and tolerant.

Mark my words once for all, my dear friend, and be clever. Men are entirely self-centred, and incapable of looking at things objectively. If you had a dog and wanted to make him fond of you, and fancied that of your hundred rare and excellent characteristics the mongrel would be sure to perceive one, and that that would be sufficient to make him devoted to you body and soul—if, I say, you fancied that, you would be a fool. Pat him, give him something to eat; and for the rest, be what you please: he will not in the least care, but will be your faithful and devoted dog. Now, believe me, it is just the same with men—exactly the same. As Goethe says, man or dog, it is a miserable wretch:

> *Denn ein erbärmlicher Schuft, so wie der Mensch, ist der Hund.*

If you ask why these contemptible fellows are so lucky, it is just because, in themselves and for themselves and to themselves, they are nothing at all. The value which they possess is merely comparative; they exist only for others; they are never more than means; they are never an end and object in themselves; they are mere bait, set to catch others.[90] I do not admit that this rule is susceptible of any exception, that is to say, complete exceptions. There are, it is true, men—though they are sufficiently rare—who enjoy some subjective moments; nay, there are perhaps some who for every hundred subjective moments enjoy a few that are objective; but a higher state of perfection scarcely ever occurs. But do not take yourself for an exception: examine your

---

[90] All this is very euphemistically expressed in the Sophoclean verse:

[Greek: *charis charin gar estin ha tiktous aei*]

This is really an *à priori* justification of politeness; but I could give a still deeper reason for it.

love, your friendship, and consider if your objective judgments are not mostly subjective judgments in disguise; consider if you duly recognise the good qualities of a man who is not fond of you. Then be tolerant: confound it! it's your duty. As you are all so self-centred, recognise your own weakness. You know that you cannot like a man who does not show himself friendly to you; you know that he cannot do so for any length of time unless he likes you, and that he cannot like you unless you show that you are friendly to him; then do it: your false friendliness will gradually become a true one. Your own weakness and subjectivity must have some illusion.

* * * * *

Consider that chance, which, with error, its brother, and folly, its aunt, and malice, its grandmother, rules in this world; which every year and every day, by blows great and small, embitters the life of every son of earth, and yours too; consider, I say, that it is to this wicked power that you owe your prosperity and independence; for it gave you what it refused to many thousands, just to be able to give it to individuals like you. Remembering all this, you will not behave as though you had a right to the possession of its gifts; but you will perceive what a capricious mistress it is that gives you her favours; and therefore when she takes it into her head to deprive you of some or all of them, you will not make a great fuss about her injustice; but you will recognise that what chance gave, chance has taken away; if needs be, you will observe that this power is not quite so favourable to you as she seemed to be hitherto. Why, she might have disposed not only of what she gave you, but also of your honest and hard-earned gains.

But if chance still remains so favourable to you as to give you more than almost all others whose path in life you may care to examine, oh! be happy; do not struggle for the possession of her presents; employ them properly; look upon them as property held from a capricious lord; use them wisely and well.

* * * * *

The Aristotelian principle of keeping the mean in all things is ill suited to the moral law for which it was intended; but it may easily be the best general rule of worldly wisdom, the best precept for a happy life. For life is so full of uncertainty; there are on all sides so many discomforts, burdens, sufferings, dangers, that a safe and happy voyage can be accomplished only by steering carefully through the rocks. As a rule, the fear of the ills we know drive us into the contrary ills; the pain of solitude, for example, drives us into society, and the first society that comes; the discomforts of society drive us into solitude; we exchange a forbidding demeanour for incautious confidence and so on. It is ever the mark of folly to avoid one vice by rushing into its contrary:

Stulti dum vitant vitia in contraria currunt.

Or else we think that we shall find satisfaction in something, and spend all our efforts on it; and thereby we omit to provide for the satisfaction of a hundred other wishes which make themselves felt at their own time. One loss and omission follows another, and there is no end to the misery.

[Greek: Maeden agan] and *nil admirari* are, therefore, excellent rules of worldly wisdom.

* * * * *

We often find that people of great experience are the most frank and cordial in their intercourse with complete strangers, in whom they have no interest whatever. The reason of this is that men of experience know that it is almost impossible for people who stand in any sort of mutual relation to be sincere and open with one another; but that there is always more or less of a strain between them, due to the fact that they are looking after their own interests, whether immediate or remote. They regret the fact, but they know that it is so; hence they leave their own people, rush into the arms of a complete stranger, and in happy confidence open their hearts to him. Thus it is that monks and the like, who have given up the world and are strangers to it, are such good people to turn to for advice.

* * * * *

It is only by practising mutual restraint and self-denial that we can act and talk with other people; and, therefore, if we have to converse at all, it can only be with a feeling of resignation. For if we seek society, it is because we want fresh impressions: these come from without, and are therefore foreign to ourselves. If a man fails to perceive this, and, when he seeks the society of others, is unwilling to practise resignation, and absolutely refuses to deny himself, nay, demands that others, who are altogether different from himself, shall nevertheless be just what he wants them to be for the moment, according to the degree of education which he has reached, or according to his intellectual powers or his mood—the man, I say, who does this, is in contradiction with himself. For while he wants some one who shall be different from himself, and wants him just because he is different, for the sake of society and fresh influence, he nevertheless demands that this other individual shall precisely resemble the imaginary creature who accords with his mood, and have no thoughts but those which he has himself.

Women are very liable to subjectivity of this kind; but men are not free from it either.

I observed once to Goethe, in complaining of the illusion and vanity of life, that when a friend is with us we do not think the same of him as when he is away. He replied: "Yes! because the absent friend is yourself, and he exists only in your head; whereas the friend who is present has an individuality of his own, and moves according to laws of his own, which cannot always be in accordance with those which you form for yourself."

* * * * *

A good supply of resignation is of the first importance in providing for the journey of life. It is a supply which we shall have to extract from disappointed hopes; and the sooner we do it, the better for the rest of the journey.

* * * * *

How should a man be content so long as he fails to obtain complete unity in his inmost being? For as long as two voices alternately speak in him, what is right for one must be wrong for the other. Thus he is always complaining. But has any man ever been completely at one with himself? Nay, is not the very thought a contradiction?

That a man shall attain this inner unity is the impossible and inconsistent pretension put forward by almost all philosophers.[91] For as a man it is natural to him to be at war with himself as long as he lives. While he can be only one thing thoroughly, he has the disposition to be everything else, and the inalienable possibility of being it. If he has made his choice of one thing, all the other possibilities are always open to him, and are constantly claiming to be realised; and he has therefore to be continuously keeping them back, and to be overpowering and killing them as long as he wants to be that one thing. For example, if he wants to think only, and not act and do business, the disposition to the latter is not thereby destroyed all at once; but as long as the thinker lives, he has every hour to keep on killing the acting and pushing man that is within him; always battling with himself, as though he were a monster whose head is no sooner struck off than it grows again. In the same way, if he is resolved to be a saint, he must kill himself so far as he is a being that enjoys and is given over to pleasure; for such he

---

[91] *Audacter licet profitearis, summum bonum esse animi concordian.*—Seneca.

remains as long as he lives. It is not once for all that he must kill himself: he must keep on doing it all his life. If he has resolved upon pleasure, whatever be the way in which it is to be obtained, his lifelong struggle is with a being that desires to be pure and free and holy; for the disposition remains, and he has to kill it every hour. And so on in everything, with infinite modifications; it is now one side of him, and now the other, that conquers; he himself is the battlefield. If one side of him is continually conquering, the other is continually struggling; for its life is bound up with his own, and, as a man, he is the possibility of many contradictions.

How is inner unity even possible under such circumstances? It exists neither in the saint nor in the sinner; or rather, the truth is that no man is wholly one or the other. For it is *men* they have to be; that is, luckless beings, fighters and gladiators in the arena of life.

To be sure, the best thing he can do is to recognise which part of him smarts the most under defeat, and let it always gain the victory. This he will always be able to do by the use of his reason, which is an ever-present fund of ideas. Let him resolve of his own free will to undergo the pain which the defeat of the other part involves. This is *character*. For the battle of life cannot be waged free from all pain; it cannot come to an end without bloodshed; and in any case a man must suffer pain, for he is the conquered as well as the conqueror. *Haec est vivendi conditio.*

* * * * *

The clever man, when he converses, will think less of what he is saying that of the person with whom he is speaking; for then he is sure to say nothing which he will afterwards regret; he is sure not to lay himself open, nor to commit an indiscretion. But his conversation will never be particularly interesting.

An intellectual man readily does the opposite, and with him the person with whom he converses is often no more than the mere occasion of a monologue; and it often happens that the other then makes up for his subordinate *rôle* by lying in wait for the man of intellect, and drawing his secrets out of him.

* * * * *

Nothing betrays less knowledge of humanity than to suppose that, if a man has a great many friends, it is a proof of merit and intrinsic value: as though men gave their friendship according to value and merit! as though they were not, rather, just like dogs, which love the person that pats them and gives them bits of meat, and never trouble themselves about anything else! The man who understands how to pat his fellows best, though they be the nastiest brutes,—that's the man who has many friends.

It is the converse that is true. Men of great intellectual worth, or, still more, men of genius, can have only very few friends; for their clear eye soon discovers all defects, and their sense of rectitude is always being outraged afresh by the extent and the horror of them. It is only extreme necessity that can compel such men not to betray their feelings, or even to stroke the defects as if they were beautiful additions. Personal love (for we are not speaking of the reverence which is gained by authority) cannot be won by a man of genius, unless the gods have endowed him with an indestructible cheerfulness of temper, a glance that makes the world look beautiful, or unless he has succeeded by degrees in taking men exactly as they are; that is to say, in making a fool of the fools, as is right and proper. On the heights we must expect to be solitary.

* * * * *

Our constant discontent is for the most part rooted in the impulse of self-preservation. This passes into a kind of selfishness, and makes a duty out of the maxim that we should always fix our minds upon what we lack, so that we may endeavour to procure it. Thus it is that we are always intent on finding out what we want, and on thinking of it; but that maxim allows us to overlook undisturbed the things which we already possess; and so, as soon as we have obtained anything, we give it much less attention than before. We seldom think of what we have, but always of what we lack.

This maxim of egoism, which has, indeed, its advantages in procuring the means to the end in view, itself concurrently destroys the ultimate end, namely, contentment; like the bear in the fable that throws a stone at the hermit to kill the fly on his nose. We ought to wait until need and privation announce themselves, instead of looking for them. Minds that are naturally content do this, while hypochondrists do the reverse.

* * * * *

A man's nature is in harmony with itself when he desires to be nothing but what he is; that is to say, when he has attained by experience a knowledge of his strength and of his weakness, and makes use of the one and conceals the other, instead of playing with false coin, and trying to show a strength which he does not possess. It is a harmony which produces an agreeable and rational character; and for the simple reason that everything which makes the man and gives him his mental and physical qualities is nothing but the manifestation of his will; is, in fact, what he *wills*. Therefore it is the greatest of all inconsistencies to wish to be other than we are.

* * * * *

People of a strange and curious temperament can be happy only under strange circumstances, such as suit their nature, in the same way as ordinary circumstances suit the ordinary man; and such circumstances can arise only if, in some extraordinary way, they happen to meet with strange people of a character different indeed, but still exactly suited to their own. That is why men of rare or strange qualities are seldom happy.

* * * * *

All this pleasure is derived from the use and consciousness of power; and the greatest of pains that a man can feel is to perceive that his powers fail just when he wants to use them. Therefore it will be advantageous for every man to discover what powers he possesses, and what powers he lacks. Let him, then, develop the powers in which he is pre-eminent, and make a strong use of them; let him pursue the path where they will avail him; and even though he has to conquer his inclinations, let him avoid the path where such powers are requisite as he possesses only in a low degree. In this way he will often have a pleasant consciousness of strength, and seldom a painful consciousness of weakness; and it will go well with him. But if he lets himself be drawn into efforts demanding a kind of strength quite different from that in which he is pre-eminent, he will experience humiliation; and this is perhaps the most painful feeling with which a man can be afflicted.

Yet there are two sides to everything. The man who has insufficient self-confidence in a sphere where he has little power, and is never ready to make a venture, will on the one hand not even learn how to use the little power that he has; and on the other, in a sphere in which he would at least be able to achieve something, there will be a complete absence of effort, and consequently of pleasure. This is always hard to bear; for a man can never draw a complete blank in any department of human welfare without feeling some pain.

* * * * *

As a child, one has no conception of the inexorable character of the laws of nature, and of the stubborn way in which everything persists in remaining what it is. The child believes that even lifeless things are disposed to yield to it; perhaps because it feels itself one with nature, or, from mere unacquaintance with the world, believes that nature is disposed to be friendly. Thus it was that when I was a child, and had thrown my shoe into a large vessel full of milk, I was discovered entreating the shoe to jump out. Nor is a child on its guard against animals until it learns that they are ill-natured and spiteful. But not before we have gained mature experience do we recognise that human character is unalterable; that no entreaty, or representation, or example, or benefit, will bring a man to give up his ways; but that, on the contrary, every man is compelled to follow his own mode of acting and thinking, with the necessity of a law of nature; and that, however we take him, he always remains the same. It is only after we have obtained a clear and profound knowledge of this fact that we give up trying to persuade people, or to alter them and bring them round to our way of thinking. We try to accommodate ourselves to theirs instead, so far as they are indispensable to us, and to keep away from them so far as we cannot possibly agree.

Ultimately we come to perceive that even in matters of mere intellect—although its laws are the same for all, and the subject as opposed to the object of thought does not really enter into individuality—there is, nevertheless, no certainty that the whole truth of any matter can be communicated to any one, or that any one can be persuaded or compelled to assent to it; because, as Bacon says, *intellectus humanus luminis sicci non est*: the light of the human intellect is coloured by interest and passion.

* * * * *

It is just because *all happiness is of a negative character* that, when we succeed in being perfectly at our ease, we are not properly conscious of it. Everything seems to pass us softly and gently, and hardly to touch us until the moment is over; and then it is the positive feeling of something lacking that tells us of the happiness which has vanished; it is then that we observe that we have failed to hold it fast, and we suffer the pangs of self-reproach as well as of privation.

* * * * *

Every happiness that a man enjoys, and almost every friendship that he cherishes, rest upon illusion; for, as a rule, with increase of knowledge they are bound to vanish. Nevertheless, here as elsewhere, a man should courageously pursue truth, and never weary of striving to settle accounts with himself and the world. No matter what happens to the right or to the left of him,—be it a chimæra or fancy that makes him happy, let him take heart and go on, with no fear of the desert which widens to his view. Of one thing only must he be quite certain: that under no circumstances will he discover any lack of worth in himself when the veil is raised; the sight of it would be the Gorgon that would kill him. Therefore, if he wants to remain undeceived, let him in his inmost being feel his own worth. For to feel the lack of it is not merely the greatest, but also the only true affliction; all other sufferings of the mind may not only be healed, but may be immediately relieved, by the secure consciousness of worth. The man who is assured of it can sit down quietly under sufferings that would otherwise bring him to despair; and though he has no pleasures, no joys and no friends, he can rest in and on himself; so powerful is the comfort to be derived from a vivid consciousness of this advantage; a comfort to be preferred to every other earthly blessing. Contrarily, nothing in the world can relieve a man who knows his own worthlessness; all that he can do is to conceal it by deceiving people or deafening them with his noise; but neither expedient will serve him very long.

* * * * *

We must always try to preserve large views. If we are arrested by details we shall get confused, and see things awry. The success or the failure of the moment, and the impression that they make, should count for nothing.[92]

* * * * *

How difficult it is to learn to understand oneself, and clearly to recognise what it is that one wants before anything else; what it is, therefore, that is most immediately necessary to our happiness; then what comes next; and what takes the third and the fourth place, and so on.

Yet, without this knowledge, our life is planless, like a captain without a compass.

* * * * *

The sublime melancholy which leads us to cherish a lively conviction of the worthlessness of everything of all pleasures and of all mankind, and therefore to long for nothing, but to feel that life is merely a burden which must be borne to an end that cannot be very distant, is a much happier state of mind than any condition of desire, which, be it never so cheerful, would have us place a value on the illusions of the world, and strive to attain them.

---

[92] *Translator's Note.*—Schopenhauer, for some reason that is not apparent, wrote this remark in French.

This is a fact which we learn from experience; and it is clear, *à priori*, that one of these is a condition of illusion, and the other of knowledge.

Whether it is better to marry or not to marry is a question which in very many cases amounts to this: Are the cares of love more endurable than the anxieties of a livelihood?

* * * * *

Marriage is a trap which nature sets for us.[93]

* * * * *

Poets and philosophers who are married men incur by that very fact the suspicion that they are looking to their own welfare, and not to the interests of science and art.

* * * * *

Habit is everything. Hence to be calm and unruffled is merely to anticipate a habit; and it is a great advantage not to need to form it.

* * * * *

"Personality is the element of the greatest happiness." Since *pain* and *boredom* are the two chief enemies of human happiness, nature has provided our personality with a protection against both. We can ward off pain, which is more often of the mind than of the body, by *cheerfulness*; and boredom by *intelligence*. But neither of these is akin to the other; nay, in any high degree they are perhaps incompatible. As Aristotle remarks, genius is allied to melancholy; and people of very cheerful disposition are only intelligent on the surface. The better, therefore, anyone is by nature armed against one of these evils, the worse, as a rule, is he armed against the other.

There is no human life that is free from pain and boredom; and it is a special favour on the part of fate if a man is chiefly exposed to the evil against which nature has armed him the better; if fate, that is, sends a great deal of pain where there is a very cheerful temper in which to bear it, and much leisure where there is much intelligence, but not *vice versâ*. For if a man is intelligent, he feels pain doubly or trebly; and a cheerful but unintellectual temper finds solitude and unoccupied leisure altogether unendurable.

---

[93] *Translator's Note.*—Also in French.

* * * * *

In the sphere of thought, absurdity and perversity remain the masters of this world, and their dominion is suspended only for brief periods. Nor is it otherwise in art; for there genuine work, seldom found and still more seldom appreciated, is again and again driven out by dullness, insipidity, and affectation.

It is just the same in the sphere of action. Most men, says Bias, are bad. Virtue is a stranger in this world; and boundless egoism, cunning and malice, are always the order of the day. It is wrong to deceive the young on this point, for it will only make them feel later on that their teachers were the first to deceive them. If the object is to render the pupil a better man by telling him that others are excellent, it fails; and it would be more to the purpose to say: Most men are bad, it is for you to be better. In this way he would, at least, be sent out into the world armed with a shrewd foresight, instead of having to be convinced by bitter experience that his teachers were wrong.

All ignorance is dangerous, and most errors must be dearly paid. And good luck must he have that carries unchastised an error in his head unto his death.[94]

* * * * *

Every piece of success has a doubly beneficial effect upon us when, apart from the special and material advantage which it brings it is accompanied by the enlivening assurance that the world, fate, or the daemon within, does not mean so badly with us, nor is so opposed to our prosperity as we had fancied; when, in fine, it restores our courage to live.

Similarly, every misfortune or defeat has, in the contrary sense, an effect that is doubly depressing.

* * * * *

If we were not all of us exaggeratedly interested in ourselves, life would be so uninteresting that no one could endure it.

* * * * *

---

[94] *Translator's Note.*—This, again, is Schopenhauer's own English.

Everywhere in the world, and under all circumstances, it is only by force that anything can be done; but power is mostly in bad hands, because baseness is everywhere in a fearful majority.

* * * * *

Why should it be folly to be always intent on getting the greatest possible enjoyment out of the moment, which is our only sure possession? Our whole life is no more than a magnified present, and in itself as fleeting.

* * * * *

As a consequence of his individuality and the position in which he is placed, everyone without exception lives in a certain state of limitation, both as regards his ideas and the opinions which he forms. Another man is also limited, though not in the same way; but should he succeed in comprehending the other's limitation he can confuse and abash him, and put him to shame, by making him feel what his limitation is, even though the other be far and away his superior. Shrewd people often employ this circumstance to obtain a false and momentary advantage.

* * * * *

The only genuine superiority is that of the mind and character; all other kinds are fictitious, affected, false; and it is good to make them feel that it is so when they try to show off before the superiority that is true.[95]

* * * * *

All the world's a stage,
And all the men and women merely players.

Exactly! Independently of what a man really is in himself, he has a part to play, which fate has imposed upon him from without, by determining his rank, education, and circumstances. The most immediate application of this truth appears to me to be that in life, as on the stage, we must distinguish between the actor and his part; distinguish, that is, the man in himself from his position and reputation—from the part which rank and circumstances have imposed

---

[95] *Translator's Note.*—In the original this also is in French.

upon him. How often it is that the worst actor plays the king, and the best the beggar! This may happen in life, too; and a man must be very *crude* to confuse the actor with his part.

* * * * *

Our life is so poor that none of the treasures of the world can make it rich; for the sources of enjoyment are soon found to be all very scanty, and it is in vain that we look for one that will always flow. Therefore, as regards our own welfare, there are only two ways in which we can use wealth. We can either spend it in ostentatious pomp, and feed on the cheap respect which our imaginary glory will bring us from the infatuated crowd; or, by avoiding all expenditure that will do us no good, we can let our wealth grow, so that we may have a bulwark against misfortune and want that shall be stronger and better every day; in view of the fact that life, though it has few delights, is rich in evils.

* * * * *

It is just because our real and inmost being is *will* that it is only by its exercise that we can attain a vivid consciousness of existence, although this is almost always attended by pain. Hence it is that existence is essentially painful, and that many persons for whose wants full provision is made arrange their day in accordance with extremely regular, monotonous, and definite habits. By this means they avoid all the pain which the movement of the will produces; but, on the other hand, their whole existence becomes a series of scenes and pictures that mean nothing. They are hardly aware that they exist. Nevertheless, it is the best way of settling accounts with life, so long as there is sufficient change to prevent an excessive feeling of boredom. It is much better still if the Muses give a man some worthy occupation, so that the pictures which fill his consciousness have some meaning, and yet not a meaning that can be brought into any relation with his will.

* * * * *

A man is *wise* only on condition of living in a world full of fools.

GENIUS AND VIRTUE.

When I think, it is the spirit of the world which is striving to express its thought; it is nature which is trying to know and fathom itself. It is not the thoughts of some other mind, which I am endeavouring to trace; but it is I who transform that which exists into something which is known and thought, and would otherwise neither come into being nor continue in it.

In the realm of physics it was held for thousands of years to be a fact beyond question that water was a simple and consequently an original element. In the same way in the realm of metaphysics it was held for a still longer period that the *ego* was a simple and consequently an indestructible entity. I have shown, however, that it is composed of two heterogeneous parts, namely, the *Will*, which is metaphysical in its character, a thing in itself, and the *knowing subject*, which is physical and a mere phenomenon.

Let me illustrate what I mean. Take any large, massive, heavy building: this hard, ponderous body that fills so much space exists, I tell you, only in the soft pulp of the brain. There alone, in the human brain, has it any being. Unless you understand this, you can go no further.

Truly it is the world itself that is a miracle; the world of material bodies. I looked at two of them. Both were heavy, symmetrical, and beautiful. One was a jasper vase with golden rim and golden handles; the other was an organism, an animal, a man. When I had sufficiently admired their exterior, I asked my attendant genius to allow me to examine the inside of them; and I did so. In the vase I found nothing but the force of gravity and a certain obscure desire, which took the form of chemical affinity. But when I entered into the other—how shall I express my astonishment at what I saw? It is more incredible than all the fairy tales and fables that were ever conceived. Nevertheless, I shall try to describe it, even at the risk of finding no credence for my tale.

In this second thing, or rather in the upper end of it, called the head, which on its exterior side looks like anything else—a body in space, heavy, and so on—I found no less an object than the whole world itself, together with the whole of the space in which all of it exists, and the whole of the time in which all of it moves, and finally everything that fills both time and space in all its variegated and infinite character; nay, strangest sight of all, I found myself walking about in it! It was no picture that I saw; it was no peep-show, but reality itself. This it is that is really and truly to be found in a thing which is no bigger than a cabbage, and which, on occasion, an executioner might strike off at a blow, and suddenly smother that world in darkness and night. The world, I say, would vanish, did not heads grow like mushrooms, and were there not always plenty of them ready to snatch it up as it is sinking down into nothing, and keep it going like a ball. This world is an idea which they all have in common, and they express the community of their thought by the word "objectivity."

In the face of this vision I felt as if I were Ardschuna when Krishna appeared to him in his true majesty, with his hundred thousand arms and eyes and mouths.

When I see a wide landscape, and realise that it arises by the operation of the functions of my brain, that is to say, of time, space, and casuality, on certain spots which have gathered on my retina, I feel that I carry it within me. I have an extraordinarily clear consciousness of the identity of my own being with that of the external world.

Nothing provides so vivid an illustration of this identity as a *dream*. For in a dream other people appear to be totally distinct from us, and to possess the most perfect objectivity, and a nature which is quite different from ours, and which often puzzles, surprises, astonishes, or terrifies us; and yet it is all our own self. It is even so with the will, which sustains the whole of the external world and gives it life; it is the same will that is in ourselves, and it is there alone that we are immediately conscious of it. But it is the intellect, in ourselves and in others, which makes all these miracles possible; for it is the intellect which everywhere divides actual being into subject and object; it is a hall of phantasmagorical mystery, inexpressibly marvellous, incomparably magical.

The difference in degree of mental power which sets so wide a gulf between the genius and the ordinary mortal rests, it is true, upon nothing else than a more or less perfect development of the cerebral system. But it is this very difference which is so important, because the whole of the real world in which we live and move possesses an existence only in relation to this cerebral system. Accordingly, the difference between a genius and an ordinary man is a total diversity of world and existence. The difference between man and the lower animals may be similarly explained.

When Momus was said to ask for a window in the breast, it was an allegorical joke, and we cannot even imagine such a contrivance to be a possibility; but it would be quite possible to imagine that the skull and its integuments were transparent, and then, good heavens! what differences should we see in the size, the form, the quality, the movement of the brain! what degrees of value! A great mind would inspire as much respect at first sight as three stars on a man's breast, and what a miserable figure would be cut by many a one who wore them!

Men of genius and intellect, and all those whose mental and theoretical qualities are far more developed than their moral and practical qualities—men, in a word, who have more mind than character—are often not only awkward and ridiculous in matters of daily life, as has been observed by Plato in the seventh book of the *Republic*, and portrayed by Goethe in his *Tasso*; but they are often, from a moral point of view, weak and contemptible creatures as well; nay, they might almost be called bad men. Of this Rousseau has given us genuine examples. Nevertheless, that better consciousness which is the source of all virtue is often stronger in them than in many of those whose actions are nobler than their thoughts; nay, it may be said that those who think nobly have a better acquaintance with virtue, while the others make a better practice of it. Full of zeal for the good and for the beautiful, they would fain fly up to heaven in a straight line; but the grosser elements of this earth oppose their flight, and they sink back again. They are like born artists, who have no knowledge of technique, or find that the marble is too hard for their fingers. Many a man who has much less enthusiasm for the good, and a far shallower acquaintance with its depths, makes a better thing of it in practice; he looks down upon the noble thinkers with contempt, and he has a right to do it; nevertheless, he does not understand them, and they despise him in their turn, and not unjustly. They are to blame; for every living man has, by the fact of his living, signed the conditions of life; but they are still more to be pitied. They achieve their redemption, not on the way of virtue, but on a path of their own; and they are saved, not by works, but by faith.

Men of no genius whatever cannot bear solitude: they take no pleasure in the contemplation of nature and the world. This arises from the fact that they never lose sight of their own will, and therefore they see nothing of the objects of the world but the bearing of such objects upon their will and person. With objects which have no such bearing there sounds within them a constant note: *It is nothing to me*, which is the fundamental base in all their music. Thus all things seem to them to wear a bleak, gloomy, strange, hostile aspect. It is only for their will that they seem to have any perceptive faculties at all; and it is, in fact, only a moral and not a theoretical tendency, only a moral and not an intellectual value, that their life possesses. The lower animals bend their heads to the ground, because all that they want to see is what touches their welfare, and they can never come to contemplate things from a really objective point of view. It is very seldom that unintellectual men make a true use of their erect position, and then it is only when they are moved by some intellectual influence outside them.

The man of intellect or genius, on the other hand, has more of the character of the eternal subject that knows, than of the finite subject that wills; his knowledge is not quite engrossed and captivated by his will, but passes beyond it; he is the son, *not of the bondwoman, but of the free*. It is not only a moral but also a theoretical tendency that is evinced in his life; nay, it might perhaps be said that to a certain extent he is beyond morality. Of great villainy he is totally incapable; and his conscience is less oppressed by ordinary sin than the conscience of the ordinary man, because life, as it were, is a game, and he sees through it.

The relation between *genius* and *virtue* is determined by the following considerations. Vice is an impulse of the will so violent in its demands that it affirms its own life by denying the life of others. The only kind of knowledge that is useful to the will is the knowledge that a given effect is produced by a certain cause. Genius itself is a kind of knowledge, namely, of ideas; and it is a knowledge which is unconcerned with any principle of causation. The man who is devoted to knowledge of this character is not employed in the business of the will. Nay, every man who is devoted to the purely objective contemplation of the world (and it is this that is meant by the knowledge of ideas) completely loses sight of his will and its objects, and pays no further regard to the interests of his own person, but becomes a pure intelligence free of any admixture of will.

Where, then, devotion to the intellect predominates over concern for the will and its objects, it shows that the man's will is not the principal element in his being, but that in proportion to his intelligence it is weak. Violent desire, which is the root of all vice, never allows a man to arrive at the pure and disinterested contemplation of the world, free from any relation to the will, such as constitutes the quality of genius; but here the intelligence remains the constant slave of the will.

Since genius consists in the perception of ideas, and men of genius _contemplate_ their object, it may be said that it is only the eye which is any real evidence of genius. For the contemplative gaze has something steady and vivid about it; and with the eye of genius it is often the case, as with Goethe, that the white membrane over the pupil is visible. With violent, passionate men the same thing may also happen, but it arises from a different cause, and may be easily distinguished by the fact that the eyes roll. Men of no genius at all have no interest in the idea expressed by an object, but only in the relations in which that object stands to others, and finally to their own person. Thus it is that they never indulge in contemplation, or are soon done with it, and rarely fix their eyes long upon any object; and so their eyes do not wear the mark of genius which I have described. Nay, the regular Philistine does the direct opposite of contemplating—he spies. If he looks at anything it is to pry into it; as may be specially observed when he screws up his eyes, which he frequently does, in order to see the clearer. Certainly, no real man of genius ever does this, at least habitually, even though he is short-sighted.

What I have said will sufficiently illustrate the conflict between genius and vice. It may be, however, nay, it is often the case, that genius is attended by a strong will; and as little as men of genius were ever consummate rascals, were they ever perhaps perfect saints either.

Let me explain. Virtue is not exactly a positive weakness of the will; it is, rather, an intentional restraint imposed upon its violence through a knowledge of it in its inmost being as manifested in the world. This knowledge of the world, the inmost being of which is communicable only in *ideas*, is common both to the genius and to the saint. The distinction between the two is that the genius reveals his knowledge by rendering it in some form of his own choice, and the product is Art. For this the saint, as such, possesses no direct faculty; he makes an immediate application of his knowledge to his own will, which is thus led into a denial of the world. With the saint knowledge is only a means to an end, whereas the genius remains at the stage of knowledge, and has his pleasure in it, and reveals it by rendering what he knows in his art.

In the hierarchy of physical organisation, strength of will is attended by a corresponding growth in the intelligent faculties. A high degree of knowledge, such as exists in the genius, presupposes a powerful will, though, at the same time, a will that is subordinate to the intellect. In other words, both the intellect and the will are strong, but the intellect is the stronger of the two. Unless, as happens in the case of the saint, the intellect is at once applied to the will, or, as in the case of the artist, it finds its pleasures in a reproduction of itself, the will remains untamed. Any strength that it may lose is due to the predominance of pure objective intelligence which is concerned with the contemplation of ideas, and is not, as in the case of the common or the bad man, wholly occupied with the objects of the will. In the interval, when the genius is no longer engaged in the contemplation of ideas, and his intelligence is again applied to the will and its objects, the will is re-awakened in all its strength. Thus it is that men of genius often have very violent desires, and are addicted to sensual pleasure and to anger. Great crimes, however, they do not commit; because, when the opportunity of them offers, they recognise their idea, and see it very vividly and clearly. Their intelligence is thus directed to the idea, and so gains the predominance over the will, and turns its course, as with the saint; and the crime is uncommitted.

The genius, then, always participates to some degree in the characteristics of the saint, as he is a man of the same qualification; and, contrarily, the saint always participates to some degree in the characteristics of the genius.

The good-natured character, which is common, is to be distinguished from the saintly by the fact that it consists in a weakness of will, with a somewhat less marked weakness of intellect. A lower degree of the knowledge of the world as revealed in ideas here suffices to check and control a will that is weak in itself. Genius and sanctity are far removed from good-nature, which is essentially weak in all its manifestations.

Apart from all that I have said, so much at least is clear. What appears under the forms of time, space, and casuality, and vanishes again, and in reality is nothing, and reveals its nothingness by death—this vicious and fatal appearance is the will. But what does not appear, and is no phenomenon, but rather the noumenon; what makes appearance possible; what is not subject to the principle of causation, and therefore has no vain or vanishing existence, but abides for ever unchanged in the midst of a world full of suffering, like a ray of light in a storm,—free, therefore, from all pain and fatality,—this, I say, is the intelligence. The man who is more intelligence than will, is thereby delivered, in respect of the greatest part of him, from nothingness and death; and such a man is in his nature a genius.

By the very fact that he lives and works, the man who is endowed with genius makes an entire sacrifice of himself in the interests of everyone. Accordingly, he is free from the obligation to make a particular sacrifice for individuals; and thus he can refuse many demands which others are rightly required to meet. He suffers and achieves more than all the others.

The spring which moves the genius to elaborate his works is not fame, for that is too uncertain a quality, and when it is seen at close quarters, of little worth. No amount of fame will make up for the labour of attaining it:

Nulla est fama tuum par æquiparare laborem.

Nor is it the delight that a man has in his work; for that too is outweighed by the effort which he has to make. It is, rather, an instinct *sui generis*; in virtue of which the genius is driven to express what he sees and feels in some permanent shape, without being conscious of any further motive.

It is manifest that in so far as it leads an individual to sacrifice himself for his species, and to live more in the species than in himself, this impulse is possessed of a certain resemblance with such modifications of the sexual impulse as are peculiar to man. The modifications to which I refer are those that confine this impulse to certain individuals of the other sex, whereby the interests of the species are attained. The individuals who are actively affected by this impulse may be said to sacrifice themselves for the species, by their passion for each other, and the disadvantageous conditions thereby imposed upon them,—in a word, by the institution of marriage. They may be said to be serving the interests of the species rather than the interests of the individual.

The instinct of the genius does, in a higher fashion, for the idea, what passionate love does for the will. In both cases there are peculiar pleasures and peculiar pains reserved for the individuals who in this way serve the interests of the species; and they live in a state of enhanced power.

The genius who decides once for all to live for the interests of the species in the way which he chooses is neither fitted nor called upon to do it in the other. It is a curious fact that the perpetuation of a man's name is effected in both ways.

In music the finest compositions are the most difficult to understand. They are only for the trained intelligence. They consist of long movements, where it is only after a labyrinthine maze that the fundamental note is recovered. It is just so with genius; it is only after a course of struggle, and doubt, and error, and much reflection and vacillation, that great minds attain their equilibrium. It is the longest pendulum that makes the greatest swing. Little minds soon come to terms with themselves and the world, and then fossilise; but the others flourish, and are always alive and in motion.

The essence of genius is a measure of intellectual power far beyond that which is required to serve the individual's will. But it is a measure of a merely relative character, and it may be reached by lowering the degree of the will, as well as by raising that of the intellect. There are men whose intellect predominates over their will, and are yet not possessed of genius in any proper sense. Their intellectual powers do, indeed, exceed the ordinary, though not to any great extent, but their will is weak. They have no violent desires; and therefore they are more concerned with mere knowledge than with the satisfaction of any aims. Such men possess talent; they are intelligent, and at the same time very contented and cheerful.

A clear, cheerful and reasonable mind, such as brings a man happiness, is dependent on the relation established between his intellect and his will—a relation in which the intellect is predominant. But genius and a great mind depend on the relation between a man's intellect and that of other people—a relation in which his intellect must exceed theirs, and at the same time his will may also be proportionately stronger. That is the reason why genius and happiness need not necessarily exist together.

When the individual is distraught by cares or pleasantry, or tortured by the violence of his wishes and desires, the genius in him is enchained and cannot move. It is only when care and desire are silent that the air is free enough for genius to live in it. It is then that the bonds of matter are cast aside, and the pure spirit—the pure, knowing subject—remains. Hence, if a man has any genius, let him guard himself from pain, keep care at a distance, and limit his desires; but those of them which he cannot suppress let him satisfy to the full. This is the only way in which he will make the best use of his rare existence, to his own pleasure and the world's profit.

To fight with need and care or desires, the satisfaction of which is refused and forbidden, is good enough work for those who, were they free of would have to fight with boredom, and so take to bad practices; but not for the man whose time, if well used, will bear fruit for centuries to come. As Diderot says, he is not merely a moral being.

Mechanical laws do not apply in the sphere of chemistry, nor do chemical laws in the sphere in which organic life is kindled. In the same way, the rules which avail for ordinary men will not do for the exceptions, nor will their pleasures either.

It is a persistent, uninterrupted activity that constitutes the superior mind. The object to which this activity is directed is a matter of subordinate importance; it has no essential bearing on the superiority in question, but only on the individual who possesses it. All that education can do is to determine the direction which this activity shall take; and that is the reason why a man's nature is so much more important than his education. For education is to natural faculty what a wax nose is to a real one; or what the moon and the planets are to the sun. In virtue of his education a man says, not what he thinks himself, but what others have thought and he has learned as a matter of training; and what he does is not what he wants, but what he has been accustomed to do.

The lower animals perform many intelligent functions much better than man; for instance, the finding of their way back to the place from which they came, the recognition of individuals, and so on. In the same way, there are many occasions in real life to which the genius is incomparably less equal and fitted than the ordinary man. Nay more: just as animals never commit a folly in the strict sense of the word, so the average man is not exposed to folly in the same degree as the genius.

The average man is wholly relegated to the sphere of *being*; the genius, on the other hand, lives and moves chiefly in the sphere of *knowledge*. This gives rise to a twofold distinction. In the first place, a man can be one thing only, but he may *know* countless things, and thereby, to some extent, identify himself with them, by participating in what Spinoza calls their *esse objectivum*. In the second place, the world, as I have elsewhere observed, is fine enough in appearance, but in reality dreadful; for torment is the condition of all life.

It follows from the first of these distinctions that the life of the average man is essentially one of the greatest boredom; and thus we see the rich warring against boredom with as much effort and as little respite as fall to the poor in their struggle with need and adversity. And from the second of them it follows that the life of the average man is overspread with a dull, turbid, uniform gravity; whilst the brow of genius glows with mirth of a unique character, which, although he has sorrows of his own more poignant than those of the average man, nevertheless breaks out afresh, like the sun through clouds. It is when the genius is overtaken by an affliction which affects others as well as himself, that this quality in him is most in evidence; for then he is seen to be like man, who alone can laugh, in comparison with the beast of the field, which lives out its life grave and dull.

It is the curse of the genius that in the same measure in which others think him great and worthy of admiration, he thinks them small and miserable creatures. His whole life long he has to suppress this opinion; and, as a rule, they suppress theirs as well. Meanwhile, he is condemned to live in a bleak world, where he meets no equal, as it were an island where there are no inhabitants but monkeys and parrots.

Moreover, he is always troubled by the illusion that from a distance a monkey looks like a man.

Vulgar people take a huge delight in the faults and follies of great men; and great men are equally annoyed at being thus reminded of their kinship with them.

The real dignity of a man of genius or great intellect, the trait which raises him over others and makes him worthy of respect, is at bottom the fact, that the only unsullied and innocent part of human nature, namely, the intellect, has the upper hand in him? and prevails; whereas, in the other there is nothing but sinful will, and just as much intellect as is requisite for guiding his steps,—- rarely any more, very often somewhat less,—and of what use is it?

It seems to me that genius might have its root in a certain perfection and vividness of the memory as it stretches back over the events of past life. For it is only by dint of memory, which makes our life in the strict sense a complete whole, that we attain a more profound and comprehensive understanding of it.

On Human Nature.

HUMAN NATURE.

Truths of the physical order may possess much external significance, but internal significance they have none. The latter is the privilege of intellectual and moral truths, which are concerned with the objectivation of the will in its highest stages, whereas physical truths are concerned with it in its lowest.

For example, if we could establish the truth of what up till now is only a conjecture, namely, that it is the action of the sun which produces thermoelectricity at the equator; that this produces terrestrial magnetism; and that this magnetism, again, is the cause of the *aurora borealis*, these would be truths externally of great, but internally of little, significance. On the other hand, examples of internal significance are furnished by all great and true philosophical systems; by the catastrophe of every good tragedy; nay, even by the observation of human conduct in the extreme manifestations of its morality and immorality, of its good and its evil character. For all these are expressions of that reality which takes outward shape as the world, and which, in the highest stages of its objectivation, proclaims its innermost nature.

To say that the world has only a physical and not a moral significance is the greatest and most pernicious of all errors, the fundamental blunder, the real perversity of mind and temper; and, at bottom, it is doubtless the tendency which faith personifies as Anti-Christ. Nevertheless, in spite of all religions—and they are systems which one and all maintain the opposite, and seek to establish it in their mythical way—this fundamental error never becomes quite extinct, but raises its head from time to time afresh, until universal indignation compels it to hide itself once more.

Yet, however certain we may feel of the moral significance of life and the world, to explain and illustrate it, and to resolve the contradiction between this significance and the world as it is, form a task of great difficulty; so great, indeed, as to make it possible that it has remained for me to exhibit the true and only genuine and sound basis of morality everywhere and at all times effective, together with the results to which it leads. The actual facts of morality are too much on my side for me to fear that my theory can ever be replaced or upset by any other.

However, so long as even my ethical system continues to be ignored by the professorial world, it is Kant's moral principle that prevails in the universities. Among its various forms the one which is most in favour at present is "the dignity of man." I have already exposed the absurdity of this doctrine in my treatise on the *Foundation of Morality*.[96] Therefore I will only say here that if the question were asked on what the alleged dignity of man rests, it would not be long before the answer was made that it rests upon his morality. In other words, his morality rests upon his dignity, and his dignity rests upon his morality.

But apart from this circular argument it seems to me that the idea of dignity can be applied only in an ironical sense to a being whose will is so sinful, whose intellect is so limited, whose body is so weak and perishable as man's. How shall a man be proud, when his conception is a crime, his birth a penalty, his life a labour, and death a necessity!—

> *Quid superbit homo? cujus conceptio culpa,*
> *Nasci pœna, labor vita, necesse mori!*

Therefore, in opposition to the above-mentioned form of the Kantian principle, I should be inclined to lay down the following rule: When you come into contact with a man, no matter whom, do not attempt an objective appreciation of him according to his worth and dignity. Do not consider his bad will, or his narrow understanding and perverse ideas; as the former may easily lead you to hate and the latter to despise him; but fix your attention only upon his sufferings, his needs, his anxieties, his pains. Then you will always feel your kinship with him; you will sympathise with him; and instead of hatred or contempt you will experience the commiseration that alone is the peace to which the

---

[96] § 8.

Gospel calls us. The way to keep down hatred and contempt is certainly not to look for a man's alleged "dignity," but, on the contrary, to regard him as an object of pity.

The Buddhists, as the result of the more profound views which they entertain on ethical and metaphysical subjects, start from the cardinal vices and not the cardinal virtues; since the virtues make their appearance only as the contraries or negations of the vices. According to Schmidt's *History of the Eastern Mongolians* the cardinal vices in the Buddhist scheme are four: Lust, Indolence, Anger, and Avarice. But probably instead of Indolence, we should read Pride; for so it stands in the *Lettres édifiantes et curieuses*,[97] where Envy, or Hatred, is added as a fifth. I am confirmed in correcting the statement of the excellent Schmidt by the fact that my rendering agrees with the doctrine of the Sufis, who are certainly under the influence of the Brahmins and Buddhists. The Sufis also maintain that there are four cardinal vices, and they arrange them in very striking pairs, so that Lust appears in connection with Avarice, and Anger with Pride. The four cardinal virtues opposed to them would be Chastity and Generosity, together with Gentleness and Humility.

When we compare these profound ideas of morality, as they are entertained by oriental nations, with the celebrated cardinal virtues of Plato, which have been recapitulated again and again—Justice, Valour, Temperance, and Wisdom—it is plain that the latter are not based on any clear, leading idea, but are chosen on grounds that are superficial and, in part, obviously false. Virtues must be qualities of the will, but Wisdom is chiefly an attribute of the Intellect. [Greek: Sophrosynae], which Cicero translates *Temperantia*, is a very indefinite and ambiguous word, and it admits, therefore, of a variety of applications: it may mean discretion, or abstinence, or keeping a level head. Courage is not a virtue at all; although sometimes it is a servant or instrument of virtue; but it is just as ready to become the servant of the greatest villainy. It is really a quality of temperament. Even Geulinx (in the preface to this *Ethics*) condemned the Platonic virtues and put the following in their place: Diligence, Obedience, Justice and Humility; which are obviously bad. The Chinese distinguish five cardinal virtues: Sympathy, Justice, Propriety, Wisdom, and Sincerity. The virtues of Christianity are theological, not cardinal: Faith, Love, and Hope.

Fundamental disposition towards others, assuming the character either of Envy or of Sympathy, is the point at which the moral virtues and vices of mankind first diverge. These two diametrically opposite qualities exist in every man; for they spring from the inevitable comparison which he draws between his own lot and that of others.

---

[97] Edit, of 1819, vol. vi., p. 372.

According as the result of this comparison affects his individual character does the one or the other of these qualities become the source and principle of all his action. Envy builds the wall between *Thee* and *Me* thicker and stronger; Sympathy makes it slight and transparent; nay, sometimes it pulls down the wall altogether; and then the distinction between self and not-self vanishes.

Valour, which has been mentioned as a virtue, or rather the Courage on which it is based (for valour is only courage in war), deserves a closer examination. The ancients reckoned Courage among the virtues, and cowardice among the vices; but there is no corresponding idea in the Christian scheme, which makes for charity and patience, and in its teaching forbids all enmity or even resistance. The result is that with the moderns Courage is no longer a virtue. Nevertheless it must be admitted that cowardice does not seem to be very compatible with any nobility of character—if only for the reason that it betrays an overgreat apprehension about one's own person.

Courage, however, may also be explained as a readiness to meet ills that threaten at the moment, in order to avoid greater ills that lie in the future; whereas cowardice does the contrary. But this readiness is of the same quality as *patience*, for patience consists in the clear consciousness that greater evils than those which are present, and that any violent attempt to flee from or guard against the ills we have may bring the others upon us. Courage, then, would be a kind of patience; and since it is patience that enables us to practise forbearance and self control, Courage is, through the medium of patience, at least akin to virtue.

But perhaps Courage admits of being considered from a higher point of view. The fear of death may in every case be traced to a deficiency in that natural philosophy—natural, and therefore resting on mere feeling—which gives a man the assurance that he exists in everything outside him just as much as in his own person; so that the death of his person can do him little harm. But it is just this very assurance that would give a man heroic Courage; and therefore, as the reader will recollect from my *Ethics*, Courage comes from the same source as the virtues of Justice and Humanity. This is, I admit, to take a very high view of the matter; but apart from it I cannot well explain why cowardice seems contemptible, and personal courage a noble and sublime thing; for no lower point of view enables me to see why a finite individual who is everything to himself—nay, who is himself even the very fundamental condition of the existence of the rest of the world—should not put his own preservation above every other aim. It is, then, an insufficient explanation of Courage to make it rest only on utility, to give it an empirical and not a transcendental character. It may have been for some such reason that Calderon once uttered a sceptical but remarkable opinion in regard to Courage, nay, actually denied its reality; and put his denial into the mouth of a wise old minister, addressing his young sovereign. "Although," he observed, "natural fear is operative in all alike, a man may be brave in not letting it be seen; and it is this that constitutes Courage":

> *Que aunque el natural temor*
> *En todos obra igualmente,*
> *No mostrarle es ser valiente*
> *Y esto es lo que hace el valor.*[98]

In regard to the difference which I have mentioned between the ancients and the moderns in their estimate of Courage as a virtue, it must be remembered that by Virtue, *virtus*, [Greek: aretae], the ancients understood every excellence or quality that was praiseworthy in itself, it might be moral or intellectual, or possibly only physical. But when Christianity demonstrated that the fundamental tendency of life was moral, it was moral superiority alone than henceforth attached to the notion of Virtue. Meanwhile the earlier usage still survived in the elder Latinists, and also in Italian writers, as is proved by the well-known meaning of the word *virtuoso*. The special attention of students should be drawn to this wider range of the idea of Virtue amongst the ancients, as otherwise it might easily be a source of secret perplexity. I may recommend two passages preserved for us by Stobæus, which will serve this purpose. One of them is apparently from the Pythagorean philosopher Metopos, in which the fitness of every bodily member is declared to be a virtue. The other pronounces that the virtue of a shoemaker is to make good shoes. This may also serve to explain why it is that in the ancient scheme of ethics virtues and vices are mentioned which find no place in ours.

As the place of Courage amongst the virtues is a matter of doubt, so is that of Avarice amongst the vices. It must not, however, be confounded with greed, which is the most immediate meaning of the Latin word *avaritia*. Let us then draw up and examine the arguments *pro et contra* in regard to Avarice, and leave the final judgment to be formed by every man for himself.

On the one hand it is argued that it is not Avarice which is a vice, but extravagance, its opposite. Extravagance springs from a brutish limitation to the present moment, in comparison with which the future, existing as it does only in thought, is as nothing. It rests upon the illusion that sensual pleasures possess a positive or real value. Accordingly, future need and misery is the price at which the spendthrift purchases pleasures that are empty, fleeting, and often no

---

[98] *La Hija del Aire*, ii., 2.

more than imaginary; or else feeds his vain, stupid self-conceit on the bows and scrapes of parasites who laugh at him in secret, or on the gaze of the mob and those who envy his magnificence. We should, therefore, shun the spendthrift as though he had the plague, and on discovering his vice break with him betimes, in order that later on, when the consequences of his extravagance ensue, we may neither have to help to bear them, nor, on the other hand, have to play the part of the friends of Timon of Athens.

At the same time it is not to be expected that he who foolishly squanders his own fortune will leave another man's intact, if it should chance to be committed to his keeping; nay, *sui profusus* and *alieni appetens* are by Sallust very rightly conjoined. Hence it is that extravagance leads not only to impoverishment but also to crime; and crime amongst the moneyed classes is almost always the result of extravagance. It is accordingly with justice that the *Koran* declares all spendthrifts to be "brothers of Satan."

But it is superfluity that Avarice brings in its train, and when was superfluity ever unwelcome? That must be a good vice which has good consequences. Avarice proceeds upon the principle that all pleasure is only negative in its operation and that the happiness which consists of a series of pleasures is a chimæra; that, on the contrary, it is pains which are positive and extremely real. Accordingly, the avaricious man foregoes the former in order that he may be the better preserved from the latter, and thus it is that *bear and forbear—sustine et abstine*—is his maxim. And because he knows, further, how inexhaustible are the possibilities of misfortune, and how innumerable the paths of danger, he increases the means of avoiding them, in order, if possible, to surround himself with a triple wall of protection. Who, then, can say where precaution against disaster begins to be exaggerated? He alone who knows where the malignity of fate reaches its limit. And even if precaution were exaggerated it is an error which at the most would hurt the man who took it, and not others. If he will never need the treasures which he lays up for himself, they will one day benefit others whom nature has made less careful. That until then he withdraws the money from circulation is no misfortune; for money is not an article of consumption: it only represents the good things which a man may actually possess, and is not one itself. Coins are only counters; their value is what they represent; and what they represent cannot be withdrawn from circulation. Moreover, by holding back the money, the value of the remainder which is in circulation is enhanced by precisely the same amount. Even though it be the case, as is said, that many a miser comes in the end to love money itself for its own sake, it is equally certain that many a spendthrift, on the other hand, loves spending and squandering for no better reason. Friendship with a miser is not only without danger, but it is profitable, because of the great advantages it can bring. For it is doubtless those who are nearest and dearest to the miser who on his death will reap the fruits of the self-control which he exercised; but even in his lifetime, too, something may be expected of him in cases of great need. At any rate one can always hope for more from him than from the spendthrift, who has lost his all and is himself helpless and in debt. *Mas dá el duro que el desnudo*, says a Spanish proverb; the man who has a hard heart will give more than the man who has an empty purse. The upshot of all this is that Avarice is not a vice.

On the other side, it may be said that Avarice is the quintessence of all vices. When physical pleasures seduce a man from the right path, it is his sensual nature—the animal part of him—which is at fault. He is carried away by its attractions, and, overcome by the impression of the moment, he acts without thinking of the consequences. When, on the other hand, he is brought by age or bodily weakness to the condition in which the vices that he could never abandon end by abandoning him, and his capacity for physical pleasure dies—if he turns to Avarice, the intellectual desire survives the sensual. Money, which represents all the good things of this world, and is these good things in the abstract, now becomes the dry trunk overgrown with all the dead lusts of the flesh, which are egoism in the abstract. They come to life again in the love of the Mammon. The transient pleasure of the senses has become a deliberate and calculated lust of money, which, like that to which it is directed, is symbolical in its nature, and, like it, indestructible.

This obstinate love of the pleasures of the world—a love which, as it were, outlives itself; this utterly incorrigible sin, this refined and sublimated desire of the flesh, is the abstract form in which all lusts are concentrated, and to which it stands like a general idea to individual particulars. Accordingly, Avarice is the vice of age, just as extravagance is the vice of youth.

This *disputatio in utramque partem*—this debate for and against—is certainly calculated to drive us into accepting the *juste milieu* morality of Aristotle; a conclusion that is also supported by the following consideration.

Every human perfection is allied to a defect into which it threatens to pass; but it is also true that every defect is allied to a perfection. Hence it is that if, as often happens, we make a mistake about a man, it is because at the beginning of our acquaintance with him we confound his defects with the kinds of perfection to which they are allied. The cautious man seems to us a coward; the economical man, a miser; the spendthrift seems liberal; the rude fellow, downright and sincere; the foolhardy person looks as if he were going to work with a noble self-confidence; and so on in many other cases.

* * * * *

No one can live among men without feeling drawn again and again to the tempting supposition that moral baseness and intellectual incapacity are closely connected, as though they both sprang direct from one source. That, however, is not so, I have shown in detail.[99] That it seems to be so is merely due to the fact that both are so often found together; and the circumstance is to be explained by the very frequent occurrence of each of them, so that it may easily happen for both to be compelled to live under one roof. At the same time it is not to be denied that they play into each other's hands to their mutual benefit; and it is this that produces the very unedifying spectacle which only too many men exhibit, and that makes the world to go as it goes. A man who is unintelligent is very likely to show his perfidy, villainy and malice; whereas a clever man understands how to conceal these qualities. And how often, on the other hand, does a perversity of heart prevent a man from seeing truths which his intelligence is quite capable of grasping!

Nevertheless, let no one boast. Just as every man, though he be the greatest genius, has very definite limitations in some one sphere of knowledge, and thus attests his common origin with the essentially perverse and stupid mass of mankind, so also has every man something in his nature which is positively evil. Even the best, nay the noblest, character will sometimes surprise us by isolated traits of depravity; as though it were to acknowledge his kinship with the human race, in which villainy—nay, cruelty—is to be found in that degree. For it was just in virtue of this evil in him, this bad principle, that of necessity he became a man. And for the same reason the world in general is what my clear mirror of it has shown it to be.

But in spite of all this the difference even between one man and another is incalculably great, and many a one would be horrified to see another as he really is. Oh, for some Asmodeus of morality, to make not only roofs and walls transparent to his favourites, but also to lift the veil of dissimulation, fraud, hypocrisy, pretence, falsehood and deception, which is spread over all things! to show how little true honesty there is in the world, and how often, even where it is least to be expected, behind all the exterior outwork of virtue, secretly and in the innermost recesses, unrighteousness sits at the helm! It is just on this account that so many men of the better kind have four-footed friends: for, to be sure, how is a man to get relief from the endless dissimulation, falsity and malice of mankind, if there were no dogs into whose honest faces he can look without distrust?

For what is our civilised world but a big masquerade? where you

---

[99] In my chief work, vol. ii., ch. xix.

meet knights, priests, soldiers, men of learning, barristers, clergymen, philosophers, and I don't know what all! But they are not what they pretend to be; they are only masks, and, as a rule, behind the masks you will find moneymakers. One man, I suppose, puts on the mask of law, which he has borrowed for the purpose from a barrister, only in order to be able to give another man a sound drubbing; a second has chosen the mask of patriotism and the public welfare with a similar intent; a third takes religion or purity of doctrine. For all sorts of purposes men have often put on the mask of philosophy, and even of philanthropy, and I know not what besides. Women have a smaller choice. As a rule they avail themselves of the mask of morality, modesty, domesticity, and humility. Then there are general masks, without any particular character attaching to them like dominoes. They may be met with everywhere; and of this sort is the strict rectitude, the courtesy, the sincere sympathy, the smiling friendship, that people profess. The whole of these masks as a rule are merely, as I have said, a disguise for some industry, commerce, or speculation. It is merchants alone who in this respect constitute any honest class. They are the only people who give themselves out to be what they are; and therefore they go about without any mask at all, and consequently take a humble rank.

It is very necessary that a man should be apprised early in life that it is a masquerade in which he finds himself. For otherwise there are many things which he will fail to understand and put up with, nay, at which he will be completely puzzled, and that man longest of all whose heart is made of better clay—

Et meliore luto finxit præcordia Titan.[100]

Such for instance is the favour that villainy finds; the neglect that merit, even the rarest and the greatest, suffers at the hands of those of the same profession; the hatred of truth and great capacity; the ignorance of scholars in their own province; and the fact that true wares are almost always despised and the merely specious ones in request. Therefore let even the young be instructed betimes that in this masquerade the apples are of wax, the flowers of silk, the fish of pasteboard, and that all things—yes, all things—are toys and trifles; and that of two men whom he may see earnestly engaged in business, one is supplying spurious goods and the other paying for them in false coin.

But there are more serious reflections to be made, and worse things to be recorded. Man is at bottom a savage, horrible beast. We know it, if only in the business of taming and restraining him which we call civilisation. Hence it is that we are terrified if now and then his nature

---

[100] Juvenal, *Sat.* 14, 34.

breaks out. Wherever and whenever the locks and chains of law and order fall off and give place to anarchy, he shows himself for what he is. But it is unnecessary to wait for anarchy in order to gain enlightenment on this subject. A hundred records, old and new, produce the conviction that in his unrelenting cruelty man is in no way inferior to the tiger and the hyæna. A forcible example is supplied by a publication of the year 1841 entitled *Slavery and the Internal Slave Trade in the United States of North America: being replies to questions transmitted by the British Anti-slavery Society to the American Anti-slavery Society.*[101] This book constitutes one of the heaviest indictments against the human race. No one can put it down with a feeling of horror, and few without tears. For whatever the reader may have ever heard, or imagined, or dreamt, of the unhappy condition of slavery, or indeed of human cruelty in general, it will seem small to him when he reads of the way in which those devils in human form, those bigoted, church-going, strictly Sabbatarian rascals—and in particular the Anglican priests among them—treated their innocent black brothers, who by wrong and violence had got into their diabolical clutches.

Other examples are furnished by Tshudi's *Travels in Peru*, in the description which he gives of the treatment of the Peruvian soldiers at the hands of their officers; and by Macleod's *Travels in Eastern Africa*, where the author tells of the cold-blooded and truly devilish cruelty with which the Portuguese in Mozambique treat their slaves. But we need not go for examples to the New World, that obverse side of our planet. In the year 1848 it was brought to life that in England, not in one, but apparently in a hundred cases within a brief period, a husband had poisoned his wife or *vice versâ*, or both had joined in poisoning their children, or in torturing them slowly to death by starving and ill-treating them, with no other object than to get the money for burying them which they had insured in the Burial Clubs against their death. For this purpose a child was often insured in several, even in as many as twenty clubs at once.[102]

Details of this character belong, indeed, to the blackest pages in the criminal records of humanity. But, when all is said, it is the inward and innate character of man, this god *par excellence* of the Pantheists, from which they and everything like them proceed. In every man there dwells, first and foremost, a colossal egoism, which breaks the bounds of right and justice with the greatest freedom, as everyday life shows on a small scale, and as history on every page of it on a large. Does not the recognised need of a balance of power in Europe, with the anxious way

---

[101] *Translator's Note.*—If Schopenhauer were writing to-day, he would with equal truth point to the miseries of the African trade. I have slightly abridged this passage, as some of the evils against which he protested no longer exist.

[102] Cf. *The Times*, 20th, 22nd and 23rd Sept., 1848, and also 12th Dec., 1853.

in which it is preserved, demonstrate that man is a beast of prey, who no sooner sees a weaker man near him than he falls upon him without fail? and does not the same hold good of the affairs of ordinary life?

But to the boundless egoism of our nature there is joined more or less in every human breast a fund of hatred, anger, envy, rancour and malice, accumulated like the venom in a serpent's tooth, and waiting only for an opportunity of venting itself, and then, like a demon unchained, of storming and raging. If a man has no great occasion for breaking out, he will end by taking advantage of the smallest, and by working it up into something great by the aid of his imagination; for, however small it may be, it is enough to rouse his anger—

Quantulacunque adeo est occasio, sufficit irae—[103]

and then he will carry it as far as he can and may. We see this in daily life, where such outbursts are well known under the name of "venting one's gall on something." It will also have been observed that if such outbursts meet with no opposition the subject of them feels decidedly the better for them afterwards. That anger is not without its pleasure is a truth that was recorded even by Aristotle;[104] and he quotes a passage from Homer, who declares anger to be sweeter than honey. But not in anger alone—in hatred too, which stands to anger like a chronic to an acute disease, a man may indulge with the greatest delight:

> *Now hatred is by far the longest pleasure,*
> *Men love in haste, but they detest at leisure*[105]

Gobineau in his work *Les Races Humaines* has called man *l'animal méchant par excellence*. People take this very ill, because they feel that it hits them; but he is quite right, for man is the only animal which causes pain to others without any further purpose than just to cause it. Other animals never do it except to satisfy their hunger, or in the rage of combat. If it is said against the tiger that he kills more than eats, he strangles his prey only for the purpose of eating it; and if he cannot eat it, the only explanation is, as the French phrase has it, that *ses yeux sont plus grands que son estomac*. No animal ever torments another for the mere purpose of tormenting, but man does it, and it is this that constitutes the diabolical feature in his character which is so much worse than the merely animal. I have already spoken of the matter in its broad aspect; but it is manifest even in small things, and

---

[103] Juvenal, *Sat.* 13, 183.

[104] *Rhet.*, i., 11; ii., 2.

[105] Byron *Don Juan*, c. xiii, 6.

every reader has a daily opportunity of observing it. For instance, if two little dogs are playing together—and what a genial and charming sight it is—and a child of three or four years joins them, it is almost inevitable for it to begin hitting them with a whip or stick, and thereby show itself, even at that age, *l'animal méchant par excellence*. The love of teasing and playing tricks, which is common enough, may be traced to the same source. For instance, if a man has expressed his annoyance at any interruption or other petty inconvenience, there will be no lack of people who for that very reason will bring it about: *animal méchant par excellence*! This is so certain that a man should be careful not to express any annoyance at small evils. On the other hand he should also be careful not to express his pleasure at any trifle, for, if he does so, men will act like the jailer who, when he found that his prisoner had performed the laborious task of taming a spider, and took a pleasure in watching it, immediately crushed it under his foot: *l'animal méchant par excellence*! This is why all animals are instinctively afraid of the sight, or even of the track of a man, that *animal méchant par excellence*! nor does their instinct them false; for it is man alone who hunts game for which he has no use and which does him no harm.

It is a fact, then, that in the heart of every man there lies a wild beast which only waits for an opportunity to storm and rage, in its desire to inflict pain on others, or, if they stand in his way, to kill them. It is this which is the source of all the lust of war and battle. In trying to tame and to some extent hold it in check, the intelligence, its appointed keeper, has always enough to do. People may, if they please, call it the radical evil of human nature—a name which will at least serve those with whom a word stands for an explanation. I say, however, that it is the will to live, which, more and more embittered by the constant sufferings of existence, seeks to alleviate its own torment by causing torment in others. But in this way a man gradually develops in himself real cruelty and malice. The observation may also be added that as, according to Kant, matter subsists only through the antagonism of the powers of expansion and contraction, so human society subsists only by the antagonism of hatred, or anger, and fear. For there is a moment in the life of all of us when the malignity of our nature might perhaps make us murderers, if it were not accompanied by a due admixture of fear to keep it within bounds; and this fear, again, would make a man the sport and laughing stock of every boy, if anger were not lying ready in him, and keeping watch.

But it is *Schadenfreude*, a mischievous delight in the misfortunes of others, which remains the worst trait in human nature. It is a feeling which is closely akin to cruelty, and differs from it, to say the truth, only as theory from practice. In general, it may be said of it that it takes the place which pity ought to take—pity which is its opposite, and the true source of all real justice and charity.

Envy is also opposed to pity, but in another sense; envy, that is to say, is produced by a cause directly antagonistic to that which produces the delight in mischief. The opposition between pity and envy on the one hand, and pity and the delight in mischief on the other, rests, in the main, on the occasions which call them forth. In the case of envy it is only as a direct effect of the cause which excites it that we feel it at all. That is just the reason why envy, although it is a reprehensible feeling, still admits of some excuse, and is, in general, a very human quality; whereas the delight in mischief is diabolical, and its taunts are the laughter of hell.

The delight in mischief, as I have said, takes the place which pity ought to take. Envy, on the contrary, finds a place only where there is no inducement to pity, or rather an inducement to its opposite; and it is just as this opposite that envy arises in the human breast; and so far, therefore, it may still be reckoned a human sentiment. Nay, I am afraid that no one will be found to be entirely free from it. For that a man should feel his own lack of things more bitterly at the sight of another's delight in the enjoyment of them, is natural; nay, it is inevitable; but this should not rouse his hatred of the man who is happier than himself. It is just this hatred, however, in which true envy consists. Least of all should a man be envious, when it is a question, not of the gifts of fortune, or chance, or another's favour, but of the gifts of nature; because everything that is innate in a man rests on a metaphysical basis, and possesses justification of a higher kind; it is, so to speak, given him by Divine grace. But, unhappily, it is just in the case of personal advantages that envy is most irreconcilable. Thus it is that intelligence, or even genius, cannot get on in the world without begging pardon for its existence, wherever it is not in a position to be able, proudly and boldly, to despise the world.

In other words, if envy is aroused only by wealth, rank, or power, it is often kept down by egoism, which perceives that, on occasion, assistance, enjoyment, support, protection, advancement, and so on, may be hoped for from the object of envy or that at least by intercourse with him a man may himself win honour from the reflected light of his superiority; and here, too, there is the hope of one day attaining all those advantages himself. On the other hand, in the envy that is directed to natural gifts and personal advantages, like beauty in women, or intelligence in men, there is no consolation or hope of one kind or the other; so that nothing remains but to indulge a bitter and irreconcilable hatred of the person who possesses these privileges; and hence the only remaining desire is to take vengeance on him.

But here the envious man finds himself in an unfortunate position; for all his blows fall powerless as soon as it is known that they come from him. Accordingly he hides his feelings as carefully as if they were secret sins, and so becomes an inexhaustible inventor of tricks and artifices and devices for concealing and masking his procedure, in order that, unperceived, he may wound the object of his envy. For instance, with an air of the utmost unconcern he will ignore the advantages which are eating his heart out; he will neither see them, nor know them, nor have observed or even heard of them, and thus make himself a master in the art of dissimulation. With great cunning he will completely overlook the man whose brilliant qualities are gnawing at his heart, and act as though he were quite an unimportant person; he will take no notice of him, and, on occasion, will have even quite forgotten his existence. But at the same time he will before all things endeavour by secret machination carefully to deprive those advantages of any opportunity of showing themselves and becoming known. Then out of his dark corner he will attack these qualities with censure, mockery, ridicule and calumny, like the toad which spurts its poison from a hole. No less will he enthusiastically praise unimportant people, or even indifferent or bad performances in the same sphere. In short, he will becomes a Proteas in stratagem, in order to wound others without showing himself. But what is the use of it? The trained eye recognises him in spite of it all. He betrays himself, if by nothing else, by the way in which he timidly avoids and flies from the object of his envy, who stands the more completely alone, the more brilliant he is; and this is the reason why pretty girls have no friends of their own sex. He betrays himself, too, by the causeless hatred which he shows—a hatred which finds vent in a violent explosion at any circumstance however trivial, though it is often only the product of his imagination. How many such men there are in the world may be recognised by the universal praise of modesty, that is, of a virtue invented on behalf of dull and commonplace people. Nevertheless, it is a virtue which, by exhibiting the necessity for dealing considerately with the wretched plight of these people, is just what calls attention to it.

For our self-consciousness and our pride there can be nothing more flattering than the sight of envy lurking in its retreat and plotting its schemes; but never let a man forget that where there is envy there is hatred, and let him be careful not to make a false friend out of any envious person. Therefore it is important to our safety to lay envy bare; and a man should study to discover its tricks, as it is everywhere to be found and always goes about *incognito*; or as I have said, like a venomous toad it lurks in dark corners. It deserves neither quarter nor sympathy; but as we can never reconcile it let our rule of conduct be to scorn it with a good heart, and as our happiness and glory is torture to it we may rejoice in its sufferings:

Den Neid wirst nimmer du versöhnen;
So magst du ihn getrost verhöhnen.
Dein Glück, dein Ruhm ist ihm ein Leiden:
Magst drum an seiner Quaal dich weiden.

We have been taking a look at the *depravity* of man, and it is a sight which may well fill us with horror. But now we must cast our eyes on the *misery* of his existence; and when we have done so, and are horrified by that too, we must look back again at his depravity. We shall then find that they hold the balance to each other. We shall perceive the eternal justice of things; for we shall recognise that the world is itself the Last Judgment on it, and we shall begin to understand why it is that everything that lives must pay the penalty of its existence, first in living and then in dying. Thus the evil of the penalty accords with the evil of the sin—*malum pœnæ* with *malum culpæ*. From the same point of view we lose our indignation at that intellectual incapacity of the great majority of mankind which in life so often disgusts us. In this *Sansara*, as the Buddhists call it, human misery, human depravity and human folly correspond with one another perfectly, and they are of like magnitude. But if, on some special inducement, we direct our gaze to one of them, and survey it in particular, it seems to exceed the other two. This, however, is an illusion, and merely the effect of their colossal range.

All things proclaim this *Sansara*; more than all else, the world of mankind; in which, from a moral point of view, villainy and baseness, and from an intellectual point of view, incapacity and stupidity, prevail to a horrifying extent. Nevertheless, there appear in it, although very spasmodically, and always as a fresh surprise, manifestations of honesty, of goodness, nay, even of nobility; and also of great intelligence, of the thinking mind of genius. They never quite vanish, but like single points of light gleam upon us out of the great dark mass. We must accept them as a pledge that this *Sansara* contains a good and redeeming principle, which is capable of breaking through and of filling and freeing the whole of it.

* * * * *

The readers of my *Ethics* know that with me the ultimate foundation of morality is the truth which in the *Vedas* and the *Vedanta* receives its expression in the established, mystical formula, *Tat twam asi* (*This is thyself*), which is spoken with reference to every living thing, be it man or beast, and is called the *Mahavakya*, the great word.

Actions which proceed in accordance with this principle, such as those of the philanthropist, may indeed be regarded as the beginning of mysticism. Every benefit rendered with a pure intention proclaims that the man who exercises it acts in direct conflict with the world of appearance; for he recognises himself as identical with another individual, who exists in complete separation from him. Accordingly, all disinterested kindness is inexplicable; it is a mystery; and hence in order to explain it a man has to resort to all sorts of fictions. When Kant had demolished all other arguments for theism, he admitted one only, that it gave the best interpretation and solution of such mysterious actions, and of all others like them. He therefore allowed it to stand as a presumption unsusceptible indeed of theoretical proof, but valid from a practical point of view. I may, however, express my doubts whether he was quite serious about it. For to make morality rest on theism is really to reduce morality to egoism; although the English, it is true, as also the lowest classes of society with us, do not perceive the possibility of any other foundation for it.

The above-mentioned recognition of a man's own true being in another individual objectively presented to him, is exhibited in a particularly beautiful and clear way in the cases in which a man, already destined to death beyond any hope of rescue, gives himself up to the welfare of others with great solicitude and zeal, and tries to save them. Of this kind is the well-known story of a servant who was bitten in a courtyard at night by a mad dog. In the belief that she was beyond hope, she seized the dog and dragged it into a stable, which she then locked, so that no one else might be bitten. Then again there is the incident in Naples, which Tischbein has immortalised in one of his *aquarelles*. A son, fleeing from the lava which is rapidly streaming toward the sea, is carrying his aged father on his back. When there is only a narrow strip of land left between the devouring elements, the father bids the son put him down, so that the son may save himself by flight, as otherwise both will be lost. The son obeys, and as he goes casts a glance of farewell on his father. This is the moment depicted. The historical circumstance which Scott represents in his masterly way in *The Heart of Midlothian*, chap, ii., is of a precisely similar kind; where, of two delinquents condemned to death, the one who by his awkwardness caused the capture of the other happily sets him free in the chapel by overpowering the guard after the execution-sermon, without at the same time making any attempt on his own behalf. Nay, in the same category must also be placed the scene which is represented in a common engraving, which may perhaps be objectionable to western readers—I mean the one in which a soldier, kneeling to be shot, is trying by waving a cloth to frighten away his dog who wants to come to him.

In all these cases we see an individual in the face of his own immediate and certain destruction no longer thinking of saving himself, so that he may direct the whole of his efforts to saving some one else.

How could there be a clearer expression of the consciousness that what is being destroyed is only a phenomenon, and that the destruction itself is only a phenomenon; that, on the other hand, the real being of the man who meets his death is untouched by that event, and lives on in the other man, in whom even now, as his action betrays, he so clearly perceives it to exist? For if this were not so, and it was his real being which was about to be annihilated, how could that being spend its last efforts in showing such an ardent sympathy in the welfare and continued existence of another?

There are two different ways in which a man may become conscious of his own existence. On the one hand, he may have an empirical perception of it, as it manifests itself externally—something so small that it approaches vanishing point; set in a world which, as regards time and space, is infinite; one only of the thousand millions of human creatures who run about on this planet for a very brief period and are renewed every thirty years. On the other hand, by going down into the depths of his own nature, a man may become conscious that he is all in all; that, in fact, he is the only real being; and that, in addition, this real being perceives itself again in others, who present themselves from without, as though they formed a mirror of himself.

Of these two ways in which a man may come to know what he is, the first grasps the phenomenon alone, the mere product of *the principle of individuation*; whereas the second makes a man immediately conscious that he is *the thing-in-itself*. This is a doctrine in which, as regards the first way, I have Kant, and as regards both, I have the *Vedas*, to support me.

There is, it is true, a simple objection to the second method. It may be said to assume that one and the same being can exist in different places at the same time, and yet be complete in each of them. Although, from an empirical point of view, this is the most palpable impossibility—nay, absurdity—it is nevertheless perfectly true of the thing-in-itself. The impossibility and the absurdity of it, empirically, are only due to the forms which phenomena assume, in accordance with the principle of individuation. For the thing-in-itself, the will to live, exists whole and undivided in every being, even in the smallest, as completely as in the sum-total of all things that ever were or are or will be. This is why every being, even the smallest, says to itself, So long as I am safe, let the world perish—*dum ego salvus sim, pereat mundus*. And, in truth, even if only one individual were left in the world, and all the rest were to perish, the one that remained would still possess the whole self-being of the world, uninjured and undiminished, and would laugh at the destruction of the world as an illusion. This conclusion *per impossibile* may be balanced by the counter-conclusion, which is on all fours with it, that if that last individual were to be annihilated in and with him the whole world would be destroyed. It was in this sense that

the mystic Angelas Silesius[106] declared that God could not live for a
moment without him, and that if he were to be annihilated God must of
necessity give up the ghost:

> *Ich weiss dass ohne mich Gott nicht ein Nu kann leben;*
> *Werd' ich zunicht, er muss von Noth den Geist aufgeben.*

But the empirical point of view also to some extent enables us to
perceive that it is true, or at least possible, that our self can exist in
other beings whose consciousness is separated and different from our
own. That this is so is shown by the experience of somnambulists.
Although the identity of their ego is preserved throughout, they know
nothing, when they awake, of all that a moment before they themselves
said, did or suffered. So entirely is the individual consciousness a
phenomenon that even in the same ego two consciousnesses can arise
of which the one knows nothing of the other.

GOVERNMENT.

It is a characteristic failing of the Germans to look in the clouds for
what lies at their feet. An excellent example of this is furnished by the
treatment which the idea of *Natural Right* has received at the hands of
professors of philosophy. When they are called upon to explain those
simple relations of human life which make up the substance of this
right, such as Right and Wrong, Property, State, Punishment and so on,
they have recourse to the most extravagant, abstract, remote and
meaningless conceptions, and out of them build a Tower of Babel
reaching to the clouds, and taking this or that form according to the
special whim of the professor for the time being. The clearest and
simplest relations of life, such as affect us directly, are thus made quite
unintelligible, to the great detriment of the young people who are
educated in such a school. These relations themselves are perfectly
simple and easily understood—as the reader may convince himself if
he will turn to the account which I have given of them in the
Foundation of Morality, § 17, and in my chief work, bk. i., § 62. But at
the sound of certain words, like Right, Freedom, the Good, Being—this
nugatory infinitive of the cupola—and many others of the same sort,
the German's head begins to swim, and falling straightway into a kind
of delirium he launches forth into high-flown phrases which have no
meaning whatever. He takes the most remote and empty conceptions,
and strings them together artificially, instead of fixing his eyes on the
facts, and looking at things and relations as they really are. It is these

---

[106] *Translator's Note.*—Angelus Silesius, see *Counsels and Maxims*, p. 39, note.

things and relations which supply the ideas of Right and Freedom, and give them the only true meaning that they possess.

The man who starts from the preconceived opinion that the conception of Right must be a positive one, and then attempts to define it, will fail; for he is trying to grasp a shadow, to pursue a spectre, to search for what does not exist. The conception of Right is a negative one, like the conception of Freedom; its content is mere negation. It is the conception of Wrong which is positive; Wrong has the same significance as *injury*—*læsio*—in the widest sense of the term. An injury may be done either to a man's person or to his property or to his honour; and accordingly a man's rights are easy to define: every one has a right to do anything that injures no one else.

To have a right to do or claim a thing means nothing more than to be able to do or take or vise it without thereby injuring any one else. *Simplex sigillum veri.* This definition shows how senseless many questions are; for instance, the question whether we have the right to take our own life, As far as concerns the personal claims which others may possibly have upon us, they are subject to the condition that we are alive, and fall to the ground when we die. To demand of a man, who does not care to live any longer for himself, that he should live on as a mere machine for the advantage of others is an extravagant pretension.

Although men's powers differ, their rights are alike. Their rights do not rest upon their powers, because Right is of a moral complexion; they rest on the fact that the same will to live shows itself in every man at the same stage of its manifestation. This, however, only applies to that original and abstract Right, which a man possesses as a man. The property, and also the honour, which a man acquires for himself by the exercise of his powers, depend on the measure and kind of power which he possesses, and so lend his Right a wider sphere of application. Here, then, equality comes to an end. The man who is better equipped, or more active, increases by adding to his gains, not his Right, but the number of the things to which it extends.

In my chief work[107] I have proved that the State in its essence is merely an institution existing for the purpose of protecting its members against outward attack or inward dissension. It follows from this that the ultimate ground on which the State is necessary is the acknowledged lack of Right in the human race. If Right were there, no one would think of a State; for no one would have any fear that his rights would be impaired; and a mere union against the attacks of wild beasts or the elements would have very little analogy with what we mean by a State. From this point of view it is easy to see how dull and stupid are the philosophasters who in pompous phrases represent that

---

[107] 1 Bk. ii., ch. xlvii.

the State is the supreme end and flower of human existence. Such a view is the apotheosis of Philistinism.

If it were Right that ruled in the world, a man would have done enough in building his house, and would need no other protection than the right of possessing it, which would be obvious. But since Wrong is the order of the day, it is requisite that the man who has built his house should also be able to protect it. Otherwise his Right is *de facto* incomplete; the aggressor, that is to say, has the right of might— *Faustrecht*; and this is just the conception of Right which Spinoza entertains. He recognises no other. His words are: *unusquisque tantum juris habet quantum potentia valet*;[108] each man has as much right as he has power. And again: *uniuscujusque jus potentia ejus definitur*; each man's right is determined by his power.[109] Hobbes seems to have started this conception of Right,[110] and he adds the strange comment that the Right of the good Lord to all things rests on nothing but His omnipotence.

Now this is a conception of Right which, both in theory and in practice, no longer prevails in the civic world; but in the world in general, though abolished in theory, it continues to apply in practice. The consequences of neglecting it may be seen in the case of China. Threatened by rebellion within and foes without, this great empire is in a defenceless state, and has to pay the penalty of having cultivated only the arts of peace and ignored the arts of war.

There is a certain analogy between the operations of nature and those of man which is a peculiar but not fortuitous character, and is based on the identity of the will in both. When the herbivorous animals had taken their place in the organic world, beasts of prey made their appearance—necessarily a late appearance—in each species, and proceeded to live upon them. Just in the same way, as soon as by honest toil and in the sweat of their faces men have won from the ground what is needed for the support of their societies, a number of individuals are sure to arise in some of these societies, who, instead of cultivating the earth and living on its produce, prefer to take their lives in their hands and risk health and freedom by falling upon those who are in possession of what they have honestly earned, and by appropriating the fruits of their labour. These are the beasts of prey in the human race; they are the conquering peoples whom we find everywhere in history, from the most ancient to the most recent times. Their varying fortunes, as at one moment they succeed and at another fail, make up the general elements of the history of the world. Hence

---

[108] *Tract. Theol. Pol.*, ch. ii., § 8.

[109] *Ethics*, IV., xxxvii., 1.

[110] Particularly in a passage in the *De Cive*, I, § 14.

Voltaire was perfectly right when he said that the aim of all war is robbery. That those who engage in it are ashamed of their doings is clear by the fact that governments loudly protest their reluctance to appeal to arms except for purposes of self-defence. Instead of trying to excuse themselves by telling public and official lies, which are almost more revolting than war itself, they should take their stand, as bold as brass, on Macchiavelli's doctrine. The gist of it may be stated to be this: that whereas between one individual and another, and so far as concerns the law and morality of their relations, the principle, *Don't do to others what you wouldn't like done to yourself*, certainly applies, it is the converse of this principle which is appropriate in the case of nations and in politics: *What you wouldn't like done to yourself do to others*. If you do not want to be put under a foreign yoke, take time by the forelock, and put your neighbour under it himself; whenever, that is to say, his weakness offers you the opportunity. For if you let the opportunity pass, it will desert one day to the enemy's camp and offer itself there. Then your enemy will put you under his yoke; and your failure to grasp the opportunity may be paid for, not by the generation which was guilty of it, but by the next. This Macchiavellian principle is always a much more decent cloak for the lust of robbery than the rags of very obvious lies in a speech from the head of the State; lies, too, of a description which recalls the well-known story of the rabbit attacking the dog. Every State looks upon its neighbours as at bottom a horde of robbers, who will fall upon it as soon as they have the opportunity.

* * * * *

Between the serf, the farmer, the tenant, and the mortgagee, the difference is rather one of form than of substance. Whether the peasant belongs to me, or the land on which he has to get a living; whether the bird is mine, or its food, the tree or its fruit, is a matter of little moment; for, as Shakespeare makes Shylock say:

> *You take my life*
> *When you do take the means whereby I live.*

The free peasant has, indeed, the advantage that he can go off and seek his fortune in the wide world; whereas the serf who is attached to the soil, *glebæ adscriptus*, has an advantage which is perhaps still greater, that when failure of crops or illness, old age or incapacity, render him helpless, his master must look after him, and so he sleeps well at night; whereas, if the crops fail, his master tosses about on his bed trying to think how he is to procure bread for his men. As long ago as Menander it was said that it is better to be the slave of a good master than to live miserably as a freeman. Another advantage possessed by the free is that if they have any talents they can improve their position; but the same advantage is not wholly withheld from the slave. If he proves himself useful to his master by the exercise of any skill, he is treated accordingly; just as in ancient Rome mechanics, foremen of workshops, architects, nay, even doctors, were generally slaves.

Slavery and poverty, then, are only two forms, I might almost say only two names, of the same thing, the essence of which is that a man's physical powers are employed, in the main, not for himself but for others; and this leads partly to his being over-loaded with work, and partly to his getting a scanty satisfaction for his needs. For Nature has given a man only as much physical power as will suffice, if he exerts it in moderation, to gain a sustenance from the earth. No great superfluity of power is his. If, then, a not inconsiderable number of men are relieved from the common burden of sustaining the existence of the human race, the burden of the remainder is augmented, and they suffer. This is the chief source of the evil which under the name of slavery, or under the name of the proletariat, has always oppressed the great majority of the human race.

But the more remote cause of it is luxury. In order, it may be said, that some few persons may have what is unnecessary, superfluous, and the product of refinement—nay, in order that they may satisfy artificial needs—a great part of the existing powers of mankind has to be devoted to this object, and therefore withdrawn from the production of what is necessary and indispensable. Instead of building cottages for themselves, thousands of men build mansions for a few. Instead of weaving coarse materials for themselves and their families, they make fine cloths, silk, or even lace, for the rich, and in general manufacture a thousand objects of luxury for their pleasure. A great part of the urban population consists of workmen who make these articles of luxury; and for them and those who give them work the peasants have to plough and sow and look after the flocks as well as for themselves, and thus have more labour than Nature originally imposed upon them. Moreover, the urban population devotes a great deal of physical strength, and a great deal of land, to such things as wine, silk, tobacco, hops, asparagus and so on, instead of to corn, potatoes and cattle-breeding. Further, a number of men are withdrawn from agriculture and employed in ship-building and seafaring, in order that sugar, coffee, tea and other goods may be imported. In short, a large part of the powers of the human race is taken away from the production of what is necessary, in order to bring what is superfluous and unnecessary within the reach of a few. As long therefore as luxury exists, there must be a corresponding amount of over-work and misery, whether it takes the name of poverty or of slavery. The fundamental difference between the two is that slavery originates in violence, and poverty in craft. The whole unnatural condition of society—the universal struggle to escape from misery, the sea-trade attended with so much loss of life, the complicated interests of commerce, and finally the wars to which it all gives rise—is due, only and alone, to luxury, which gives no happiness even to those who enjoy it, nay, makes them ill and bad-tempered. Accordingly it looks as if the most effective way of alleviating human misery would be to diminish luxury, or even abolish it altogether.

There is unquestionably much truth in this train of thought. But the conclusion at which it arrives is refuted by an argument possessing this advantage over it—that it is confirmed by the testimony of experience. A certain amount of work is devoted to purposes of luxury. What the human race loses in this way in the *muscular power* which would otherwise be available for the necessities of existence is gradually made up to it a thousand fold by the *nervous power*, which, in a chemical sense, is thereby released. And since the intelligence and sensibility which are thus promoted are on a higher level than the muscular irritability which they supplant, so the achievements of mind exceed those of the body a thousand fold. One wise counsel is worth the work of many hands:

[Greek: Hos en sophon bouleuma tas pollon cheiras nika.]

A nation of nothing but peasants would do little in the way of discovery and invention; but idle hands make active heads. Science and the Arts are themselves the children of luxury, and they discharge their debt to it. The work which they do is to perfect technology in all its branches, mechanical, chemical and physical; an art which in our days has brought machinery to a pitch never dreamt of before, and in particular has, by steam and electricity, accomplished things the like of which would, in earlier ages, have been ascribed to the agency of the devil. In manufactures of all kinds, and to some extent in agriculture, machines now do a thousand times more than could ever have been done by the hands of all the well-to-do, educated, and professional classes, and could ever have been attained if all luxury had been abolished and every one had returned to the life of a peasant. It is by no means the rich alone, but all classes, who derive benefit from these industries. Things which in former days hardly any one could afford are now cheap and abundant, and even the lowest classes are much better off in point of comfort. In the Middle Ages a King of England once borrowed a pair of silk stockings from one of his lords, so that he might wear them in giving an audience to the French ambassador. Even Queen Elizabeth was greatly pleased and astonished to receive a pair as a New Year's present; to-day every shopman has them. Fifty years ago ladies wore the kind of calico gowns which servants wear now. If mechanical science continues to progress at the same rate for any length of time, it may end by saving human labour almost entirely, just as horses are even now being largely superseded by machines. For it is possible to conceive that intellectual culture might in some degree become general in the human race; and this would be impossible as long as bodily labour was incumbent on any great part of it. Muscular irritability and nervous sensibility are always and everywhere, both generally and particularly, in antagonism; for the simple reason that it is one and the same vital power which underlies both. Further, since the arts have a softening effect on character, it is possible that quarrels great and small, wars and duels, will vanish from the world; just as both have become much rarer occurrences. However, it is not my object here to write a *Utopia.*

But apart from all this the arguments used above in favour of the abolition of luxury and the uniform distribution of all bodily labour are open to the objection that the great mass of mankind, always and everywhere, cannot do without leaders, guides and counsellors, in one shape or another, according to the matter in question; judges, governors, generals, officials, priests, doctors, men of learning, philosophers, and so on, are all a necessity. Their common task is to lead the race for the greater part so incapable and perverse, through the labyrinth of life, of which each of them according to his position and capacity has obtained a general view, be his range wide or narrow. That these guides of the race should be permanently relieved of all bodily labour as well as of all vulgar need and discomfort; nay, that in proportion to their much greater achievements they should necessarily own and enjoy more than the common man, is natural and reasonable. Great merchants should also be included in the same privileged class, whenever they make far-sighted preparations for national needs.

The question of the sovereignty of the people is at bottom the same as the question whether any man can have an original right to rule a people against its will. How that proposition can be reasonably maintained I do not see. The people, it must be admitted, is sovereign; but it is a sovereign who is always a minor. It must have permanent guardians, and it can never exercise its rights itself, without creating dangers of which no one can foresee the end; especially as like all minors, it is very apt to become the sport of designing sharpers, in the shape of what are called demagogues.

Voltaire remarks that the first man to become a king was a successful soldier. It is certainly the case that all princes were originally victorious leaders of armies, and for a long time it was as such that they bore sway. On the rise of standing armies princes began to regard their people as a means of sustaining themselves and their soldiers, and treated them, accordingly, as though they were a herd of cattle, which had to be tended in order that it might provide wool, milk, and meat. The why and wherefore of all this, as I shall presently show in detail, is the fact that originally it was not right, but might, that ruled in the world. Might has the advantage of having been the first in the field. That is why it is impossible to do away with it and abolish it altogether; it must always have its place; and all that a man can wish or ask is that it should be found on the side of right and associated with it. Accordingly says the prince to his subjects: "I rule you in virtue of the power which I possess. But, on the other hand, it excludes that of any one else, and I shall suffer none but my own, whether it comes from without, or arises within by one of you trying to oppress another. In this way, then, you are protected." The arrangement was carried out; and just because it was carried out the old idea of kingship developed with time and progress into quite a different idea, and put the other one in the background, where it may still be seen, now and then, flitting about like a spectre. Its place has been taken by the idea of the king as father of his people, as the firm and unshakable pillar which alone supports and maintains the whole organisation of law and order, and consequently the rights of every man.[111] But a king can accomplish this only by inborn prerogative which reserves authority to him and to him alone—an authority which is supreme, indubitable, and beyond all attack, nay, to which every one renders instinctive obedience. Hence the king is rightly said to rule "by the grace of God." He is always the most useful person in the State, and his services are never too dearly repaid by any Civil List, however heavy.

But even as late a writer as Macchiavelli was so decidedly imbued with the earlier or mediaeval conception of the position of a prince that he treats it as a matter which is self-evident: he never discusses it, but tacitly takes it as the presupposition and basis of his advice. It may be said generally that his book is merely the theoretical statement and consistent and systematic exposition of the practice prevailing in his time. It is the novel statement of it in a complete theoretical form that lends it such a poignant interest. The same thing, I may remark in passing, applies to the immortal little work of La Rochefaucauld, who, however, takes private and not public life for his theme, and offers, not advice, but observations. The title of this fine little book is open, perhaps, to some objection: the contents are not, as a rule, either *maxims* or *reflections*, but *aperçus*; and that is what they should be called. There is much, too, in Macchiavelli that will be found also to apply to private life.

Right in itself is powerless; in nature it is Might that rules. To enlist might on the side of right, so that by means of it right may rule, is the problem of statesmanship. And it is indeed a hard problem, as will

---

[111] We read in Stobæus, *Florilegium*, ch. xliv., 41, of a Persian custom, by which, whenever a king died, there was a five days' anarchy, in order that people might perceive the advantage of having kings and laws.

be obvious if we remember that almost every human breast is the seat
of an egoism which has no limits, and is usually associated with an
accumulated store of hatred and malice; so that at the very start feelings
of enmity largely prevail over those of friendship. We have also to bear
in mind that it is many millions of individuals so constituted who have
to be kept in the bonds of law and order, peace and tranquillity;
whereas originally every one had a right to say to every one else: *I am
just as good as you are*! A consideration of all this must fill us with
surprise that on the whole the world pursues its way so peacefully and
quietly, and with so much law and order as we see to exist. It is the
machinery of State which alone accomplishes it. For it is physical
power alone which has any direct action on men; constituted as they
generally are, it is for physical power alone that they have any feeling
or respect.

If a man would convince himself by experience that this is the
case, he need do nothing but remove all compulsion from his fellows,
and try to govern them by clearly and forcibly representing to them
what is reasonable, right, and fair, though at the same time it may be
contrary to their interests. He would be laughed to scorn; and as things
go that is the only answer he would get. It would soon be obvious to
him that moral force alone is powerless. It is, then, physical force alone
which is capable of securing respect. Now this force ultimately resides
in the masses, where it is associated with ignorance, stupidity and
injustice. Accordingly the main aim of statesmanship in these difficult
circumstances is to put physical force in subjection to mental force—to
intellectual superiority, and thus to make it serviceable. But if this aim
is not itself accompanied by justice and good intentions the result of the
business, if it succeeds, is that the State so erected consists of knaves
and fools, the deceivers and the deceived. That this is the case is made
gradually evident by the progress of intelligence amongst the masses,
however much it may be repressed; and it leads to revolution. But if,
contrarily, intelligence is accompanied by justice and good intentions,
there arises a State as perfect as the character of human affairs will
allow. It is very much to the purpose if justice and good intentions not
only exist, but are also demonstrable and openly exhibited, and can be
called to account publicly, and be subject to control. Care must be
taken, however, lest the resulting participation of many persons in the
work of government should affect the unity of the State, and inflict a
loss of strength and concentration on the power by which its home and
foreign affairs have to be administered. This is what almost always
happens in republics. To produce a constitution which should satisfy all
these demands would accordingly be the highest aim of statesmanship.
But, as a matter of fact, statesmanship has to consider other things as
well. It has to reckon with the people as they exist, and their national
peculiarities. This is the raw material on which it has to work, and the

ingredients of that material will always exercise a great effect on the completed scheme.

Statesmanship will have achieved a good deal if it so far attains its object as to reduce wrong and injustice in the community to a minimum. To banish them altogether, and to leave no trace of them, is merely the ideal to be aimed at; and it is only approximately that it can be reached. If they disappear in one direction, they creep in again in another; for wrong and injustice lie deeply rooted in human nature. Attempts have been made to attain the desired aim by artificial constitutions and systematic codes of law; but they are not in complete touch with the facts—they remain an asymptote, for the simple reason that hard and fast conceptions never embrace all possible cases, and cannot be made to meet individual instances. Such conceptions resemble the stones of a mosaic rather than the delicate shading in a picture. Nay, more: all experiments in this matter are attended with danger; because the material in question, namely, the human race, is the most difficult of all material to handle. It is almost as dangerous as an explosive.

No doubt it is true that in the machinery of the State the freedom of the press performs the same function as a safety-valve in other machinery; for it enables all discontent to find a voice; nay, in doing so, the discontent exhausts itself if it has not much substance; and if it has, there is an advantage in recognising it betimes and applying the remedy. This is much better than to repress the discontent, and let it simmer and ferment, and go on increasing until it ends in an explosion. On the other hand, the freedom of the press may be regarded as a permission to sell poison—poison for the heart and the mind. There is no idea so foolish but that it cannot be put into the heads of the ignorant and incapable multitude, especially if the idea holds out some prospect of any gain or advantage. And when a man has got hold of any such idea what is there that he will not do? I am, therefore, very much afraid that the danger of a free press outweighs its utility, particularly where the law offers a way of redressing wrongs. In any case, however, the freedom of the press should be governed by a very strict prohibition of all and every anonymity.

Generally, indeed, it may be maintained that right is of a nature analogous to that of certain chemical substances, which cannot be exhibited in a pure and isolated condition, but at the most only with a small admixture of some other substance, which serves as a vehicle for them, or gives them the necessary consistency; such as fluorine, or even alcohol, or prussic acid. Pursuing the analogy we may say that right, if it is to gain a footing in the world and really prevail, must of necessity be supplemented by a small amount of arbitrary force, in order that, notwithstanding its merely ideal and therefore ethereal nature, it may be able to work and subsist in the real and material world, and not evaporate and vanish into the clouds, as it does in Hesiod. Birth-right of every description, all heritable privileges, every form of national religion, and so on, may be regarded as the necessary chemical base or alloy; inasmuch as it is only when right has some such firm and actual foundation that it can be enforced and consistently vindicated. They form for right a sort of [Greek: os moi pou sto]—a fulcrum for supporting its lever.

Linnæus adopted a vegetable system of an artificial and arbitrary character. It cannot be replaced by a natural one, no matter how reasonable the change might be, or how often it has been attempted to make it, because no other system could ever yield the same certainty and stability of definition. Just in the same way the artificial and arbitrary basis on which, as has been shown, the constitution of a State rests, can never be replaced by a purely natural basis. A natural basis would aim at doing away with the conditions that have been mentioned: in the place of the privileges of birth it would put those of personal merit; in the place of the national religion, the results of rationalistic inquiry, and so on. However agreeable to reason this might all prove, the change could not be made; because a natural basis would lack that certainty and fixity of definition which alone secures the stability of the commonwealth. A constitution which embodied abstract right alone would be an excellent thing for natures other than human, but since the great majority of men are extremely egoistic, unjust, inconsiderate, deceitful, and sometimes even malicious; since in addition they are endowed with very scanty intelligence there arises the necessity for a power that shall be concentrated in one man, a power that shall be above all law and right, and be completely irresponsible, nay, to which everything shall yield as to something that is regarded as a creature of a higher kind, a ruler by the grace of God. It is only thus that men can be permanently held in check and governed.

The United States of North America exhibit the attempt to proceed without any such arbitrary basis; that is to say, to allow abstract right to prevail pure and unalloyed. But the result is not attractive. For with all the material prosperity of the country what do we find? The prevailing sentiment is a base Utilitarianism with its inevitable companion, ignorance; and it is this that has paved the way for a union of stupid Anglican bigotry, foolish prejudice, coarse brutality, and a childish veneration of women. Even worse things are the order of the day: most iniquitous oppression of the black freemen, lynch law, frequent assassination often committed with entire impunity, duels of a savagery elsewhere unknown, now and then open scorn of all law and justice, repudiation of public debts, abominable political rascality towards a neighbouring State, followed by a mercenary raid on its rich territory,—afterwards sought to be excused, on the part of the chief authority of the State, by lies which every one in the country knew to be such and laughed at—an ever-increasing ochlocracy, and finally all the disastrous influence which this abnegation of justice in high quarters must have exercised on private morals. This specimen of a pure constitution on the obverse side of the planet says very little for republics in general, but still less for the imitations of it in Mexico, Guatemala, Colombia and Peru.

A peculiar disadvantage attaching to republics—and one that might not be looked for—is that in this form of government it must be more difficult for men of ability to attain high position and exercise direct political influence than in the case of monarchies. For always and everywhere and under all circumstances there is a conspiracy, or instinctive alliance, against such men on the part of all the stupid, the weak, and the commonplace; they look upon such men as their natural enemies, and they are firmly held together by a common fear of them. There is always a numerous host of the stupid and the weak, and in a republican constitution it is easy for them to suppress and exclude the men of ability, so that they may not be outflanked by them. They are fifty to one; and here all have equal rights at the start.

In a monarchy, on the other hand, this natural and universal league of the stupid against those who are possessed of intellectual advantages is a one-sided affair; it exists only from below, for in a monarchy talent and intelligence receive a natural advocacy and support from above. In the first place, the position of the monarch himself is much too high and too firm for him to stand in fear of any sort of competition. In the next place, he serves the State more by his will than by his intelligence; for no intelligence could ever be equal to all the demands that would in his case be made upon it. He is therefore compelled to be always availing himself of other men's intelligence. Seeing that his own interests are securely bound up with those of his country; that they are inseparable from them and one with them, he will naturally give the preference to the best men, because they are his most serviceable instruments, and he will bestow his favour upon them—as soon, that is, as he can find them; which is not so difficult, if only an honest search be made. Just in the same way even ministers of State have too much advantage over rising politicians to need to regard them with jealousy; and accordingly for analogous reasons they are glad to single out distinguished men and set them to work, in order to make use of their powers for themselves. It is in this way that intelligence has always under a monarchical government a much better chance against its irreconcilable and ever-present foe, stupidity; and the advantage which it gains is very great.

In general, the monarchical form of government is that which is natural to man; just as it is natural to bees and ants, to a flight of cranes, a herd of wandering elephants, a pack of wolves seeking prey in common, and many other animals, all of which place one of their number at the head of the business in hand. Every business in which men engage, if it is attended with danger—every campaign, every ship at sea—must also be subject to the authority of one commander; everywhere it is one will that must lead. Even the animal organism is constructed on a monarchical principle: it is the brain alone which guides and governs, and exercises the hegemony. Although heart, lungs, and stomach contribute much more to the continued existence of the whole body, these philistines cannot on that account be allowed to guide and lead. That is a business which belongs solely to the brain; government must proceed from one central point. Even the solar system is monarchical. On the other hand, a republic is as unnatural as it is unfavourable to the higher intellectual life and the arts and sciences. Accordingly we find that everywhere in the world, and at all times, nations, whether civilised or savage, or occupying a position between the two, are always under monarchical government. The rule of many as Homer said, is not a good thing: let there be one ruler, one king;

> [Greek: Ouk agathon polykoiraniae-eis koiranos esto
> Eis basoleus.][112]

How would it be possible that, everywhere and at all times, we should see many millions of people, nay, even hundreds of millions, become the willing and obedient subjects of one man, sometimes even one woman, and provisionally, even, of a child, unless there were a monarchical instinct in men which drove them to it as the form of government best suited to them? This arrangement is not the product of reflection. Everywhere one man is king, and for the most part his dignity is hereditary. He is, as it were, the personification, the monogram, of the whole people, which attains an individuality in him. In this sense he can rightly say: *l'etat c'est moi.* It is precisely for this reason that in Shakespeare's historical plays the kings of England and France mutually address each other as *France* and *England*, and the Duke of Austria goes by the name of his country. It is as though the kings regarded themselves as the incarnation of their nationalities. It is all in accordance with human nature; and for this very reason the hereditary monarch cannot separate his own welfare and that of his family from the welfare of his country; as, on the other hand, mostly happens when the monarch is elected, as, for instance, in the States of the Church.[113] The Chinese can conceive of a monarchical government only; what a republic is they utterly fail to understand. When a Dutch

---

[112] *Iliad*, ii., 204.
[113] *Translator's Note.*—The reader will recollect that Schopenhauer was writing long before the Papal territories were absorbed into the kingdom of Italy.

legation was in China in the year 1658, it was obliged to represent that the Prince of Orange was their king, as otherwise the Chinese would have been inclined to take Holland for a nest of pirates living without any lord or master.[114] Stobæus, in a chapter in his *Florilegium*, at the head of which he wrote *That monarchy is best*, collected the best of the passages in which the ancients explained the advantages of that form of government. In a word, republics are unnatural and artificial; they are the product of reflection. Hence it is that they occur only as rare exceptions in the whole history of the world. There were the small Greek republics, the Roman and the Carthaginian; but they were all rendered possible by the fact that five-sixths, perhaps even seven-eighths, of the population consisted of slaves. In the year 1840, even in the United States, there were three million slaves to a population of sixteen millions. Then, again, the duration of the republics of antiquity, compared with that of monarchies, was very short. Republics are very easy to found, and very difficult to maintain, while with monarchies it is exactly the reverse. If it is Utopian schemes that are wanted, I say this: the only solution of the problem would be a despotism of the wise and the noble, of the true aristocracy and the genuine nobility, brought about by the method of generation—that is, by the marriage of the noblest men with the cleverest and most intellectual women. This is my Utopia, my Republic of Plato.

Constitutional kings are undoubtedly in much the same position as the gods of Epicurus, who sit upon high in undisturbed bliss and tranquillity, and do not meddle with human affairs. Just now they are the fashion. In every German duodecimo-principality a parody of the English constitution is set up, quite complete, from Upper and Lower Houses down to the Habeas Corpus Act and trial by jury. These institutions, which proceed from English character and English circumstances, and presuppose both, are natural and suitable to the English people. It is just as natural to the German people to be split up into a number of different stocks, under a similar number of ruling Princes, with an Emperor over them all, who maintains peace at home, and represents the unity of the State board. It is an arrangement which has proceeded from German character and German circumstances. I am of opinion that if Germany is not to meet with the same fate as Italy, it must restore the imperial crown, which was done away with by its arch-enemy, the first Napoleon; and it must restore it as effectively as possible.[115] For German unity depends on it, and without the imperial

---

[114] See Jean Nieuhoff, *L'Ambassade de la Compagnie Orientale des Provinces Unies vers L'Empereur de la Chine*, traduit par Jean le Charpentier à Leyde, 1665; ch. 45.

[115] *Translator's Note.*—Here, again, it is hardly necessary to say that Schopenhauer, who died in 1860, and wrote this passage at least some years previously, cannot be

crown it will always be merely nominal, or precarious. But as we no longer live in the days of Günther of Schwarzburg, when the choice of Emperor was a serious business, the imperial crown ought to go alternately to Prussia and to Austria, for the life of the wearer. In any case, the absolute sovereignty of the small States is illusory. Napoleon I. did for Germany what Otto the Great did for Italy: he divided it into small, independent States, on the principle, *divide et impera.*

The English show their great intelligence, amongst other ways, by clinging to their ancient institutions, customs and usages, and by holding them sacred, even at the risk of carrying this tenacity too far, and making it ridiculous. They hold them sacred for the simple reason that those institutions and customs are not the invention of an idle head, but have grown up gradually by the force of circumstance and the wisdom of life itself, and are therefore suited to them as a nation. On the other hand, the German Michel[116] allows himself to be persuaded by his schoolmaster that he must go about in an English dress-coat, and that nothing else will do. Accordingly he has bullied his father into giving it to him; and with his awkward manners this ungainly creature presents in it a sufficiently ridiculous figure. But the dress-coat will some day be too tight for him and incommode him. It will not be very long before he feels it in trial by jury. This institution arose in the most barbarous period of the Middle Ages—the times of Alfred the Great, when the ability to read and write exempted a man from the penalty of death. It is the worst of all criminal procedures. Instead of judges, well versed in law and of great experience, who have grown grey in daily unravelling the tricks and wiles of thieves, murderers and rascals of all sorts, and so are well able to get at the bottom of things, it is gossiping tailors and tanners who sit in judgment; it is their coarse, crude, unpractised, and awkward intelligence, incapable of any sustained attention, that is called upon to find out the truth from a tissue of lies and deceit. All the time, moreover, they are thinking of their cloth and their leather, and longing to be at home; and they have absolutely no clear notion at all of the distinction between probability and certainty. It is with this sort of a calculus of probabilities in their stupid heads that they confidently undertake to seal a man's doom.

The same remark is applicable to them which Dr. Johnson made of

---

referring to any of the events which culminated in 1870. The whole passage forms a striking illustration of his political sagacity.

[116] *Translator's Note.*—It may be well to explain that "Michel" is sometimes used by the Germans as a nickname of their nation, corresponding to "John Bull" as a nickname of the English. Flügel in his German-English Dictionary declares that *der deutsche Michel* represents the German nation as an honest, blunt, unsuspicious fellow, who easily allows himself to be imposed upon, even, he adds, with a touch of patriotism, "by those who are greatly his inferiors in point of strength and real worth."

a court-martial in which he had little confidence, summoned to decide a very important case. He said that perhaps there was not a member of it who, in the whole course of his life, had ever spent an hour by himself in balancing probabilities.[117] Can any one imagine that the tailor and the tanner would be impartial judges? What! the vicious multitude impartial! as if partiality were not ten times more to be feared from men of the same class as the accused than from judges who knew nothing of him personally, lived in another sphere altogether, were irremovable, and conscious of the dignity of their office. But to let a jury decide on crimes against the State and its head, or on misdemeanors of the press, is in a very real sense to set the fox to keep the geese.

Everywhere and at all times there has been much discontent with governments, laws and public regulations; for the most part, however, because men are always ready to make institutions responsible for the misery inseparable from human existence itself; which is, to speak mythically, the curse that was laid on Adam, and through him on the whole race. But never has that delusion been proclaimed in a more mendacious and impudent manner than by the demagogues of the *Jetstzeit*—of the day we live in. As enemies of Christianity, they are, of course, optimists: to them the world is its own end and object, and accordingly in itself, that is to say, in its own natural constitution, it is arranged on the most excellent principles, and forms a regular habitation of bliss. The enormous and glaring evils of the world they attribute wholly to governments: if governments, they think, were to do their duty, there would be a heaven upon earth; in other words, all men could eat, drink, propagate and die, free from trouble and want. This is what they mean when they talk of the world being "its own end and object"; this is the goal of that "perpetual progress of the human race," and the other fine things which they are never tired of proclaiming.

Formerly it was *faith* which was the chief support of the throne; nowadays it is *credit*. The Pope himself is scarcely more concerned to retain the confidence of the faithful than to make his creditors believe in his own good faith. If in times past it was the guilty debt of the world which was lamented, now it is the financial debts of the world which arouse dismay. Formerly it was the Last Day which was prophesied; now it is the [Greek: seisachtheia] the great repudiation, the universal bankruptcy of the nations, which will one day happen; although the prophet, in this as in the other case, entertains a firm hope that he will not live to see it himself.

From an ethical and a rational point of view, the *right of possession* rests upon an incomparably better foundation than the *right of birth*; nevertheless, the right of possession is allied with the right of

---

[117] Boswell's *Johnson*, 1780, set. 71.

birth and has come to be part and parcel of it, so that it would hardly be possible to abolish the right of birth without endangering the right of possession. The reason of this is that most of what a man possesses he inherited, and therefore holds by a kind of right of birth; just as the old nobility bear the names only of their hereditary estates, and by the use of those names do no more than give expression to the fact that they own the estates. Accordingly all owners of property, if instead of being envious they were wise, ought also to support the maintenance of the rights of birth.

The existence of a nobility has, then, a double advantage: it helps to maintain on the one hand the rights of possession, and on the other the right of birth belonging to the king. For the king is the first nobleman in the country, and, as a general rule, he treats the nobility as his humble relations, and regards them quite otherwise than the commoners, however trusty and well-beloved. It is quite natural, too, that he should have more confidence in those whose ancestors were mostly the first ministers, and always the immediate associates, of his own. A nobleman, therefore, appeals with reason to the name he bears, when on the occurrence of anything to rouse distrust he repeats his assurance of fidelity and service to the king. A man's character, as my readers are aware, assuredly comes to him from his father. It is a narrow-minded and ridiculous thing not to consider whose son a man is.

FREE-WILL AND FATALISM.

No thoughtful man can have any doubt, after the conclusions reached in my prize-essay on *Moral Freedom*, that such freedom is to be sought, not anywhere in nature, but outside of it. The only freedom that exists is of a metaphysical character. In the physical world freedom is an impossibility. Accordingly, while our several actions are in no wise free, every man's individual character is to be regarded as a free act. He is such and such a man, because once for all it is his will to be that man. For the will itself, and in itself, and also in so far as it is manifest in an individual, and accordingly constitutes the original and fundamental desires of that individual, is independent of all knowledge, because it is antecedent to such knowledge. All that it receives from knowledge is the series of motives by which it successively develops its nature and makes itself cognisable or visible; but the will itself, as something that lies beyond time, and so long as it exists at all, never changes. Therefore every man, being what he is and placed in the circumstances which for the moment obtain, but which on their part also arise by strict necessity, can absolutely never do anything else than just what at that moment he does do. Accordingly, the whole course of a man's life, in all its incidents great and small, is as necessarily predetermined as the course of a clock.

The main reason of this is that the kind of metaphysical free act which I have described tends to become a knowing consciousness—a perceptive intuition, which is subject to the forms of space and time. By means of those forms the unity and indivisibility of the act are represented as drawn asunder into a series of states and events, which are subject to the Principle of Sufficient Reason in its four forms—and it is this that is meant by *necessity*. But the result of it all assumes a moral complexion. It amounts to this, that by what we do we know what we are, and by what we suffer we know what we deserve.

Further, it follows from this that a man's *individuality* does not rest upon the principle of individuation alone, and therefore is not altogether phenomenal in its nature. On the contrary, it has its roots in the thing-in-itself, in the will which is the essence of each individual. The character of this individual is itself individual. But how deep the roots of individuality extend is one of the questions which I do not undertake to answer.

In this connection it deserves to be mentioned that even Plato, in his own way, represented the individuality of a man as a free act.[118] He represented him as coming into the world with a given tendency, which was the result of the feelings and character already attaching to him in accordance with the doctrine of metempsychosis. The Brahmin philosophers also express the unalterable fixity of innate character in a mystical fashion. They say that Brahma, when a man is produced, engraves his doings and sufferings in written characters on his skull, and that his life must take shape in accordance therewith. They point to the jagged edges in the sutures of the skull-bones as evidence of this writing; and the purport of it, they say, depends on his previous life and actions. The same view appears to underlie the Christian, or rather, the Pauline, dogma of Predestination.

But this truth, which is universally confirmed by experience, is attended with another result. All genuine merit, moral as well as intellectual, is not merely physical or empirical in its origin, but metaphysical; that is to say, it is given *a priori* and not *a posteriori*; in other words, it lies innate and is not acquired, and therefore its source is not a mere phenomenon, but the thing-in-itself. Hence it is that every man achieves only that which is irrevocably established in his nature, or is born with him. Intellectual capacity needs, it is true, to be developed just as many natural products need to be cultivated in order that we may enjoy or use them; but just as in the case of a natural product no cultivation can take the place of original material, neither can it do so in the case of intellect. That is the reason why qualities

---

[118] *Phædrus* and *Laws, bk.* x.

which are merely acquired, or learned, or enforced—that is, qualities *a posteriori*, whether moral or intellectual—are not real or genuine, but superficial only, and possessed of no value. This is a conclusion of true metaphysics, and experience teaches the same lesson to all who can look below the surface. Nay, it is proved by the great importance which we all attach to such innate characteristics as physiognomy and external appearance, in the case of a man who is at all distinguished; and that is why we are so curious to see him. Superficial people, to be sure,—and, for very good reasons, commonplace people too,—will be of the opposite opinion; for if anything fails them they will thus be enabled to console themselves by thinking that it is still to come.

The world, then, is not merely a battlefield where victory and defeat receive their due recompense in a future state. No! the world is itself the Last Judgment on it. Every man carries with him the reward and the disgrace that he deserves; and this is no other than the doctrine of the Brahmins and Buddhists as it is taught in the theory of metempsychosis.

The question has been raised, What two men would do, who lived a solitary life in the wilds and met each other for the first time. Hobbes, Pufendorf, and Rousseau have given different answers. Pufendorf believed that they would approach each other as friends; Hobbes, on the contrary, as enemies; Rousseau, that they would pass each other by In silence. All three are both right and wrong. This is just a case in which the incalculable difference that there is in innate moral disposition between one individual and another would make its appearance. The difference is so strong that the question here raised might be regarded as the standard and measure of it. For there are men in whom the sight of another man at once rouses a feeling of enmity, since their inmost nature exclaims at once: That is not me! There are, others in whom the sight awakens immediate sympathy; their inmost nature says: *That is me over again!* Between the two there are countless degrees. That in this most important matter we are so totally different is a great problem, nay, a mystery.

In regard to this *a priori* nature of moral character there is matter for varied reflection in a work by Bastholm, a Danish writer, entitled *Historical Contributions to the Knowledge of Man in the Savage State.* He is struck by the fact that intellectual culture and moral excellence are shown to be entirely independent of each other, inasmuch as one is often found without the other. The reason of this, as we shall find, is simply that moral excellence in no wise springs from reflection, which is developed by intellectual culture, but from the will itself, the constitution of which is innate and not susceptible in itself of any improvement by means of education. Bastholm represents most nations as very vicious and immoral; and on the other hand he reports that excellent traits of character are found amongst some savage peoples; as, for instance, amongst the Orotchyses, the inhabitants of the island Savu, the Tunguses, and the Pelew islanders. He thus attempts to solve the problem, How it is that some tribes are so remarkably good, when their neighbours are all bad.

It seems to me that the difficulty may be explained as follows: Moral qualities, as we know, are heritable, and an isolated tribe, such as is described, might take its rise in some one family, and ultimately in a single ancestor who happened to be a good man, and then maintain its purity. Is it not the case, for instance, that on many unpleasant occasions, such as repudiation of public debts, filibustering raids and so on, the English have often reminded the North Americans of their descent from English penal colonists? It is a reproach, however, which can apply only to a small part of the population.

It is marvellous how *every man's individuality* (that is to say, the union of a definite character with a definite intellect) accurately determines all his actions and thoughts down to the most unimportant details, as though it were a dye which pervaded them; and how, in consequence, one man's whole course of life, in other words, his inner and outer history, turns out so absolutely different from another's. As a botanist knows a plant in its entirety from a single leaf; as Cuvier from a single bone constructed the whole animal, so an accurate knowledge of a man's whole character may be attained from a single characteristic act; that is to say, he himself may to some extent be constructed from it, even though the act in question is of very trifling consequence. Nay, that is the most perfect test of all, for in a matter of importance people are on their guard; in trifles they follow their natural bent without much reflection. That is why Seneca's remark, that even the smallest things may be taken as evidence of character, is so true: *argumenta morum ex minimis quoque licet capere.*[119] If a man shows by his absolutely unscrupulous and selfish behaviour in small things that a sentiment of justice is foreign to his disposition, he should not be trusted with a penny unless on due security. For who will believe that the man who every day shows that he is unjust in all matters other than those which concern property, and whose boundless selfishness everywhere protrudes through the small affairs of ordinary life which are subject to no scrutiny, like a dirty shirt through the holes of a ragged jacket— who, I ask, will believe that such a man will act honourably in matters of *meum* and *tuum* without any other incentive but that of justice? The man who has no conscience in small things will be a scoundrel in big things. If we neglect small traits of character, we have only ourselves to blame if we afterwards learn to our disadvantage what this character is in the great affairs of life. On the same principle, we ought to break

---

[119] *Ep.*, 52.

with so-called friends even in matters of trifling moment, if they show a
character that is malicious or bad or vulgar, so that we may avoid the
bad turn which only waits for an opportunity of being done us. The
same thing applies to servants. Let it always be our maxim: Better
alone than amongst traitors.

Of a truth the first and foremost step in all knowledge of mankind
is the conviction that a man's conduct, taken as a whole, and in all its
essential particulars, is not governed by his reason or by any of the
resolutions which he may make in virtue of it. No man becomes this or
that by wishing to be it, however earnestly. His acts proceed from his
innate and unalterable character, and they are more immediately and
particularly determined by motives. A man's conduct, therefore, is the
necessary product of both character and motive. It may be illustrated by
the course of a planet, which is the result of the combined effect of the
tangential energy with which it is endowed, and the centripetal energy
which operates from the sun. In this simile the former energy represents
character, and the latter the influence of motive. It is almost more than
a mere simile. The tangential energy which properly speaking is the
source of the planet's motion, whilst on the other hand the motion is
kept in check by gravitation, is, from a metaphysical point of view, the
will manifesting itself in that body.

To grasp this fact is to see that we really never form anything more
than a conjecture of what we shall do under circumstances which are
still to happen; although we often take our conjecture for a resolve.
When, for instance, in pursuance of a proposal, a man with the greatest
sincerity, and even eagerness, accepts an engagement to do this or that
on the occurrence of a certain future event, it is by no means certain
that he will fulfil the engagement; unless he is so constituted that the
promise which he gives, in itself and as such, is always and everywhere
a motive sufficient for him, by acting upon him, through considerations
of honour, like some external compulsion. But above and beyond this,
what he will do on the occurrence of that event may be foretold from
true and accurate knowledge of his character and the external
circumstances under the influence of which he will fall; and it may with
complete certainty be foretold from this alone. Nay, it is a very easy
prophecy if he has been already seen in a like position; for he will
inevitably do the same thing a second time, provided that on the first
occasion he had a true and complete knowledge of the facts of the case.
For, as I have often remarked, a final cause does not impel a man by
being real, but by being known; *causa finalis non movet secundum
suum esse reale, sed secundum esse cognitum.*[120] Whatever he failed to
recognise or understand the first time could have no influence upon his

---

[120] Suarez, *Disp. Metaph.*, xxiii.; §§7 and 8.

will; just as an electric current stops when some isolating body hinders the action of the conductor. This unalterable nature of character, and the consequent necessity of our actions, are made very clear to a man who has not, on any given occasion, behaved as he ought to have done, by showing a lack either of resolution or endurance or courage, or some other quality demanded at the moment. Afterwards he recognises what it is that he ought to have done; and, sincerely repenting of his incorrect behaviour, he thinks to himself, *If the opportunity were offered to me again, I should act differently.* It is offered once more; the same occasion recurs; and to his great astonishment he does precisely the same thing over again.[121]

The best examples of the truth in question are in every way furnished by Shakespeare's plays. It is a truth with which he was thoroughly imbued, and his intuitive wisdom expressed it in a concrete shape on every page. I shall here, however, give an instance of it in a case in which he makes it remarkably clear, without exhibiting any design or affectation in the matter; for he was a real artist and never set out from general ideas. His method was obviously to work up to the psychological truth which he grasped directly and intuitively, regardless of the fact that few would notice or understand it, and without the smallest idea that some dull and shallow fellows in Germany would one day proclaim far and wide that he wrote his works to illustrate moral commonplaces. I allude to the character of the Earl of Northumberland, whom we find in three plays in succession, although he does not take a leading part in any one of them; nay, he appears only in a few scenes distributed over fifteen acts. Consequently, if the reader is not very attentive, a character exhibited at such great intervals, and its moral identity, may easily escape his notice, even though it has by no means escaped the poet's. He makes the earl appear everywhere with a noble and knightly grace, and talk in language suitable to it; nay, he sometimes puts very beautiful and even elevated passages, into his mouth. At the same time he is very far from writing after the manner of Schiller, who was fond of painting the devil black, and whose moral approval or disapproval of the characters which he presented could be heard in their own words. With Shakespeare, and also with Goethe, every character, as long as he is on the stage and speaking, seems to be absolutely in the right, even though it were the devil himself. In this respect let the reader compare Duke Alba as he appears in Goethe with the same character in Schiller.

We make the acquaintance of the Earl of Northumberland in the play of *Richard II.*, where he is the first to hatch a plot against the King in favour of Bolingbroke, afterwards Henry IV., to whom he even

---

[121] Cf. *World as Will*, ii., pp. 251 ff. *sqq.* (third edition).

offers some personal flattery (Act II., Sc. 3). In the following act he suffers a reprimand because, in speaking of the King he talks of him as "Richard," without more ado, but protests that he did it only for brevity's sake. A little later his insidious words induce the King to surrender. In the following act, when the King renounces the crown, Northumberland treats him with such harshness and contempt that the unlucky monarch is quite broken, and losing all patience once more exclaims to him: *Fiend, thou torment'st me ere I come to hell*! At the close, Northumberland announces to the new King that he has sent the heads of the former King's adherents to London.

In the following tragedy, *Henry IV.*, he hatches a plot against the new King in just the same way. In the fourth act we see the rebels united, making preparations for the decisive battle on the morrow, and only waiting impatiently for Northumberland and his division. At last there arrives a letter from him, saying that he is ill, and that he cannot entrust his force to any one else; but that nevertheless the others should go forward with courage and make a brave fight. They do so, but, greatly weakened by his absence, they are completely defeated; most of their leaders are captured, and his own son, the valorous Hotspur, falls by the hand of the Prince of Wales.

Again, in the following play, the *Second Part of Henry IV.*, we see him reduced to a state of the fiercest wrath by the death of his son, and maddened by the thirst for revenge. Accordingly he kindles another rebellion, and the heads of it assemble once more. In the fourth act, just as they are about to give battle, and are only waiting for him to join them, there comes a letter saying that he cannot collect a proper force, and will therefore seek safety for the present in Scotland; that, nevertheless, he heartily wishes their heroic undertaking the best success. Thereupon they surrender to the King under a treaty which is not kept, and so perish.

So far is character from being the work of reasoned choice and consideration that in any action the intellect has nothing to do but to present motives to the will. Thereafter it looks on as a mere spectator and witness at the course which life takes, in accordance with the influence of motive on the given character. All the incidents of life occur, strictly speaking, with the same necessity as the movement of a clock. On this point let me refer to my prize-essay on *The Freedom of the Will*. I have there explained the true meaning and origin of the persistent illusion that the will is entirely free in every single action; and I have indicated the cause to which it is due. I will only add here the following teleological explanation of this natural illusion.

Since every single action of a man's life seems to possess the freedom and originality which in truth only belong to his character as he apprehends it, and the mere apprehension of it by his intellect is what constitutes his career; and since what is original in every single action seems to the empirical consciousness to be always being performed anew, a man thus receives in the course of his career the strongest possible moral lesson. Then, and not before, he becomes thoroughly conscious of all the bad sides of his character. Conscience accompanies every act with the comment: *You should act differently*, although its true sense is: *You could be other than you are.* As the result of this immutability of character on the one hand, and, on the other, of the strict necessity which attends all the circumstances in which character is successively placed, every man's course of life is precisely determined from Alpha right through to Omega. But, nevertheless, one man's course of life turns out immeasurably happier, nobler and more worthy than another's, whether it be regarded from a subjective or an objective point of view, and unless we are to exclude all ideas of justice, we are led to the doctrine which is well accepted in Brahmanism and Buddhism, that the subjective conditions in which, as well as the objective conditions under which, every man is born, are the moral consequences of a previous existence.

Macchiavelli, who seems to have taken no interest whatever in philosophical speculations, is drawn by the keen subtlety of his very unique understanding into the following observation, which possesses a really deep meaning. It shows that he had an intuitive knowledge of the entire necessity with which, characters and motives being given, all actions take place. He makes it at the beginning of the prologue to his comedy *Clitia. If*, he says, *the same men were to recur in the world in the way that the same circumstances recur, a hundred years would never elapse without our finding ourselves together once more, and doing the same things as we are doing now—Se nel mondo tornassino i medesimi uomini, como tornano i medesimi casi, non passarebbono mai cento anni che noi non ci trovassimo un altra volta insieme, a fare le medesime cose che hora.* He seems however to have been drawn into the remark by a reminiscence of what Augustine says in his *De Civitate Dei*, bk. xii., ch. xiii.

Again, Fate, or the [Greek: eimarmenae] of the ancients, is nothing but the conscious certainty that all that happens is fast bound by a chain of causes, and therefore takes place with a strict necessity; that the future is already ordained with absolute certainty and can undergo as little alteration as the past. In the fatalistic myths of the ancients all that can be regarded as fabulous is the prediction of the future; that is, if we refuse to consider the possibility of magnetic clairvoyance and second sight. Instead of trying to explain away the fundamental truth of Fatalism by superficial twaddle and foolish evasion, a man should attempt to get a clear knowledge and comprehension of it; for it is demonstrably true, and it helps us in a very important way to an understanding of the mysterious riddle of our life. Predestination and Fatalism do not differ in the main. They differ only in this, that with

Predestination the given character and external determination of human action proceed from a rational Being, and with Fatalism from an irrational one. But in either case the result is the same: that happens which must happen.

On the other hand the conception of *Moral Freedom* is inseparable from that of *Originality*. A man may be said, but he cannot be conceived, to be the work of another, and at the same time be free in respect of his desires and acts. He who called him into existence out of nothing in the same process created and determined his nature—in other words, the whole of his qualities. For no one can create without creating a something, that is to say, a being determined throughout and in all its qualities. But all that a man says and does necessarily proceeds from the qualities so determined; for it is only the qualities themselves set in motion. It is only some external impulse that they require to make their appearance. As a man is, so must he act; and praise or blame attaches, not to his separate acts, but to his nature and being.

That is the reason why Theism and the moral responsibility of man are incompatible; because responsibility always reverts to the creator of man and it is there that it has its centre. Vain attempts have been made to make a bridge from one of these incompatibles to the other by means of the conception of moral freedom; but it always breaks down again. What is *free* must also be *original*. If our will is *free*, our will is also *the original element*, and conversely. Pre-Kantian dogmatism tried to separate these two predicaments. It was thereby compelled to assume two kinds of freedom, one cosmological, of the first cause, and the other moral and theological, of human will. These are represented in Kant by the third as well as the fourth antinomy of freedom.

On the other hand, in my philosophy the plain recognition of the strictly necessary character of all action is in accordance with the doctrine that what manifests itself even in the organic and irrational world is *will*. If this were not so, the necessity under which irrational beings obviously act would place their action in conflict with will; if, I mean, there were really such a thing as the freedom of individual action, and this were not as strictly necessitated as every other kind of action. But, as I have just shown, it is this same doctrine of the necessary character of all acts of will which makes it needful to regard a man's existence and being as itself the work of his freedom, and consequently of his will. The will, therefore, must be self-existent; it must possess so-called *a-se-ity*. Under the opposite supposition all responsibility, as I have shown, would be at an end, and the moral like the physical world would be a mere machine, set in motion for the amusement of its manufacturer placed somewhere outside of it. So it is that truths hang together, and mutually advance and complete one another; whereas error gets jostled at every corner.

What kind of influence it is that *moral instruction* may exercise on conduct, and what are the limits of that influence, are questions which I have sufficiently examined in the twentieth section of my treatise on the *Foundation of Morality*. In all essential particulars an analogous influence is exercised by *example*, which, however, has a more powerful effect than doctrine, and therefore it deserves a brief analysis.

In the main, example works either by restraining a man or by encouraging him. It has the former effect when it determines him to leave undone what he wanted to do. He sees, I mean, that other people do not do it; and from this he judges, in general, that it is not expedient; that it may endanger his person, or his property, or his honour. He rests content, and gladly finds himself relieved from examining into the matter for himself. Or he may see that another man, who has not refrained, has incurred evil consequences from doing it; this is example of the deterrent kind. The example which encourages a man works in a twofold manner. It either induces him to do what he would be glad to leave undone, if he were not afraid lest the omission might in some way endanger him, or injure him in others' opinion; or else it encourages him to do what he is glad to do, but has hitherto refrained from doing from fear of danger or shame; this is example of the seductive kind. Finally, example may bring a man to do what he would have otherwise never thought of doing. It is obvious that in this last case example works in the main only on the intellect; its effect on the will is secondary, and if it has any such effect, it is by the interposition of the man's own judgment, or by reliance on the person who presented the example.

The whole influence of example—and it is very strong—rests on the fact that a man has, as a rule, too little judgment of his own, and often too little knowledge, o explore his own way for himself, and that he is glad, therefore, to tread in the footsteps of some one else. Accordingly, the more deficient he is in either of these qualities, the more is he open to the influence of example; and we find, in fact, that most men's guiding star is the example of others; that their whole course of life, in great things and in small, comes in the end to be mere imitation; and that not even in the pettiest matters do they act according to their own judgment. Imitation and custom are the spring of almost all human action. The cause of it is that men fight shy of all and any sort of reflection, and very properly mistrust their own discernment. At the same time this remarkably strong imitative instinct in man is a proof of his kinship with apes.

But the kind of effect which example exercises depends upon a man's character, and thus it is that the same example may possibly seduce one man and deter another. An easy opportunity of observing this is afforded in the case of certain social impertinences which come into vogue and gradually spread. The first time that a man notices anything of the kind, he may say to himself: *For shame! how can he do it*! *how selfish and inconsiderate of him*! *really, I shall take care never to do anything like that.* But twenty others will think: *Aha*! *if he does that, I may do it too.*

As regards morality, example, like doctrine, may, it is true, promote civil or legal amelioration, but not that inward amendment which is, strictly speaking, the only kind of moral amelioration. For example always works as a personal motive alone, and assumes, therefore, that a man is susceptible to this sort of motive. But it is just the predominating sensitiveness of a character to this or that sort of motive that determines whether its morality is true and real; though, of whatever kind it is, it is always innate. In general it may be said that example operates as a means of promoting the good and the bad qualities of a character, but it does not create them; and so it is that Seneca's maxim, *velle non discitur—will cannot be learned*—also holds good here. But the innateness of all truly moral qualities, of the good as of the bad, is a doctrine that consorts better with the metempsychosis of the Brahmins and Buddhists, according to which a man's good and bad deeds follow him from one existence to another like his shadow, than with Judaism. For Judaism requires a man to come into the world as a moral blank, so that, in virtue of an inconceivable free will, directed to objects which are neither to be sought nor avoided—*liberum arbitrium indifferentiæ*—and consequently as the result of reasoned consideration, he may choose whether he is to be an angel or a devil, or anything else that may lie between the two. Though I am well aware what the Jewish scheme is, I pay no attention to it; for my standard is truth. I am no professor of philosophy, and therefore I do not find my vocation in establishing the fundamental ideas of Judaism at any cost, even though they for ever bar the way to all and every kind of philosophical knowledge. *Liberum arbitrium indifferentiæ* under the name of *moral freedom* is a charming doll for professors of philosophy to dandle; and we must leave it to those intelligent, honourable and upright gentlemen.

CHARACTER.

Men who aspire to a happy, a brilliant and a long life, instead of to a virtuous one, are like foolish actors who want to be always having the great parts,—the parts that are marked by splendour and triumph. They fail to see that the important thing is not *what* or *how much*, but *how* they act.

Since *a man does not alter*, and his *moral character* remains absolutely the same all through his life; since he must play out the part which he has received, without the least deviation from the character; since neither experience, nor philosophy, nor religion can effect any improvement in him, the question arises, What is the meaning of life at all? To what purpose is it played, this farce in which everything that is essential is irrevocably fixed and determined?

It is played that a man may come to understand himself, that he may see what it is that he seeks and has sought to be; what he wants, and what, therefore, he is. *This is a knowledge which must be imparted to him from without.* Life is to man, in other words, to will, what chemical re-agents are to the body: it is only by life that a man reveals what he is, and it is only in so far as he reveals himself that he exists at all. Life is the manifestation of character, of the something that we understand by that word; and it is not in life, but outside of it, and outside time, that character undergoes alteration, as a result of the self-knowledge which life gives. Life is only the mirror into which a man gazes not in order that he may get a reflection of himself, but that he may come to understand himself by that reflection; that he may see *what* it is that the mirror shows. Life is the proof sheet, in which the compositors' errors are brought to light. How they become visible, and whether the type is large or small, are matters of no consequence. Neither in the externals of life nor in the course of history is there any significance; for as it is all one whether an error occurs in the large type or in the small, so it is all one, as regards the essence of the matter, whether an evil disposition is mirrored as a conqueror of the world or a common swindler or ill-natured egoist. In one case he is seen of all men; in the other, perhaps only of himself; but that he should see himself is what signifies.

Therefore if egoism has a firm hold of a man and masters him, whether it be in the form of joy, or triumph, or lust, or hope, or frantic grief, or annoyance, or anger, or fear, or suspicion, or passion of any kind—he is in the devil's clutches and how he got into them does not matter. What is needful is that he should make haste to get out of them; and here, again, it does not matter how.

I have described *character* as *theoretically* an act of will lying beyond time, of which life in time, or *character in action*, is the development. For matters of practical life we all possess the one as well as the other; for we are constituted of them both. Character modifies our life more than we think, and it is to a certain extent true that every man is the architect of his own fortune. No doubt it seems as if our lot were assigned to us almost entirely from without, and imparted to us in something of the same way in which a melody outside us reaches the ear. But on looking back over our past, we see at once that our life consists of mere variations on one and the same theme, namely, our character, and that the same fundamental bass sounds through it all. This is an experience which a man can and must make in and by himself.

Not only a man's life, but his intellect too, may be possessed of a clear and definite character, so far as his intellect is applied to matters of theory. It is not every man, however, who has an intellect of this kind; for any such definite individuality as I mean is genius—an original view of the world, which presupposes an absolutely exceptional individuality, which is the essence of genius. A man's intellectual character is the theme on which all his works are variations. In an essay which I wrote in Weimar I called it the knack by which every genius produces his works, however various. This intellectual character determines the physiognomy of men of genius—what I might call *the theoretical physiognomy*—and gives it that distinguished expression which is chiefly seen in the eyes and the forehead. In the case of ordinary men the physiognomy presents no more than a weak analogy with the physiognomy of genius. On the other hand, all men possess *the practical physiognomy*, the stamp of will, of practical character, of moral disposition; and it shows itself chiefly in the mouth.

Since character, so far as we understand its nature, is above and beyond time, it cannot undergo any change under the influence of life. But although it must necessarily remain the same always, it requires time to unfold itself and show the very diverse aspects which it may possess. For character consists of two factors: one, the will-to-live itself, blind impulse, so-called impetuosity; the other, the restraint which the will acquires when it comes to understand the world; and the world, again, is itself will. A man may begin by following the craving of desire, until he comes to see how hollow and unreal a thing is life, how deceitful are its pleasures, what horrible aspects it possesses; and this it is that makes people hermits, penitents, Magdalenes. Nevertheless it is to be observed that no such change from a life of great indulgence in pleasure to one of resignation is possible, except to the man who of his own accord renounces pleasure. A really bad life cannot be changed into a virtuous one. The most beautiful soul, before it comes to know life from its horrible side, may eagerly drink the sweets of life and remain innocent. But it cannot commit a bad action; it cannot cause others suffering to do a pleasure to itself, for in that case it would see clearly what it would be doing; and whatever be its youth and inexperience it perceives the sufferings of others as clearly as its own pleasures. That is why one bad action is a guarantee that numberless others will be committed as soon as circumstances give occasion for them. Somebody once remarked to me, with entire justice, that every man had something very good and humane in his disposition, and also something very bad and malignant; and that according as he was moved one or the other of them made its appearance. The sight of others' suffering arouses, not only in different men, but in one and the same man, at one moment an inexhaustible sympathy, at another a certain satisfaction; and this satisfaction may increase until it becomes the cruelest delight in pain. I observe in myself that at one moment I regard all mankind with heartfelt pity, at another with the greatest indifference, on occasion with hatred, nay, with a positive enjoyment of their pain.

All this shows very clearly that we are possessed of two different, nay, absolutely contradictory, ways of regarding the world: one according to the principle of individuation, which exhibits all creatures as entire strangers to us, as definitely not ourselves. We can have no feelings for them but those of indifference, envy, hatred, and delight that they suffer. The other way of regarding the world is in accordance with what I may call the *Tat-twam-asi—this-is-thyself* principle. All creatures are exhibited as identical with ourselves; and so it is pity and love which the sight of them arouses.

The one method separates individuals by impassable barriers; the other removes the barrier and brings the individuals together. The one makes us feel, in regard to every man, *that is what I am*; the other, *that is not what I am*. But it is remarkable that while the sight of another's suffering makes us feel our identity with him, and arouses our pity, this is not so with the sight of another's happiness. Then we almost always feel some envy; and even though we may have no such feeling in certain cases,—as, for instance, when our friends are happy,—yet the interest which we take in their happiness is of a weak description, and cannot compare with the sympathy which we feel with their suffering. Is this because we recognise all happiness to be a delusion, or an impediment to true welfare? No! I am inclined to think that it is because the sight of the pleasure, or the possessions, which are denied to us, arouses envy; that is to say, the wish that we, and not the other, had that pleasure or those possessions.

It is only the first way of looking at the world which is founded on any demonstrable reason. The other is, as it were, the gate out of this world; it has no attestation beyond itself, unless it be the very abstract and difficult proof which my doctrine supplies. Why the first way predominates in one man, and the second in another—though perhaps it does not exclusively predominate in any man; why the one or the other emerges according as the will is moved—these are deep problems. The paths of night and day are close together:

[Greek: Engus gar nuktos de kai aematos eisi keleuthoi.]

It is a fact that there is a great and original difference between one empirical character and another; and it is a difference which, at bottom, rests upon the relation of the individual's will to his intellectual faculty. This relation is finally determined by the degree of will in his father and of intellect in his mother; and the union of father and mother is for the most part an affair of chance. This would all mean a revolting injustice in the nature of the world, if it were not that the difference between parents and son is phenomenal only and all chance is, at bottom, necessity.

As regards the freedom of the will, if it were the case that the will manifested itself in a single act alone, it would be a free act. But the will manifests itself in a course of life, that is to say, in a series of acts. Every one of these acts, therefore, is determined as a part of a complete whole, and cannot happen otherwise than it does happen. On the other hand, the whole series is free; it is simply the manifestation of an individualised will.

If a man feels inclined to commit a bad action and refrains, he is kept back either (1) by fear of punishment or vengeance; or (2) by superstition in other words, fear of punishment in a future life; or (3) by the feeling of sympathy, including general charity; or (4) by the feeling of honour, in other words, the fear of shame; or (5) by the feeling of justice, that is, an objective attachment to fidelity and good-faith, coupled with a resolve to hold them sacred, because they are the foundation of all free intercourse between man and man, and therefore often of advantage to himself as well. This last thought, not indeed as a thought, but as a mere feeling, influences people very frequently. It is this that often compels a man of honour, when some great but unjust advantage is offered him, to reject it with contempt and proudly exclaim: *I am an honourable man*! For otherwise how should a poor man, confronted with the property which chance or even some worse agency has bestowed on the rich, whose very existence it is that makes him poor, feel so much sincere respect for this property, that he refuses to touch it even in his need; and although he has a prospect of escaping punishment, what other thought is it that can be at the bottom of such a man's honesty? He is resolved not to separate himself from the great community of honourable people who have the earth in possession, and whose laws are recognised everywhere. He knows that a single dishonest act will ostracise and proscribe him from that society for ever. No! a man will spend money on any soil that yields him good fruit, and he will make sacrifices for it.

With a good action,—that, every action in which a man's own advantage is ostensibly subordinated to another's,—the motive is either (1) self-interest, kept in the background; or (2) superstition, in other words, self-interest in the form of reward in another life; or (3) sympathy; or (4) the desire to lend a helping hand, in other words, attachment to the maxim that we should assist one another in need, and the wish to maintain this maxim, in view of the presumption that some day we ourselves may find it serve our turn. For what Kant calls a good action done from motives of duty and for the sake of duty, there is, as will be seen, no room at all. Kant himself declares it to be doubtful whether an action was ever determined by pure motives of duty alone. I affirm most certainly that no action was ever so done; it is mere babble; there is nothing in it that could really act as a motive to any man. When he shelters himself behind verbiage of that sort, he is always actuated by one of the four motives which I have described. Among these it is obviously sympathy alone which is quite genuine and sincere.

Good and *bad* apply to character only *à potiori*; that is to say, we prefer the good to the bad; but, absolutely, there is no such distinction. The difference arises at the point which lies between subordinating one's own advantage to that of another, and not subordinating it. If a man keeps to the exact middle, he is *just*. But most men go an inch in their regard for others' welfare to twenty yards in regard for their own.

The source of *good* and of *bad character*, so far as we have any real knowledge of it, lies in this, that with the bad character the thought of the external world, and especially of the living creatures in it, is accompanied—all the more, the greater the resemblance between them and the individual self—by a constant feeling of *not I, not I, not I.*

Contrarily, with the good character (both being assumed to exist in a high degree) the same thought has for its accompaniment, like a fundamental bass, a constant feeling of *I, I, I.* From this spring benevolence and a disposition to help all men, and at the same time a cheerful, confident and tranquil frame of mind, the opposite of that which accompanies the bad character.

The difference, however, is only phenomenal, although it is a difference which is radical. But now we come to *the hardest of all problems*: How is it that, while the will, as the thing-in-itself, is identical, and from a metaphysical point of view one and the same in all its manifestations, there is nevertheless such an enormous difference between one character and another?—the malicious, diabolical wickedness of the one, and set off against it, the goodness of the other, showing all the more conspicuously. How is it that we get a Tiberius, a Caligula, a Carcalla, a Domitian, a Nero; and on the other hand, the Antonines, Titus, Hadrian, Nerva? How is it that among the animals, nay, in a higher species, in individual animals, there is a like difference?—the malignity of the cat most strongly developed in the tiger; the spite of the monkey; on the other hand, goodness, fidelity and love in the dog and the elephant. It is obvious that the principle of wickedness in the brute is the same as in man.

We may to some extent modify the difficulty of the problem by observing that the whole difference is in the end only one of degree. In every living creature, the fundamental propensities and instincts all exist, but they exist in very different degrees and proportions. This, however, is not enough to explain the facts.

We must fall back upon the intellect and its relation to the will; it is the only explanation that remains. A man's intellect, however, by no means stands in any direct and obvious relation with the goodness of his character. We may, it is true, discriminate between two kinds of intellect: between understanding, as the apprehension of relation in accordance with the Principle of Sufficient Reason, and cognition, a faculty akin to genius, which acts more directly, is independent of this law, and passes beyond the Principle of Individuation. The latter is the faculty which apprehends Ideas, and it is the faculty which has to do with morality. But even this explanation leaves much to be desired. *Fine minds are seldom fine souls* was the correct observation of Jean Paul; although they are never the contrary. Lord Bacon, who, to be sure, was less a fine soul than a fine mind, was a scoundrel.

I have declared space and time to be part of the Principle of Individuation, as it is only space and time that make the multiplicity of similar objects a possibility. But multiplicity itself also admits of variety; multiplicity and diversity are not only quantitative, but also qualitative. How is it that there is such a thing as qualitative diversity, especially in ethical matters? Or have I fallen into an error the opposite of that in which Leibnitz fell with his *identitas indiscernibilium*?

The chief cause of intellectual diversity is to be found in the brain and nervous system. This is a fact which somewhat lessens the obscurity of the subject. With the brutes the intellect and the brain are strictly adapted to their aims and needs. With man alone there is now and then, by way of exception, a superfluity, which, if it is abundant, may yield genius. But ethical diversity, it seems, proceeds immediately from the will. Otherwise ethical character would not be above and beyond time, as it is only in the individual that intellect and will are united. The will is above and beyond time, and eternal; and character is innate; that is to say, it is sprung from the same eternity, and therefore it does not admit of any but a transcendental explanation.

Perhaps some one will come after me who will throw light into this dark abyss.

MORAL INSTINCT.

An act done by instinct differs from every other kind of act in that an understanding of its object does not precede it but follows upon it. Instinct is therefore a rule of action given *à priori*. We may be unaware of the object to which it is directed, as no understanding of it is necessary to its attainment. On the other hand, if an act is done by an exercise of reason or intelligence, it proceeds according to a rule which the understanding has itself devised for the purpose of carrying out a preconceived aim. Hence it is that action according to rule may miss its aim, while instinct is infallible.

On the *à priori* character of instinct we may compare what Plato says in the *Philebus*. With Plato instinct is a reminiscence of something which a man has never actually experienced in his lifetime; in the same way as, in the *Phædo* and elsewhere, everything that a man learns is regarded as a reminiscence. He has no other word to express the *à priori* element in all experience.

There are, then, three things that are *à priori*:

(1) Theoretical Reason, in other words, the conditions which make all experience possible.

(2) Instinct, or the rule by which an object promoting the life of the senses may, though unknown, be attained.

(3) The Moral Law, or the rule by which an action takes place without any object.

Accordingly rational or intelligent action proceeds by a rule laid down in accordance with the object as it is understood. Instinctive action proceeds by a rule without an understanding of the object of it. Moral action proceeds by a rule without any object at all.

Theoretical Reason is the aggregate of rules in accordance with which all my knowledge—that is to say, the whole world of experience—necessarily proceeds. In the same manner *Instinct* is the aggregate of rules in accordance with which all my action necessarily proceeds if it meets with no obstruction. Hence it seems to me that Instinct may most appropriately be called *practical reason*, for like theoretical reason it determines the *must* of all experience.

The so-called moral law, on the other hand, is only one aspect of *the better consciousness*, the aspect which it presents from the point of view of instinct. This better consciousness is something lying beyond all experience, that is, beyond all reason, whether of the theoretical or the practical kind, and has nothing to do with it; whilst it is in virtue of the mysterious union of it and reason in the same individual that the better consciousness comes into conflict with reason, leaving the individual to choose between the two.

In any conflict between the better consciousness and reason, if the individual decides for reason, should it be theoretical reason, he becomes a narrow, pedantic philistine; should it be practical, a rascal.

If he decides for the better consciousness, we can make no further positive affirmation about him, for if we were to do so, we should find ourselves in the realm of reason; and as it is only what takes place within this realm that we can speak of at all it follows that we cannot speak of the better consciousness except in negative terms.

This shows us how it is that reason is hindered and obstructed; that *theoretical reason* is suppressed in favour of *genius*, and *practical reason* in favour of *virtue*. Now the better consciousness is neither theoretical nor practical; for these are distinctions that only apply to reason. But if the individual is in the act of choosing, the better consciousness appears to him in the aspect which it assumes in vanquishing and overcoming the practical reason (or instinct, to use the common word). It appears to him as an imperative command, an *ought*. It so appears to him, I say; in other words, that is the shape which it takes for the theoretical reason which renders all things into objects and ideas. But in so far as the better consciousness desires to vanquish and overcome the theoretical reason, it takes no shape at all; on the simple ground that, as it comes into play, the theoretical reason is suppressed and becomes the mere servant of the better consciousness. That is why genius can never give any account of its own works.

In the morality of action, the legal principle that both sides are to be heard must not be allowed to apply; in other words, the claims of self and the senses must not be urged. Nay, on the contrary, as soon as the pure will has found expression, the case is closed; *nec audienda altera pars.*

The lower animals are not endowed with moral freedom. Probably this is not because they show no trace of the better consciousness which in us is manifested as morality, or nothing analogous to it; for, if that were so, the lower animals, which are in so many respects like ourselves in outward appearance that we regard man as a species of animal, would possess some *raison d'être* entirely different from our own, and actually be, in their essential and inmost nature, something quite other than ourselves. This is a contention which is obviously refuted by the thoroughly malignant and inherently vicious character of certain animals, such as the crocodile, the hyæna, the scorpion, the snake, and the gentle, affectionate and contented character of others, such as the dog. Here, as in the case of men, the character, as it is manifested, must rest upon something that is above and beyond time. For, as Jacob Böhme says,[122] *there is a power in every animal which is indestructible, and the spirit of the world draws it into itself, against the final separation at the Last Judgment.* Therefore we cannot call the lower animals free, and the reason why we cannot do so is that they are wanting in a faculty which is profoundly subordinate to the better consciousness in its highest phase, I mean reason. Reason is the faculty of supreme comprehension, the idea of totality. How reason manifests itself in the theoretical sphere Kant has shown, and it does the same in the practical: it makes us capable of observing and surveying the whole of our life, thought, and action, in continual connection, and therefore of acting according to general maxims, whether those maxims originate in the understanding as prudential rules, or in the better consciousness as moral laws.

If any desire or passion is aroused in us, we, and in the same way the lower animals, are for the moment filled with this desire; we are all anger, all lust, all fear; and in such moments neither the better consciousness can speak, nor the understanding consider the consequences. But in our case reason allows us even at that moment to see our actions and our life as an unbroken chain,—a chain which

---

[122] *Epistles,* 56.

connects our earlier resolutions, or, it may be, the future consequences of our action, with the moment of passion which now fills our whole consciousness. It shows us the identity of our person, even when that person is exposed to influences of the most varied kind, and thereby we are enabled to act according to maxims. The lower animal is wanting in this faculty; the passion which seizes it completely dominates it, and can be checked only by another passion—anger, for instance, or lust, by fear; even though the vision that terrifies does not appeal to the senses, but is present in the animal only as a dim memory and imagination. Men, therefore, may be called irrational, if, like the lower animals, they allow themselves to be determined by the moment.

So far, however, is reason from being the source of morality that it is reason alone which makes us capable of being rascals, which the lower animals cannot be. It is reason which enables us to form an evil resolution and to keep it when the provocation to evil is removed; it enables us, for example, to nurse vengeance. Although at the moment that we have an opportunity of fulfilling our resolution the better consciousness may manifest itself as love or charity, it is by force of reason, in pursuance of some evil maxim, that we act against it. Thus Goethe says that a man may use his reason only for the purpose of being more bestial than any beast:

> *Er hat Vernunft, doch braucht er sie allein*
> *Um theirischer als jedes Thier zu sein.*

For not only do we, like the beasts, satisfy the desires of the moment, but we refine upon them and stimulate them in order to prepare the desire for the satisfaction.

Whenever we think that we perceive a trace of reason in the lower animals, it fills us with surprise. Now our surprise is not excited by the good and affectionate disposition which some of them exhibit—we recognise that as something other than reason—but by some action in them which seems to be determined not by the impression of the moment, but by a resolution previously made and kept. Elephants, for instance, are reported to have taken premeditated revenge for insults long after they were suffered; lions, to have requited benefits on an opportunity tardily offered. The truth of such stories has, however, no bearing at all on the question, What do we mean by reason? But they enable us to decide whether in the lower animals there is any trace of anything that we can call reason.

Kant not only declares that all our moral sentiments originate in reason, but he lays down that reason, *in my sense of the word*, is a condition of moral action; as he holds that for an action to be virtuous and meritorious it must be done in accordance with maxims, and not spring from a resolve taken under some momentary impression. But in both contentions he is wrong. If I resolve to take vengeance on some one, and when an opportunity offers, the better consciousness in the form of love and humanity speaks its word, and I am influenced by it rather than by my evil resolution, this is a virtuous act, for it is a manifestation of the better consciousness. It is possible to conceive of a very virtuous man in whom the better consciousness is so continuously active that it is never silent, and never allows his passions to get a complete hold of him. By such consciousness he is subject to a direct control, instead of being guided indirectly, through the medium of reason, by means of maxims and moral principles. That is why a man may have weak reasoning powers and a weak understanding and yet have a high sense of morality and be eminently good; for the most important element in a man depends as little on intellectual as it does on physical strength. Jesus says, *Blessed are the poor in spirit.* And Jacob Böhme has the excellent and noble observation: *Whoso lies quietly in his own will, like a child in the womb, and lets himself be led and guided by that inner principle from which he is sprung, is the noblest and richest on earth.*[123]

ETHICAL REFLECTIONS.

The philosophers of the ancient world united in a single conception a great many things that had no connection with one another. Of this every dialogue of Plato's furnishes abundant examples. The greatest and worst confusion of this kind is that between ethics and politics. The State and the Kingdom of God, or the Moral Law, are so entirely different in their character that the former is a parody of the latter, a bitter mockery at the absence of it. Compared with the Moral Law the State is a crutch instead of a limb, an automaton instead of a man.

* * * * *

The *principle of honour* stands in close connection with human freedom. It is, as it were, an abuse of that freedom. Instead of using his freedom to fulfil the moral law, a man employs his power of voluntarily undergoing any feeling of pain, of overcoming any momentary impression, in order that he may assert his self-will, whatever be the object to which he directs it. As he thereby shows that, unlike the lower animals, he has thoughts which go beyond the welfare of his body and whatever makes for that welfare, it has come about that the principle of honour is often confused with virtue. They are regarded as if they were twins. But wrongly; for although the principle of honour is something

---

[123] *Epistles*, 37.

which distinguishes man from the lower animals, it is not, in itself, anything that raises him above them. Taken as an end and aim, it is as dark a delusion as any other aim that springs from self. Used as a means, or casually, it may be productive of good; but even that is good which is vain and frivolous. It is the misuse of freedom, the employment of it as a weapon for overcoming the world of feeling, that makes man so infinitely more terrible than the lower animals; for they do only what momentary instinct bids them; while man acts by ideas, and his ideas may entail universal ruin before they are satisfied.

There is another circumstance which helps to promote the notion that honour and virtue are connected. A man who can do what he wants to do shows that he can also do it if what he wants to do is a virtuous act. But that those of our actions which we are ourselves obliged to regard with contempt are also regarded with contempt by other people serves more than anything that I have here mentioned to establish the connection. Thus it often happens that a man who is not afraid of the one kind of contempt is unwilling to undergo the other. But when we are called upon to choose between our own approval and the world's censure, as may occur in complicated and mistaken circumstances, what becomes of the principle of honour then?

Two characteristic examples of the principle of honour are to be found in Shakespeare's *Henry VI.*, Part II., Act IV., Sc. 1. A pirate is anxious to murder his captive instead of accepting, like others, a ransom for him; because in taking his captive he lost an eye, and his own honour and that of his forefathers would in his opinion be stained, if he were to allow his revenge to be bought off as though he were a mere trader. The prisoner, on the other hand, who is the Duke of Suffolk, prefers to have his head grace a pole than to uncover it to such a low fellow as a pirate, by approaching him to ask for mercy.

Just as civic honour—in other words, the opinion that we deserve to be trusted—is the palladium of those whose endeavour it is to make their way in the world on the path of honourable business, so knightly honour—in other words, the opinion that we are men to be feared—is the palladium of those who aim at going through life on the path of violence; and so it was that knightly honour arose among the robber-knights and other knights of the Middle Ages.

* * * * *

A theoretical philosopher is one who can supply in the shape of ideas for the reason, a copy of the presentations of experience; just as what the painter sees he can reproduce on canvas; the sculptor, in marble; the poet, in pictures for the imagination, though they are pictures which he supplies only in sowing the ideas from which they sprang.

A so-called practical philosopher, on the other hand, is one who, contrarily, deduces his action from ideas. The theoretical philosopher transforms life into ideas. The practical philosopher transforms ideas into life; he acts, therefore, in a thoroughly reasonable manner; he is consistent, regular, deliberate; he is never hasty or passionate; he never allows himself to be influenced by the impression of the moment.

And indeed, when we find ourselves among those full presentations of experience, or real objects, to which the body belongs—since the body is only an objectified will, the shape which the will assumes in the material world—it is difficult to let our bodies be guided, not by those presentations, but by a mere image of them, by cold, colourless ideas, which are related to experience as the shadow of Orcus to life; and yet this is the only way in which we can avoid doing things of which we may have to repent.

The theoretical philosopher enriches the domain of reason by adding to it; the practical philosopher draws upon it, and makes it serve him.

* * * * *

According to Kant the truth of experience is only a hypothetical truth. If the suppositions which underlie all the intimations of experience—subject, object, time, space and causality—were removed, none of those intimations would contain a word of truth. In other words, experience is only a phenomenon; it is not knowledge of the thing-in-itself.

If we find something in our own conduct at which we are secretly pleased, although we cannot reconcile it with experience, seeing that if we were to follow the guidance of experience we should have to do precisely the opposite, we must not allow this to put us out; otherwise we should be ascribing an authority to experience which it does not deserve, for all that it teaches rests upon a mere supposition. This is the general tendency of the Kantian Ethics.

* * * * *

Innocence is in its very nature stupid. It is stupid because the aim of life (I use the expression only figuratively, and I could just as well speak of the essence of life, or of the world) is to gain a knowledge of our own bad will, so that our will may become an object for us, and that we may undergo an inward conversion. Our body is itself our will objectified; it is one of the first and foremost of objects, and the deeds that we accomplish for the sake of the body show us the evil inherent in our will. In the state of innocence, where there is no evil because there is no experience, man is, as it were, only an apparatus for living, and the object for which the apparatus exists is not yet disclosed. An empty form of life like this, a stage untenanted, is in itself, like the so-called real world, null and void; and as it can attain a meaning only by action, by error, by knowledge, by the convulsions of the will, it wears a character of insipid stupidity. A golden age of innocence, a fools' paradise, is a notion that is stupid and unmeaning, and for that very reason in no way worthy of any respect. The first criminal and murderer, Cain, who acquired a knowledge of guilt, and through guilt acquired a knowledge of virtue by repentance, and so came to understand the meaning of life, is a tragical figure more significant, and almost more respectable, than all the innocent fools in the world put together.

* * * * *

If I had to write about *modesty* I should say: I know the esteemed public for which I have the honour to write far too well to dare to give utterance to my opinion about this virtue. Personally I am quite content to be modest and to apply myself to this virtue with the utmost possible circumspection. But one thing I shall never admit—that I have ever required modesty of any man, and any statement to that effect I repel as a slander.

The paltry character of most men compels the few who have any merit or genius to behave as though they did not know their own value, and consequently did not know other people's want of value; for it is only on this condition that the mob acquiesces in tolerating merit. A virtue has been made out of this necessity, and it is called modesty. It is a piece of hypocrisy, to be excused only because other people are so paltry that they must be treated with indulgence.

* * * * *

Human misery may affect us in two ways, and we may be in one of two opposite moods in regard to it.

In one of them, this misery is immediately present to us. We feel it in our own person, in our own will which, imbued with violent desires, is everywhere broken, and this is the process which constitutes suffering. The result is that the will increases in violence, as is shown in all cases of passion and emotion; and this increasing violence comes to a stop only when the will turns and gives way to complete resignation, in other words, is redeemed. The man who is entirely dominated by this mood will regard any prosperity which he may see in others with envy, and any suffering with no sympathy.

In the opposite mood human misery is present to us only as a fact of knowledge, that is to say, indirectly. We are mainly engaged in looking at the sufferings of others, and our attention is withdrawn from our own. It is in their person that we become aware of human misery; we are filled with sympathy; and the result of this mood is general benevolence, philanthropy. All envy vanishes, and instead of feeling it, we are rejoiced when we see one of our tormented fellow-creatures experience any pleasure or relief.

After the same fashion we may be in one of two opposite moods in regard to human baseness and depravity. In the one we perceive this baseness indirectly, in others. Out of this mood arise indignation, hatred, and contempt of mankind. In the other we perceive it directly, in ourselves. Out of it there arises humiliation, nay, contrition.

In order to judge the moral value of a man, it is very important to observe which of these four moods predominate in him. They go in pairs, one out of each division. In very excellent characters the second mood of each division will predominate.

* * * * *

The categorical imperative, or absolute command, is a contradiction. Every command is conditional. What is unconditional and necessary is a *must*, such as is presented by the laws of nature.

It is quite true that the moral law is entirely conditional. There is a world and a view of life in which it has neither validity nor significance. That world is, properly speaking, the real world in which, as individuals, we live; for every regard paid to morality is a denial of that world and of our individual life in it. It is a view of the world, however, which does not go beyond the principle of sufficient reason; and the opposite view proceeds by the intuition of Ideas.

* * * * *

If a man is under the influence of two opposite but very strong motives, A and B, and I am greatly concerned that he should choose A, but still more that he should never be untrue to his choice, and by changing his mind betray me, or the like, it will not do for me to say anything that might hinder the motive B from having its full effect upon him, and only emphasise A; for then I should never be able to reckon on his decision. What I have to do is, rather, to put both motives before him at the same time, in as vivid and clear a way as possible, so that they may work upon him with their whole force. The choice that he then makes is the decision of his inmost nature, and stands firm to all eternity. In saying *I will do this*, he has said *I must do this*. I have got at his will, and I can rely upon its working as steadily as one of the forces of nature. It is as certain as fire kindles and water wets that he will act according to the motive which has proved to be stronger for him.

Insight and knowledge may be attained and lost again; they may be changed, or improved, or destroyed; but will cannot be changed. That is why *I apprehend, I perceive, I see,* is subject to alteration and uncertainty; *I will,* pronounced on a right apprehension of motive, is as firm as nature itself. The difficulty, however, lies in getting at a right apprehension. A man's apprehension of motive may change, or be corrected or perverted; and on the other hand, his circumstances may undergo an alteration.

* * * * *

A man should exercise an almost boundless toleration and placability, because if he is capricious enough to refuse to forgive a single individual for the meanness or evil that lies at his door, it is doing the rest of the world a quite unmerited honour.

But at the same time the man who is every one's friend is no one's friend. It is quite obvious what sort of friendship it is which we hold out to the human race, and to which it is open to almost every man to return, no matter what he may have done.

* * * * *

With the ancients *friendship* was one of the chief elements in morality. But friendship is only limitation and partiality; it is the restriction to one individual of what is the due of all mankind, namely, the recognition that a man's own nature and that of mankind are identical. At most it is a compromise between this recognition and selfishness.

* * * * *

A lie always has its origin in the desire to extend the dominion of one's own will over other individuals, and to deny their will in order the better to affirm one's own. Consequently a lie is in its very nature the product of injustice, malevolence and villainy. That is why truth, sincerity, candour and rectitude are at once recognised and valued as praiseworthy and noble qualities; because we presume that the man who exhibits them entertains no sentiments of injustice or malice, and therefore stands in no need of concealing such sentiments. He who is open cherishes nothing that is bad.

* * * * *

There is a certain kind of courage which springs from the same source as good-nature. What I mean is that the good-natured man is almost as clearly conscious that he exists in other individuals as in himself. I have often shown how this feeling gives rise to good-nature. It also gives rise to courage, for the simple reason that the man who possesses this feeling cares less for his own individual existence, as he lives almost as much in the general existence of all creatures. Accordingly he is little concerned for his own life and its belongings. This is by no means the sole source of courage for it is a phenomenon due to various causes. But it is the noblest kind of courage, as is shown by the fact that in its origin it is associated with great gentleness and patience. Men of this kind are usually irresistible to women.

* * * * *

All general rules and precepts fail, because they proceed from the false assumption that men are constituted wholly, or almost wholly, alike; an assumption which the philosophy of Helvetius expressly makes. Whereas the truth is that the original difference between individuals in intellect and morality is immeasurable.

* * * * *

The question as to whether morality is something real is the question whether a well-grounded counter-principle to egoism actually exists.

As egoism restricts concern for welfare to a single individual, *viz.*, the man's own self, the counter-principle would have to extend it to all other individuals.

* * * * *

It is only because the will is above and beyond time that the stings of conscience are ineradicable, and do not, like other pains, gradually wear away. No! an evil deed weighs on the conscience years afterwards as heavily as if it had been freshly committed.

* * * * *

Character is innate, and conduct is merely its manifestation; the occasion for great misdeeds comes seldom; strong counter-motives keep us back; our disposition is revealed to ourselves by our desires, thoughts, emotions, when it remains unknown to others. Reflecting on all this, we might suppose it possible for a man to possess, in some sort, an innate evil conscience, without ever having done anything very bad.

* * * * *

Don't do to others what you wouldn't like done to yourself. This is, perhaps, one of those arguments that prove, or rather ask, too much. For a prisoner might address it to a judge.

* * * * *

Stupid people are generally malicious, for the very same reason as the ugly and the deformed.

Similarly, genius and sanctity are akin. However simple-minded a saint may be, he will nevertheless have a dash of genius in him; and however many errors of temperament, or of actual character, a genius may possess, he will still exhibit a certain nobility of disposition by which he shows his kinship with the saint.

* * * * *

The great difference between Law without and Law within, between the State and the Kingdom of God, is very clear. It is the State's business to see that *every one should have justice done to him*; it regards men as passive beings, and therefore takes no account of anything but their actions. The Moral Law, on the other hand, is concerned that *every one should do justice*; it regards men as active, and looks to the will rather than the deed. To prove that this is the true distinction let the reader consider what would happen if he were to say, conversely, that it is the State's business that every one should do justice, and the business of the Moral Law that every one should have justice done to him. The absurdity is obvious.

As an example of the distinction, let me take the case of a debtor and a creditor disputing about a debt which the former denies. A lawyer and a moralist are present, and show a lively interest in the matter. Both desire that the dispute should end in the same way, although what they want is by no means the same. The lawyer says, *I want this man to get back what belongs to him*; and the moralist, *I want that man to do his duty.*

It is with the will alone that morality is concerned. Whether external force hinders or fails to hinder the will from working does not in the least matter. For morality the external world is real only in so far as it is able or unable to lead and influence the will. As soon as the will is determined, that is, as soon as a resolve is taken, the external world and its events are of no further moment and practical do not exist. For if the events of the world had any such reality—that is to say, if they possessed a significance in themselves, or any other than that derived from the will which is affected by them—what a grievance it would be that all these events lie in the realm of chance and error! It is, however, just this which proves that the important thing is not what happens, but what is willed. Accordingly, let the incidents of life be left to the play of chance and error, to demonstrate to man that he is as chaff before the wind.

The State concerns itself only with the incidents—with what happens; nothing else has any reality for it. I may dwell upon thoughts of murder and poison as much as I please: the State does not forbid me, so long as the axe and rope control my will, and prevent it from becoming action.

Ethics asks: What are the duties towards others which justice imposes upon us? in other words, What must I render? The Law of Nature asks: What need I not submit to from others? that is, What must I suffer? The question is put, not that I may do no injustice, but that I may not do more than every man must do if he is to safeguard his existence, and than every man will approve being done, in order that he may be treated in the same way himself; and, further, that I may not do more than society will permit me to do. The same answer will serve for both questions, just as the same straight line can be drawn from either of two opposite directions, namely, by opposing forces; or, again, as the angle can give the sine, or the sine the angle.

It has been said that the historian is an inverted prophet. In the same way it may be said that a teacher of law is an inverted moralist (*viz.*, a teacher of the duties of justice), or that politics are inverted ethics, if we exclude the thought that ethics also teaches the duty of benevolence, magnanimity, love, and so on. The State is the Gordian knot that is cut instead of being untied; it is Columbus' egg which is made to stand by being broken instead of balanced, as though the business in question were to make it stand rather than to balance it. In this respect the State is like the man who thinks that he can produce fine weather by making the barometer go up.

* * * * *

The pseudo-philosophers of our age tell us that it is the object of the State to promote the moral aims of mankind. This is not true; it is rather the contrary which is true. The aim for which mankind exists—the expression is parabolic—is not that a man should act in such and such a manner; for all *opera operata*, things that have actually been done, are in themselves matters of indifference. No! the aim is that the Will, of which every man is a complete specimen—nay, is the very Will itself—should turn whither it needs to turn; that the man himself (the union of Thought and Will) should perceive what this will is, and what horrors it contains; that he should show the reflection of himself in his own deeds, in the abomination of them. The State, which is wholly concerned with the general welfare, checks the manifestation of the bad will, but in no wise checks the will itself; the attempt would be impossible. It is because the State checks the manifestation of his will that a man very seldom sees the whole abomination of his nature in the mirror of his deeds. Or does the reader actually suppose there are no people in the world as bad as Robespierre, Napoleon, or other murderers? Does he fail to see that there are many who would act like them if only they could?

Many a criminal dies more quietly on the scaffold than many a non-criminal in the arms of his family. The one has perceived what his will is and has discarded it. The other has not been able to discard it, because he has never been able to perceive what it is. The aim of the State is to produce a fool's paradise, and this is in direct conflict with the true aim of life, namely, to attain a knowledge of what the will, in its horrible nature, really is.

* * * * *

Napoleon was not really worse than many, not to say most, men. He was possessed of the very ordinary egoism that seeks its welfare at the expense of others. What distinguished him was merely the greater power he had of satisfying his will, and greater intelligence, reason and courage; added to which, chance gave him a favourable scope for his operations. By means of all this he did for his egoism what a thousand other men would like to do for theirs, but cannot. Every feeble lad who by little acts of villainy gains a small advantage for himself by putting others to some disadvantage, although it may be equally small, is just as bad as Napoleon.

Those who fancy that retribution comes after death would demand that Napoleon should by unutterable torments pay the penalty for all the numberless calamities that he caused. But he is no more culpable than all those who possess the same will, unaccompanied by the same power.

The circumstance that in his case this extraordinary power was added allowed him to reveal the whole wickedness of the human will; and the sufferings of his age, as the necessary obverse of the medal, reveal the misery which is inextricably bound up with this bad will. It is the general manipulation of this will that constitutes the world. But it is precisely that it should be understood how inextricably the will to live is bound up with, and is really one and the same as, this unspeakable misery, that is the world's aim and purpose; and it is an aim and purpose which the appearance of Napoleon did much to assist. Not to be an unmeaning fools' paradise but a tragedy, in which the will to live understands itself and yields—that is the object for which the world exists. Napoleon is only an enormous mirror of the will to live.

The difference between the man who causes suffering and the man who suffers it, is only phenomenal. It is all a will to live, identical with great suffering; and it is only by understanding this that the will can mend and end.

* * * * *

What chiefly distinguishes ancient from modern times is that in ancient times, to use Napoleon's expression, it was affairs that reigned: *les paroles aux choses*. In modern times this is not so. What I mean is that in ancient times the character of public life, of the State, and of Religion, as well as of private life, was a strenuous affirmation of the will to live. In modern times it is a denial of this will, for such is the character of Christianity. But now while on the one hand that denial has suffered some abatement even in public opinion, because it is too repugnant to human character, on the other what is publicly denied is secretly affirmed. Hence it is that we see half measures and falsehood everywhere; and that is why modern times look so small beside antiquity.

* * * * *

The structure of human society is like a pendulum swinging between two impulses, two evils in polar opposition, *despotism* and *anarchy*. The further it gets from the one, the nearer it approaches the other. From this the reader might hit on the thought that if it were exactly midway between the two, it would be right. Far from it. For these two evils are by no means equally bad and dangerous. The former is incomparably less to be feared; its ills exist in the main only as possibilities, and if they come at all it is only one among millions that they touch. But, with anarchy, possibility and actuality are inseparable; its blows fall on every man every day. Therefore every constitution should be a nearer approach to a despotism than to anarchy; nay, it must contain a small possibility of despotism.

THE END

9 781420 970623